ROMANESQUE ART

in the MNAC collections

Museu Nacional d'Art de Catalunya
Palau Nacional. Parc de Montjuïc
08038 Barcelona. www.mnac.cat

Lunwerg S.L.
Diagonal 662-664
08034 Barcelona www.lunwerg.com

Design and production:
Lunwerg Editores

© *texts:*
Manuel Castiñeiras González, Jordi Camps Sòria, Joan Duran-Porta
(*The Romanesque Art. Collection of the MNAC*)

© *photographs:*
as listed on page 223
© Auguste Herbin,
Francis Picabia, VEGAP, Barcelona, 2008

© *translation:*
Andrew Langdon-Davies, Andrew Stacey

Editorial coordination:
Montse Gumà (Publishing Department of the MNAC) and María García Freire (Lunwerg)

Graphic design:
Bettina Benet (Lunwerg)

ISBN (Lunwerg): 978-84-9785-548-8
ISBN (MNAC): 978-84-8043-196-5

Depósito legal: B-53134-2008

Printed in Spain

SPONSORS
Abertis
Banco Santander Central Hispano
Bassat Ogilvy
Cadena Ser
Consorci de la Zona Franca de Barcelona
El País
El Periódico de Catalunya
Fira Barcelona
Freixenet, SA
Fundació Agbar
Fundación Telefónica
Gas Natural SDG
Grupo Sacyr Vallehermoso
La Vanguardia
Presència
Ràdio Televisió Espanyola a Catalunya
Televisió de Catalunya / Catalunya Ràdio

COLLABORATORS
Barcelona tv, Caja Mediterráneo, El Punt, Emte SA, Fundació DAMM, Fundación REPSOL, Hewlett-Packard Española SL, Magma Serveis Culturals, Seguridad Expres

ROMANESQUE ART

in the MNAC collections

Texts

Manuel Castiñeiras and Jordi Camps

in collaboration with Joan Duran-Porta

MNAC abertis LUNWERG EDITORES

Index

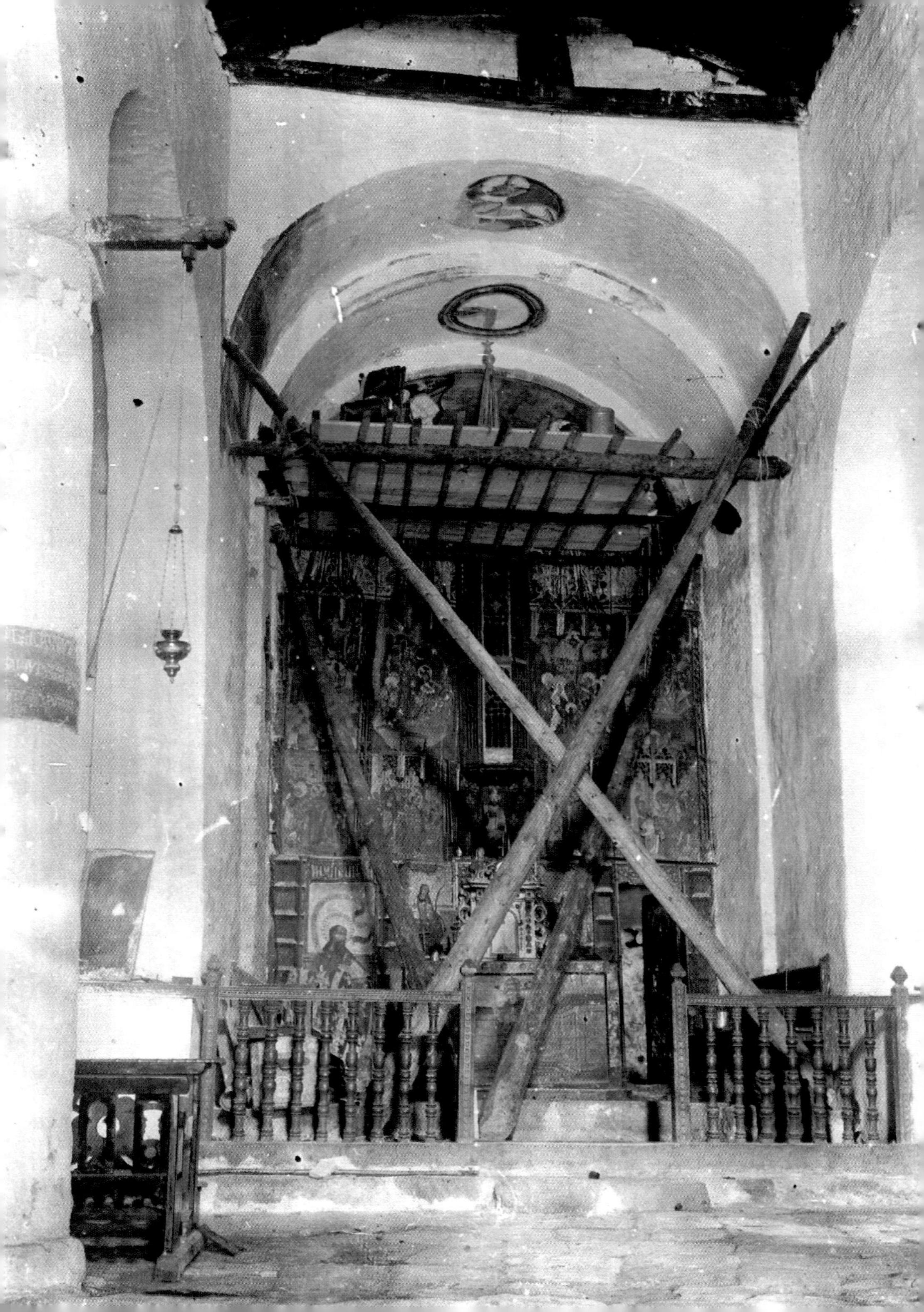

An Introduction to Catalan Romanesque

Manuel Castiñeiras
Jordi Camps

1. THE INTERIOR OF SANT CLIMENT DE TAÜLL IN 1904.
At the back, the paintings in the apse can be seen half hidden by the Gothic altarpiece.

THE STUDY AND PRESERVATION OF ROMANESQUE ART IN CATALONIA. SPECIAL CHARACTERISTICS

The term 'Romanesque art' is used to designate a period in medieval art comprising roughly the eleventh to thirteenth centuries and spanning longer or shorter times in different regions of the European West. It was adopted in the nineteenth century in order to refer to a return to the architectural and sculptural monumentality that had disappeared in Europe after the end of the Roman Empire. In the course of time, researchers have gradually discovered many variations and have established several stages and variants of the art of that time, although the word 'Romanesque' is still generally applied. The introduction of the term in Catalonia coincided with a surge in studies of the Middle Ages and growing interest in the period. In fact, Elies Rogent, who restored Santa Maria de Ripoll and Sant Llorenç de Munt, in writing the syllabus for the 1873-1874 academic year at the Escola d'Arquitectura de Barcelona, already used the concept of a 'Romanesque style', which he identified mainly with eleventh-century architectural works. The term also crops up in various studies in the 1880s, applied to the churches in the Vall de Boí and other buildings such as the tower of Sant Martí del Canigó.

The rediscovery in modern times of Catalan Romanesque struck a chord in the cultural movement known as *La Renaixença* ('Rebirth') and the search for the defining elements of a Catalan national identity, which it was felt went back to the Middle Ages. With this in mind, the period we now include in the Romanesque was the moment when the dominions of the Catalan counties were being consolidated and when the country's own cultural identity, its legal system and customs were all beginning to take shape. Scientific field trips, or 'excursionism', played a decisive role in this context. Various associations organised this activity, whose object it was to gather a series of researchers on trips to bring to light the country's scientific, artistic and literary wealth, taking advantage of the nascent railway and finding its inspiration in Catalanist thinking. Thanks to the work of organisations like the Associació Catalana d'Excursions, which was set up in 1876 and became the Centre Excursionista de Catalunya in 1891, there was therefore a growing awareness of the value of the heritage of the past in forming an identity. This was fed by numerous publications (yearbooks, guides) and by the work of certain figures who drew up and compiled information on monuments, amongst them the *modernista* architect Lluís Domènech i Montaner, who between 1901 and 1906 gathered a large amount of material for the *Història de l'art romànic a Catalunya* which he never finished. The awareness of Catalonia's own artistic heritage also showed itself in the restoration of large monuments, like that of the monastery of Ripoll under Bishop Josep Morgades of Vic, which was inaugurated in 1886 once the architect Elies Rogent had completed his work. This was also the context for the inauguration of the Museu Episcopal de Vic in 1891.

Romanesque art in Catalonia, in its different periods and manifestations, shared fully in international trends, sometimes playing a predominant role, sometimes following in the wake of novelties arising in other places. No-one is in any doubt as to the innovation inherent in eleventh-century Catalan architecture, of how advanced its monumental decoration was, or of the wealth and diversity of the mural painting and the panel painting of the twelfth century. On the other hand, it's true that the renewal in the great monumental sculpture of the true Romanesque arrived in Catalonia with some delay. One feature worth pointing out is the persistence of Romanesque formulas after the twelfth century, a common occurrence in southern European countries, where the Romanesque, refreshed by the trends of the '1200 style', lived on for the whole of the thirteenth century alongside the advance of Gothic from the north.

Eleventh-century architecture. 'First Romanesque' and its variants

Architecture, with its structures and spaces arising from the needs of worship and the liturgy, undoubtedly provides the framework for artistic activity. From the middle of the tenth century, the gradual rise of feudalism, the growth in population and the spread of various technical breakthroughs generated feverish building activity that gave the European West what the famous Burgundy chronicler Rodolphus Glaber in about 1000 called a 'white mantle of churches'. Catalonia also took part in this early movement. We see this in the work in important monasteries, which materialised in buildings of some size, like the church of Sant Miquel de Cuixà, for example. The presence of Abbot Garí, who had been a monk in the great Burgundy monastery of Cluny, explains the extraordinary innovation of the large east end with its five apses and seven altars, very similar to the one in Cluny II.

However, the real boom in building activity in Catalonia took place in the course of the eleventh century, and can be seen in monasteries (Sant Pere de Rodes, Santa Maria de Ripoll, Sant Miquel de Cuixà) and in cathedrals (Vic, Girona, Barcelona, Elne). Sometimes these buildings were brand-new and sometimes they were older ones that were remodelled and enlarged. The originality of the floor plans, the technical innovations (with the barrel vault in perfect consonace with the building's supporting elements) and the artistic treatment of the walls, led Josep Puig i Cadafalch to call it 'first Romanesque'.

One group of buildings, headed by Sant Pere de Rodes, made use of formulas rooted in the traditions of the Ancient World and the Early Middle Ages. Rodes, built mainly in the first third of the eleventh century, stands out for its system of supports and the separation of nave and aisles by pillars, artistically reinforced by pilasters, which on the side corresponding to the central nave are arranged on two levels, with superimposed orders that bring to mind resources from Antiquity and the Carolingian world. Furthermore, Sant Pere de Rodes also exemplifies the use of sculptural decoration, especially on capitals of a Corinthian type and with systematically arranged interlacing, an example which was partly followed in the Roussillonese complex of Sant Andreu de Sureda. It's important to emphasise that it was precisely in this part of the eastern Pyrenees between Roussillon and Empordà that the first Romanesque sculptural façades in the whole of Europe made their revolutionary appearance. They were decorated with Theophanic visions in very flat relief, based on chiaroscuro effects, and framed with bevel-carved borders of plant and geometrical motifs. This is the case especially of the famous lintels of Sant Genís de Fontanes (dated from an inscription to 1019-1020) and of Sant Andreu de Sureda. In the course of the eleventh century, these technical ap-

2. Sant Pere de Rodes.
The interior of the monastery church.
The system for supporting of the body of the naves, which comes from Roman architecture, is outstanding, as are the elaborate Corinthian or interweaving capitals, prime examples of European sculpture from the first half of the 11th century.

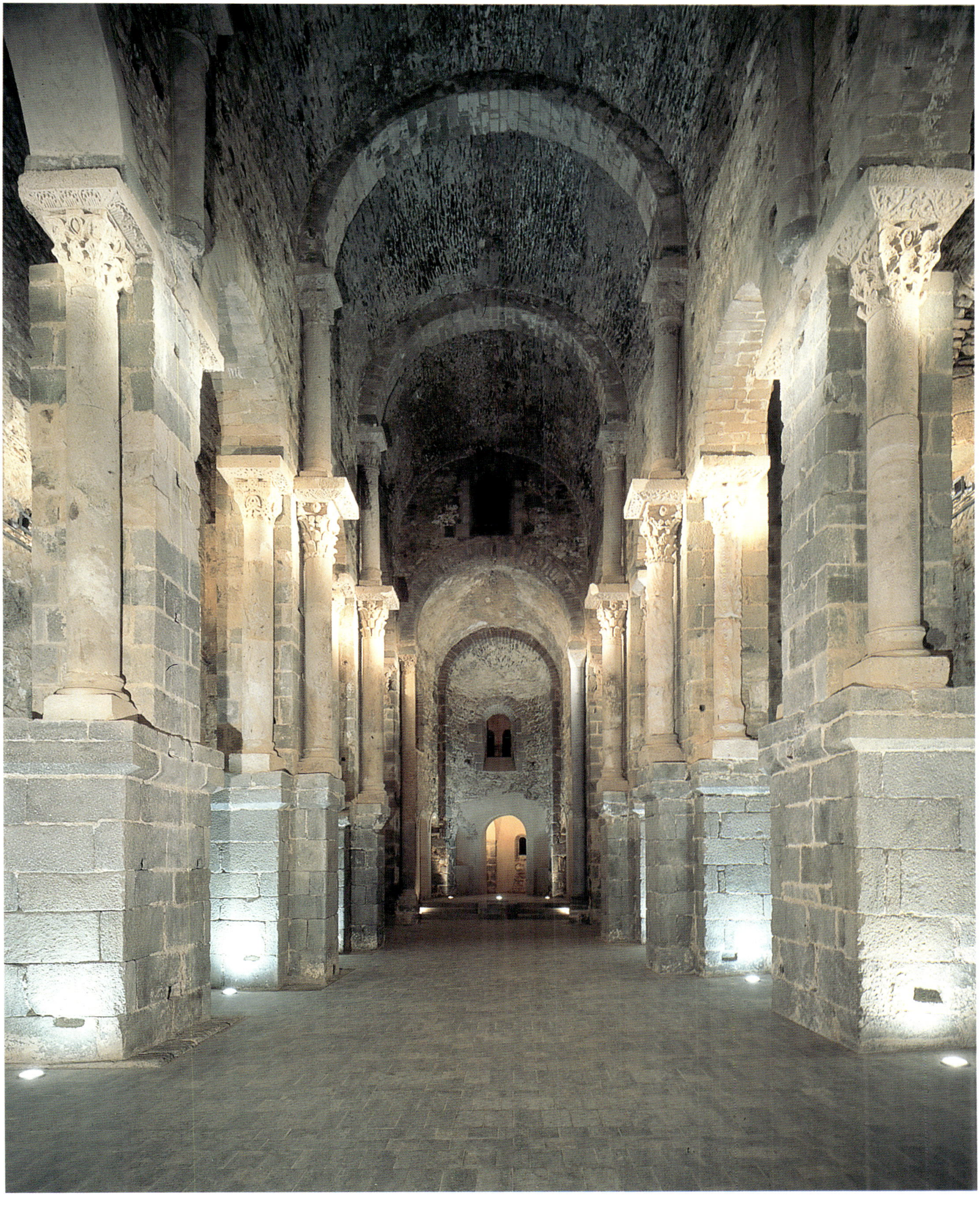

2

3

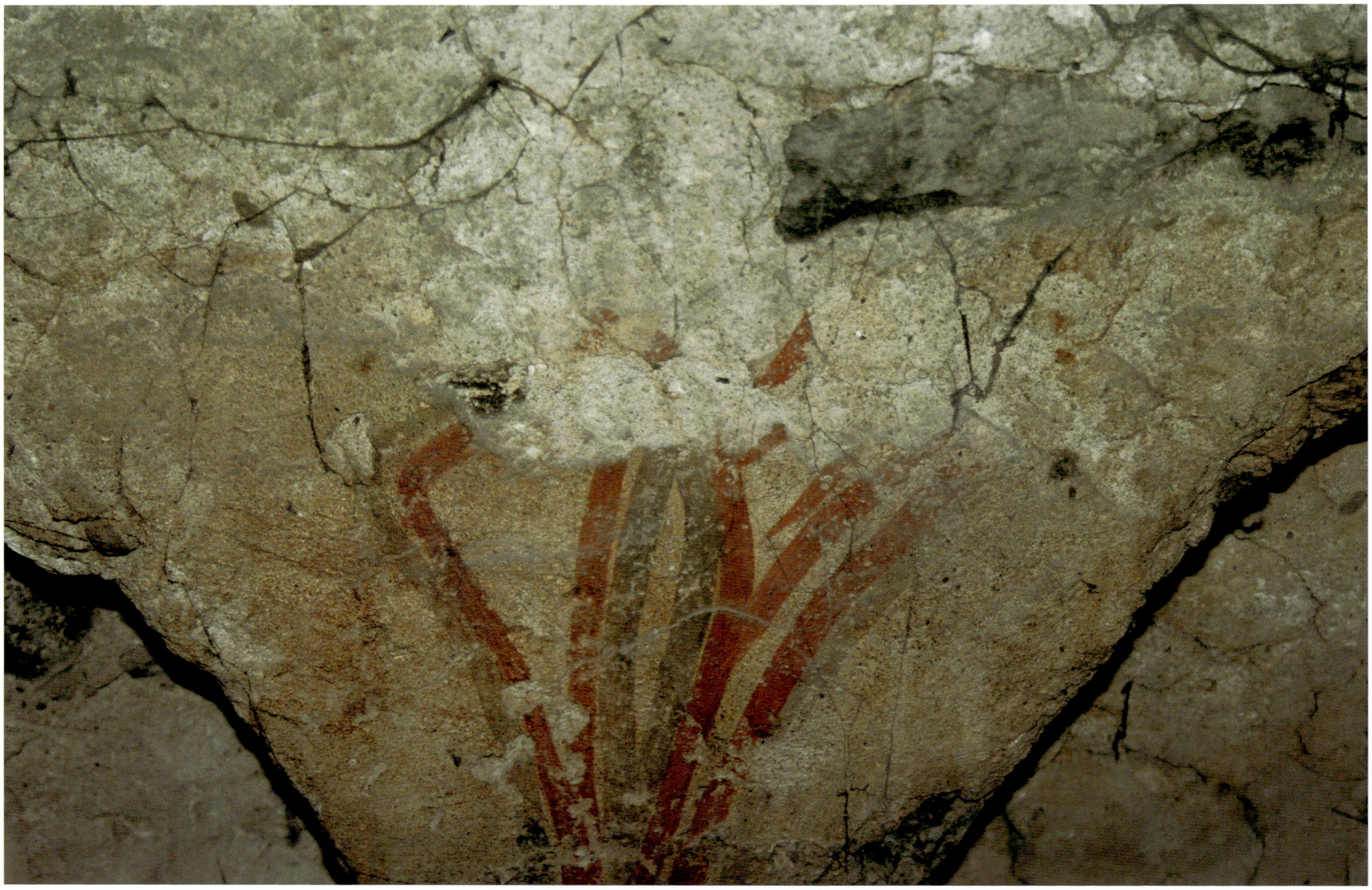

3. SANTA MARIA DE RIPOLL.
Remains of the early portal.
Surviving from the early portal of the church in Ripoll, beneath the 12th-century façade, are the remains of a wall archading with pictorial decoration.
In the photograph, remains of a floral motif are visible.

proaches can be found in sites farther south, like the Romanesque cathedral of Barcelona (consecrated in 1058) and in the decoration of the capitals in the interior of Sant Pere d'Àger.

Within this varied outlook, though, one type of construction extends throughout the eleventh century. It stands out for the decorative treatment given the external surfaces of the exterior of churches (apses, side walls, façades), in the form of vertical bands, or lesenes, and blind arches that stand out from the background and produce an ornamental effect through the play of light and dark. Normally, the small, irregularly-shaped bond is an imitation of the ancient *opus laeteritium* of the Romans, which was sometimes finished with either a coat of whitewash or polychromy. This is borne out by remains of the rendering as well as of the exterior paint, such as those from the early façade of Santa Maria de Ripoll, which are hidden behind the large, twelfth-century portal.

The numerous analogies between this model of architecture and buildings in the Lombardy region in the north of Italy have reinforced the myth of the so-called 'Lombard Romanesque', according to which the first Romanesque constructions in the Catalan counties were the work of stonemasons and artists from Lombardy, the Lombard masters or *magistri comacini*, to use a Latin term of uncertain origin (possibly related to the city of Como or deriving from the fact that these masters worked *cum machinis*).

The existence of these Lombard masters was argued for by Josep Puig i Cadafalch in his publications in the first third of the twentieth century, always in the wider and

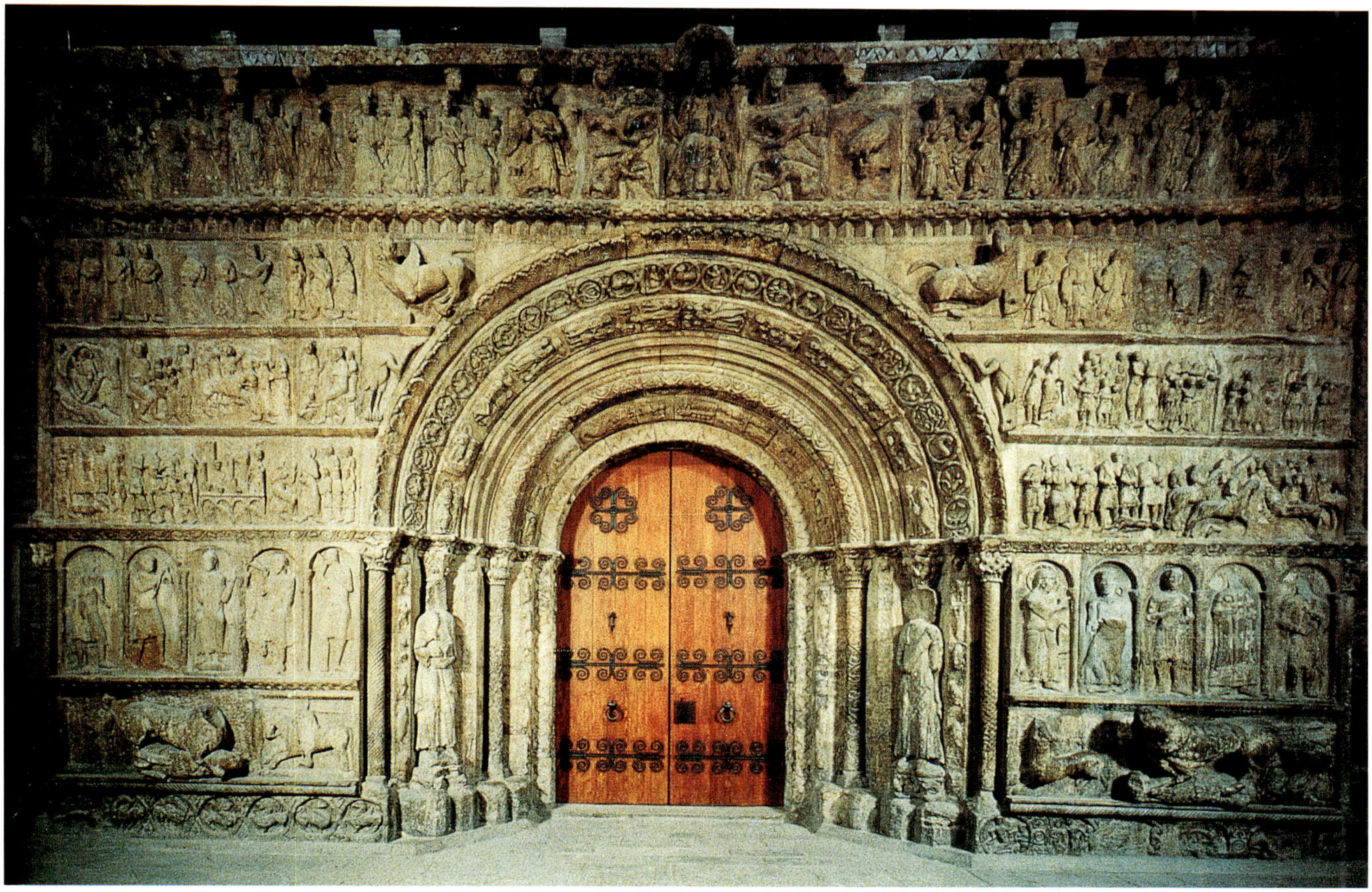

4

4. The portal of Santa Maria de Ripoll.
Despite the degradation of the stonework, due mainly to the humidity, the portal of Ripoll is the most significant and monumental work of sculpture in Catalan Romanesque art.

more complex theoretical framework with which he characterised that 'first Romanesque'. Puig can undoubtedly be credited with having brought eleventh-century Catalan architecture into the international historiographic picture, but today his theories need to be discussed or at least qualified. Thus without denying certain analogies or possible contacts with the north of Italy, this early Romanesque Catalan architecture is seen as a quite unique combination of various traditions—Lombard, Carolingian and Roman—that give it a very particular personality of its own.

Many of the large sites from this period in Catalonia have been lost and are only known to us from a few remains, as they were later replaced or partly destroyed and sometimes largely renovated. The one great building of the time must have been the monastery church in Ripoll, with its broad transept and seven apsidal chapels, all modelled on Saint Peter's in Rome. The building was consecrated in 1032, under the auspices of the Abbot-Bishop Oliba, who had a good knowledge of the Roman point of reference. A member of the family of the Counts of Cerdanya and Besalú, Oliba was unquestionably one of the great driving forces of this period in Catalonia thanks to his connections with monasteries and cathedrals.

Perhaps one of the masterpieces of this architecture is the canonical church of Sant Vicenç de Cardona, consecrated in 1040. The building shows an exemplary arrangement of the interior space, which is totally covered by stone vaults, where each section of the main nave with its barrel vault is matched by three sections of the aisles, with groin vaults. The success of this early Romanesque architectural model is illustrated in Catalonia by its prolonged survival into the second half of the eleventh century, sometimes in simpler structures with wooden roofs, as we see in the Vall de Boí and other parts of the Pyrenees.

The flourishing of mural painting

Judging from the examples that have survived, another of the great contributions by Catalan Romanesque is the series of mural paintings, many of them in the Pyrenees, in buildings that have not been replaced in the course of time and that have preserved their original decoration behind later altarpieces and under layers of modern-day rendering. Later we shall tell the story of their discovery and of their removal to Barcelona, since which time they have become works of an emblematic nature and a central feature of the MNAC. Apart from a few earlier cases known to us, like the churches of Terrassa, the first large campaigns in pictorial decoration took place around 1100 or in the first decades of the twelfth century, as we see, for example, in the churches in the valleys of Pallars and Ribagorça. There are signs, though, that large churches like the monastery of Ripoll must also have been decorated with important cycles of paintings, a common practice in other parts of Europe.

Most of the groups preserved in Catalonia, then, are from dates that go from the very end of the eleventh century to well into the twelfth. Although a lot of information about the way the workshops worked and the nature of the artists is missing, attempts have been made to classify the different groups in trends and circles, on the basis of likely influences and of a comparison of styles. Some of these groups have been stylistically associated with central or southern France (the case of Sant Joan de Boí), while others come closer to schemes from the north of Italy and a relation has been sought for them with groups from Lombardy (Sant Quirze de Pedret, Sant Pere del Burgal). Nevertheless, in a large part of the works the similarities with Italian sites can be explained by the effect of the ecclesiastical reform of the second half of the eleventh century, known as the Gregorian Reform, and by the artistic dictates issuing from Rome as a result of it. Whatever the case, the circulation of artistic models didn't depend only on the movements of workshops and artists; an important part was also played by the sketchbooks, illustrated with collections of repertories, as well as the references provided by objects and books, in a demonstration of the transposition of small-format elements to monumental scale. The paintings from Sant Joan de Boí are a good example of the influence of miniatures in large-format decorative work.

So far as we can tell from the surviving remains, the iconographic programme could extend over the whole of the interior of the building, following a coherent global plan presided by the representation of the Divinity in the apse. The Old and New Testaments could be illustrated on the walls of the nave and aisles, while on the west wall the counter-façade depicted the Last Judgement, as we see in Santa Maria de Taüll. The pictorial decoration could reach other parts of the church or attached buildings, either on the exterior or in certain points in the cloister.

5. Ripoll Bible. Folio 1.
The Ripoll Bible, copied and illustrated in the middle of the 11th century, was used as a direct source for several motifs on the great 12th-century portal, especially for the scenes from the Book of Exodus.

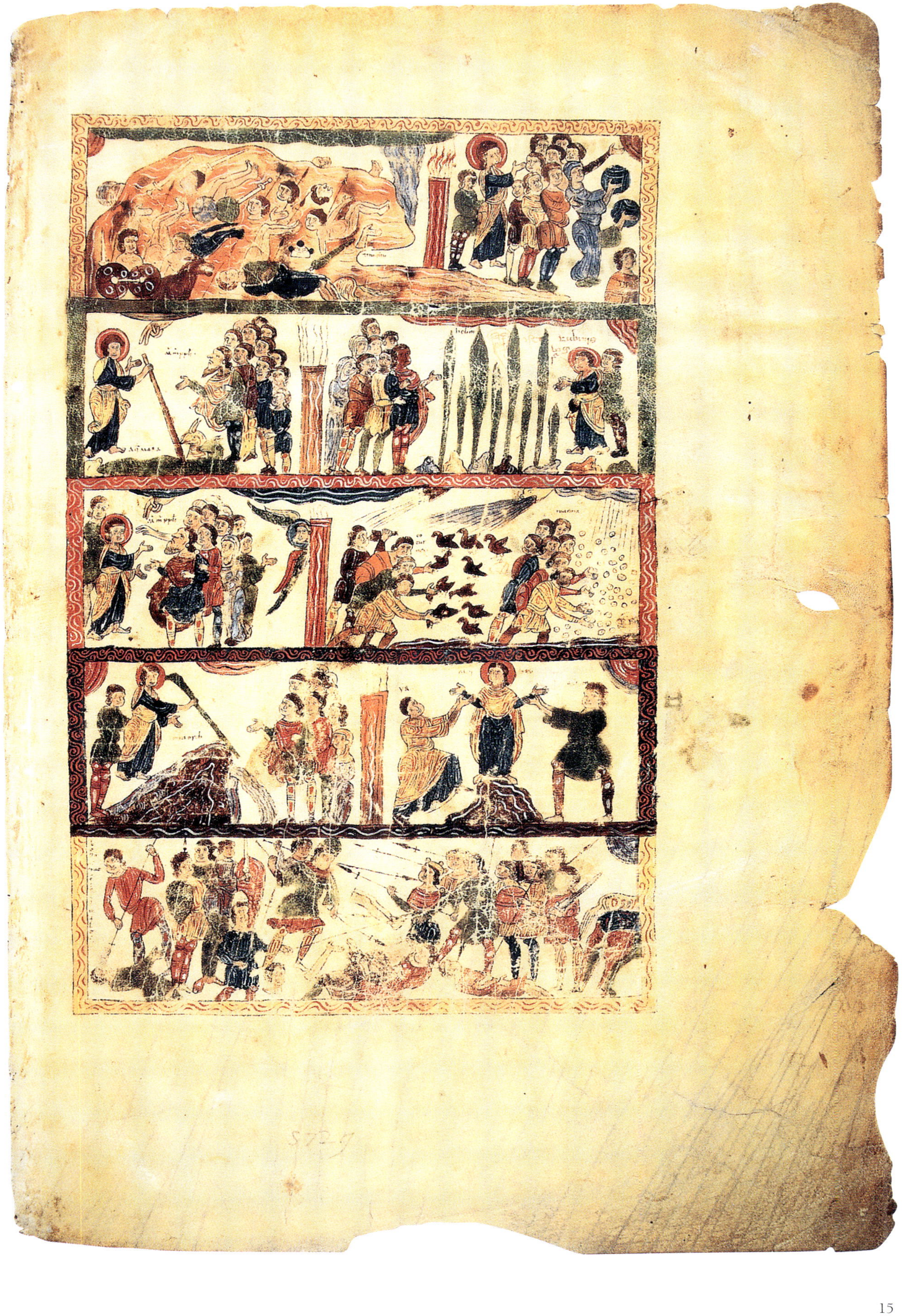

The twelfth-century renewal: monumental sculpture

Building construction gradually underwent technical innovations that were to lead to the use of structures based on stonework of regular cut stone blocks of a considerable size. At the same time, another of the great offerings of Romanesque was being made: the generalised rise of monumental sculpture integrated in the supports and the openings of churches, on façades and in cloisters, with a great increase in figurative and storied subject matter. Technically, it marks the recovery of a sense of volume and modelling, almost in a return to Roman Antiquity. Over much of Europe, as in northern Spain and Languedoc, it began in the last quarter of the eleventh century. In Catalonia, though, and despite the pioneering venture of the Roussillonese lintels of the early eleventh century, the large-scale incorporation of sculpture into architectural work came later, in about 1120. After that moment, some of the great buildings of the previous century were the object of renovations involving structural changes, changes in the decorative programmes and in the liturgical furnishings. In other cases buildings were entirely rebuilt, as happened in La Seu d'Urgell cathedral, the churches in Besalú and Sant Pere de Galligans in Girona. Here the sculpture is perfectly integrated with the walls, emphasising important elements such as entrances (gateways, façades), openings, the interior spaces, especially around the altar (the areas of the apses and the crossing) and the colonnades in the cloisters.

One example of the wealth and of the technical possibilities contributed by materials like marble can be seen in sites in Roussillon, which are especially rich both in the decoration of new cloisters (Sant Miquel de Cuixà, Elne cathedral) and in other elements, like the famous tribunes in Serrabona and in Cuixà itself. Closely related to the Roussillonese sphere, the Master of Cabestany illustrates the circulation of workshops, sculptors and their technical formulas, with a production dotted around various points of the western Mediterranean like Languedoc, Catalonia and Tuscany, showing how wide-reaching the work of a given workshop or circle could be. It's also an example of the survival and the interpretation of formulas from Antiquity, taking as a point of reference ancient sarcophagi, especially from the fourth century.

However, the masterpiece of Romanesque sculpture in Catalonia, as well as the most controversial work, is undoubtedly the portal of Santa Maria de Ripoll. It was added on top of the eleventh-century façade like a piece of furniture and its general composition takes the form of a Roman triumphal arch, with a complex iconographic programme covering every surface. Partly inspired in the illustrations in the eleventh-century Ripoll Bible, the work is also a reminder of the days of Oliba.

Around the altar: liturgical furnishings

Architectural renovations and new buildings also called for the production of items for the altar and liturgical furnishings. In some cases, these works took on a monumental format, like the tribunes mentioned at Cuixà and Serrabona, truly monumental constructions located in the middle of the nave that acted as an element dividing the interior space and organising movement there.

However, the largest and most significant production was intended for the altar (or altars), the focal point of the building insomuch as it was the place where the Eucharist was celebrated. Here we find the sacred ornaments and the images for veneration, with polychrome wooden carvings that were often also decorated with plaster reliefs with colradura (gold-coloured varnish) to give them a more sumptuous appearance. We mustn't forget that the models for objects of this sort were generally to be found in metalwork objects decorated with enamel and precious stones. In the case of Catalonia, though, what is especially unique and outstanding is the extraordinary series of polychrome altar frontals in tempera, comparable only, at the height of the twelfth century, with the painted crosses of central Italy. As we shall see, many of them should be seen as being directly related to other pictorial traditions, such as miniatures and mural painting. In addition, amongst the different types of altar furnishing, Catalonia offers a very varied panorama. Over the altar table there were frequently wooden canopies decorated with figurative cycles, either with the classical structure of the temple-canopy or else with a structure that was only ever found in Catalonia: the ceiling-canopy.

In this field too Ripoll stands out as a paradigmatic focus which, along with other workshops like, probably, those of La Seu d'Urgell or Vic, developed an ample production directed not only at satisfying the needs of the centre itself but also those of other monasteries and parish churches. It's therefore not difficult to understand the similarities between the compositional scheme of the portal in Ripoll and that of the altar frontal from Martinet (Worcester Art Museum), or similarities of style between the reliefs on the same portal and some wooden sculptural productions, something clearly visible in the frontal from Sant Pere de Ripoll (Museu Episcopal de Vic). In Ripoll, furthermore, there was considerable understanding of the painting technique and the preparation of the constituent materials, applied to the altar frontals or the ceiling-canopies. In all these workshops, the polychrome work was closely coordinated with the carving when it came to producing images for veneration, such as crucifixes or Madonnas, although some of the prototypes are of foreign origin and generally arrived by way of the pilgrim's routes, which were a very important means of entry. As in architecture, the connections with international trends and relations with the main centres of the period produced first-rate pieces, always also in connection with the local tradition, which was especially successful in the case of Ripoll.

SUMPTUOUS OBJECTS: FROM METALWORK TO ENAMELS

There are more written accounts of the metalwork sof the Romanesque period in Catalonia than there are remains. We know of the existence of liturgical objects and altar furnishings covered with precious stones, like those in Girona cathedral. A box-wood Madonna (Museu del Tresor de la Catedral) from this cathedral has survived that was covered with silver. Of the many objects made in metal the majority must come from foreign workshops, especially the enamels made in Limoges, a centre with plentiful production and exports all over Europe (favoured by conciliar decisions) after the last quarter of the twelfth century. The arrival of these products, though, doesn't remove the possibility that some local workshop might have been operating in Catalonia on a smaller scale. Nevertheless, at the beginning of the thirteenth century some images covered in an alloy of lead and tin also arrived in Catalonia, like the ones from Tuir and Plandogau (Museu Frederic Marès, Barcelona), closely related to the Auvergne region through the pilgrims' routes connected with the cult of Mary.

The end of Romanesque: the transformations of '1200 art'

After the period 1140-1150 a series of changes took place in certain parts of Europe and the Mediterranean which gradually penetrated the artistic culture of the second half of the twelfth century. For one, Gothic art took off in France in the area around Paris, under figures like Abbot Suger of Saint-Denis, with the introduction of new approaches to composition and new subject matter in painting, sculpture, stained glass and the sumptuous arts. Subsequently, these gradually spread to other parts of Europe. For another, the Byzantine world under the Komnenian dynasty was characterised by an art full of humanism, with varied expressiveness and corporeity in its treatment of the characters and scenes. These novelties were introduced into Western European art in the features of what is called the '1200 style' or, in a broader sense, '1200 art', often also marked by the imprint of the Ancient Roman world. These developments also filtered into different aspects of Spanish art and Catalan art, at a time when the courts, whose power was growing, were culturally stimulated through contact with other European dynasties as a result of diplomatic relations or matrimonial alliances.

Once the County of Barcelona had consolidated its dominance over the south, known as Catalunya Nova, work began on building the two large new cathedrals of Tarragona and Lleida, as well as the great Cistercian monasteries. In this way, during the last centuries of the twelfth century and a large part of the thirteenth, all aspects of sculpture and painting were to bear the mark of Byzantine art and the Ancient World, to differing degrees according to the site and to the international trend associated with it. Without forgetting their own twelfth-century tradition, some works of architectural sculpture showed this somewhat heterogeneous air in which memories of the Italian world, of Tuscany or Emiglia, overlapped with the influence of the workshops of Languedoc and Provence or even other parts of Europe. In this situation, then, it's not surprising that in Barcelona or in buildings connected with powerful feudal lords there is work that can reflect influences from the workshop of the Pórtico de la Gloria on Santiago de Compostela cathedral, as well as from central France, under the rule of the Plantagenets. As regards the pictorial arts, the workshops producing panel paintings were the ones that most readily absorbed the new possibilities, intensifying those elements of Byzantine origin, through Italian, English or Germanic intermediaries or directly from the Eastern Mediterranean. This moment was to give Catalonia real masterpieces of this pictorial art, which brought the world of Romanesque art to a brilliant close.

6. The chapter house of Sigena. The paintings from the chapter house of the Aragonese nunnery are an extraordinary example of the power of the 1200 style south of the Pyrenees. MNAC/MAC 68703-68709

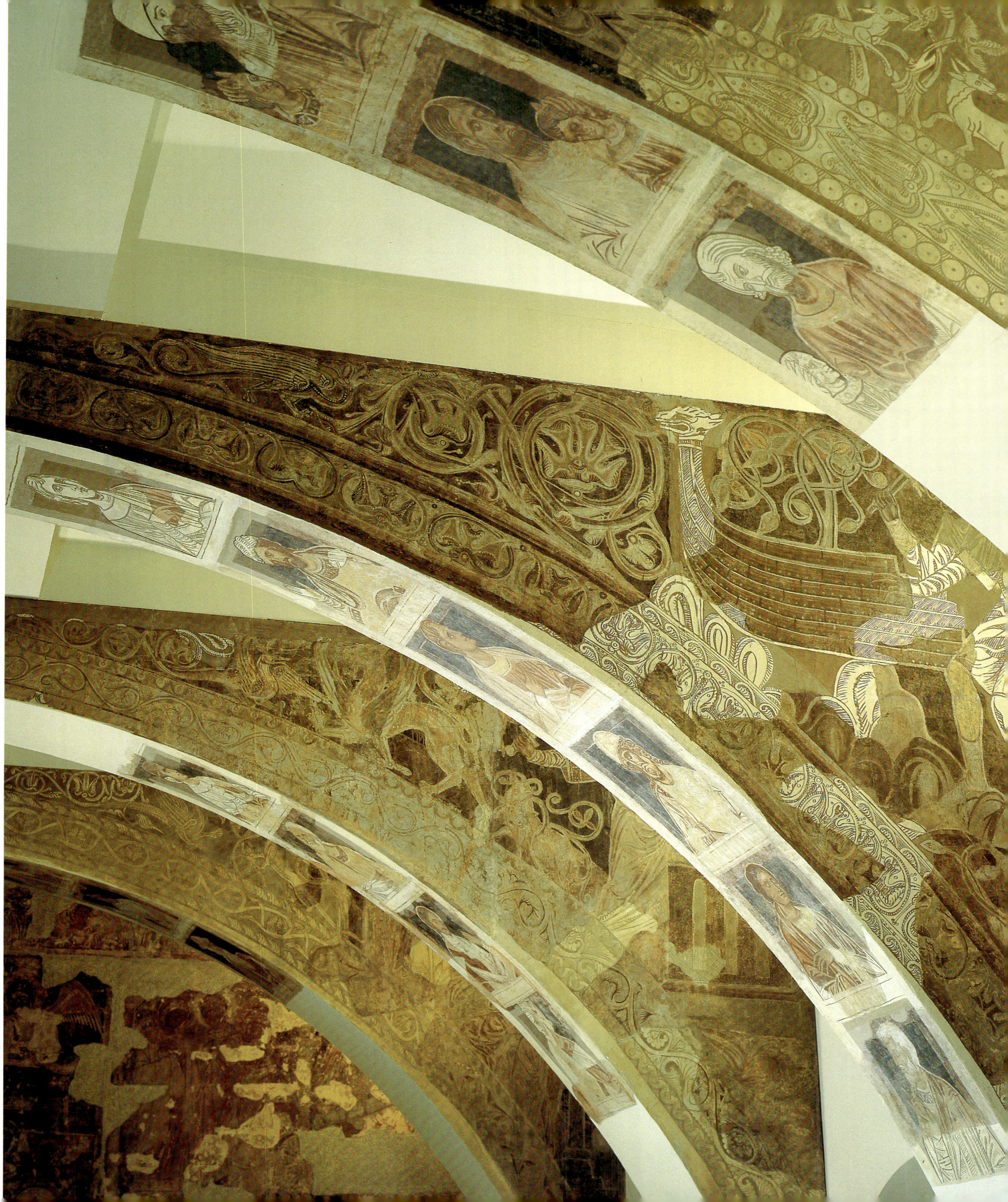

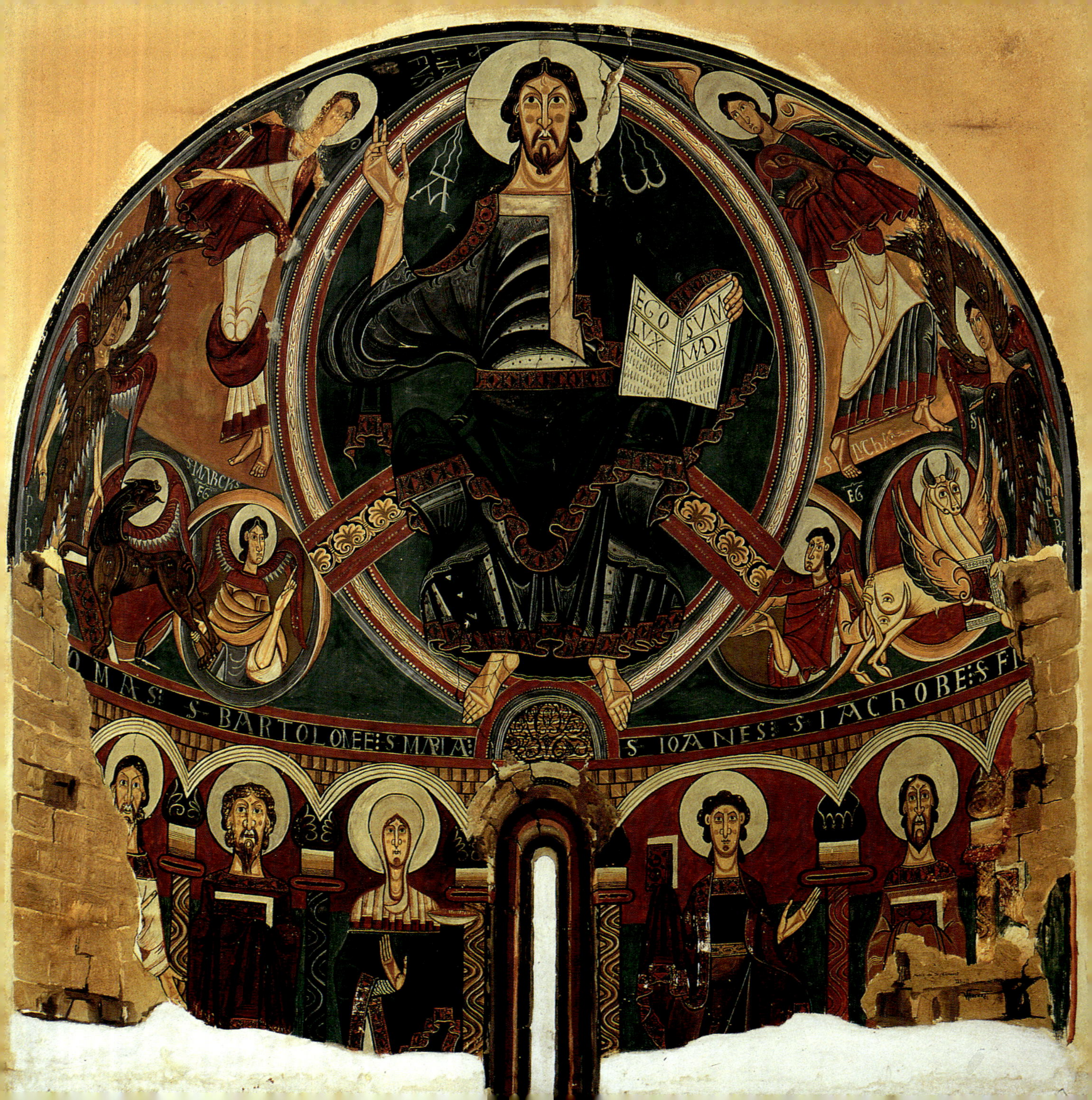
EGO SVM
LVX MVDI
OMAS S BARTOLOMEE S MARIA
S IOANES S IACHOBE S FI

Mural Painting

Manuel Castiñeiras

'This work is of an importance beyond all imagining. Extremely valuable examples of Catalan Romanesque art have been saved from total destruction which now, safeguarded in our Museum, make it extraordinarily important',

'Pintures murals romàniques',
La Veu de Catalunya,
Sunday, 26 March 1922, p. 5.

7. JOAN VALLHONRAT
Reproduction of the mural paintings from the apse of Sant Climent de Taüll.
1908
Tempera on paper stuck to a canvas mounted on a wooden frame.
130 × 130 cm
MNAC/MAC 63862

DISCOVERY, REMOVAL AND FIRST INSTALLATIONS

It's still easy today to imagine the surprise of those first travellers as they gazed on the impressive paintings hidden behind a Gothic altarpiece in the central apse of Sant Climent de Taüll. Few then would have dared to predict the long journey in store for this and so many other works now making up the MNAC's exceptional collection of Romanesque painting. In fact, their first illustrious visitors, like Lluís Domènech i Montaner in 1904, Adolf Mas and Josep Gudiol i Cunill in 1907 and Josep Salvany, only managed to take general photographs in black and white of the east end of the church, sometimes accompanied by a sketchy description, in which the imposing 'Pantocrator' can be glimpsed between the pointed pinnacles of the Gothic altarpiece. The honour of being the first person to draw them in their entirety fell to Joan Vallhonrat, who in 1908 painted a watercolour for the Junta de Museus for the third instalment of *Les Pintures Murals Catalanes* (1911), a copy of which is kept in the MNAC's collections. In fact it was the publication of this collection, thanks to which the Catalan Pyrenees' magnificent heritage of Romanesque painting was made known to the world, that provoked or rather stirred up the greed of antiquarians and collectors who a few years later tried to export this work and others like it. Fortunately, the Junta de Museus managed to stop the operation and, as a safety measure, decided to purchase the work and have it removed and transported to Barcelona by Italian experts, in a campaign carried out between 1919 and 1923. Once installed in the new Museu d'Art i Arqueologia in the Parc de la Ciutadella, and later in the Palau Nacional de Montjuïc, the paintings from Sant Climent became the masterpiece of Catalan Romanesque art and, thanks to the admiration of avant-garde artists like Picabia, Picasso, Breton and Tàpies, an undisputed icon of universal art.

In fact, the international fame of the Museu Nacional d'Art de Catalunya is due mainly to its extraordinary collection of Romanesque paintings. First of all, no other museum in the world has such a large collection of works in this technique. Because of the large size of this sort of work, they are not usually kept in museums but, as in France, are kept on their original site. Secondly, the very fact of their removal and transfer to the Museum made them the stars of an odyssey we shall be narrating in detail later. Thirdly and lastly, apart from its unquestionable aesthetic value, Romanesque art has an added value in Catalonia as it coincides with the country's historical and political beginnings: the Catalonia of the counts. This is why the defence of the country's past during the second half of the nineteenth century by the *Renaixença* movement, later refreshed during the *Noucentista* period, took a particular interest in the recovery, study and dissemination of Romanesque art.

As regards the story of the discovery of Romanesque painting in Catalonia, there are still a few questions to be answered. Nevertheless, in recent decades important progress has been made. We know that at the end of the nineteenth century some Romanesque mural paintings in Catalonia were already known of and had been published, amongst them those of Sant Quirze de Pedret and Sant Martí de Fonollar. Years later, the architect and scholar Lluís Domènech i Montaner, in the course of writing his *Història de l'art romànic a Catalunya* (which was never published), made a series of trips in 1904 to the *comarques* of Pallars and Ribagorça. On these trips he was able for the first time to see, describe and, in some cases, to draw and photograph the murals of El Burgal, Àneu and

Taüll. Later, thanks to the *Missió Arqueològica-jurídica a la ratlla d'Aragó*, a field-trip organised by the Institut d'Estudis Catalans in 1907 in which Josep Puig i Cadafalch, Josep Gudiol i Cunill, the photographer Adolf Mas and others took part, the rich Romanesque patrimony of the Vall de Boí finally received due appreciation. In fact, following on from this trip, the Junta de Museus, the body in charge of overseeing the museums belonging to the Mancomunitat de Catalunya, had a series of copies made of the mural paintings known or under study. These were used by the Institut d'Estudis Catalans to illustrate the instalments of the series *Pintures murals catalanes* by Josep Pijoan. Between 1907 and 1921 this publication was to make known to the public the most important series of Romanesque mural paintings (Pedret, Sant Martí de Fonollar, Sant Miquel de la Seu d'Urgell, Sant Climent de Taüll and Santa Maria de Taüll, Sant Joan de Boí, Santa Maria d'Àneu, Sant Pere del Burgal, Ginestarre de Cardós, Esterri de Cardós, Santa Eulàlia d'Estaon, Santa Maria de Mur and Sant Pere d'Àger), but as well as making them famous it also stirred the interest of the growing international art market of the time.

It was in this context that the Hungarian-born North-American art dealer Ignacio Pollak, in partnership with the French-born Gabriel Dereppe, purchased the mural paintings in the central apse of Santa Maria de Mur and had them removed. These paintings were subsequently acquired by the Barcelona collector Lluís Plandiura. The plan, executed in the summer of 1919, was possible thanks to the hired services of an Italian expert in the removal of mural painting, the *estrattista* Franco Steffanoni. When the Junta de Museus de Barcelona heard that the paintings in the apse of the church at Santa Maria de Mur were being removed, J. Folch i Torres informed the President of the Mancomunitat, J. Puig i Cadafalch, about what was happening. Puig tried to have the church declared a Historical and Artistic Monument, but this came about too late (1920). In 1921 the paintings were sold by their new owner, Lluís Plandiura, to the Museum of Fine Arts in Boston, United States, where they have remained ever since. However, thanks to the alarm raised by the removal of paintings from Santa Maria de Mur, it was revealed that this was part of a larger operation affecting another ten series in the region. In a move to stop it, between 1919 and 1920 the Junta de Museus, through a loan from the firm of Fàbrega y Recassens, negotiated with I. Pollak for the purchase and removal of the paintings and their installation in the Museu d'Art i Arqueologia in Barcelona's Parc de la Ciutadella, where there was already an important collection of medieval art.

The process of removing the paintings was carried out between 1920 and 1923 by Franco Steffanoni with the help of Arturo Dalmati and his apprentice Arturo Cividini, using a technique known as *strappo*, which involves stripping off the chromatic surface of a mural painting in such a way that the pictorial film is separated from the *intonaco* or rendering of the wall. The operation consisted of five steps. First of all, a careful examination was made of the wall and the surface was cleaned of remains of whitewash, dust or retouching. Secondly, a water-soluble organic glue was made and cotton cloths were soaked in it. Thirdly, up to three layers of these cloths were applied uniformly over the picture surface to be removed, so as to ensure a safe, flexible covering of even thickness. Fourthly, once the glued cloths had dried and the glue had contracted, the actual removal (the *strappo*) took place. This consisted in slowly pulling the cloth away with the help of a palette knife and rolling it up. Once the paintings had been moved to Barcelona, the fifth and final step took place,

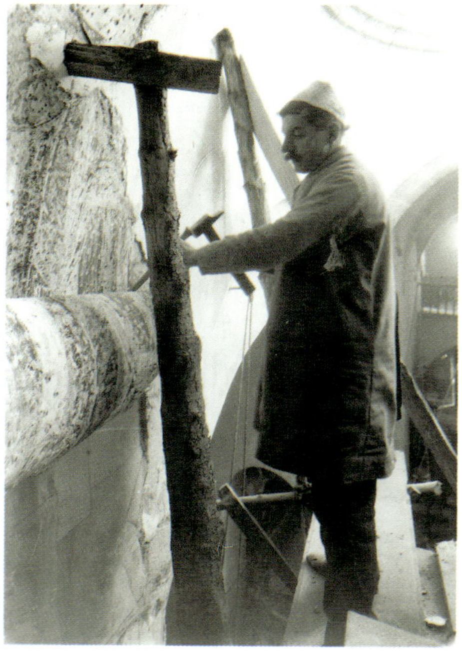

8 9

8. Santa Maria de Taüll.
The removal of the paintings from Santa Maria de Taüll. 1922

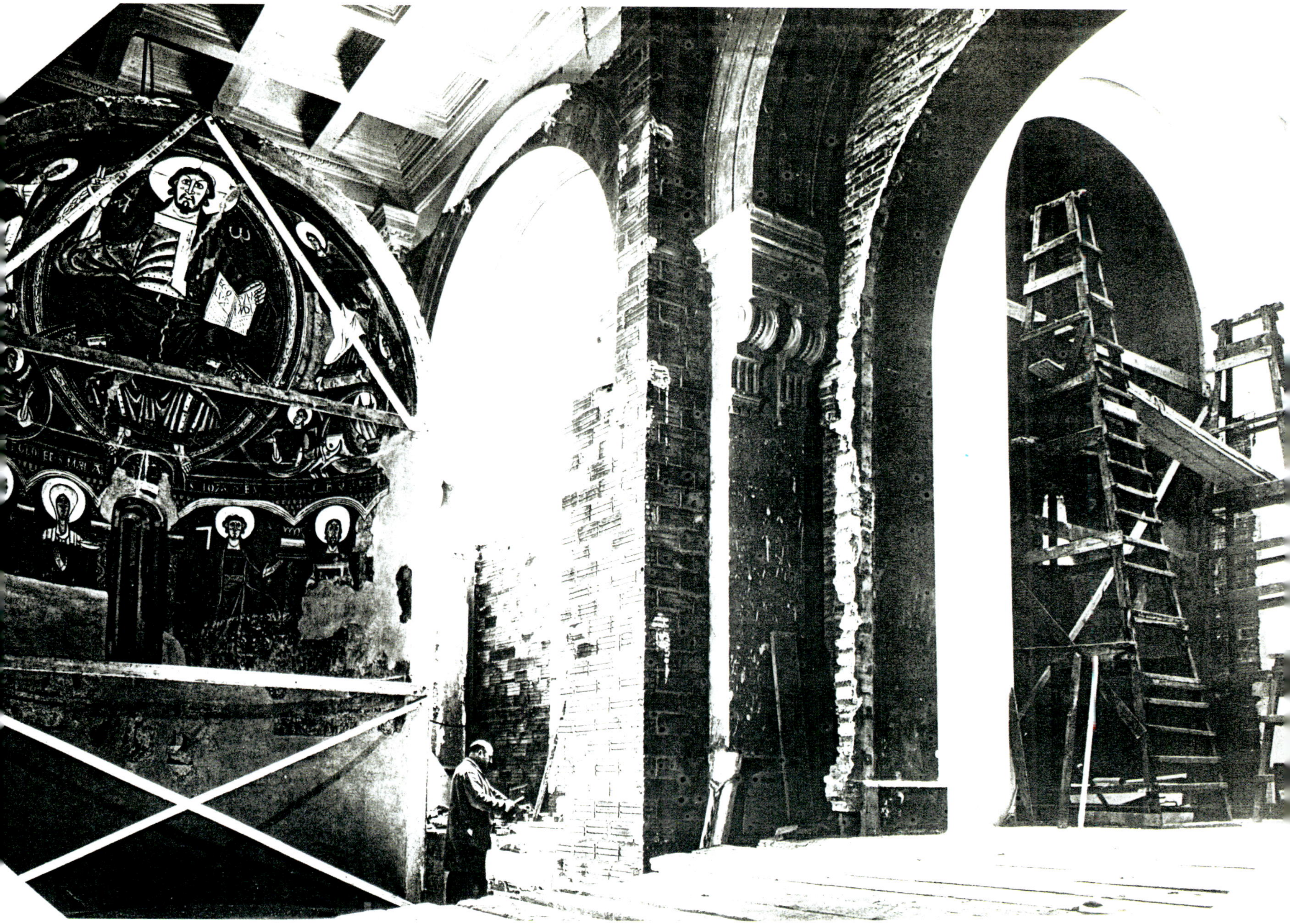

9. The assembly of the apse 1922-1924. The installation of the paintings in the old Museu d'Art i Arqueología. 1923

in which the surface was released again after giving it a new cloth support. First the rear surface of the cloth was checked and smoothed with a palette knife to eliminate possible remains of *intonaco* or preparatory mortar. A calcium casseinate adhesive was then prepared which was insoluble in water and gauze and sacking or linen cloth were glued to the back. Finally the cotton cloths covering the surface of the painting were easily eliminated with water and once transferred to cloth the works were set in wooden frameworks using plaster and tow. These frameworks were designed by the architect J. F. Ràfols as reproductions of the original apses and were built by the firm of Priu i Simon.

This procedure was suitable for removing al fresco painting and differed from the *stacco* method, which was normally applied to stuccoes, mural painting in oil, varnish or wax, all of which had to be removed complete with the *intonaco* or preparatory mortar by cutting out a section of wall. The revolutionary *strappo* procedure was perfected by an Italian nobleman from Bergamo, Count Giovanni Secco Suardo, who was a collector and restorer and who described the procedure in his handbook *Manuale ragionato per la parte meccanica dell'Arte del Ristauratore dei dipinti* in 1866. It was in his laboratory in Bergamo that Antonio Zanchi (1823-1886) studied. Zanchi was the first *estrattista* to specialise in removing paintings using this method and it was he who taught Giuseppe Steffanoni (1841-1902). Steffanoni, who started out as a carpenter, was the founder of a dynasty of restorers and *estrattisti* who made their name in northern Italy and abroad working for *sorprintendenze*, collectors, private dealers and museums. In 1880 he started his own business with his sons Francesco (1870-1942) and Fedele (1867-1921) as 'Dita Giuseppe Steffanoni e figli', which after his death became 'Steffanoni f.li'. It was Francesco, or Franco, who decades later, between 1919 and 1923, was in charge of removing the Catalan mural paintings along with his colleague Arturo Cividini. Some famous works removed by the Steffanoni in Italy at the end of the nineteenth century were Pier Francesco Mazzucchielli's *Vulcan's Forge* and the paintings in the bridal chamber of the castle of Roccabianca, both kept at the Pinacoteca in the Castello Sforzesco in Milan, and also the Tiepolo frescoes in the Villa Contarini alla Mira (Venice) for the French collector Edouard André, now in the museum devoted to him in Paris, the Musée Jacquemart-André. The Steffanoni family actively served the *Uffici Regionali per la Conservazioni dei Monumenti*, set up in 1888, in operations to rescue frescoes from buildings in ruins or about to be demolished, and for the Academia di Brera in Milan, where between 1900 and 1901, under the supervision of Corrado Ricci, they set up a new installation for the Pinacoteca of the mural paintings transferred to cloth on wooden frameworks, as they would do later in Barcelona.

Franco Steffanoni was an expert in removing paintings but he was not a smuggler of works of art. In fact, he came to Catalonia in 1919 under contract to Ignacio Pollack, to remove the mural paintings from Santa Maria de Mur and following that, between 1920 and 1923, those of ten more churches in the Catalan Pyrenees, most of them in the Bishopric of La Seu d'Urgell (Santa Maria de Taüll and Sant Climent de Taüll, Sant Joan de Boí, Santa Eulàlia d'Estaon, Ginestarre, Esterri de Cardós, Sant Miquel de la Seu d'Urgell, Sant Miquel d'Engolasters, Santa Maria d'Àneu and Sant Quirze de Pedret), all of which remained in Barcelona. The operation was undoubtedly a somewhat complex one, because first of all a sketch of the paintings had to be made so as to divide them up into pieces, as Secco Suardo recommended that these should be of a small size. Secondly, these divisions had to coincide with the figures in the composition. Thirdly and lastly, many of the churches involved had to be inspected first, as part of the original decoration was hidden under layers of whitewash, as in the case of Sant Joan de Boí and much of Santa Maria de Taüll. Hence the importance of the work of Joaquim Folch i Torres, who was the Director of the Museum's medieval and modern art section at the time and in 1920 was appointed supervisor for the operation.

All together, more than 345 square metres of paintings were removed, using a procedure hitherto unknown in Spain. These paintings were later to form part of one of the most avant-garde installations in the European museography of the time: the Romanesque section at the Museu d'Art i Arqueologia in the Parc de la Ciutadella, in the building's north-east wing. Although some of the works were shown to the public for the first time

10. SANT PERE DE LA SEU D'URGELL: APSE.
Mural paintings from the central apse of the church of Sant Pere (today Sant Miquel and Sant Pere), in the cathedral complex of La Seu d'Urgell. Middle of the 12th century
705 × 565 × 300 cm
MNAC/MAC 15867

10

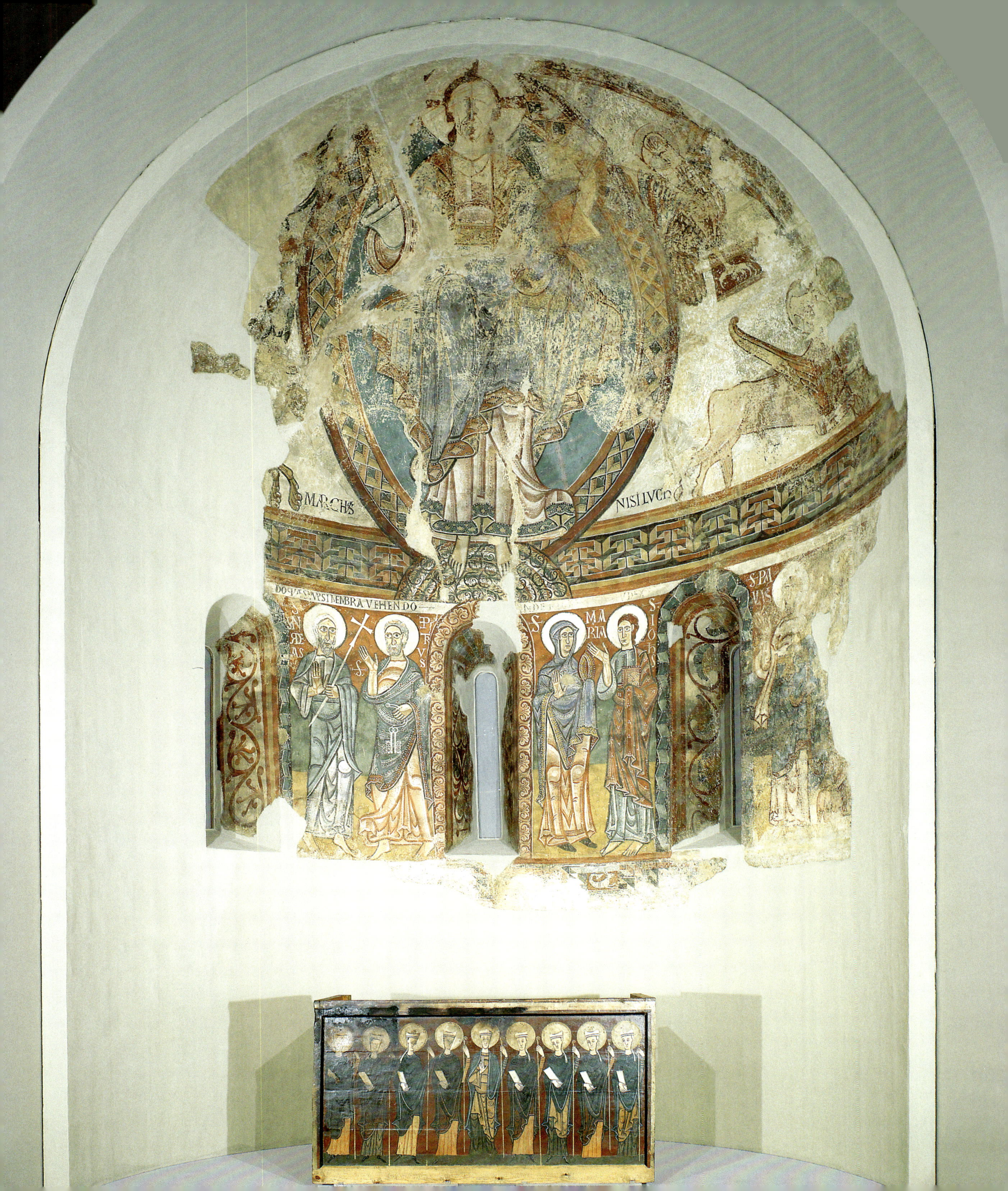

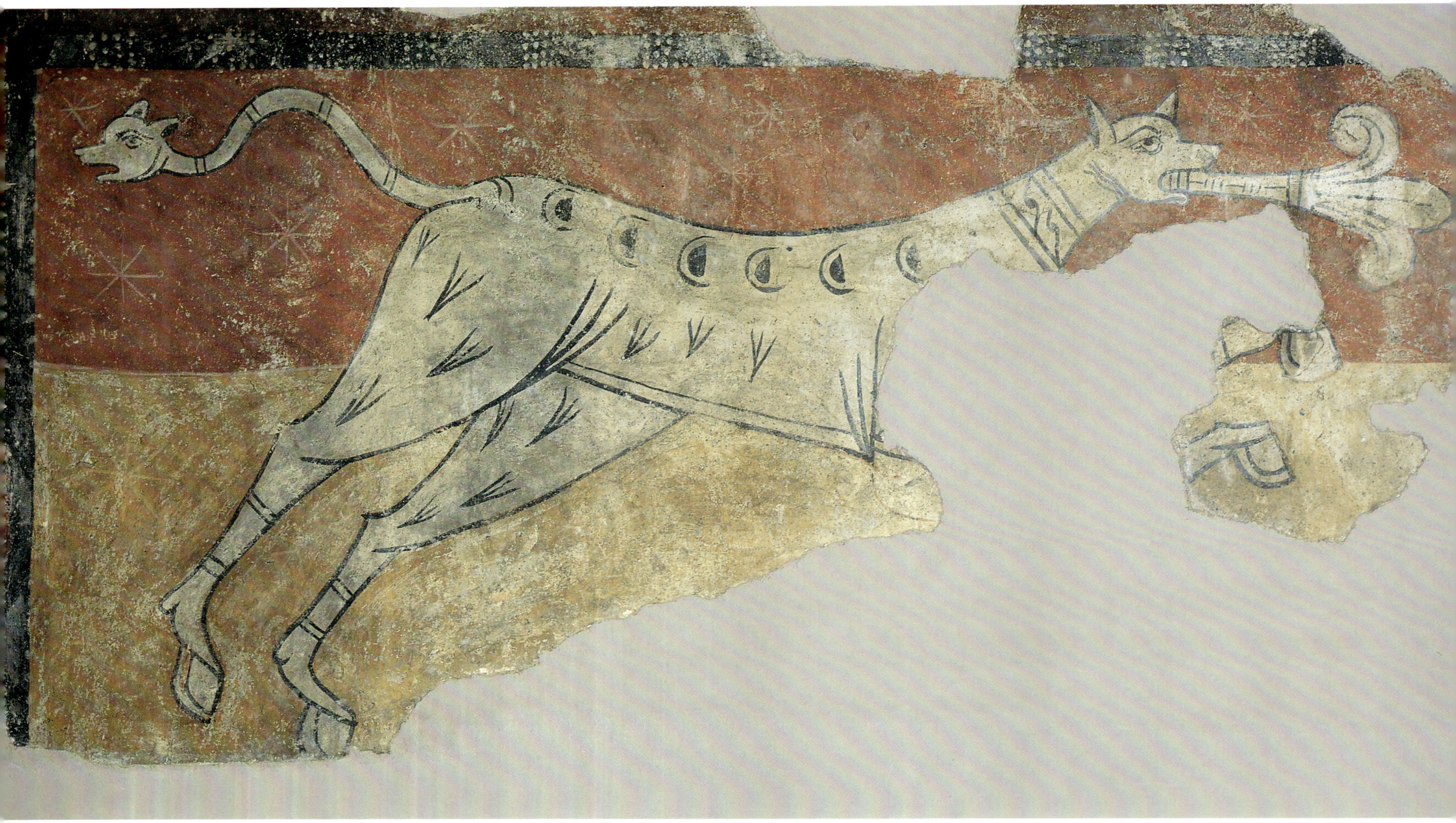

on 25 March 1922, when an exhibition was held of the works acquired by the Junta de Museus between 1919 and 1922, the section wasn't officially inaugurated until 12 June 1924. The installation was the painstaking work of J. Folch i Torres, Director of the Museu d'Art i Arqueologia since 1920, and was an immediate success with the public, a fact recorded in the press of the time:

> 'The installation of the mural paintings is worthy of sincere applause, both for the care with which they have been moved to their new site and for the admirable success presiding their arrangement, thanks to which they preserve the same appearance as in their place of origin, increased by a level of light they were lacking in the old churches they came from, which makes it possible to appreciate their every detail, constituting a part of the museum that Barcelona can be proud of'.
>
> 'En el Museo del Parque', *Las Noticias*, 26 March 1922.

Over the years, fulfilling its role as a leading museum of Romanesque mural painting, the institution purchased more of these works, some of them newly removed, others that had already been removed, with the object of adding to its magnificent collection but also of ensuring they were properly preserved. This is the case of the se-

11. BOÍ: ANIMAL
Imaginary animal with fleur-de-lis, which originally decorated the south wall of the north aisle of the church of Sant Joan de Boí (Alta Ribagorça).
Around 1100
230 × 276 cm
MNAC/MAC 15951

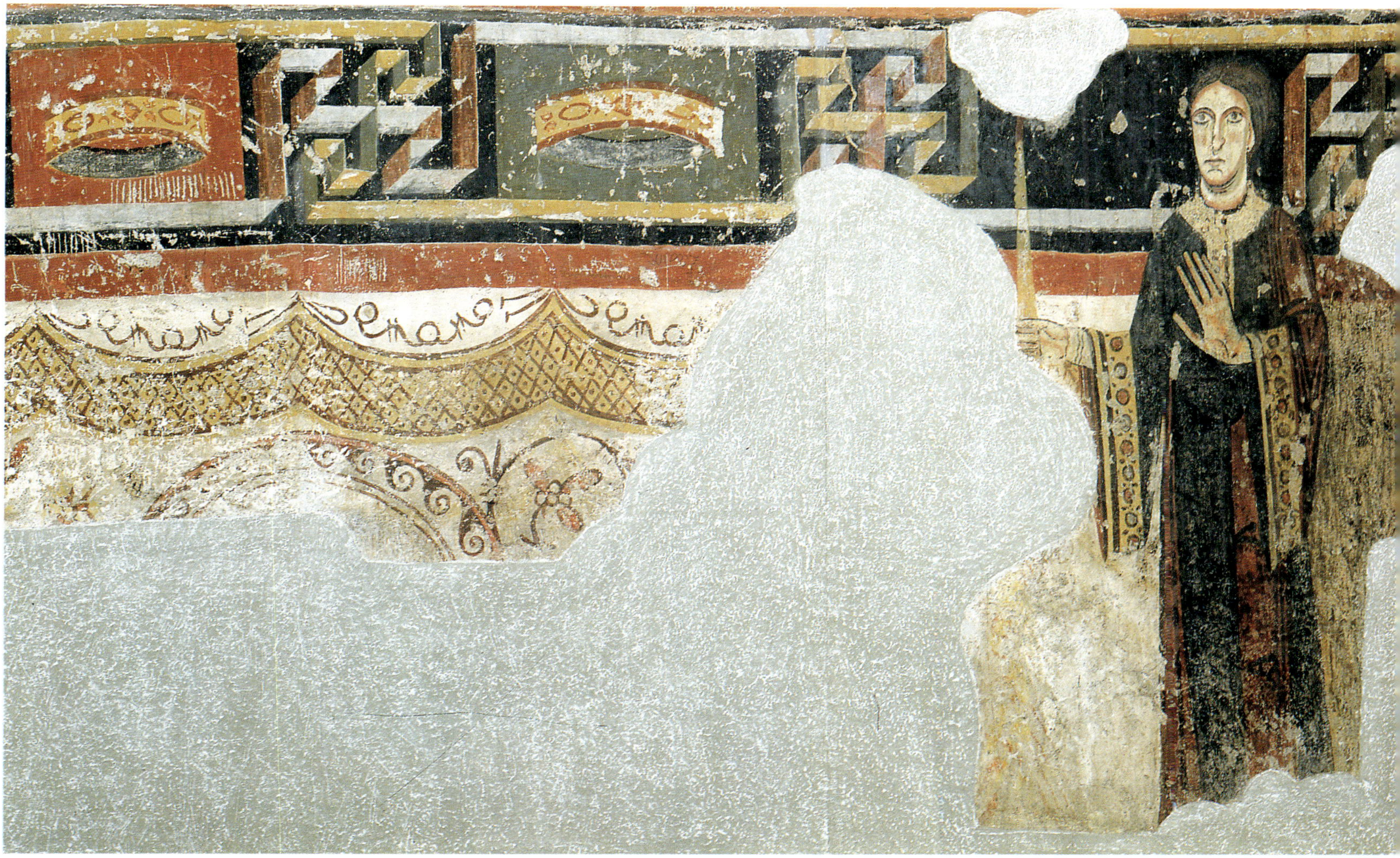

11 12

12. El Burgal: detail of Countess Llúcia of Pallars. Lady donor identified as Countess Llúcia of Pallars, from the lower register of the apse of the church of Sant Pere del Burgal. Around 1095-1120 From the monastery church of Sant Pere del Burgal MNAC/MAC 113138

ries from El Burgal, Argolell and Orcau, acquired in 1932 when the Plandiura collection was purchased, the one from Sorpe, exhibited for the first time in 1934, the paintings from Sigena, removed during the Spanish Civil War, the ones from Toses and from the lateral apse in Santa Maria de Mur, in 1950-1953, to which were added in the 1960s and 1970s other fragments that served to complete Sorpe, Estaon, Santa Maria de Taüll, El Burgal and Boí.

In addition, there have been three successive installations since the collection was moved to the new Museu d'Art de Catalunya in the Palau Nacional on Montjuïc inaugurated in 1934. One was by by Folch i Torres in 1934, one by Joan Ainaud in 1973 and one by the Italian architect Gae Aulenti in 1995, while Eduard Carbonell was Director. The overhead natural light that predominated in Folch's museography was later replaced with artificial light, which in Ainaud's arrangement suggested a withdrawn, candle-lit church atmosphere, whereas in Aulenti's installation this gave way to more modern and aseptic lighting. Similarly, the wood and plaster structures of the apses, which were concealed in the earlier Museum installations, were considered by the Italian architect to be true museum pieces, mute witnesses to the history of the removal of the paintings, and therefore worthy of being admired.

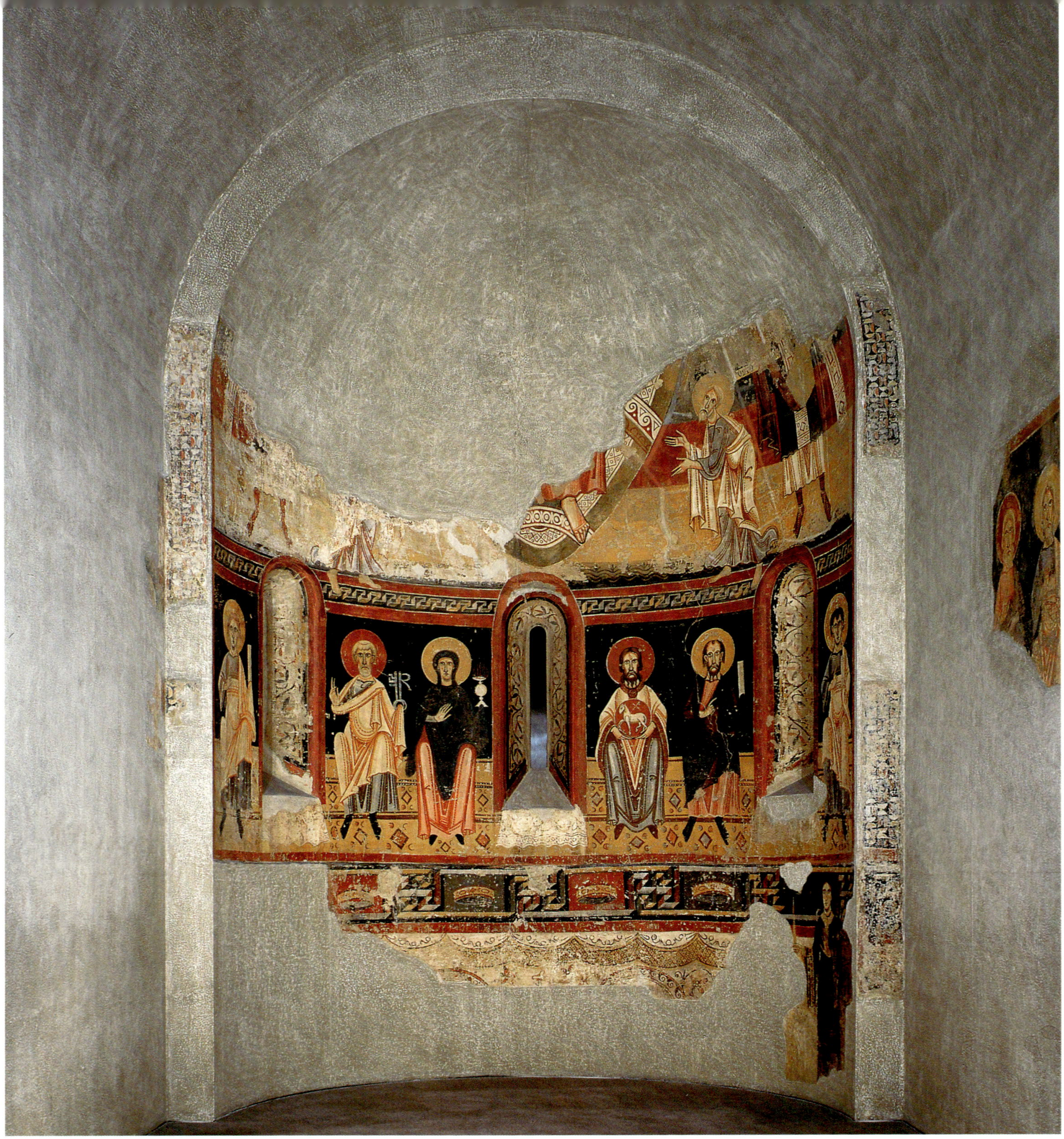

13 14

13. El Burgal: central apse.
Mural paintings from the apse of the monastery church of Sant Pere del Burgal. In the vault, the Maiestas Domini *flanked by the figures of Isaiah and Ezekiel, and enclosing the composition archangels Gabriel and Michael. In the central register, an unidentified apostle, Saint Peter and the Virgin, Saint John the Baptist with the* Agnus Dei*, Saint Paul and Saint John the Evangelist. In the lower register, a lady donor identified as Llúcia of Pallars. Around 1095-1120*
860 × 470 × 500 cm. MNAC/MAC 113138

14. El Burgal: detail.
Detail of the Virgin with the chalice of the Holy Grail and Saint John the Baptist with the clypeus of the Agnus Dei*, from the decoration of the central register of Sant Pere del Burgal.*

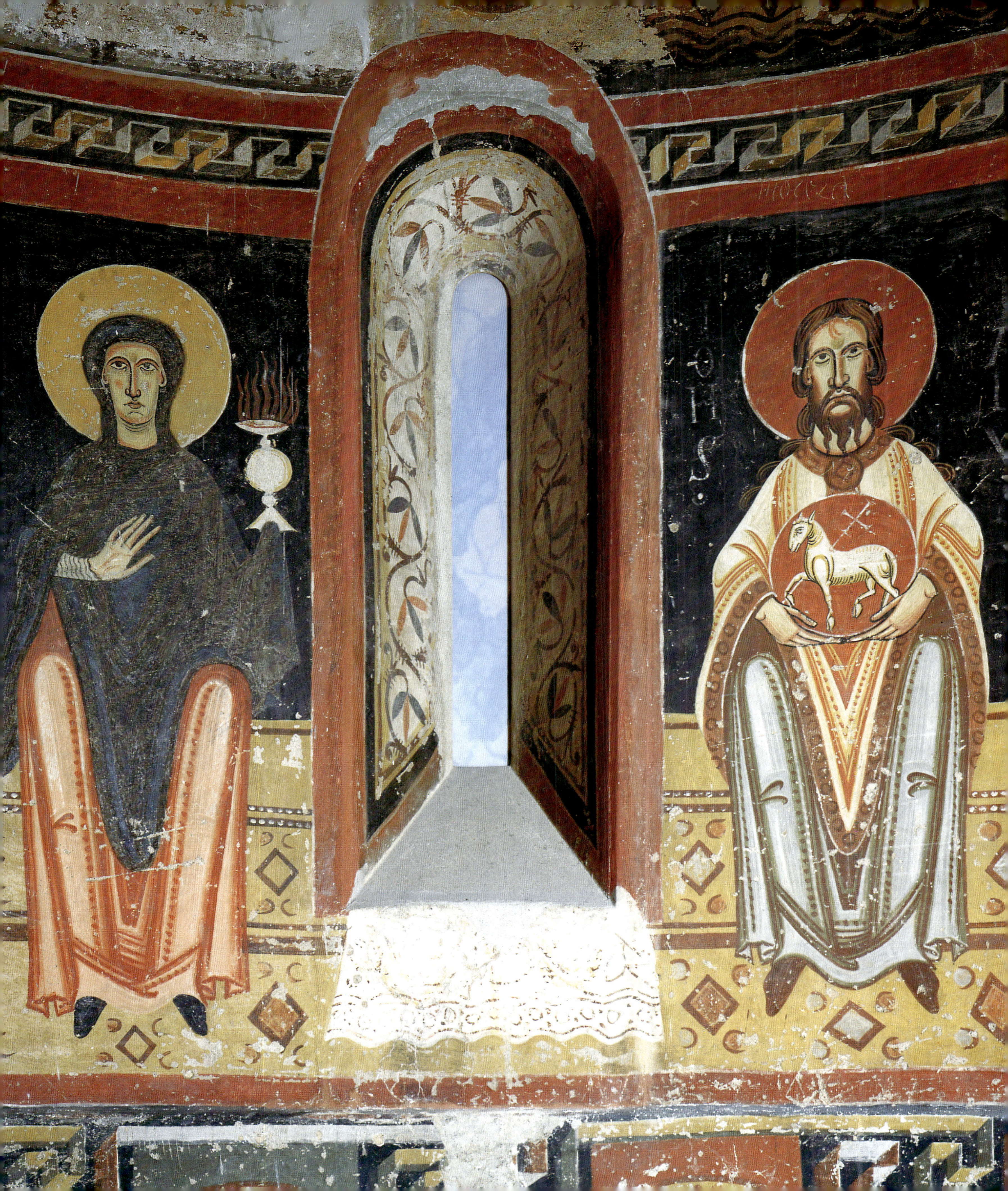

15

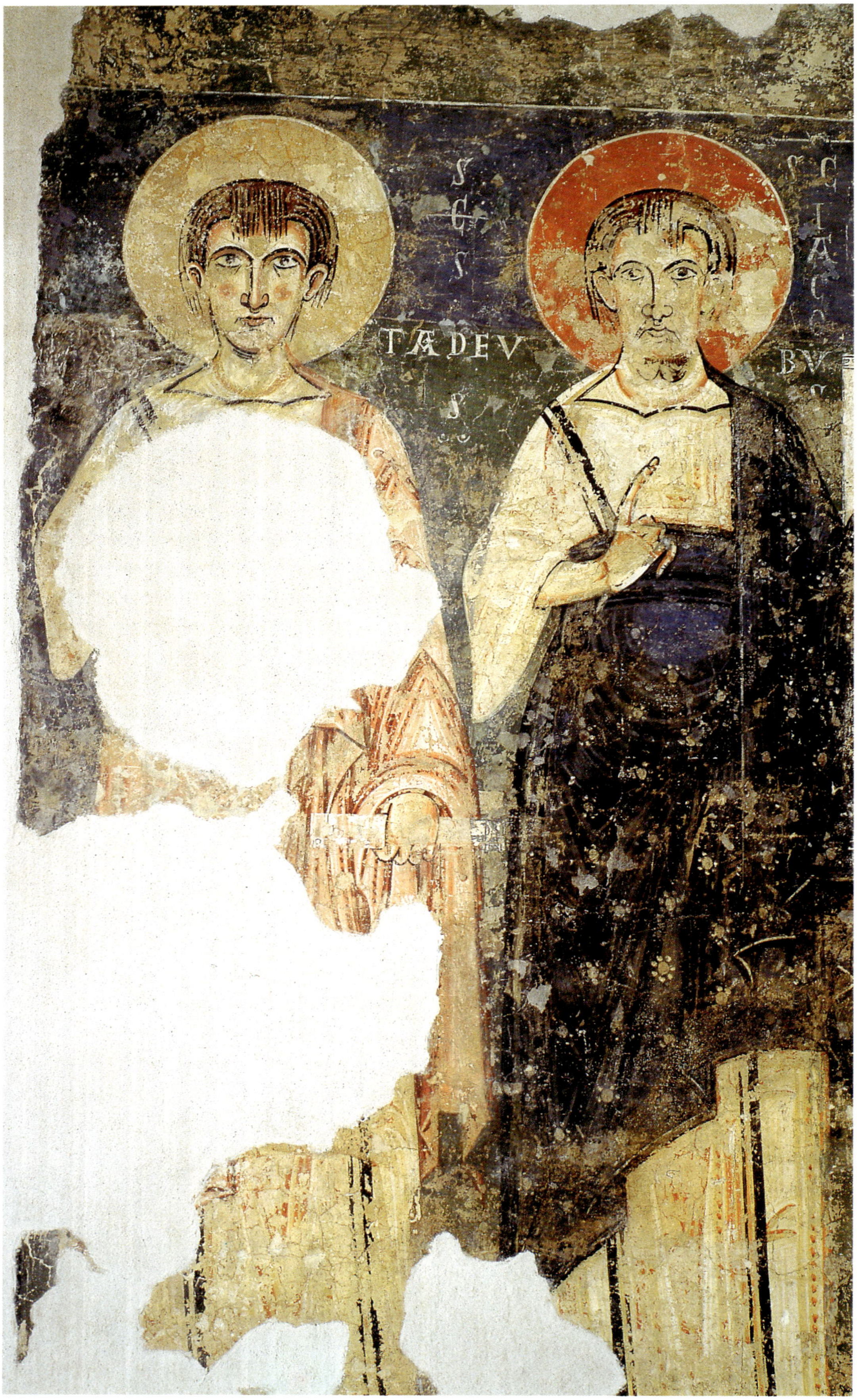

15. ÀGER: SAINT THADDEUS AND SAINT JAMES.
Saint Thaddeus and Saint James, from the decoration of the central apse of the canonical church of Sant Pere d'Àger.
Late 11th – early 12th century.

16. ÀNEU: APSE.
Mural paintings from the central apse of the church of Santa Maria d'Àneu.
Late 11th – early 12th century.
760 × 460 × 240 cm
MNAC/MAC 15874

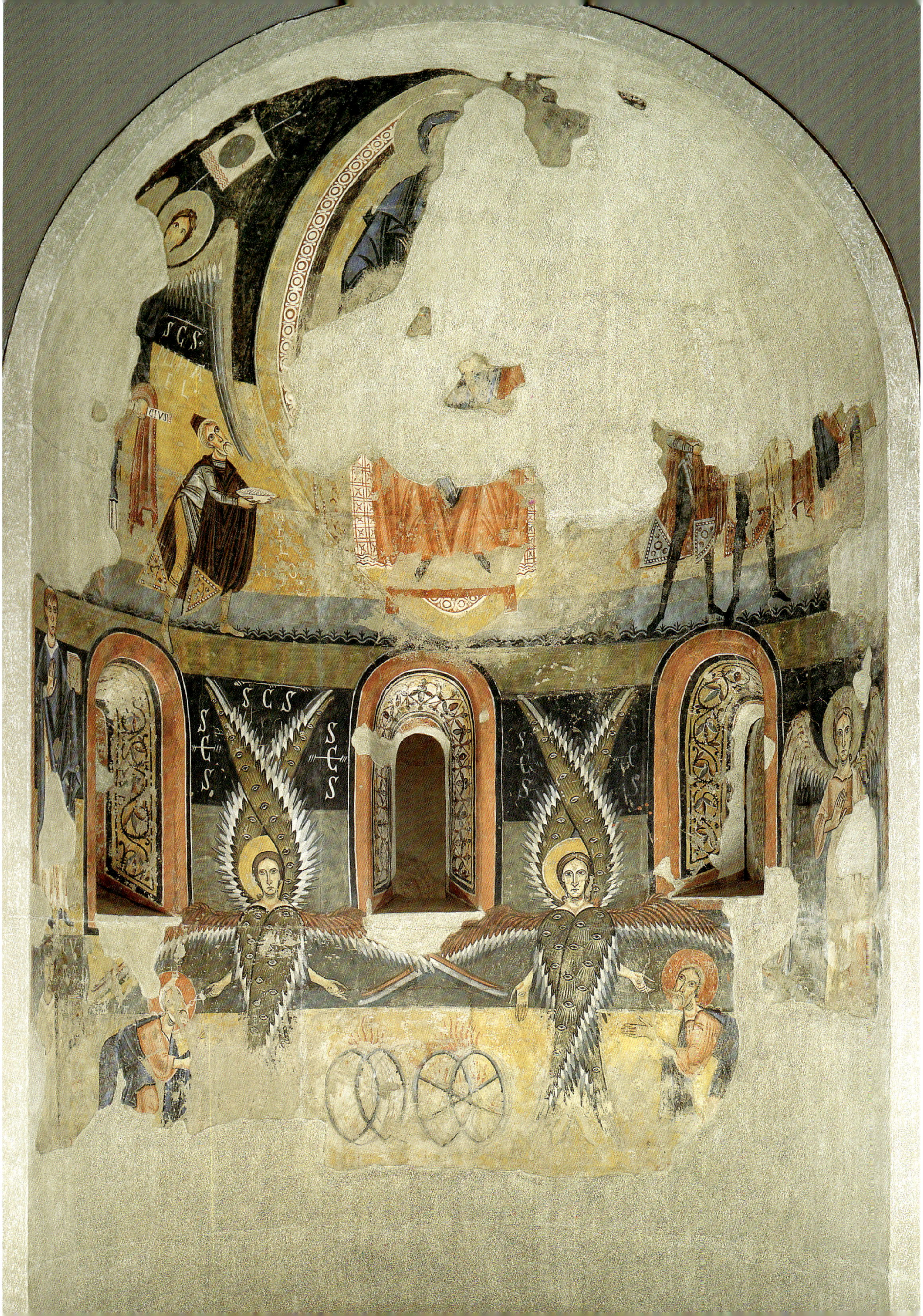
SCS

In spite of the large number of testimonies of mural painting that have survived in Catalonia, we know next to nothing about who the artists were, where they came from, their social status or their technical training, how work was organised in the workshop or their relationship with their patrons or the people who commissioned their work. In fact, we have neither their signatures nor accounts to go by, so that all we can say about them is based on a comparison with other better-documented cases of European Romanesque art, especially in Italy. What we do know for a fact is that their work was an absolutely fundamental part of the building, as a church wasn't considered finished until it was given a coat of whitewash or paint. In fact, when the building was handed over it usually included incisions in the whitewash imitating cut stone blocks, which were then outlined in tempera with red pigment to give the inside of the buildings a more luxurious aspect than simple bare stone. This was an ancient formula, accounts of which go right back to the first and second Pompeian styles. The technique was often used in eleventh-century Catalan architecture, even in buildings that were subsequently painted with figurative mural paintings, as in the case of Santa Maria de Taüll.

However, we have no way of knowing if the presence of large figurative mural programmes in the apses, like those kept in the MNAC, was as widespread as it might at first sight appear. In fact, the only more or less complete testimonies to have come down to us in Catalonia are these cycles from small rural churches, most of them in the Pyrenean *comarques* of Pallars and Ribagorça, whose preservation it has been suggested could be due to their isolation and the fact that the buildings weren't renovated over the years. But we don't know if the large monastery churches like Ripoll, or cathedrals like Barcelona, Girona or La Seu d'Urgell also had extensive figurative programmes of mural paintings that might have provided a model or inspiration for these other churches. Perhaps, on the other hand, as we can deduce from surviving written accounts, these large churches decorated altar tables and the walls of naves, aisles and apses on the main liturgical feast days with tapestries and embroideries, a much more expensive and fragile technique than mural painting. There are magnificent examples of this in the *Tapestry of the Creation* in Girona cathedral, the *Witches' Cloth* (Museu Episcopal de Vic) and the *Embrodery of La Seu d'Urgell* (Victoria & Albert Museum, London). In fact, we ought to ask if the Catalan mural decorations of the twelfth century are not to some extent a cheaper and more permanent way of ornamenting church interiors in far-flung areas. The bottoms of many Catalan mural paintings do indeed imitate curtains or hangings and, like these, are decorated with *clipeus* with the Bestiary (Santa Maria de Taüll) or scenes of Psychomachy (Estaon), for which we find parallels in Italian examples such as Santa Maria in Foro Claudio or the Crypt of Aquileia.

As regards the mural painters' training and technical skills, their craft is usually set apart from other techniques of the time, such as miniature painting, which may have been the work of monks and was carried out in ecclesiastical settings. In this case, it was the works that travelled, rather than the artists. The mural painter, on the other hand, would have been a layman who worked in a travelling workshop and who might even undertake long journeys in response to commissions. This, for example, is the biography that has been

17. ÀNEU: DETAIL OF THE SERAPHIM.
Detail of one of the seraphim and vision of the prophet Isaiah, from the decoration of the lower register of the central apse of the church of Santa Maria d'Àneu.

18. ÀNEU: DETAIL.
Detail of the two seraphim in Isaiah's vision bring the pincers with the red-hot coals close to the lips of the prophets Elias and Isaiah.
Late 11th – early 12th century
MNAC/MAC 15874 17

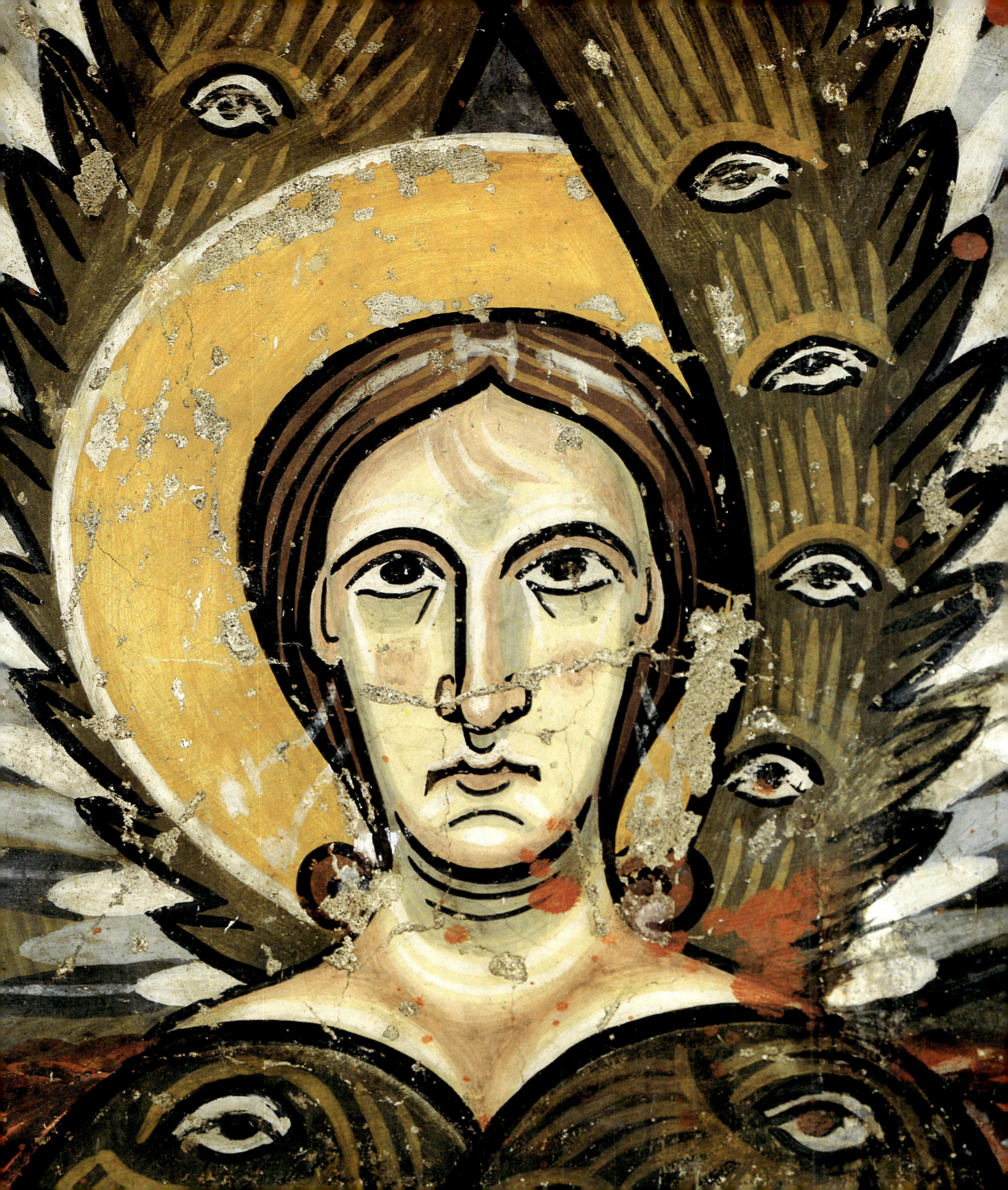

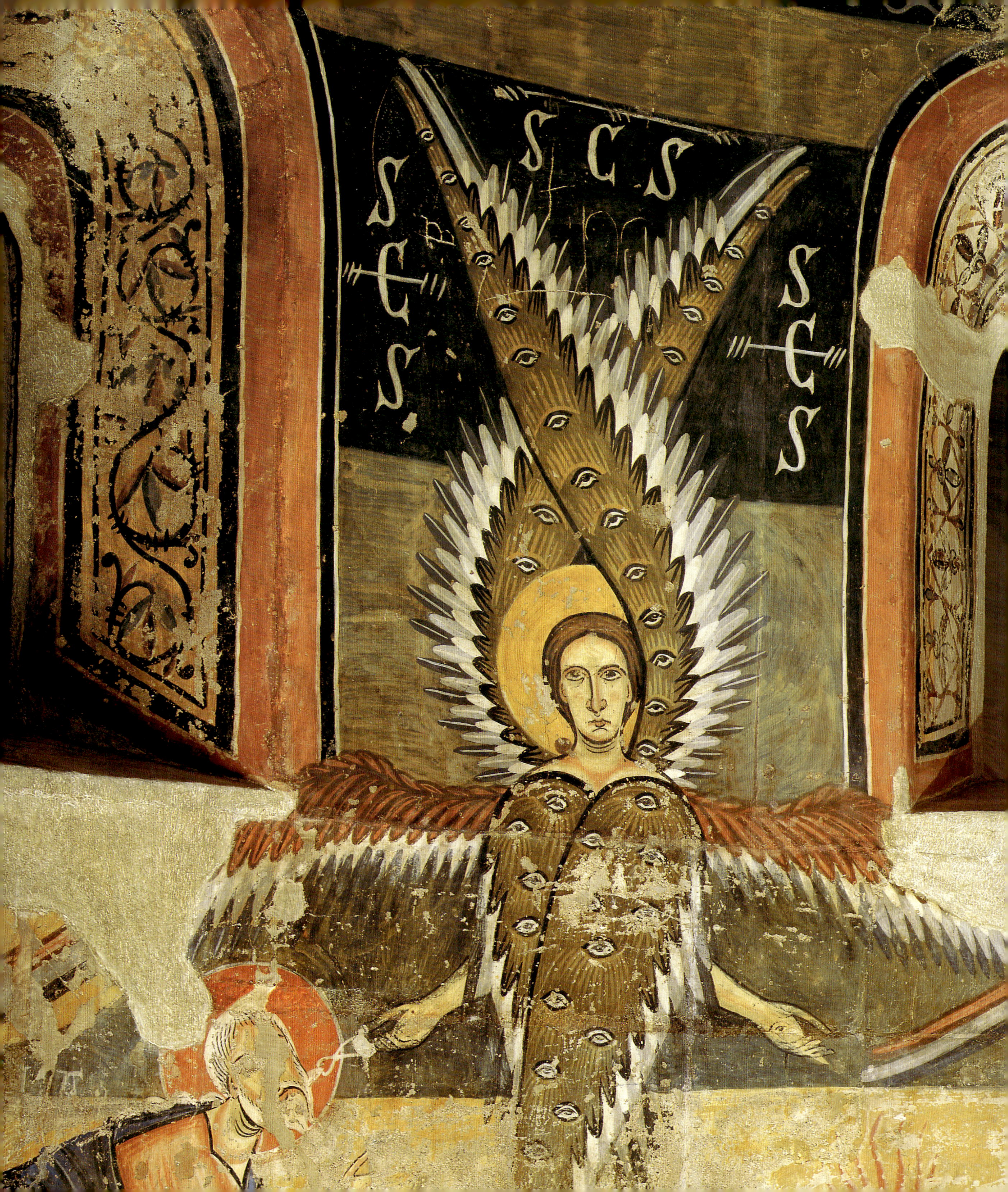
SCS
S
SCS
S
S
SCS
S

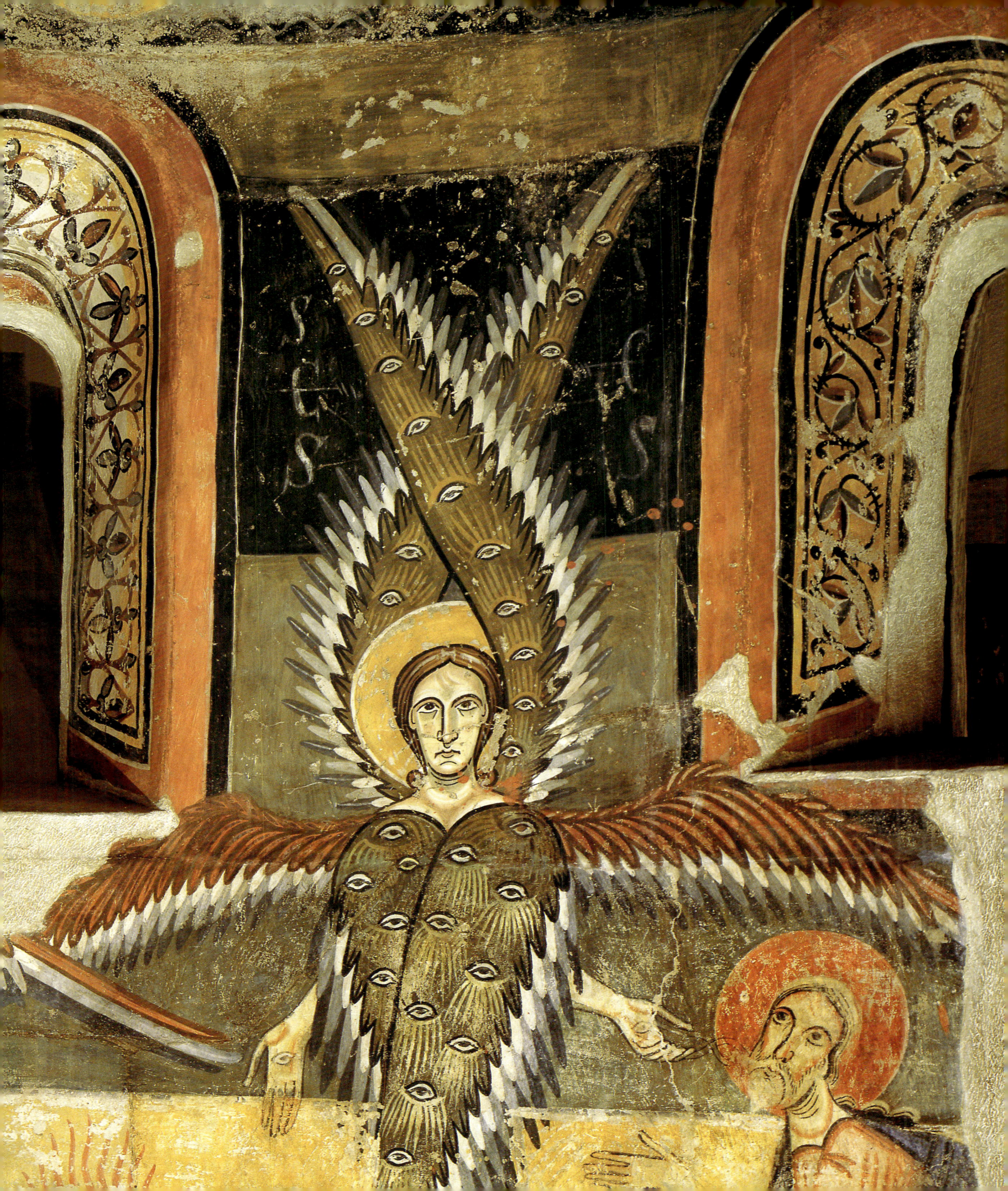

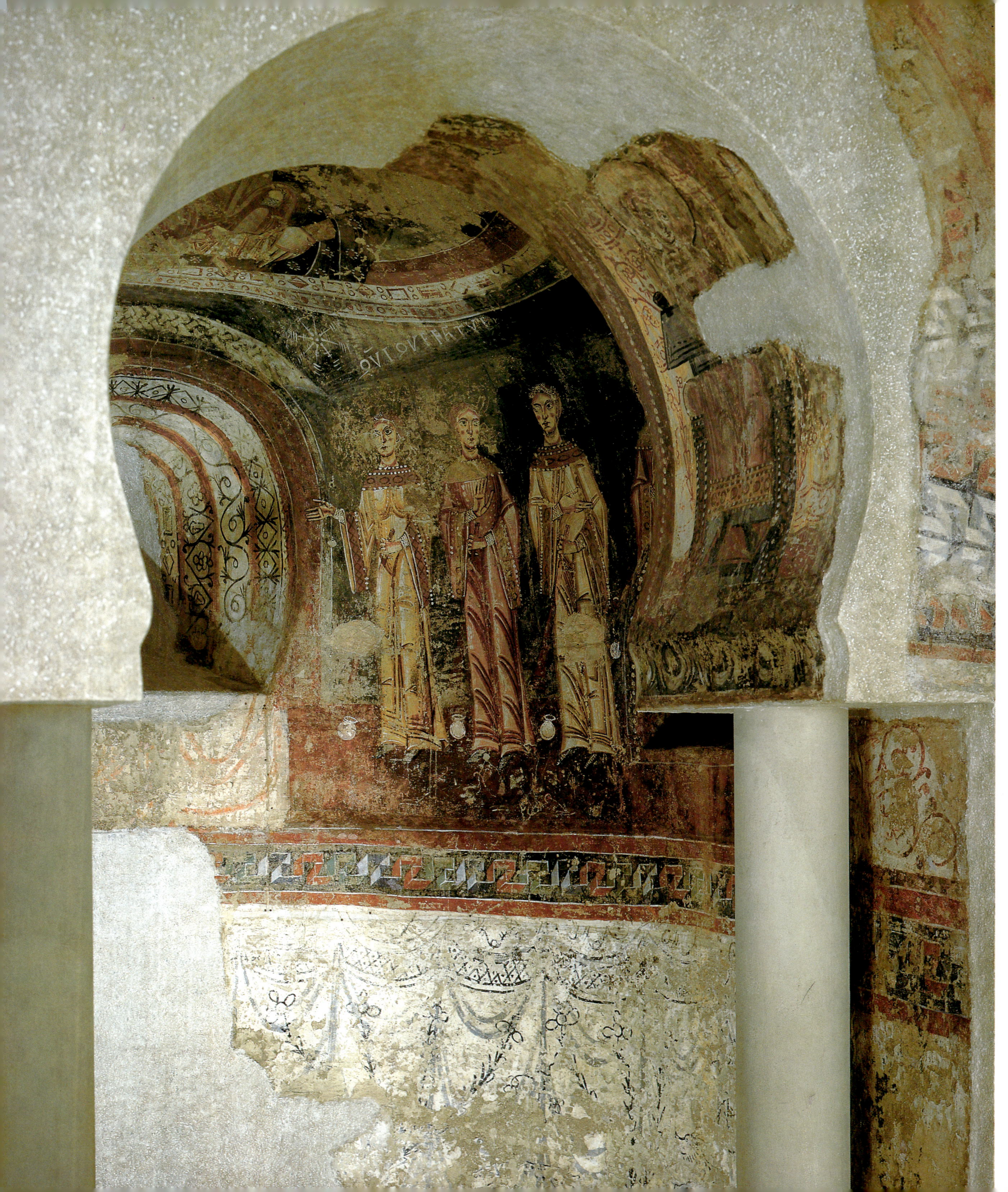

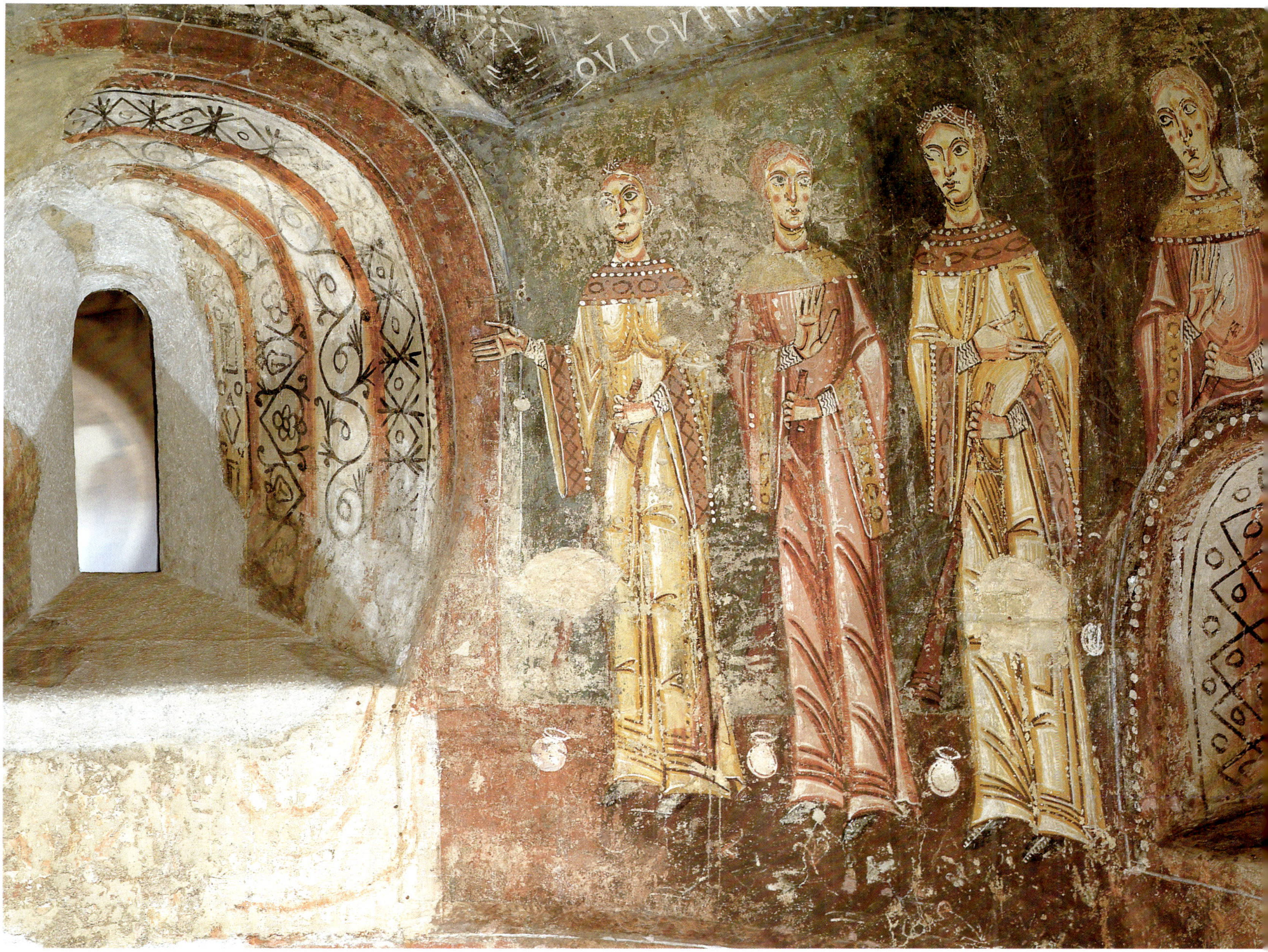

19 20

19. Pedret: small apse.
Parable of the Wise and Foolish Virgins and curtains with figures on, from the decoration in the small apse on the right-hand side of the church of Sant Quirze de Pedret (Berguedà). Late 11th – early 12th century
325 × 315 × 325 cm
MNAC/MAC 15973

20. Pedret: detail of Foolish Virgins.
Detail of the Foolish Virgins, from the decoration of the apse on the right-hand side of the church of Sant Quirze de Pedret.

suggested for the 'Master of Pedret', who was supposedly of Lombardic origin and the person behind a series of mural groups like Pedret, Àger, Àneu and El Burgal. However, as we shall see, this radiating model for Romanesque painting, in which everything spreads outwards from one particular point in Europe, raises serious doubts, as it doesn't seem to be supported by technical analyses. Similarly, at least in the early stages of development, we mustn't disregard the possible existence of ecclesiastical painters or at least of *clerici vagantes*, whose training would have given them access not only to the repertories of the miniature but also to the technical handbooks kept in the monastery libraries.

Thanks to the numerous analyses of mural painting and painted panels promoted by the MNAC's Restoration Laboratory and to the comparative study of their results in relation with the recipes in the technical treatises known at the time, like the one by Heraclius, the one by the monk Theophilus or the later one by Cennini, good progress has been

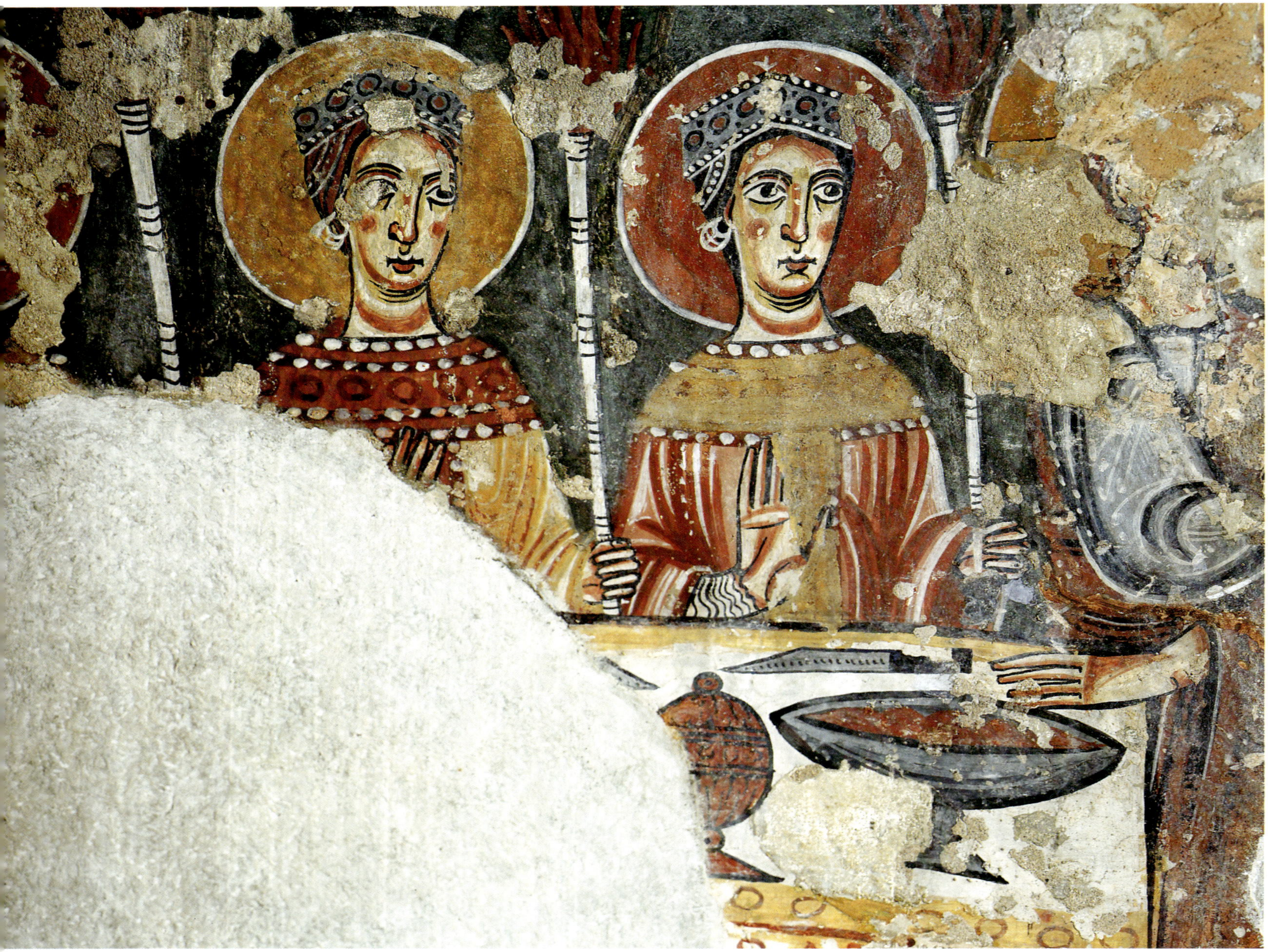

21 22

made in our understanding of this matter. For example, the pigments used in Romanesque painting are of an inorganic nature, hence their stability and resistance, as plant lacquers are only found in later series like Sigena. Furthermore, in Catalonia most of these paints were made from minerals that can be found in the Pyrenees: earth such as haematite for red, goethite for yellow ochre, carbon for black, calcite and gypsum for white and finally, the most characteristic in the region, aerinite for blue or green (when mixed with ochre). One of the few exceptions is the use of cinnabar for red in Sant Climent de Taüll, a sulphide of mercury imported from Al-Andalus, where it was found in the mines at Almadén (Ciudad Real), or the use of azurite in Àneu and El Burgal for some bright blues, azurite being a mineral of copper which is characteristic in work in the north of Italy. The use of these two pigments, azurite and cinnabar, which were not only more expensive but also produced better effects, probably denotes greater ambition in the decorative programme

21-22. PEDRET: DETAILS.
Detail of the Wise Virgins and allegory of the Church, from the mural decoration of the small apse on the right-hand side of the church of Sant Quirze de Pedret

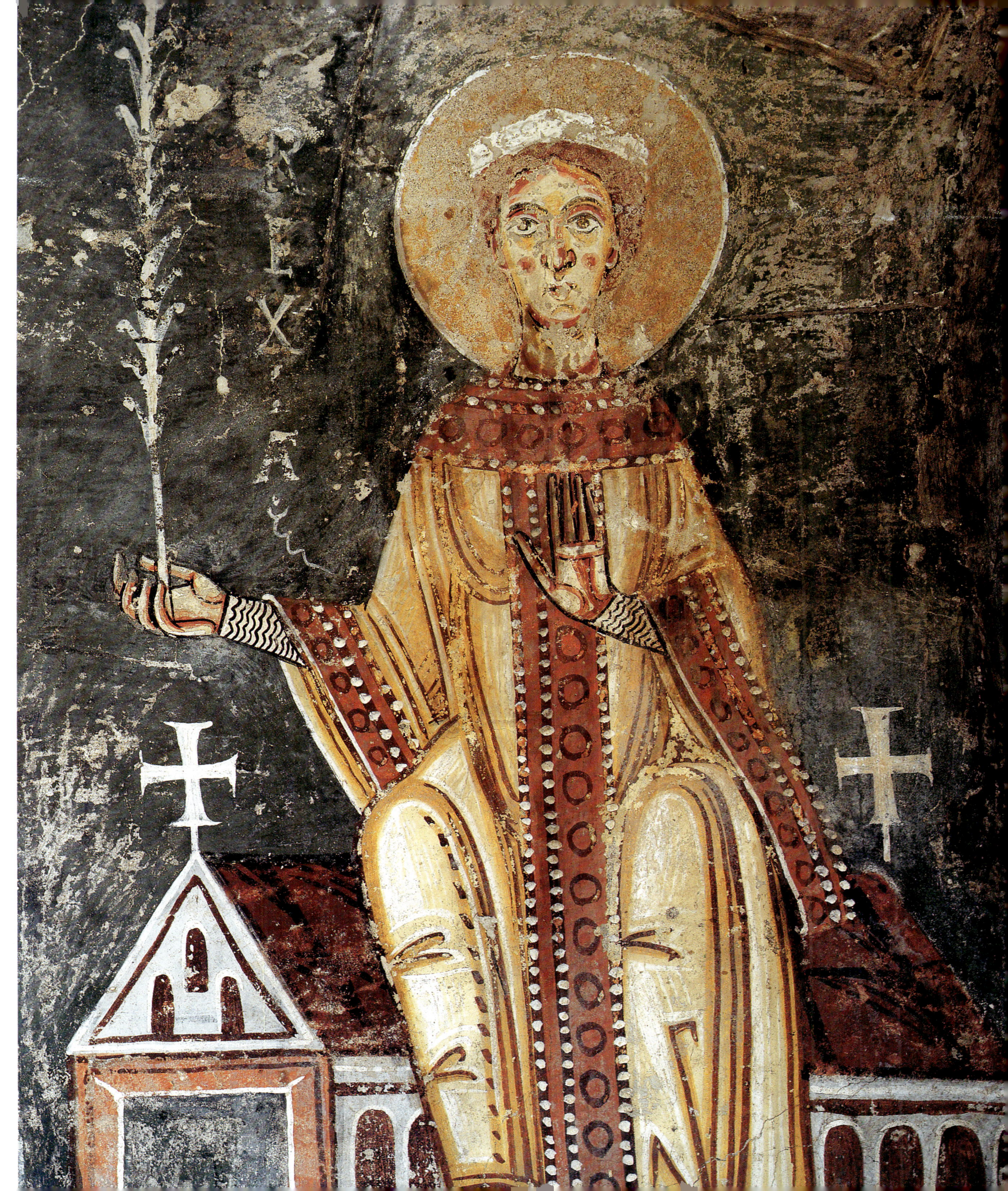

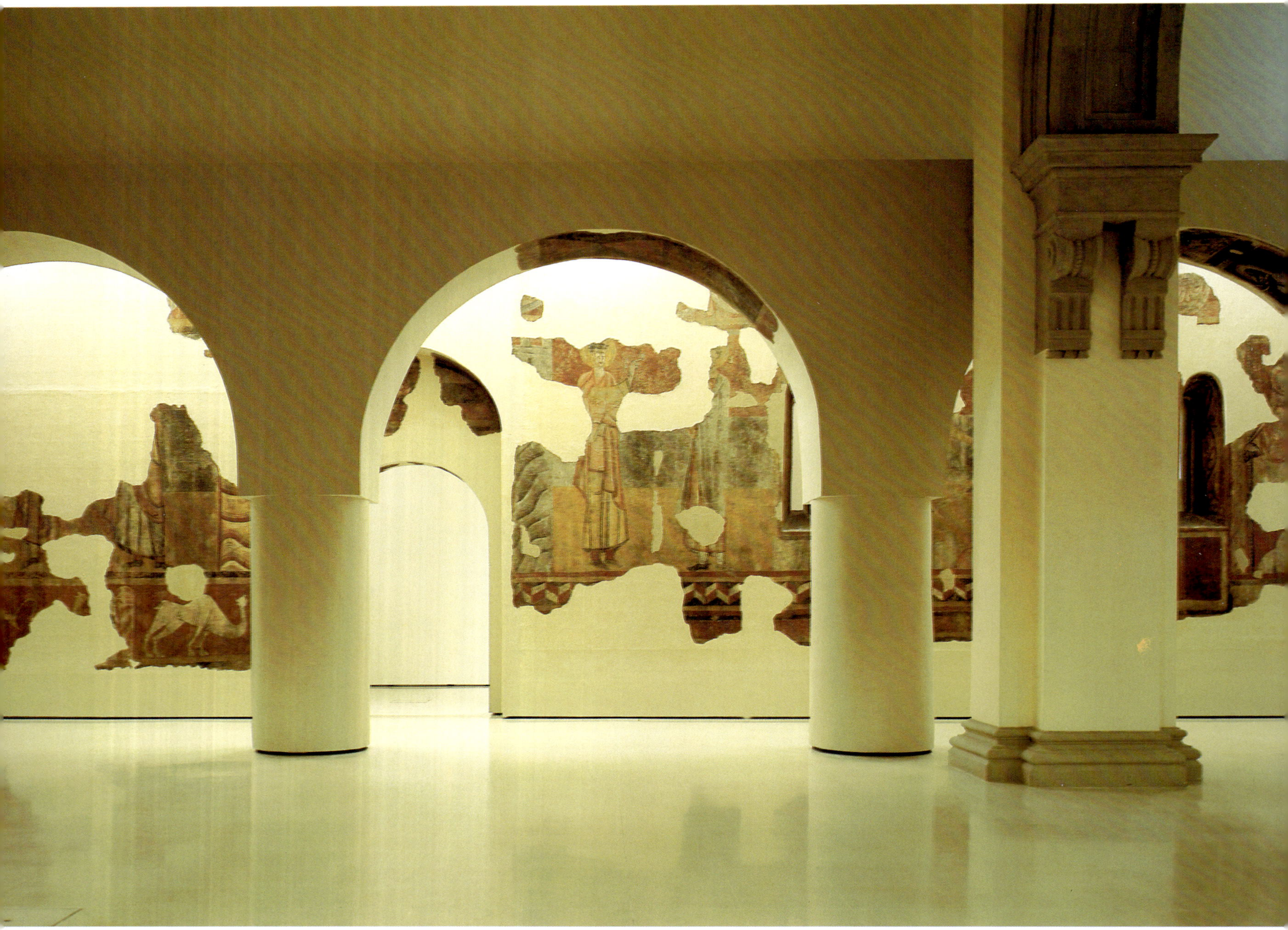

23

23. Boí – general view.
General view of the wall paintings of the north aisle of Sant Joan de Boí. Around 1100

24. Boí: Detail
Figures of saints from the decoration of the south aisle of the church of Sant Joan de Boí

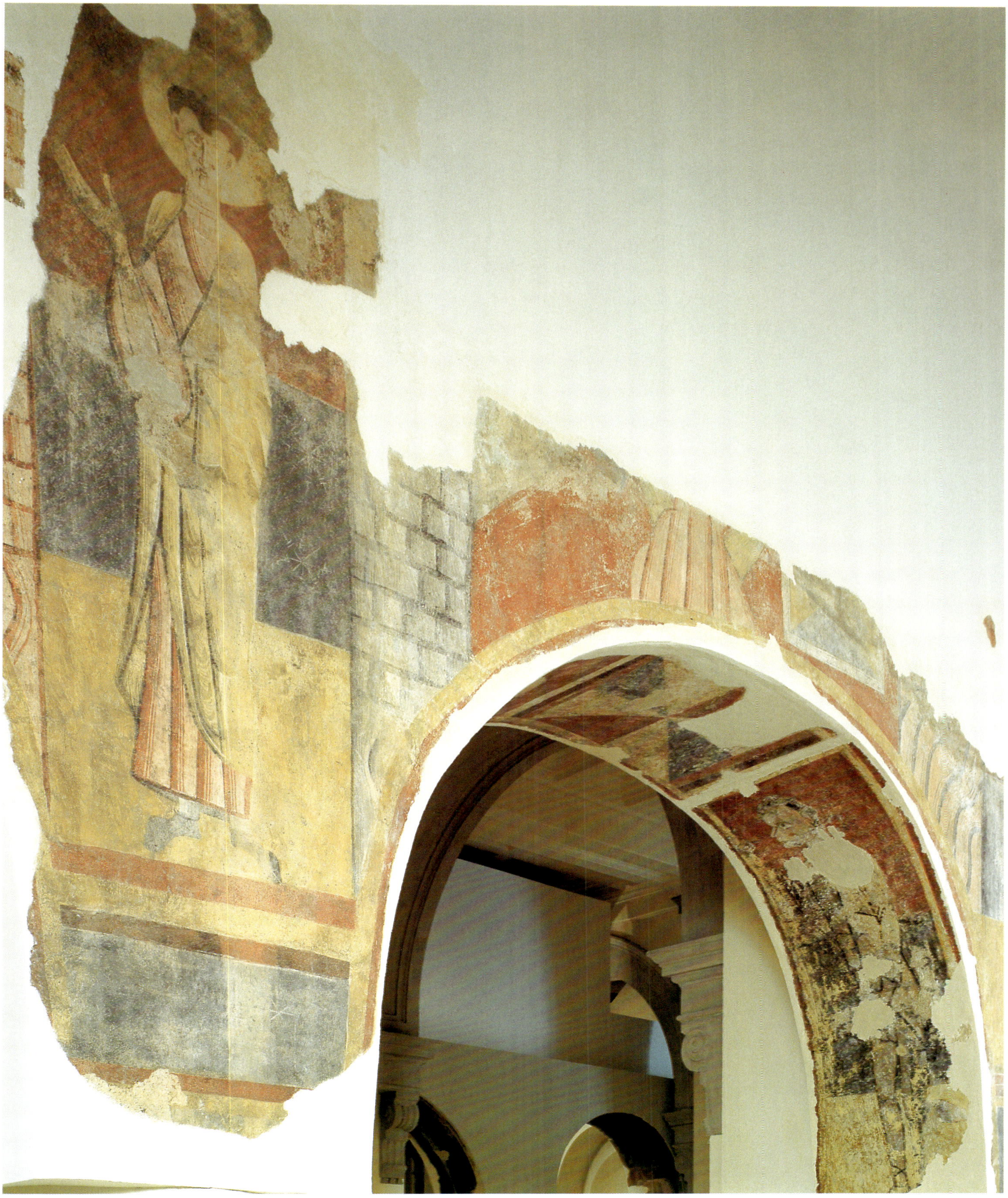

24

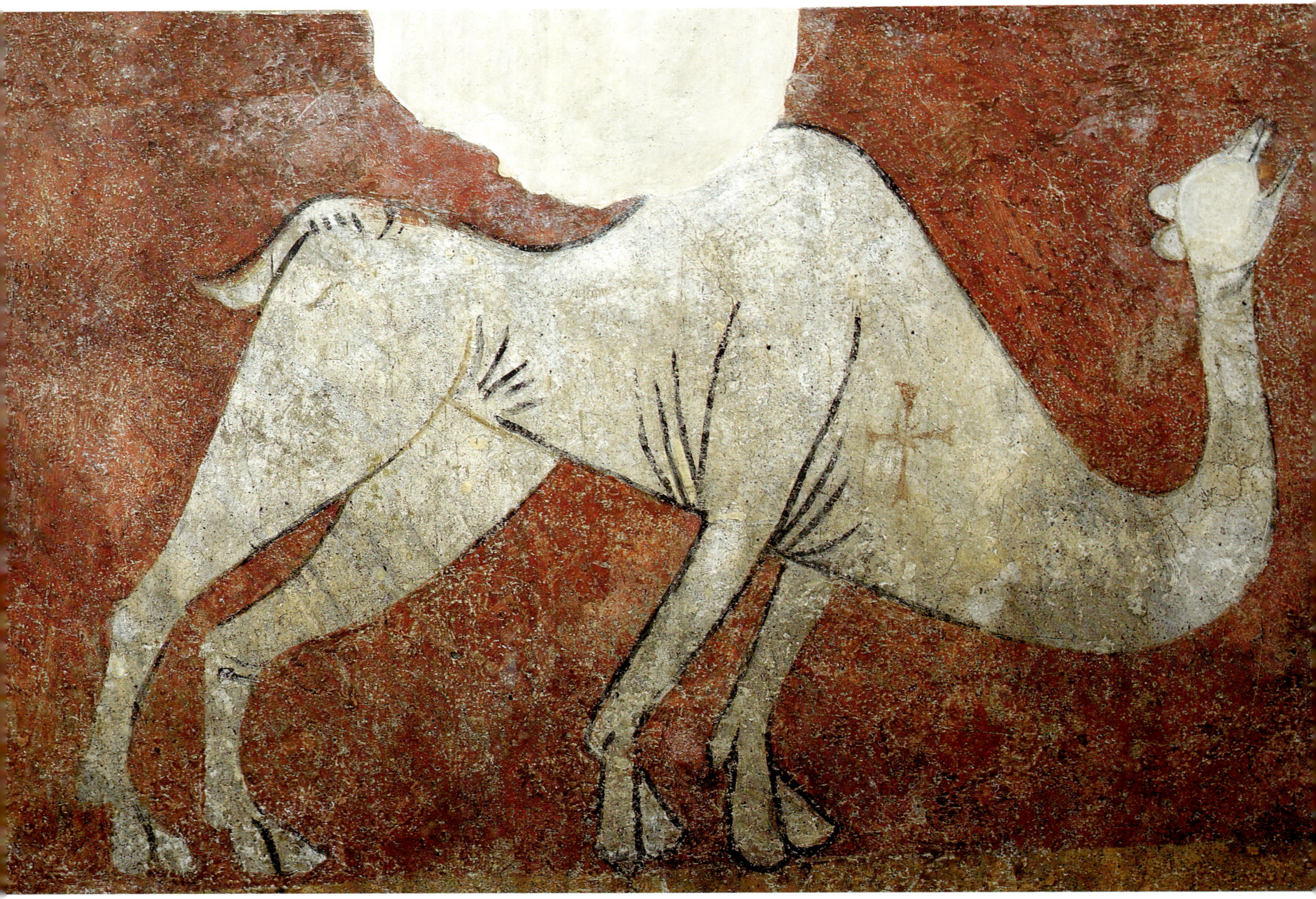

25

26

on the part of the commissioners, though the one great absence in these Catalan works, (except in the case of Sant Pere de Sorpe) is the navy blue *par excellence*, lapis lazuli, an import from Afghanistan, which cost the earth and can be found in the mural paintings in Papal Rome, in Catalan panel painting (the *Esquius Panel*) and in miniatures.

But over and above the use of aerinite for the blue, it's possibly in the pictorial technique where the recourse to local recipes in Catalonia can best be glimpsed. This technique consisted in a simple or abbreviated fresco, called *a secco* as it contained numerous finishes in tempera. The process consisted in the following stages. First of all, the wall was covered with coarse lime mortar, the *arricio*, over which was applied a smoother layer of rendering, the *intonaco*, which was very compact and was made up of sand mixed with slaked lime. Lines or incisions were made directly onto this surface to mark out the composition and figures, and three pictorial layers were applied, sometimes over a layer of black to imitate the effect of expensive pigments, as in the case of Sant Climent de Taüll.

25-26. BOÍ: ANIMALS
Camel decorating the lower register of the north wall of the church of Sant Joan de Boí.
Figures of imaginary animals from the decoration on the intrados of one of the arches separating the north aisle from the central one in the church. The animal in the lower register has been identified as an elephant

27. BOÍ: THE LAPIDATION OF SAINT STEPHEN.
The Lapidatation of Saint Stephen, which originally decorated the south wall of the north aisle of the church of Sant Joan de Boí (Alta Ribagorça)

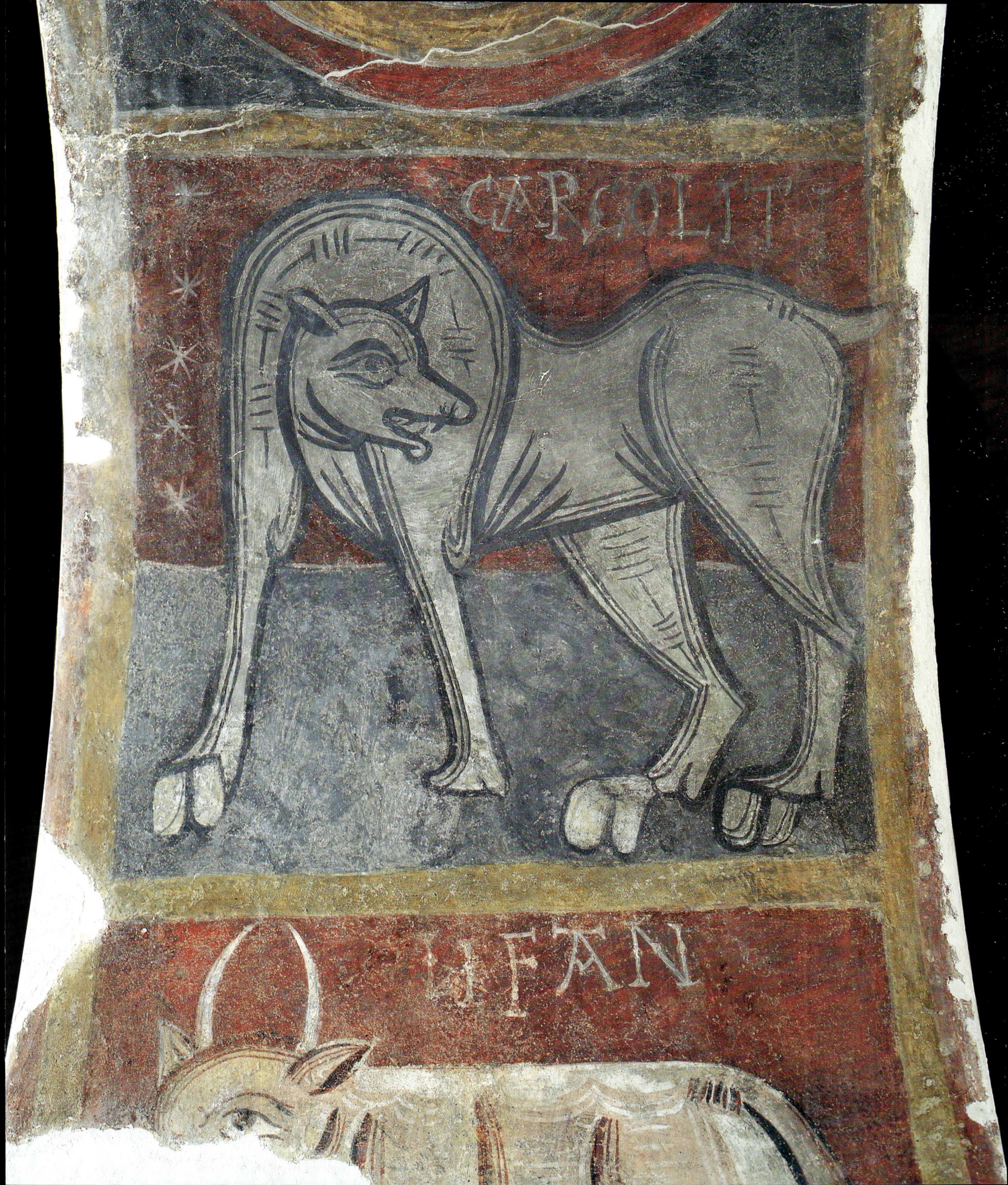
CARCOLIT
FAN

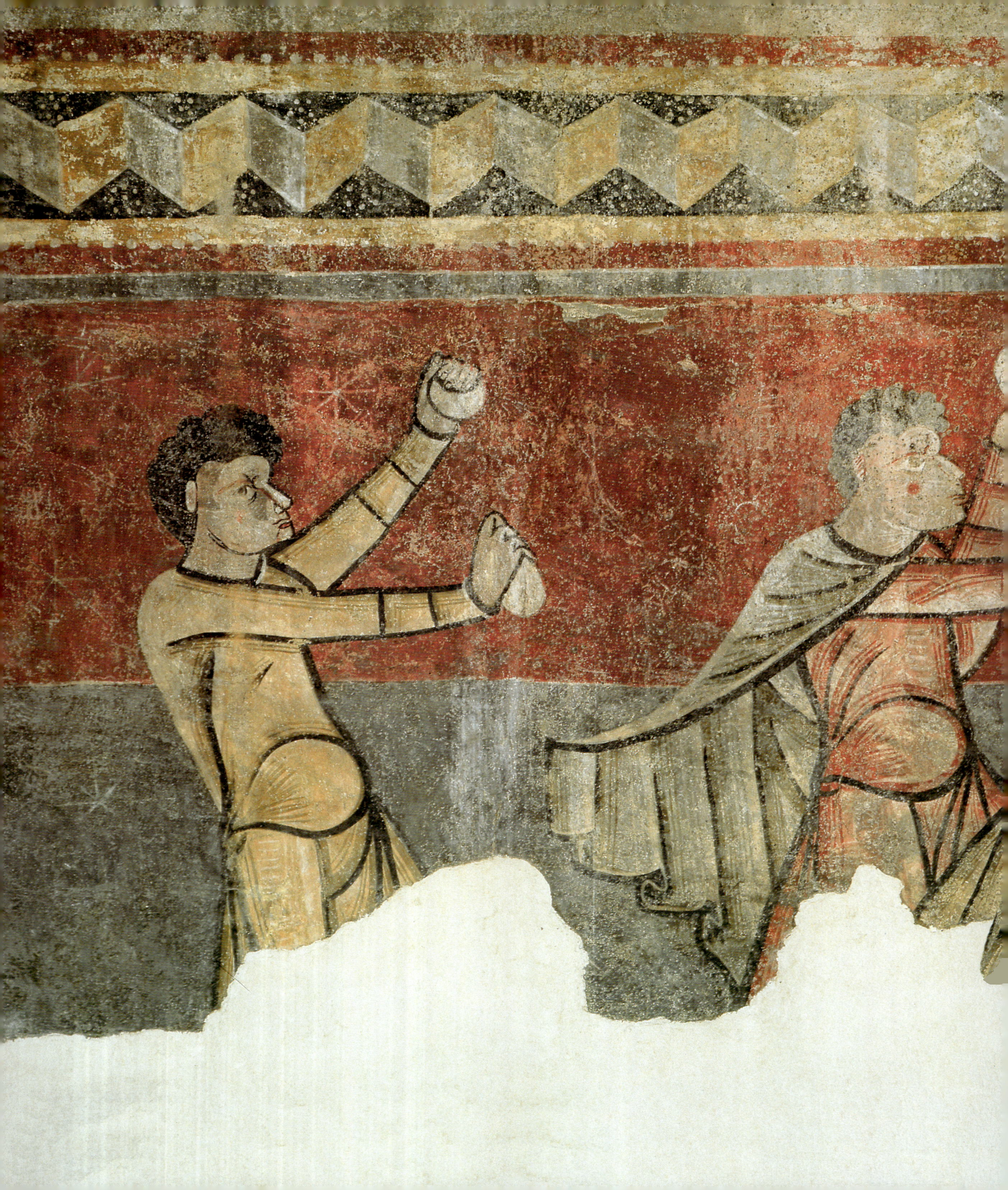

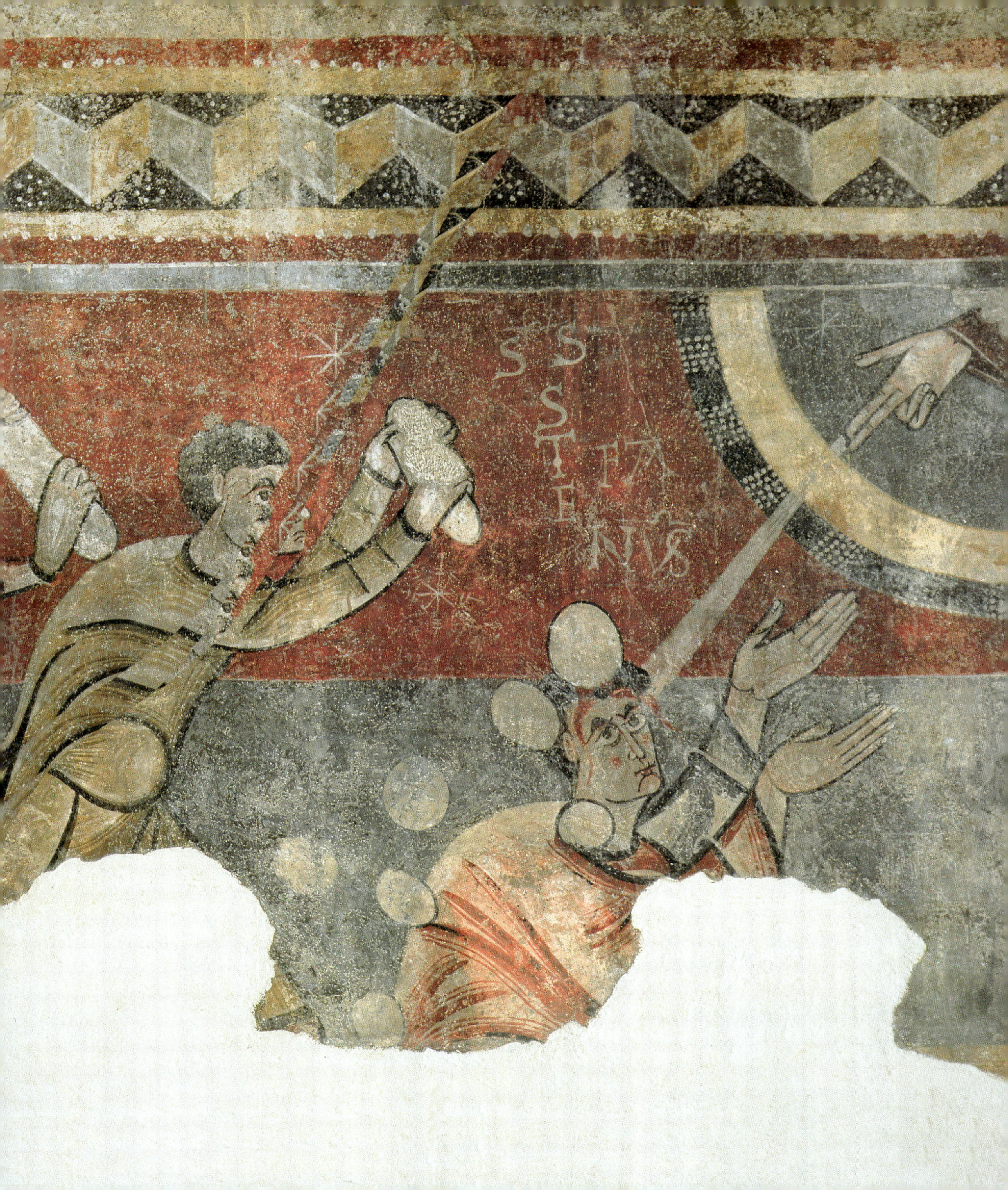
SS
STEFANVS

On drying in contact with the air, which contains carbon dioxide and oxygen, the calcium hydroxide of the rendering, mixed with the pigments, became carbonated to form a compact, resistant surface that fixed the pigments perfectly. The whole work process was divided up into days, which are visible in the topography of the *intonaco* as *giornate*, and in *pontate*, which correspond to the marks left at different levels by the scaffolding used in the work. Nevertheless, some colours were applied in the dry, using lime water or tempera, to outline or to finish off details, hence the more extensive retouching involved for the restorers in removing the mural paintings and installing them in their new home, as the tempera finishes weren't equally attached to the picture surface.

However, the tendency to study the pictorial arts in Catalonia (mural painting, panel painting and miniatures) as airtight compartments doesn't seem to respond to an obvious fact, which is the indisputable interrelationship and overlapping in time of these arts. In fact, apart from the issue of the Master of Pedret or the Pedret Circle, which we shall be going into later, the revolution that seems to have taken place in Catalan painting around 1120, with the emergence of the first painted frontals and the production of mural paintings with more obviously local features, like Sant Climent de Taüll and Santa Maria de Taüll, should be explained as the product of a common dialogue. There's nothing unusual in the idea that painters might have gone through a progressive apprenticeship, starting with the practice of panel painting and leading up to the production of mural paintings. Indeed, according to the later recommendations by Cennino Cennini (1398-1401), painters underwent extensive training. During an apprenticeship lasting thirteen years they began by drawing on wood, then moved onto painted and stuccoed panels, until they finally started to work at mural painting. This course wasn't actually very different to the one followed by Byzantine icon painters, according to the well-known *Painter's Manual* of Mount Athos. This curious 'syllabus' could explain the unusual personality of the Master of Sant Climent de Taüll, whose work makes a complete break with the illusionism of the so-called Master of Pedret's Circle and seems to ignore the teachings of this mural tradition in favour of new forms of experimenting, both in composition and in the use of colour. This puts him closer to the aesthetic of the emerging panel painting (*Urgell Altar Frontal* and *Esquius Panel*) and therefore suggests a common apprenticeship and an exchange of recipes between the two techniques.

The original pictorial style of the Master of the Apse of Sant Climent de Taüll, at once stiff and ornamental, probably derives from previous experience in panel painting. This explains the strange pictorial technique he uses in Christ's cloak, which is alien to the tradition of al fresco painting. The blue mantle is treated with subtly superimposed regular layers applied over black to achieve shades which, especially in the centre of the upper legs, produce a three-dimensional visual effect like a hollow that contrasts with the grey tunic. Brought to life by white varnish, it gives an impression of a volume coming towards us. This overlaying of dark and light colours or gradation in the tones to give relief to the figure is typical of panel painting, as we see in Cennino's *Craftsman's Handbook*. Similarly, the unusual choice of white as the colour of the haloes in Taüll can also be found in the *Urgell Altar Frontal* and the *Ix Altar Frontal*. Amongst these shared resources, one formula worth noting is that of painting an inscription in a colourful table in registers, which in Sant Climent de Taüll contains the date of consecration by Saint Raymond,

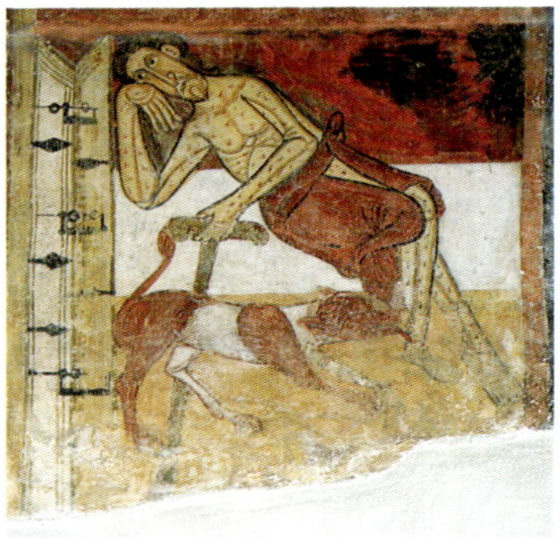

28

28. SANT CLIMENT DE TAÜLL: LAZARUS.
The parable of the poor man Lazarus in front of the rich man Epulon's door, from the presbytery arch in the church of Sant Climent de Taüll.

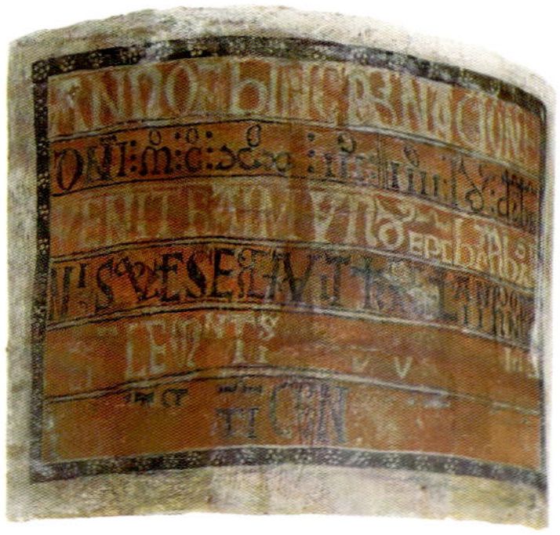

29

29. SANT CLIMENT DE TAÜLL: INSCRIPTION.
Inscription redone from the first column on the left with the date of the consecration, December 10th, 1123, of the church of Sant Climent de Taüll.

30. SANT CLIMENT DE TAÜLL: APSE.
General view of the mural paintings from the central and left-hand apses of the church of Sant Climent de Taüll.
Around 1123
MNAC/MAC 15966

31-32. SANT CLIMENT DE TAÜLL:
MAIESTAS DOMINI.
Maiestas Domini, *from the decoration in the vault of the church of Sant Climent de Taüll (Alta Ribagorça)*
Detail of the book with the inscription «EGO SVM LVX MVNDI».

30

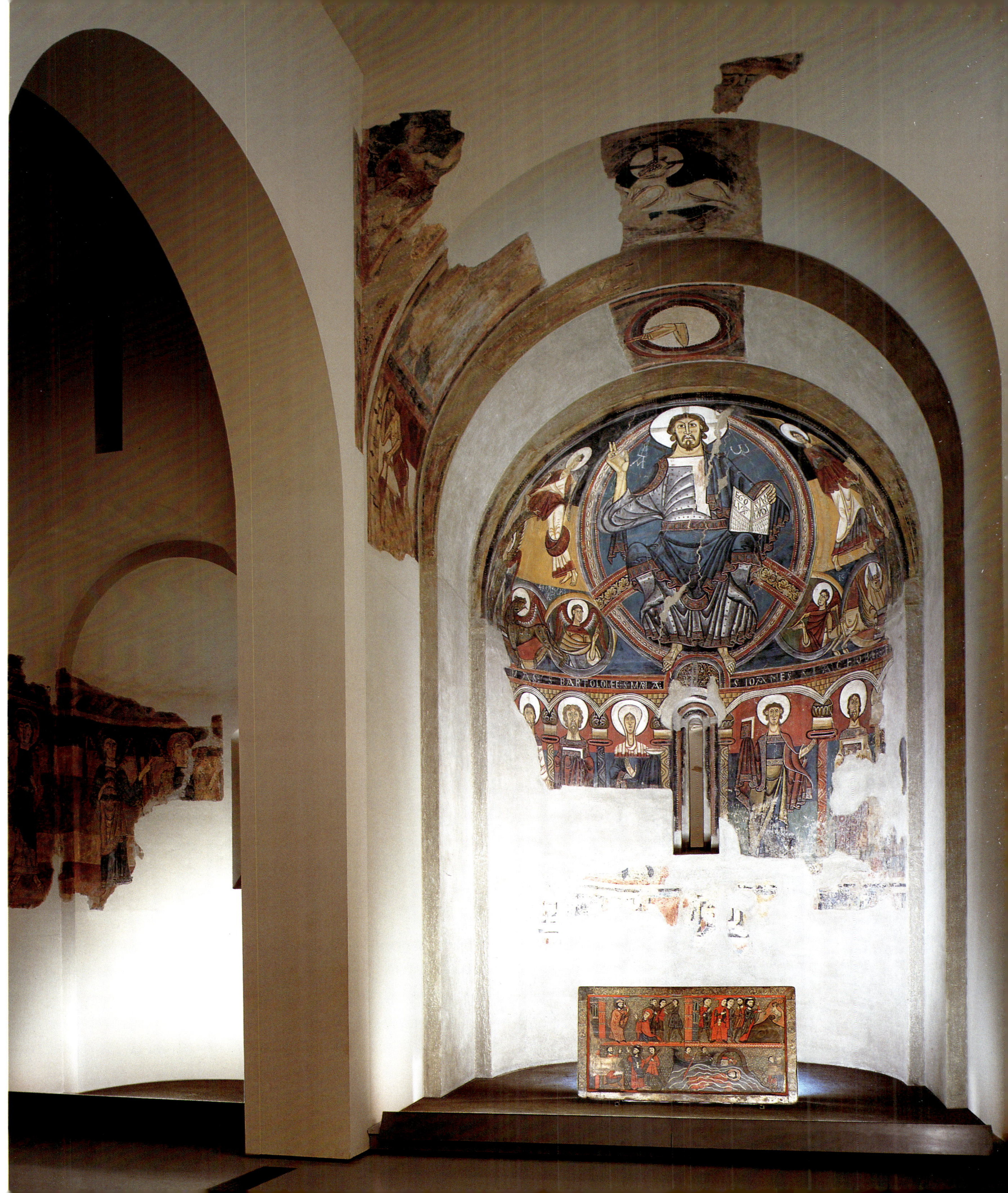

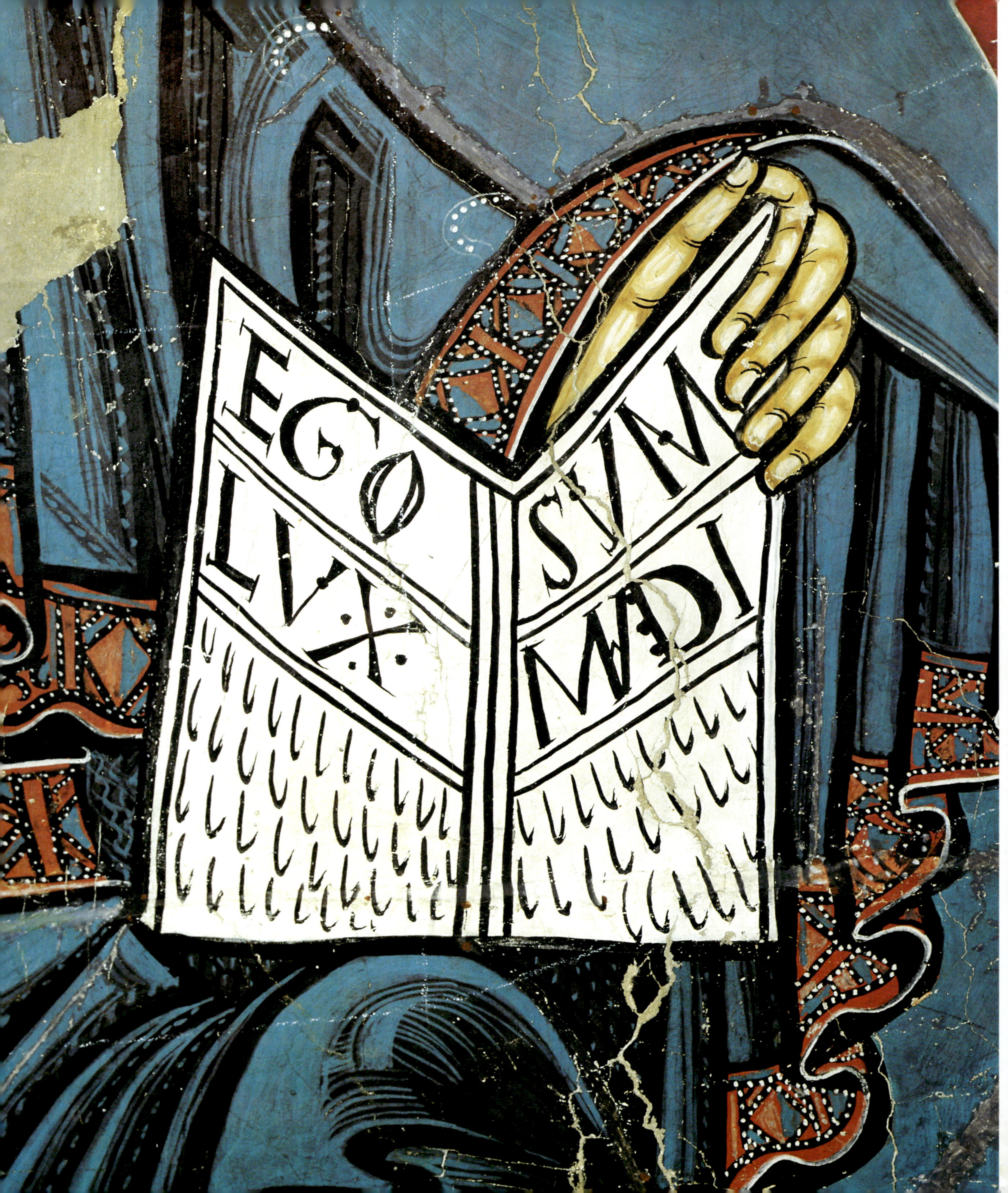
EGO
LVX
SVM
MVDI

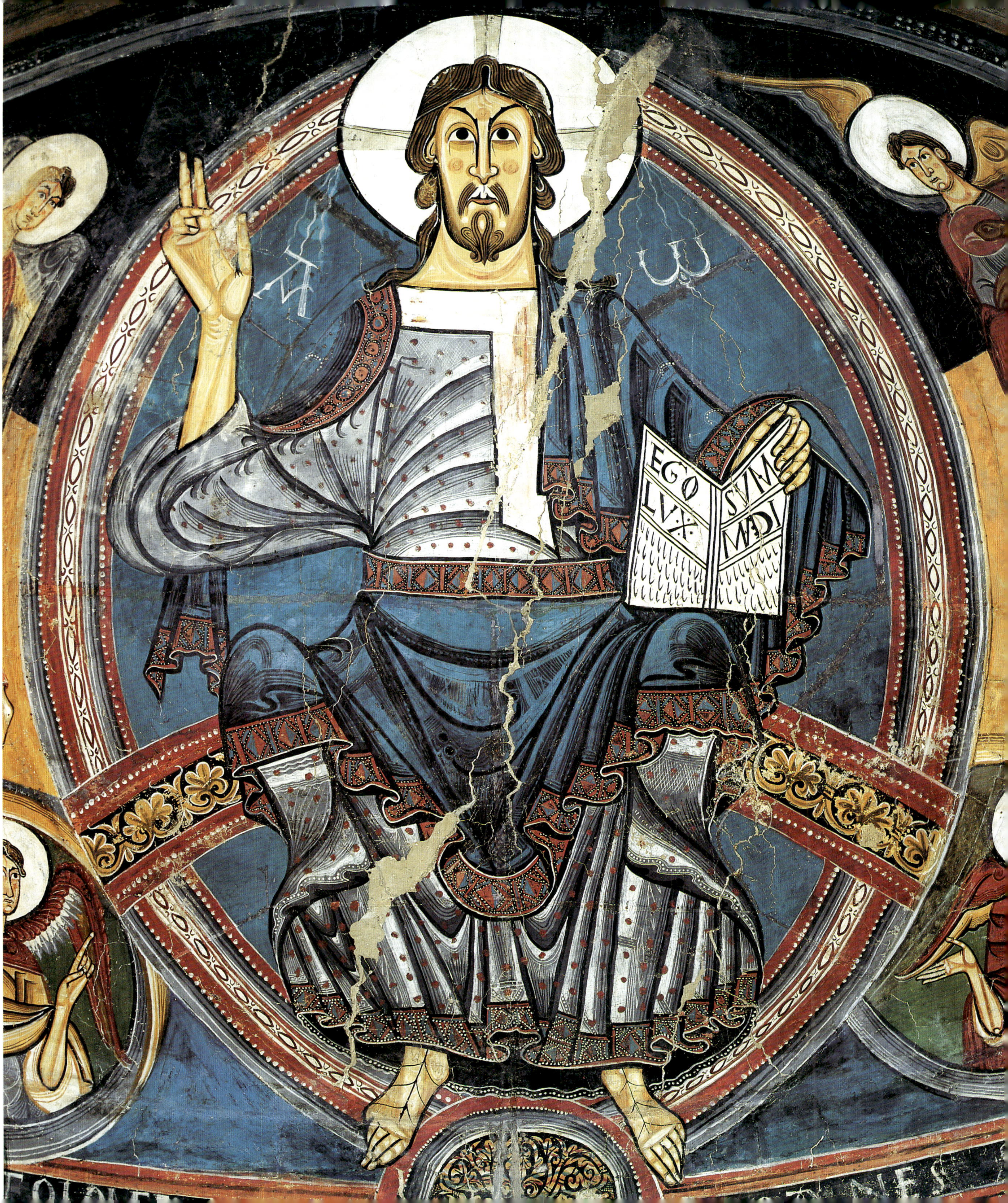
EGO SVM
LVX MVDI

Bishop of Roda, in 1123, while on the altar frontal from Sant Llorenç de Dosmunts (Museu Episcopal de Vic) it serves to gloss the scene of the saint's martyrdom. Similarly, some of the recipes used in the Crucifix from the group in Sant Pere de Sorpe (lapis lazuli in the *perizonium* and silver leaf on the *suppedaneum*) indicate a knowledge of the recipes typical of panel painting in Catalonia, where lapis lazuli and metal leafs were indeed used (Esquius, Planès, etc.) and are described in a technical handbook in Ripoll in 1134 (Madrid, Biblioteca Nacional, Ms. 19).

Masterpieces and workshops

The MNAC's superb collection of Romanesque painting is without a doubt the finest exponent of the birth and development of this technique in Catalonia. Nevertheless, when it comes to appraising it and explaining it, we still come up against numerous doubts as regards its date, filiation and meaning. We must never lose sight of the fact that this is architectural decoration and is therefore inseparably tied to the history of the buildings housing it. Since the main works of Romanesque mural painting surviving in Catalonia, apart from a few exceptions like the Holy Sepulchre in Olèrdola, are no earlier than the end of the eleventh century or even the beginning of the twelfth, it has been taken for granted that the great Catalan architecture of the eleventh century (Sant Martí del Canigó, Santa Maria de Ripoll, Sant Vicenç de Cardona) was characterised by bare stone walls. It's practically impossible to review the original appearance of these churches due to their state of ruin or the abusive restorations they have undergone, which have eliminated all trace of the decoration. This goes for Sant Llorenç de Munt, which in about 1960 still had the rendering of a large part of its walls. In fact J. Puig i Cadafalch himself said that 'all the churches were destined to be polychromed', as in the absence of figurative paintings they were 'rendered with lime and whitewashed.'

This is why historiography has frequently toyed with the possibility that the magnificent basilica consecrated by Abbot Oliba in Ripoll in 1032 had its interior painted following the prestigious model of Saint Peter's in Rome. This hypothesis, based on accounts of the remains of paintings and inscriptions seen by nineteenth-century researchers, seems to be supported by the fact that there is still polychromy today on the original façade (behind the monumental twelfth-century stone portal) as well as other fragments in the interior. This would cover the large gap of the eleventh century, would provide a reference model that was contemporary with the Lombardic groups (Galliano, Novara) with which Catalan Romanesque painting has always been associated and would back up the parallel between the Abbot of Ripoll and Abbot Gauzlino of Fleury, who hired a Lombardic painter by the name of Nivardus to decorate his church. Furthermore, in the Ripoll and Rodes Bibles, produced mainly during the time of Abbot Oliba, we find many of the recurring themes from later pictorial cycles which at one time may also have decorated Oliba's church: Isaiah's Vision of the Seraphim (Àneu), the Wheels in Ezekiel's Vision (Àneu, Sant Climent de Taüll), the Annunciation with a servant girl (Sorpe), the Wise and Foolish Virgins (Pedret), the Last Judgement (Santa Maria de Taüll) and minstrels and tumblers (Boí). Ripoll, for its part, provides the earliest testimony of a painted

33. Sant Climent de Taüll: details of the apse.
Agnus Dei and Dextera Domini, Maiestas Domini *with the symbols of evangelists Matthew and John from the central apse of Sant Climent de Taüll.*
Around 1123
From the presbytery arch and the vault of the central apse of Sant Climent de Taüll (Alta Ribagorça).
MNAC/MAC 15968/15806/15966 33

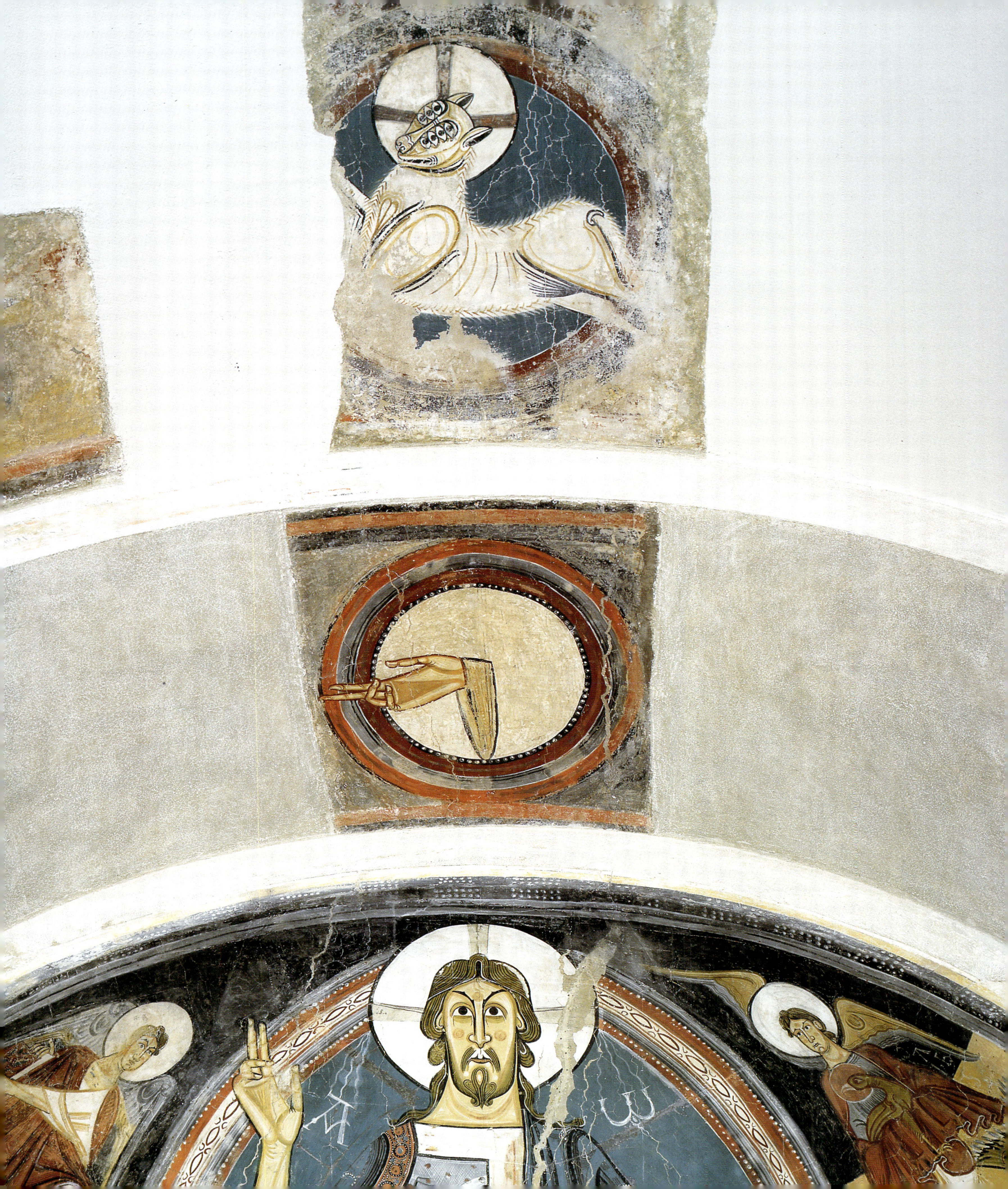

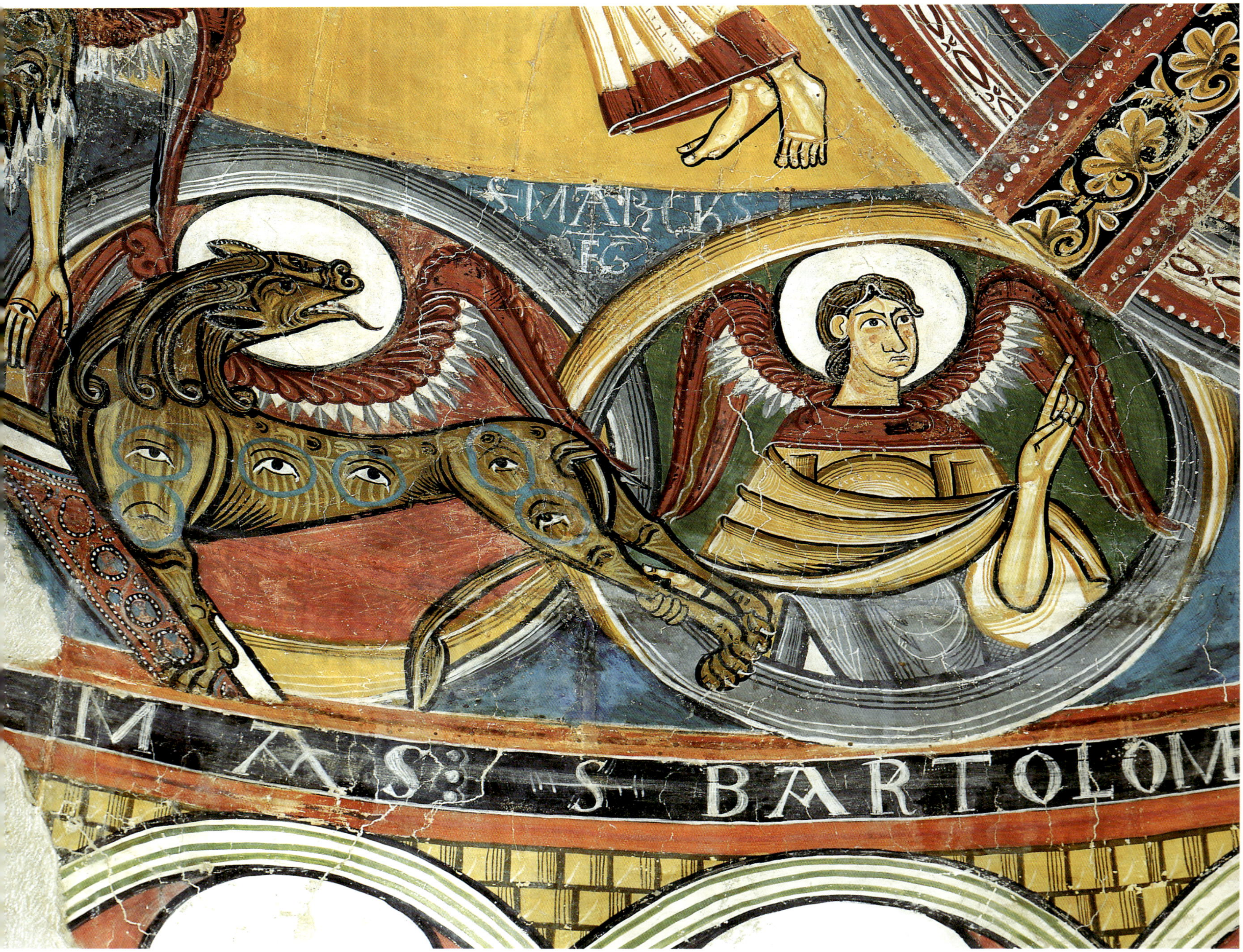

34. Sant Climent de Taüll:
detail of apse.
Angel carrying the symbol of the evangelist Mark from the central apse of Sant Climent de Taüll (Alta Ribagorça).

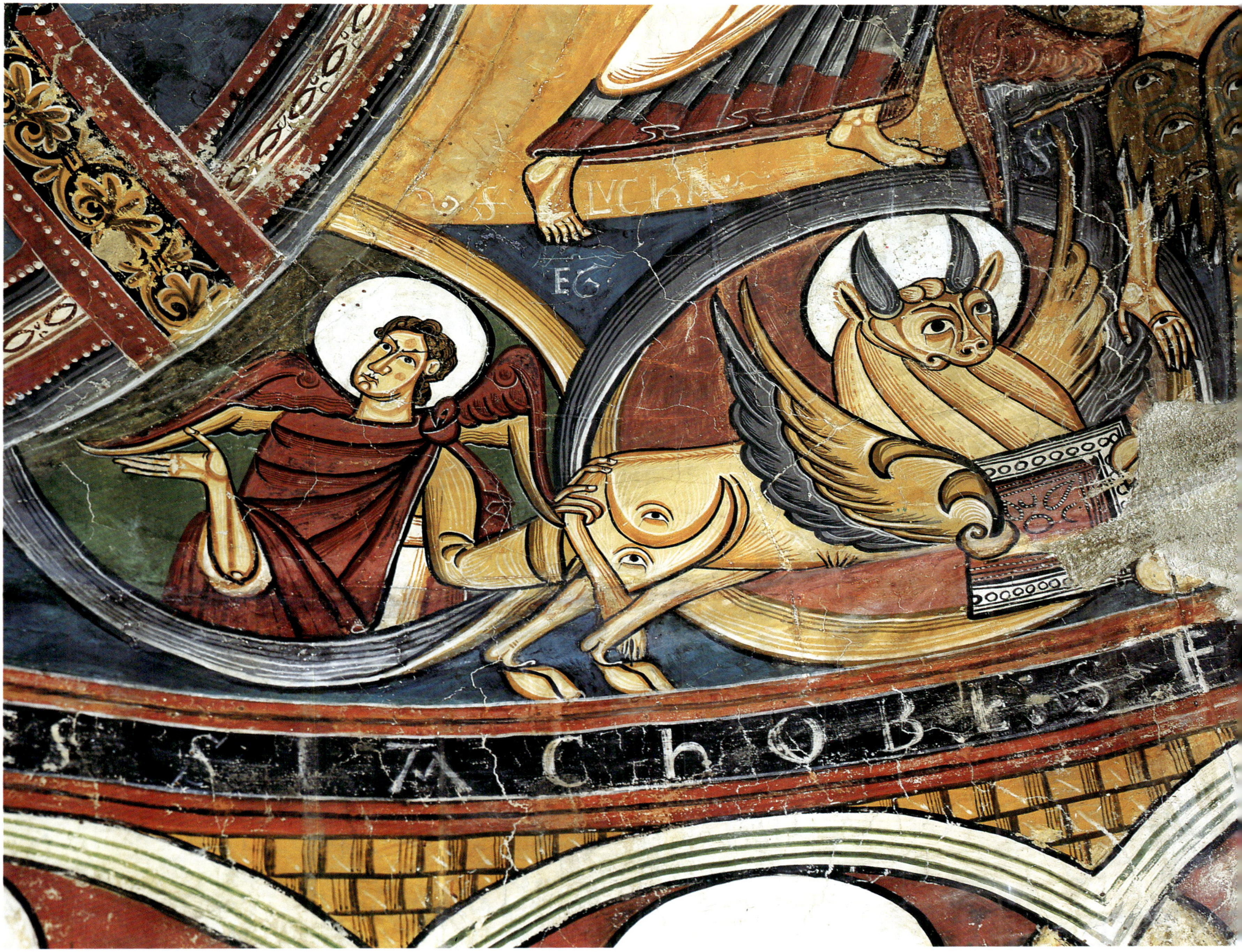

35. SANT CLIMENT DE TAÜLL:
DETAIL OF APSE.
Angel carrying the symbol of the evangelist Luke from the central apse of Sant Climent de Taüll (Alta Ribagorça)

36-37. SANT CLIMENT DE TAÜLL:
DETAIL OF APSE.
The Virgin with the chalice and Saints John and James from the central register of the decoration of the central apse of Sant Climent de Taüll (Alta Ribagorça)

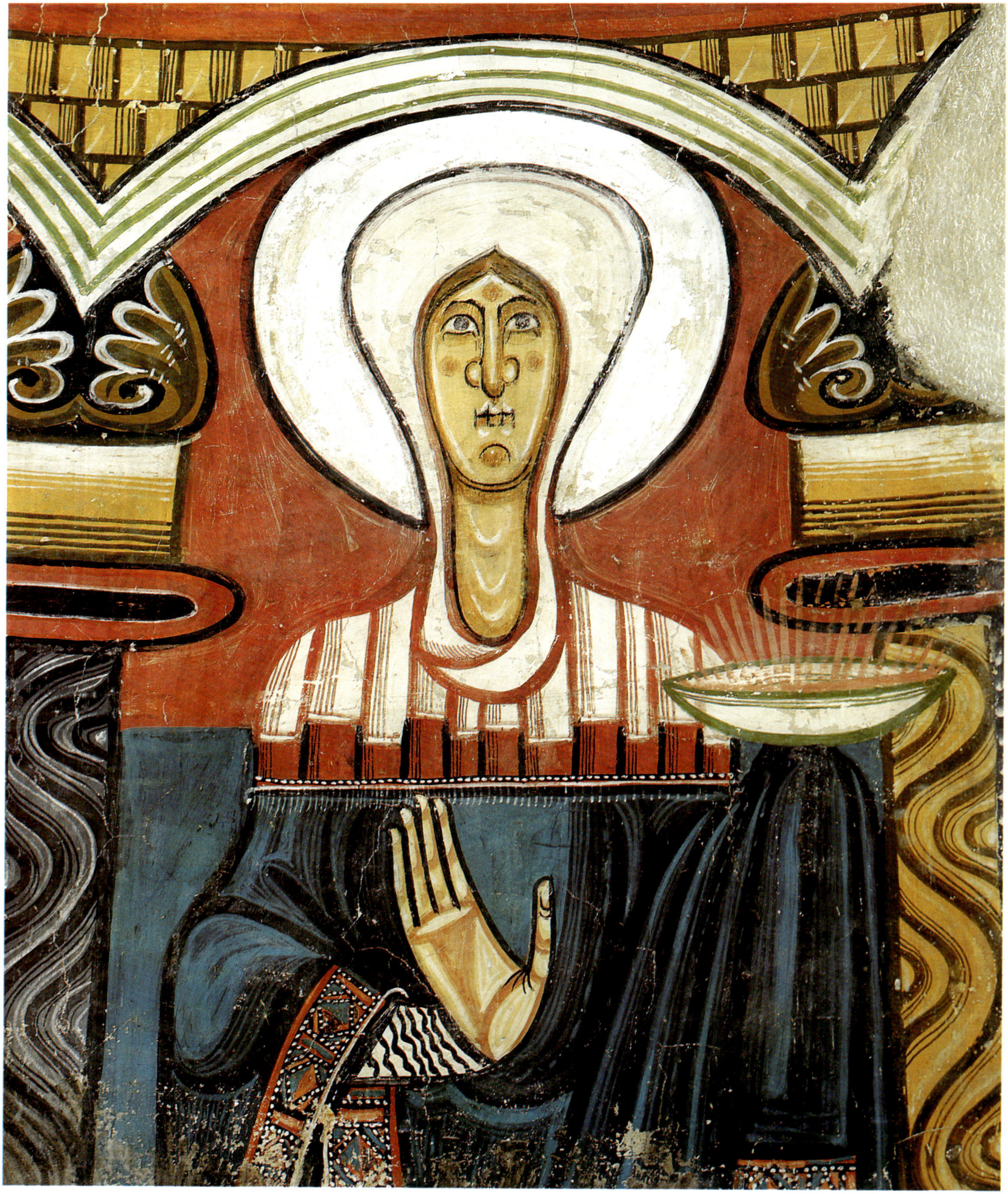

36

37

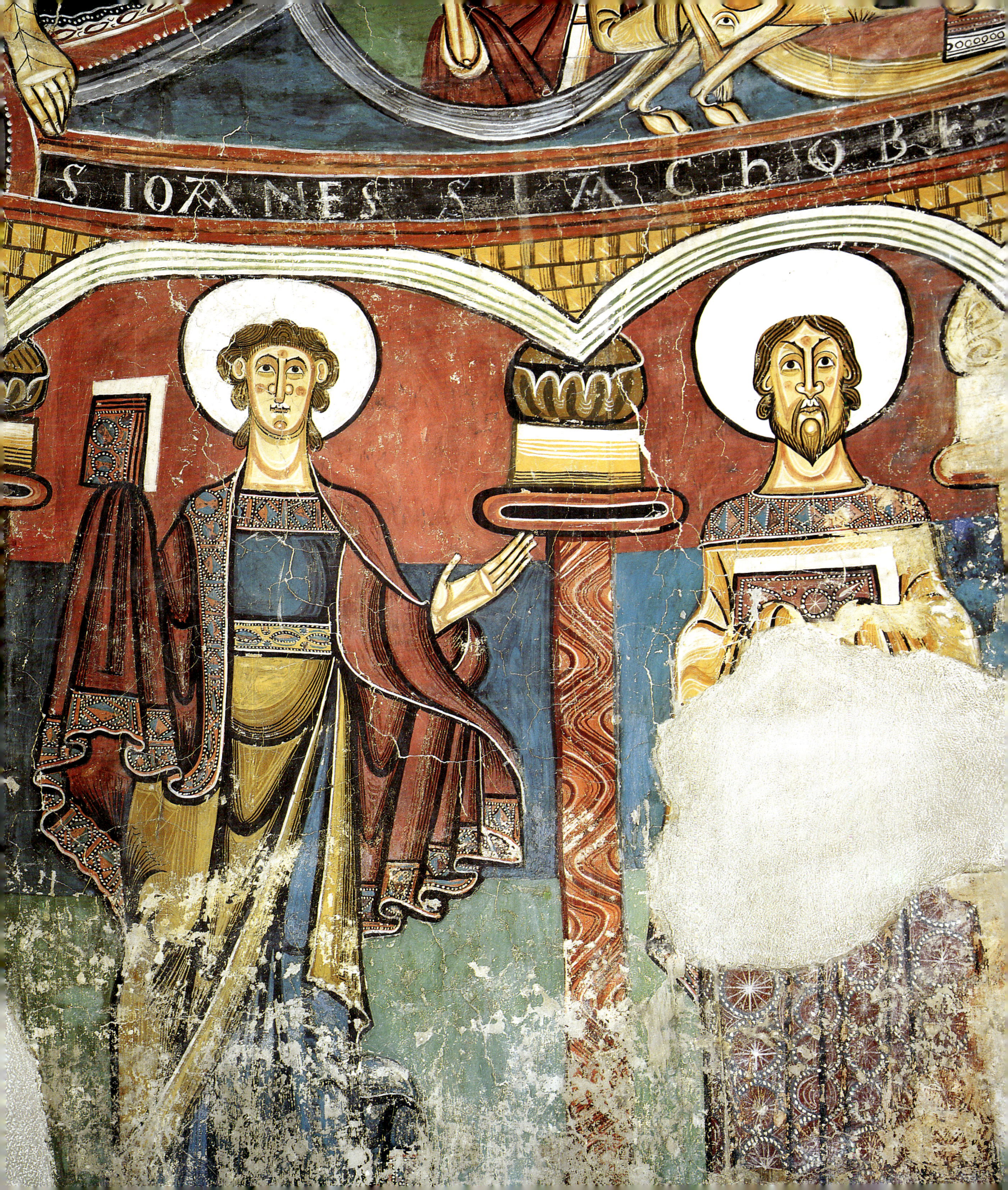
S IOANNES S IACHOBE

outer door, something which a few decades later was to be found in Sant Joan de Boí (*c.* 1100). I would mention in this respect that pictorial decoration of doors using figurative programmes is something that is also recorded in areas like Veneto or Greece, though at later dates in the twelfth century. This is the case of the church of Saints Felice and Fortunato in Vicenza (*c.* 1154) or the Byzantine church of Kastoria.

Luckily, we have two dates that help establish the flourishing of Romanesque mural painting in Catalonia, to which the cycles of Pedret (Berguedà), Àneu and El Burgal (Pallars Sobirà) and Àger (Noguera) belong. The first, the terminus *post quem*, is given by the female lay figure depicted at the bottom of the apse from Sant Pere del Burgal dressed in a beautiful *brial* (a rich silk dress with long, wide sleeves) and holding a candle. The accompanying inscription reads '(LUC)IA CONMITESA, Joan Ainaud identified her as the Countess Llúcia of Pallars, wife of Count Artau I of Pallars, who in 1081, following her husband's death, took over the government of the county until 1090 and whose presence here, according to Ainaud, indicates the date of the paintings, which were done under her patronage. The second date, however, which provides the terminus *ante quem*, comes from a series not in the MNAC's collection, the paintings in the cathedral of Saint-Lizier (France), consecrated in 1117, which show many similarities with the Àger cycle. In other words, the period from 1081 to 1117 has been put forward as the timeframe for the activity of a hypothetical travelling workshop known as the Master of Pedret's Circle, which presumably worked in all these places and which historiography has associated with Lombard painting, more precisely the frescoes of San Pietro al Monte in Civate (*c.* 1100), Prugiasco and Carugo. This is certainly an unusual figurative language, still heir to the illusionism of late Antiquity and Byzantine art, with figures occupying different planes, glimpses of landscape, faces tinged with flesh tones (forehead, cheek and throat) and loose clothes with shadowing that give the figures a certain corporeity and spatial three-dimensionality. While the luxurious jewelled clothing (and crowns) of the Virgins of Pedret or the Archangels of El Burgal and Àneu are reminiscent of Byzantium, the way the faces are built up follows the technique of the three concentric circles of Byzantine art: their centres between the eyes and the circumferences marking, at top and bottom, respectively, the start of the hair and the base of the nose, the top of the head and the beard, and finally the halo. The thematic and ornamental repertory is also highly original. To the figures of the Archangels Gabriel and Michael, with standards and with the inscriptions 'PETICIVS' and 'POSTOLATIVS', as they appear in Àneu, El Burgal and in Santa Maria de Cap d'Aran (The Cloisters, New York), as well as in the later examples from Esterri de Cardós and Estaon, are added the prophets making the sign of *proskynesis* or adoration in Àneu (Isaiah and Elijah) and El Burgal. Similarly, the Greek fret ornamental motif appears in Pedret and El Burgal.

As we saw, an explanation for all this repertory, with its roots deep in Byzantine and late Antiquity art, has been sought in a direct relationship with Lombardy, specifically with the example of San Vincenzo di Galliano (1007), a century earlier, where we find the same Archangels with the inscriptions 'PETICIO' and 'POSTULATIO' and the prophets Jeremiah and Ezekiel in a similar posture, as well as a Greek fret frieze. Nevertheless, the style of the apse at Galliano has a powerful imprint of late Antiquity and the figures show a metallic corporeity typical of the Imperial art. This is a long way from the graceful fig-

38. SANTA MARIA DE TAÜLL: APSE.
Mural paintings from the central apse of the church of Santa Maria de Taüll. Around 1123
MNAC/MAC 15861

39-40. SANTA MARIA DE TAÜLL: APSE.
Magi Caspar and Balthasar and the Maiestas Mariae, *from the vault of the central apse of the church of Santa Maria de Taüll*

38

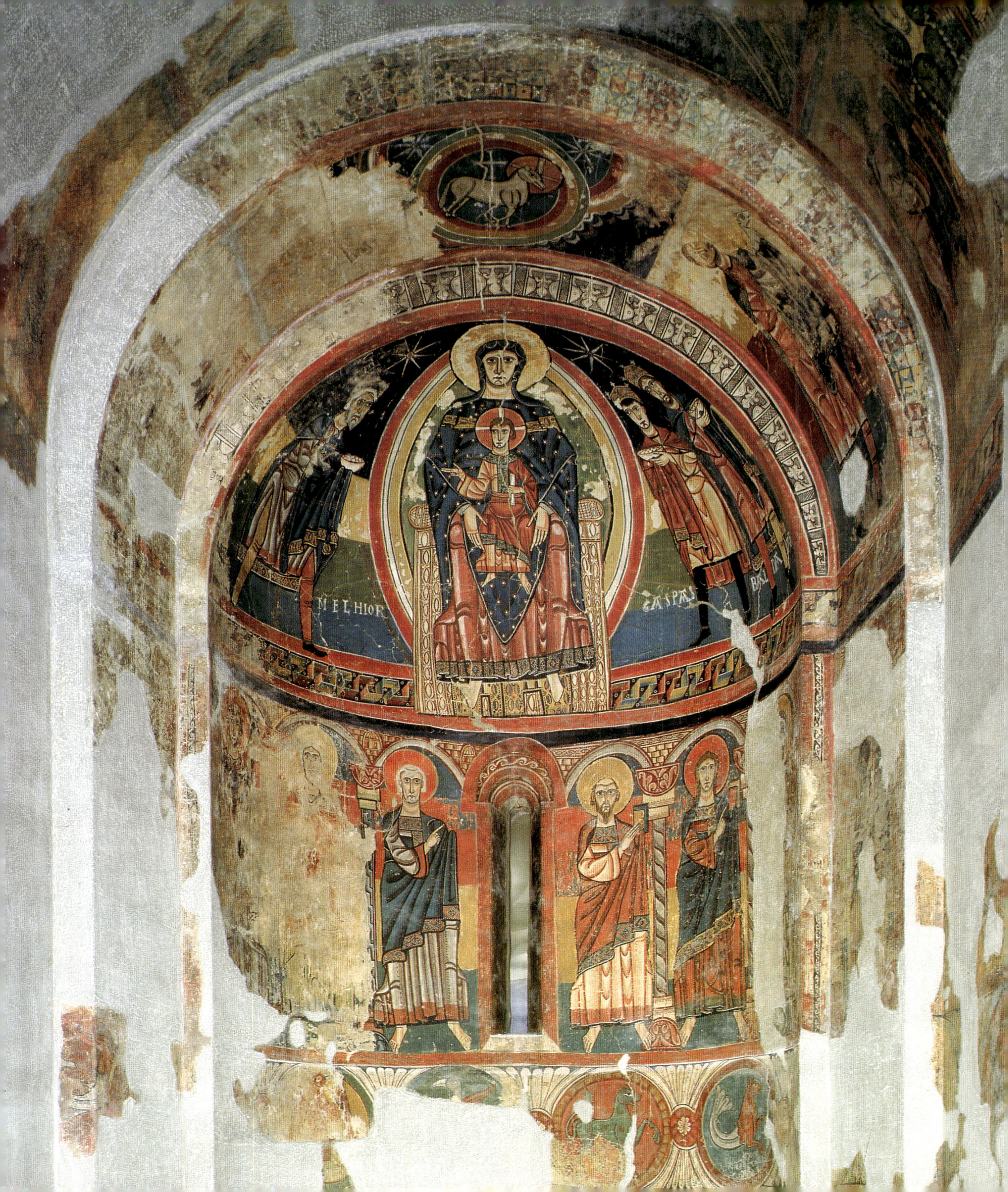
MELHIOR
GASPAS

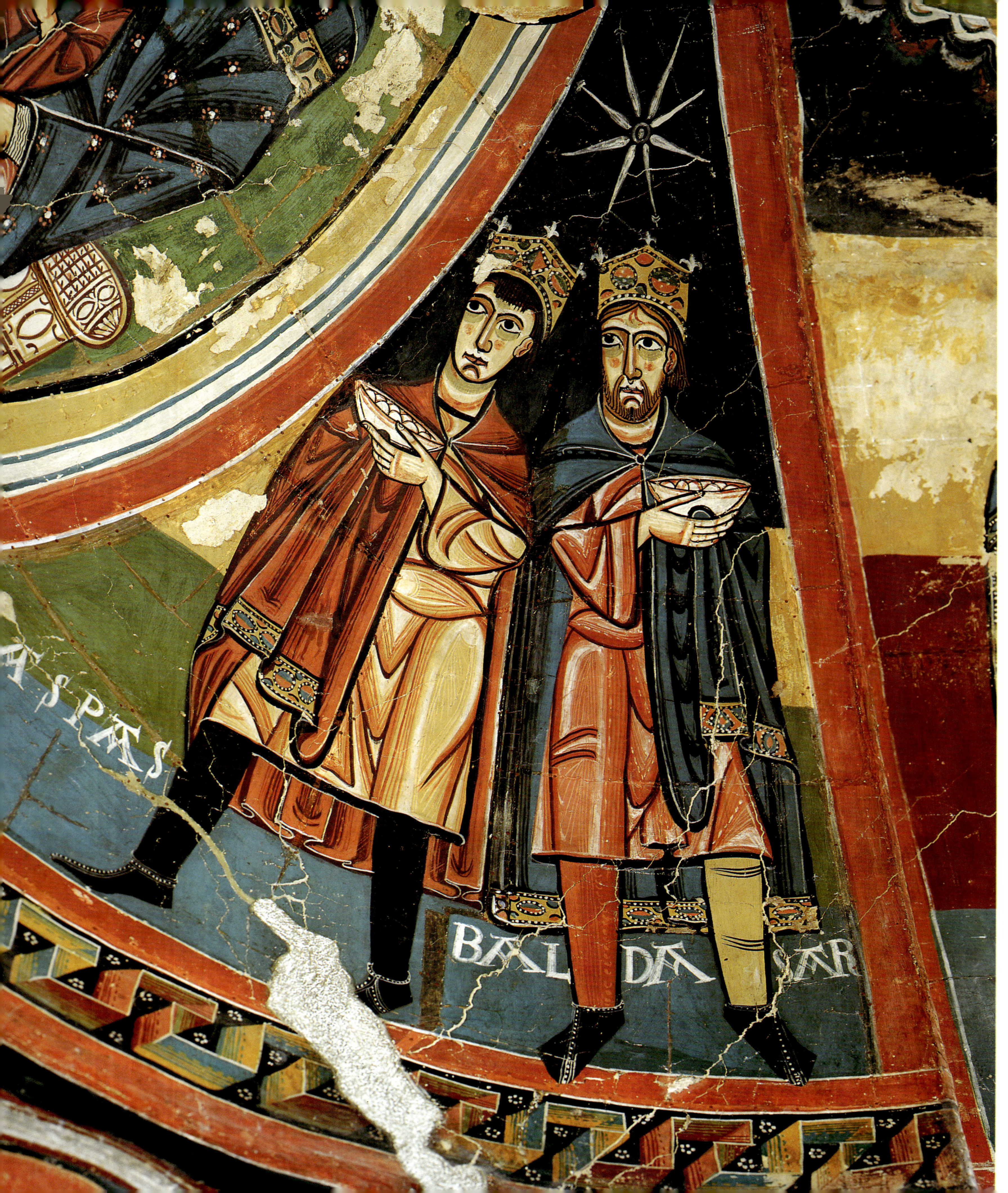

ASPAR
BALDASAR

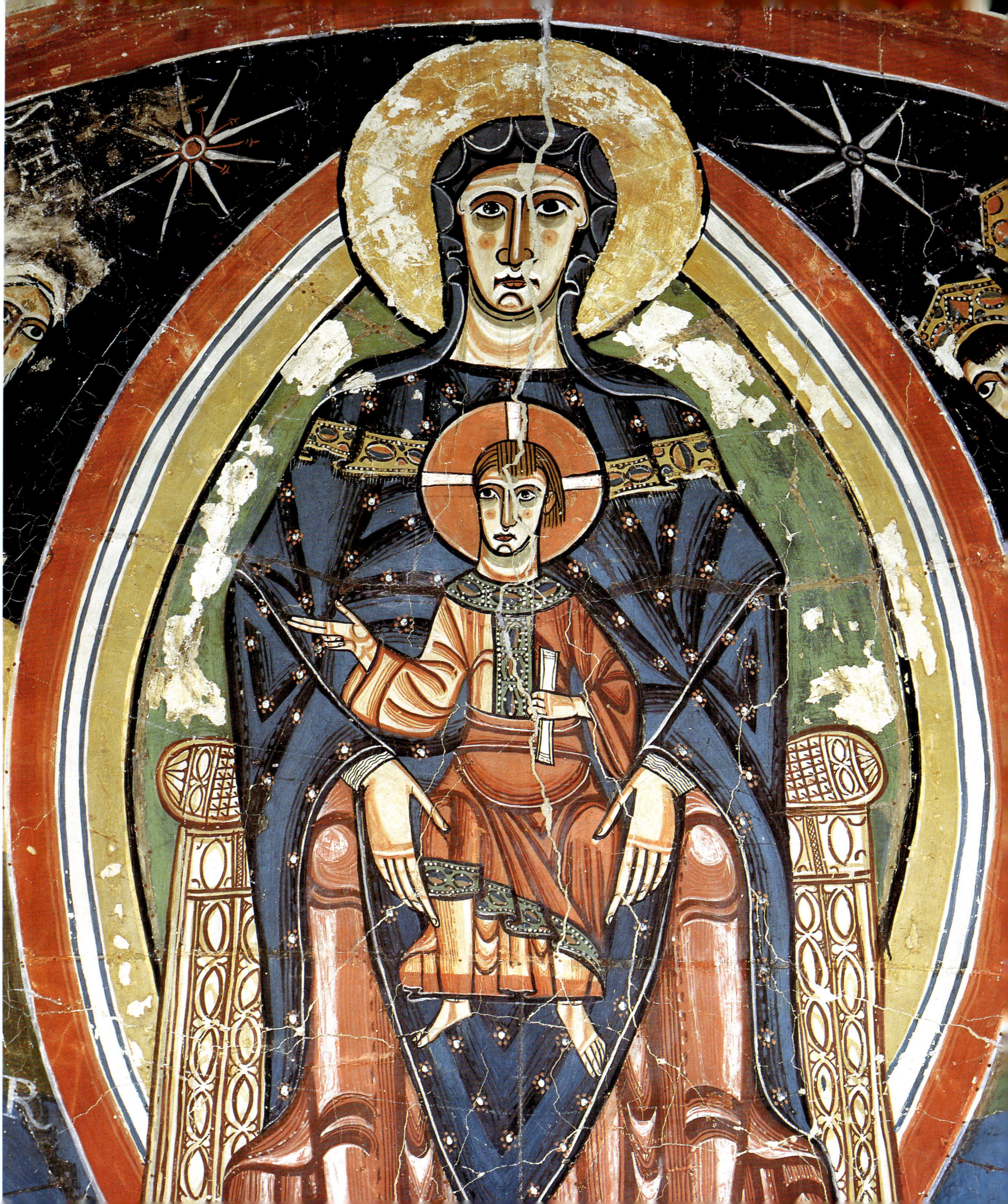

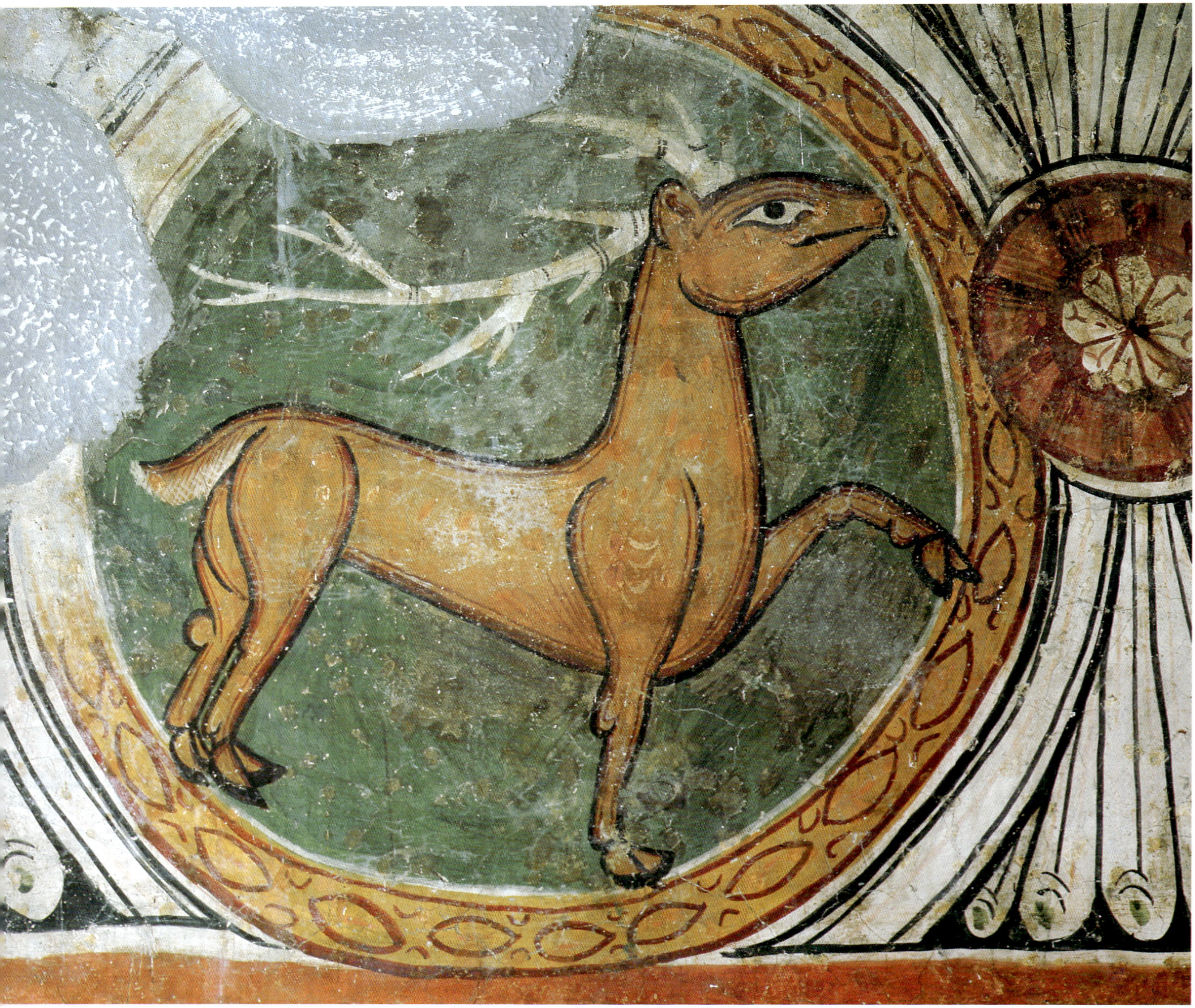

41-42. Santa Maria de Taüll: apse.
A deer and an imaginary animal from the decoration of the lower register of the church of Santa Maria de Taüll

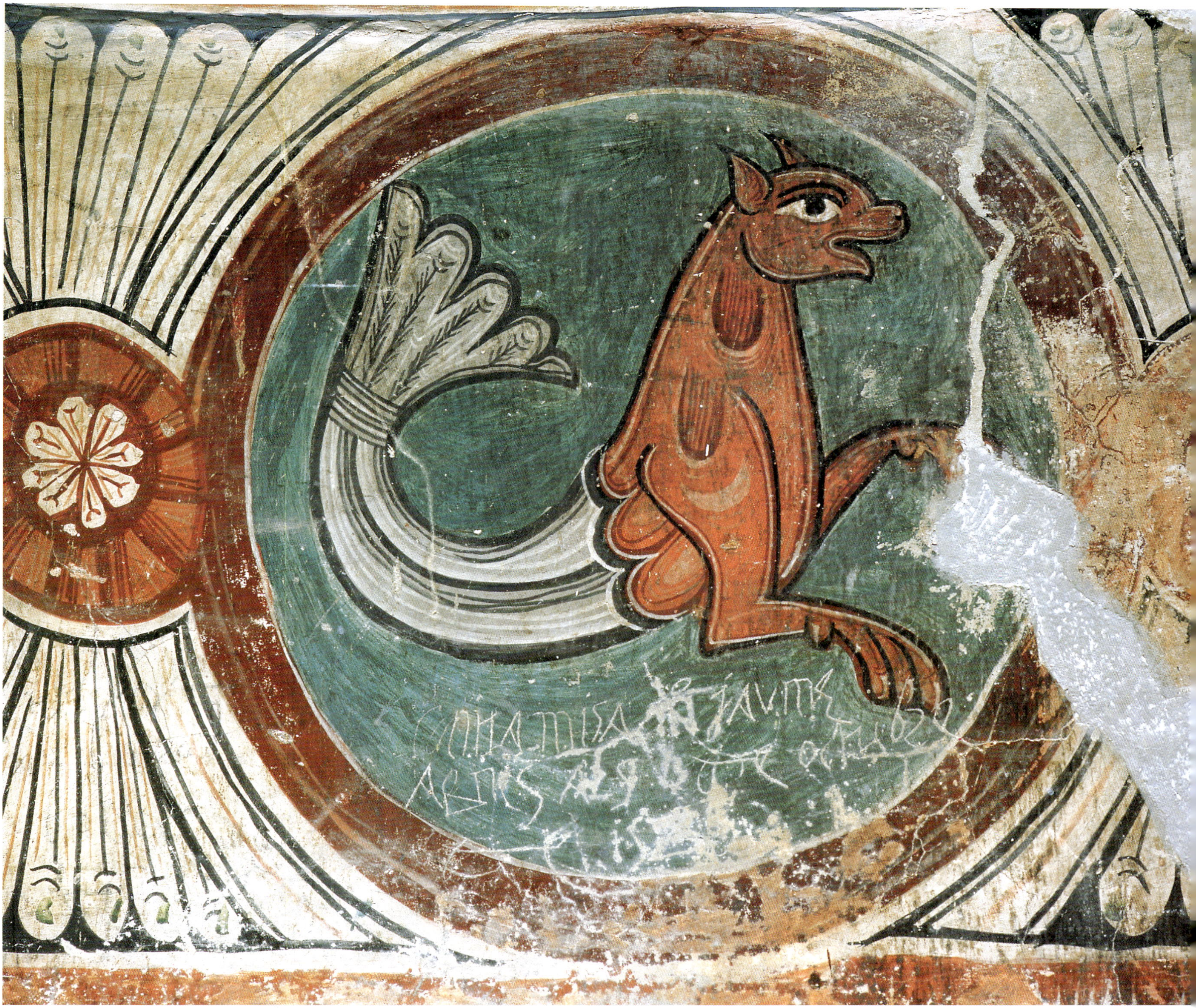

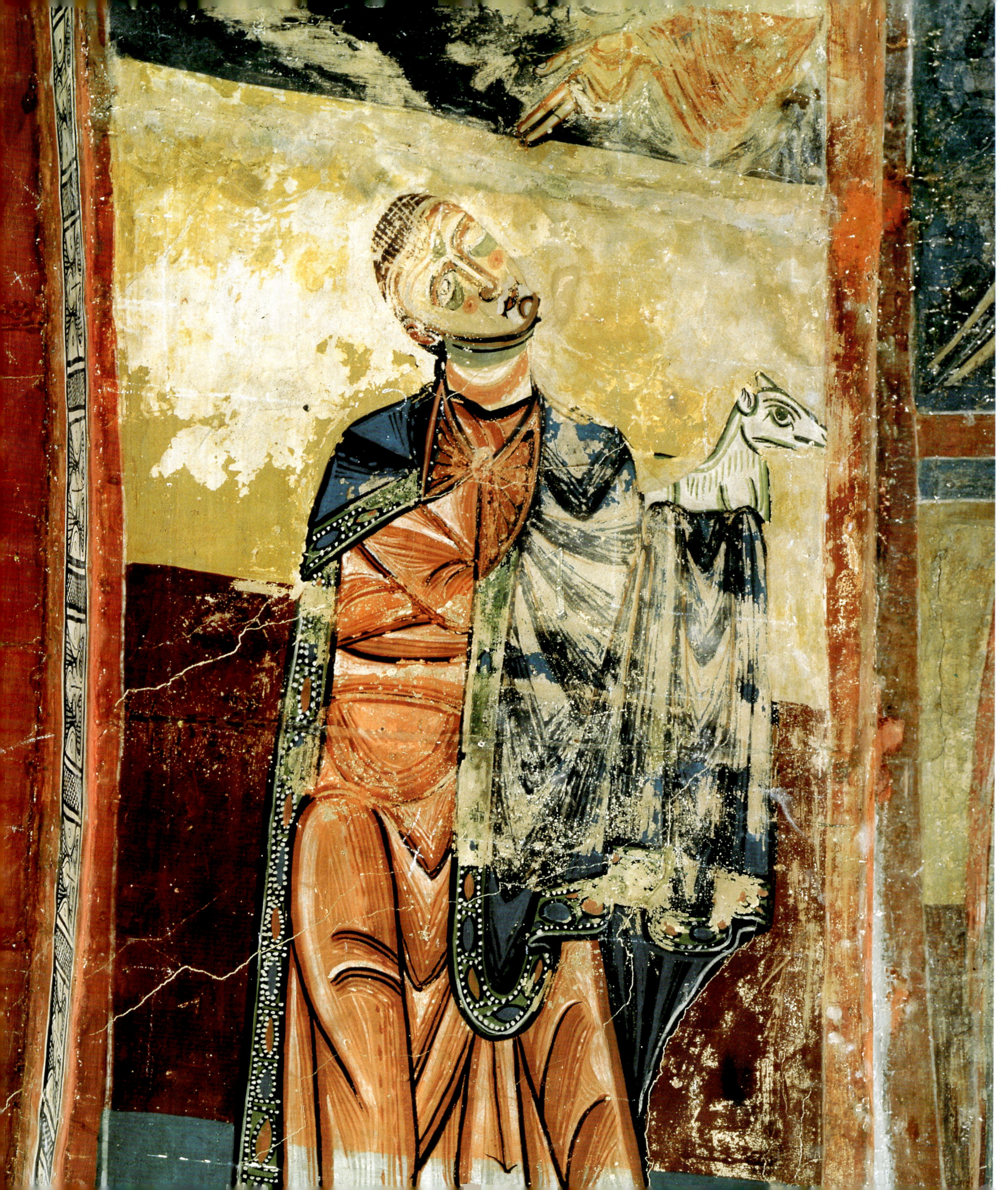

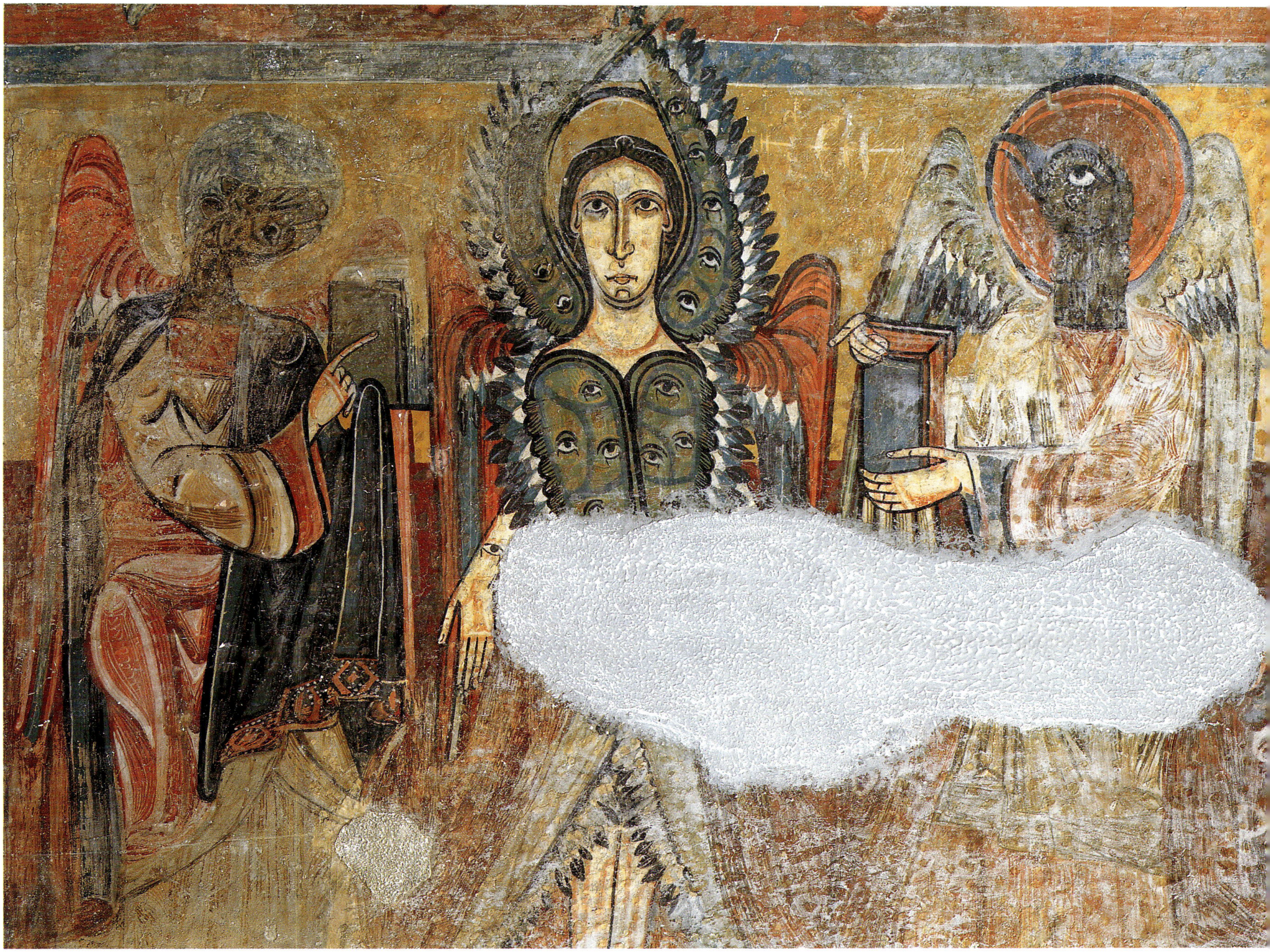

43. Santa Maria de Taüll: apse.
Abel offering the lamb, from the decoration on the presbytery arch of the church of Santa Maria de Taüll

44. Santa Maria de Taüll: Detail of the apse.
A seraphim flanked by the symbols of evangelists Mark and John, from the decoration on the presbytery vault of the church of Santa Maria de Taüll

ures of the Pedret Circle, whose style connects more closely with the paintings on the north wall of the nave in Galliano, and in particular w.th the master who painted the cycles of Judith and Saint Margaret, which are normally dated later than the apse. Whatever the case, the Lombardic connection doesn't seem to have been the only path of inspiration for the Pedret Circle, since as well as the local legacy already mentioned, close links have always been seen with the painting of Lazio and the South of Italy. In fact the liturgical cloth with facing birds that covers the altar of the holocaust in the central apse of Pedret (Museu Diocesà de Solsona) is reminiscent cf the decoration of San Nicola in Carcere (*c.* 1120); the representation of the Apocalypse in that same central apse in Pedret is reminiscent of the cycle of Sant'Anastasio in Castel Sant'Elia (*c.* 1110-1125) or that

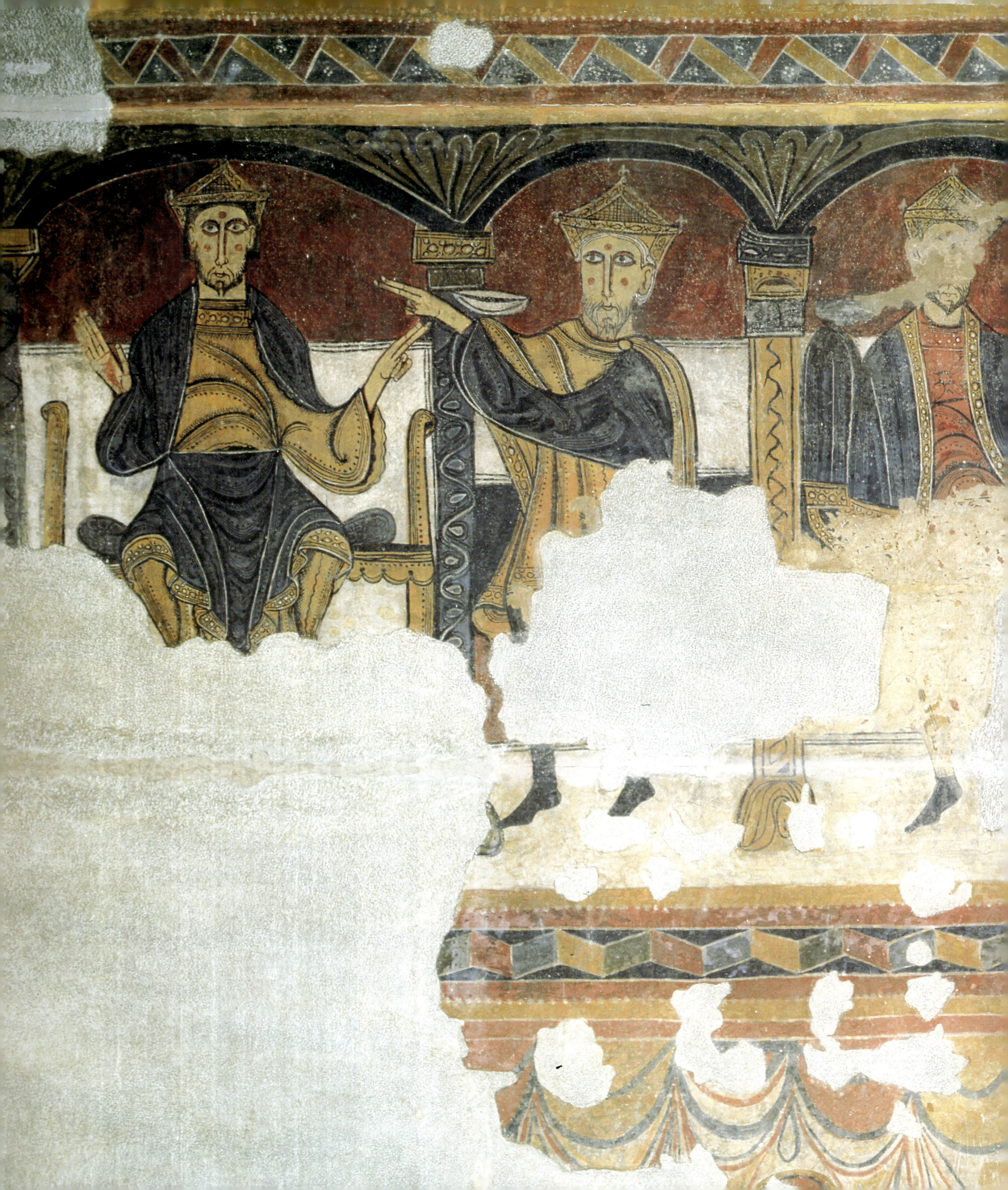

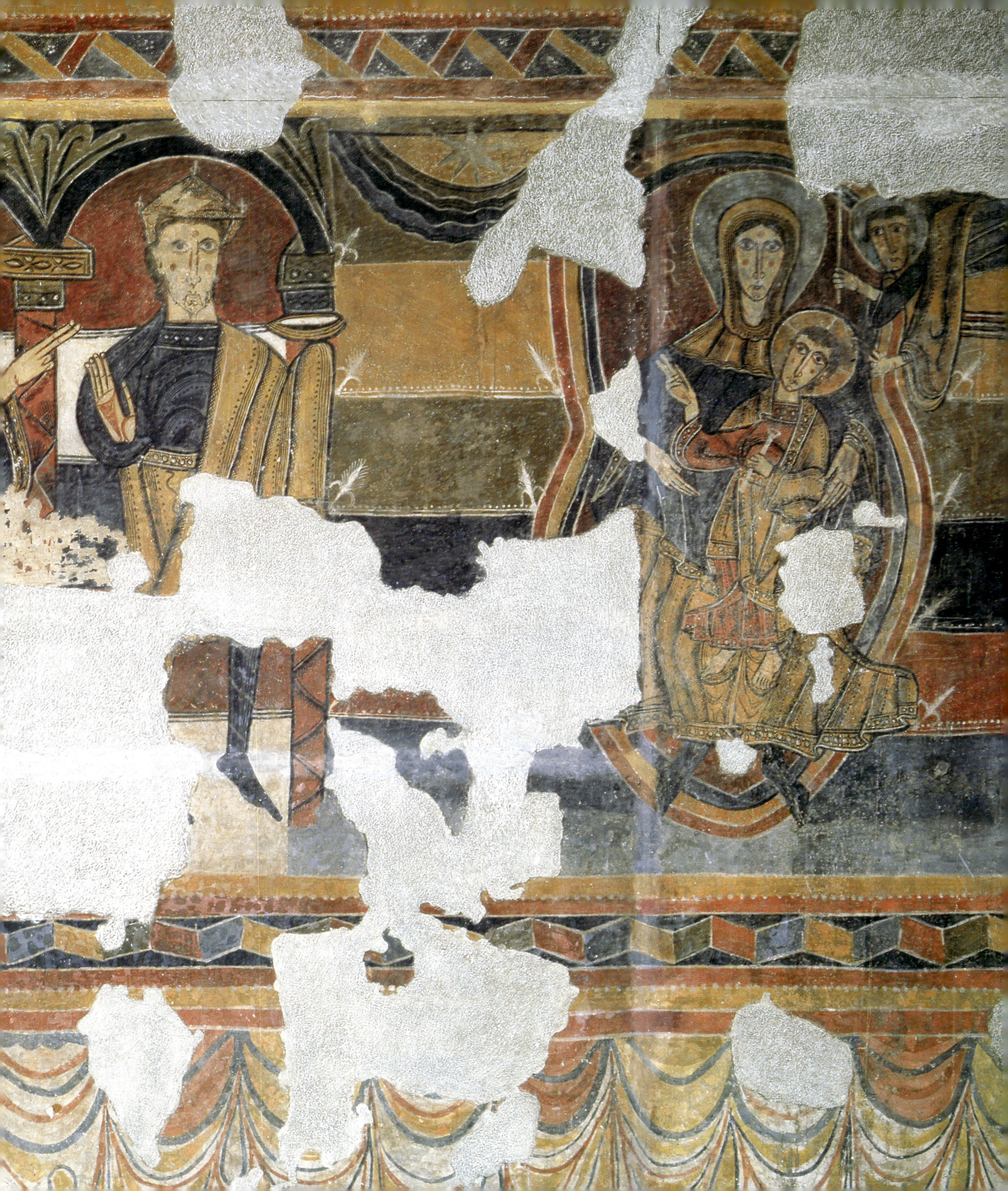

of the crypt of Anagni cathedral (thirteenth century); and the theme of the Wise Virgins crowned brings to mind the ones in the Roman tradition (Santa Prassede, San Sebastiano in Pallara, Santa Pudenziana, Castel Sant'Elia, Anagni). Even though the wheels and the kneeling prophets can be found on a painted panel of the Last Judgement from Santa Maria di Campo Marzio (Vatican Museums), the subject of the Archangels with standards is also found in the paintings in the tribune in Saint Lawrence outside the Walls, both of which date from the second half of the eleventh century.

Having established these points, we can return to the problem of the early date of these Catalan sites and try to focus them more clearly in relation to the cultural movement they form part of, the Gregorian Reform. It's most likely that the inscription and representation of Llúcia of Pallars in El Burgal had a funerary or commemorative value and were therefore not done while she was alive but under the reign of her sons, Artau II, Count of Pallars (1090-1124), and Saint Otto, Bishop of Urgell (1095-1122), after the counts of Pallars Sobirà had recovered the monastery in 1095. In fact, the established Catalan tradition of offering candles to the souls of deceased church benefactors seems to explain the appearance of Llúcia, after death, carrying a candle and accompanied by members of her family (her sons), whose portraits appeared a few years ago *in situ* on the left of the entrance wall to the central apse. In addition to this, the countess is not depicted as an old woman but as ideally young, more or less the same age as that of Christ at his death, as she would have to resuscitate with this appearance on the Day of Judgement. However, the inclusion of lay figures at the bottom of a sacred theme is a recurring formula in Byzantine pictorial cycles as well as those of central and southern Italy, as we see from the paintings in Kiev cathedral (eleventh century), San Pietro di Crepacore in Apulia (ninth century), San Clemente in Rome (1078-1084) and San Pietro in Valle in Ferentillo (twelfth century).

We have to understand the cycles of El Burgal, Àneu and Pedret in this context of church reform, known as the Gregorian Reform, in which iconographic programmes served to express the attempt to return to the origins of the Church of Rome. In El Burgal, the decoration in the apse shows a division into three registers that was to be repeated endlessly in Catalan Romanesque. At the top, Christ in Majesty on the Day of Judgement is flanked by the Archangels Gabriel and Michael, who would originally have had the complete inscriptions *Petitius* and *Postulatius*, and the figures of two prophets at their feet, as in Galliano and Àneu. Below the heaven is a central register in the form of a semi-circular bench like the *synthronon* in a church, where some of the Apostles, the Virgin and Saint John the Baptist are seated. Finally, in the lower register, against a background of curtains, there appears the figure of Llúcia of Pallars, who in a daring *trompe-l'oeil* is projected forward into the observer's space. The central role of the visible heads of the Roman Church, Saint Peter and Saint Paul, and the emphasis on the Eucharist implicit in the attributes held by Mary (the chalice containing the blood of Christ) and Saint John the Baptist (the clipeus with the Lamb of God) seem to connect with the principles of the Gregorian Reform as regards the primacy of the Pope and the defence of the dogma of the real presence of Christ in the Eucharist against the ideas of Berengarius of Tours.

45. Santa Maria de Taüll
Synoptic scene with the Three Wise Men from the Orient approaching Herod before adoring the Messiah, from the wall paintings of the south aisle of the church of Santa Maria de Taüll

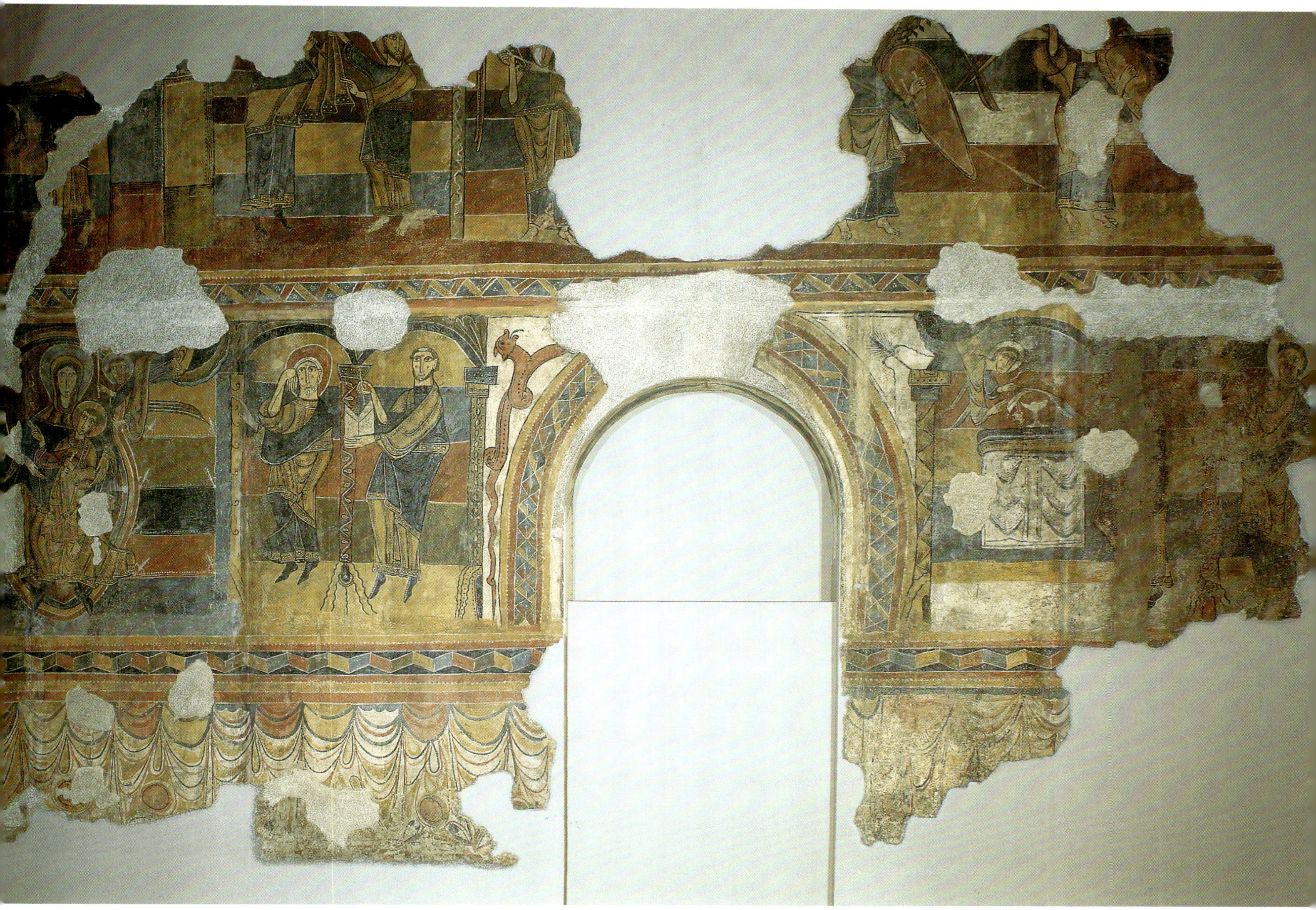

46

46. SANTA MARIA DE TAÜLL.
From left to right in the central register, the revelation of the birth of Saint John the Baptist, which the angel made to Zachariah while he was officiating in the Temple. The naming of John the Baptist by Zachariah, from the paintings on the wall of the south aisle in the church of Santa Maria de Taüll

47. SANTA MARIA DE TAÜLL.
The fight between David and Goliath, from the decoration on the inside of the west façade of the church of Santa Maria de Taüll

The pictorial decoration of Santa Maria d'Àneu, a church returned to the Bishopric of La Seu d'Urgell in 1087-1088 by the Count of Pallars, doesn't seem to be earlier than this date either. Although its ambitious iconographic programme has been interpreted as proof of its links with Lombardic painting, a detailed analysis reveals an important debt to Oliba.

First of all, the prominence given the three Archangels (Michael, Gabriel and Raphael) seems to translate into images the recurrent sacred topography of the great Catalan monasteries of the eleventh century: Ripoll, with its altar dedicated to Saint Michael and Saint Raphael, Cuixà, with the famous trilogy of Archangels on the rotunda in the west block, and the altars of Saint Michael in the monastery of Sant Pere de Rodes and Vic cathedral. Remember that the Catalan mints of the eleventh century, in Besalú and Girona, issued coin with the images of Raphael and Michael. This obsession with angels and, especially, with Michael, persisted until the twelfth century, as we can see in the decoration of the left lateral apse in Sant Climent de Taüll.

Secondly, there is the magnificent representation on the lower register of the Seraphim, with their six wings of peacock feathers covered with eyes, from Isaiah's Vision in the Temple of Jerusalem, singing 'S(AN)C(TU)S, S(AN)C(TU)S, S(AN)C(TU)S' (Isa. 6:3). What's more, the Seraphim, located at the level of the church's original altar (evoking the sacrificial altar), as though flanking it, are depicted holding out tongs with burning coals to the lips of the prophets Elijah ('ELHIA') and Isaiah ('I(SAIAS)') to purify their words (Isa. 6:6). This image is very common in Byzantine miniatures and can also be found in the part of the Bible of Rodes probably completed in Ripoll in the third quarter of the eleventh century. It was intended as a metaphorical allusion to the tabernacle or the Ark of the Covenant in the Old Testament and, by extension, to Mary, Mother of God, represented in the upper register in a scene from the Epiphany, as the new Tabernacle.

Thirdly, there is the unusual importance given to the wheels from Ezekiel's Vision (Ez. 1:15), located in the centre of the lower register. This is something that was common in the Ripoll Bible and even reached the apse of Sant Climent de Taüll, where the four wheels are also depicted at the bottom of the representation of the four living beings.

Finally, on the left of the semi-cylinder of the apse, overlapping one another, are two mysterious characters, probably a presbyter and a deacon, making an identical gesture as they present a closed book. These figures, which so far have proved impossible to identify from the remaining inscriptions but are presumably donors, corroborate the ecclesiological tone of the work, as it extols their acts in the manner of contemporary portraits, like the ones of Desiderius of Montecassino in the paintings in Sant'Angelo in Formis. Similarly, the exaltation of Mary in this programme, which presents Mary in Majesty as the union between the Old and New Testaments, is characteristic of Catalan mural painting, where it was to have some success (Santa Maria de Cap d'Aran, Santa Maria de Taüll). We need to ask ourselves whether the origins of this iconographic particularity are related to the Marian cult documented during Oliba's time in Ripoll and Cuixà.

As regards the site of Sant Quirze de Pedret, the subject matter of the right lateral apse, devoted to the Parable of the Ten Virgins (Mat. 25:1-13), takes on a marked theatrical tone in which the Wise Virgins ('QUI(N)QUE PRVDENTE'), their torches alight, are happily seated at the banquet with Christ, while the Foolish ones ('QUI(N)QUE FATVE'), their empty torches on the ground, are left standing forlornly at the entrance to the gates of Paradise. It's not surprising, then, that it should have been associated with the liturgical play *Sponsus*, written in the French abbey of Saint Martial in Limoges at the end of the eleventh century, at the end of which Christ makes a small speech to them about the consequences of their actions. This eschatological and ecclesiological tone can be seen in Pedret in the representation of Christ before the Gate of Paradise, in the fact that the central apse is dedicated to the Apocalypse and in the personification of the Church ('ECREXIA') as a crowned woman seated on a temple, an iconography very like the one in the *Exultet* in Benevento. Once more the main emphasis is on Mary, who, as *Theotokus* ('S(AN)C(T)A MARIA') presides the vault in a bust formula quite definitely tied to Byzantine art.

For their part, the cycles from Ribagorça in the collection (Sant Joan de Boí, Sant Climent de Taüll and Santa Maria de Taüll) seem to point to another area of church reform,

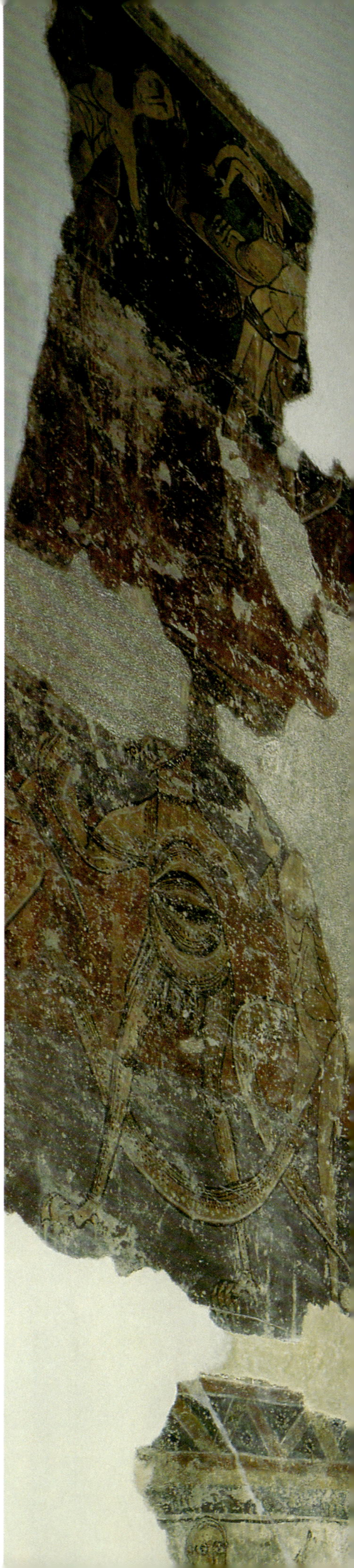

47

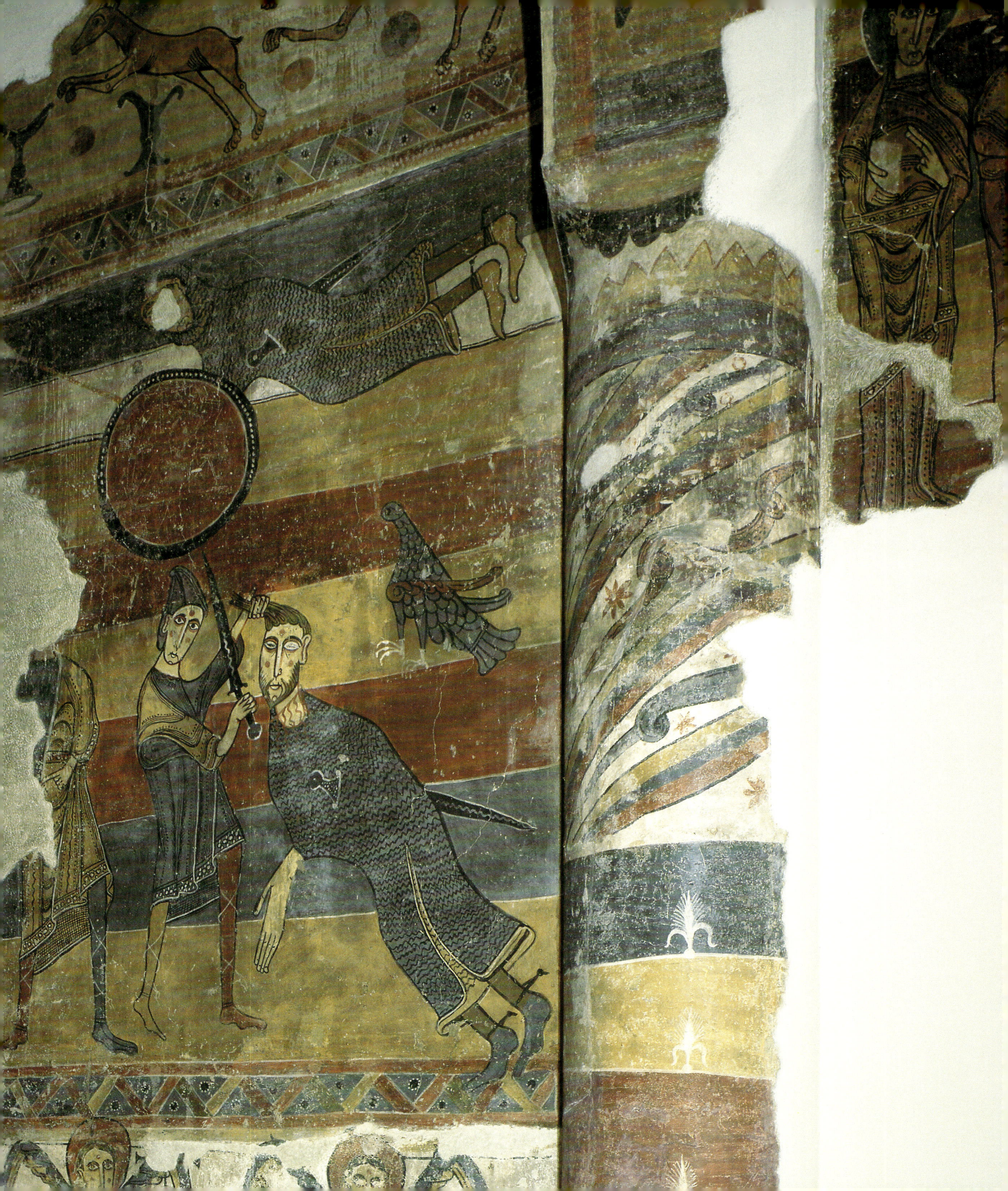

the Bishopric of Roda d'Isàvena, and to another approach to mural decoration. Two of the bishops who held office there during those years, Pons (1095-1104) and Ramon (1104-1126), both from Occitania, embarked on a policy of parish reorganisation and endorsement of liturgical reform. For that reason it has recently been suggested that all these cycles (Boí, Sant Climent de Taüll and Santa Maria de Taüll) were indebted to the pictorial traditions of southern France. In the case of Boí, dated around 1100, the decoration of the intradoses of the arches, which are covered with animals from the Bestiary, obviously takes its inspiration from the illustrations in the margins of the manuscripts produced by the *scriptorium* of Saint Martial in Limoges or its associated centres. In the church interior there were also other subjects equally widespread in Southern France, like the Lapidation of Saint Stephen or the representation of Abraham's Bosom along with Hell, which normally appeared in stone façades in association with the Parable of Poor Lazarus and the Rich Man (Moissac, Ripoll). Whatever the case, its dynamic narrative nature based on outlined figures and flat colours, of which a good example is the scene with minstrels and tumblers (which may reflect the church's festive consecration ceremony), has led the Boí style to be described as 'a miniature enlarged to monumental format', typical of the moment around 1100 when the tradition of mural painting began to take off.

Few works have been so unanimously hailed by specialised critics as a masterpiece of European Romanesque art as the paintings in the apse of Sant Climent de Taüll. They are normally dated on the basis of the inscription painted on one of the columns in the nave, which celebrates the consecration of the church by Bishop Ramon of Roda on December 10th, 1123, a date which while not absolute ties up with the production of other very similar paintings in the chapel of Sant Agustí in Roda d'Isàvena cathedral, which was consecrated in 1117. As regards the programmes by the what is called the 'Pedret Circle' analysed earlier, Taüll presents a monumental and synthetic Theophanic view filled with tension and movement, in which experiments previously carried out on the tympanum of large sculptural portals in the south of France are successfully transferred to apse paintings. We therefore find the same liking for a synoptic composition, with a masterly and unitary combination of different biblical visions, both in Taüll and on the portal of Saint-Pierre in Moissac (*c.* 1120). The centre is dominated by the Vision of the Apocalypse with the Christ of the end of time and the Tetramorph (Rev. 1:8; 1:13-14; 4:6-7), while on either side are arranged the Seraphim from the Vision of Isaiah and Cherubim from the Ark of the Covenant, already present in the reliefs by Gilduinus in the ambulatory of Saint-Sernin in Toulouse (*c.* 1096) and which we later find everywhere in Romanesque painting (Esterri de Cardós, Estaon, etc.). Finally, as I said earlier, the original four wheels that frame the symbols of Mark and Luke are a reference to the ones in Ezekiel's Vision of the Chariot (1:5-21).

Another important point is that the same movement and centrifugal agitation visible especially on Christ's legs and sleeves, in the rumpled clothes of Matthew's angel and in the impulsive forward motion in Saint Mark's are also found in the figures on the tympanum in Moissac. In fact, the Occitanian miniature is precisely where we find some of the keys to the Taüll style, with its pinched folds, of an almost metallic consistency, which are only brought to life in the upward movement of the *plis soufflés* (flying folds). This is

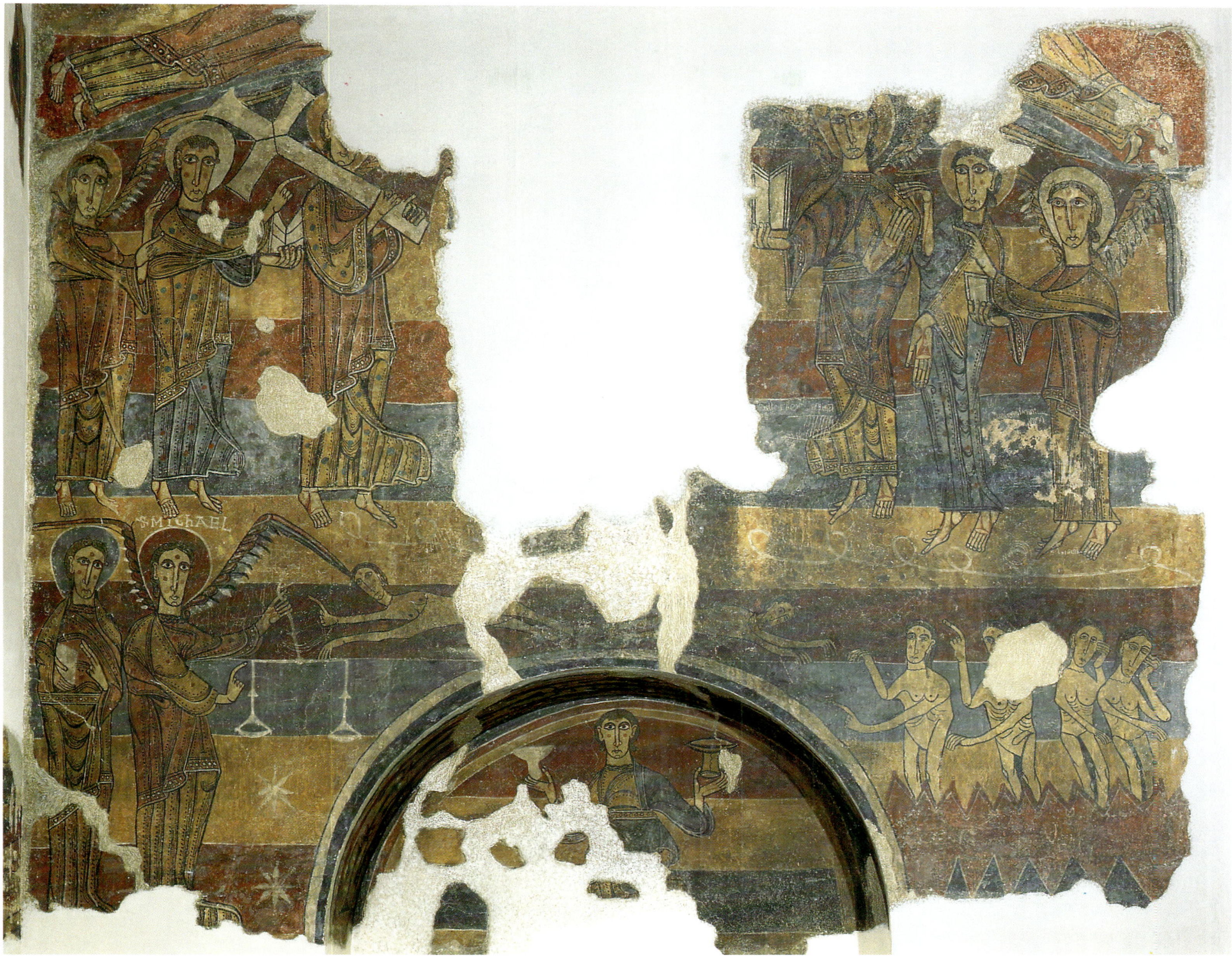

48. Santa Maria de Taüll: The Last Judgement.
The Last Judgement, from the decoration on the inside of the west façade of the church of Santa Maria de Taüll

the case of the manuscript by Flavius Josephus, *De Bello Judaico* (Paris, BNF, ms. Lat. 5058, fols. 2v-3r), produced in the Moissac scriptorium in about 1100, which shows a similar tendency to paint elongated faces with pronounced bulging eyes.

However, there's no denying the innovative creative force that shows itself in the stylised forms, in which fluctuating lines are fundamental, as we see in the wavy hair, the emphatic eyebrows, the ornamental beard or the fictitious white threads hanging from Christ's eyes. Similarly, the chromatic range, as mentioned above, is outstandingly rich and its application in layers achieves incredible effects of volume in certain areas of the Pantocrator, like the stomach or the legs. In addition, the original use of calcium white in the haloes gives the work a mysterious light that gives the text of the book Christ is holding in his hand its meaning: 'EGO SUM LUX MUNDI' (Jn. 8:12).

Arranged beneath arches and occupying the middle register of windows in imaginary architecture that may be an allusion to the Celestial Jerusalem are the Apostles (Thomas, Bartholomew, John, James, Philip) and the Virgin. The Virgin is holding a shiny paten holding the blood of Christ, a reference to the sacrifice of the Eucharist, the same as in El Burgal, which it has also been suggested is an evocation of the legend of the Holy Grail. The acknowledged genius of the Master of Taüll, expressed in masterly fashion in the figures of Christ and of some of the Apostles in the apse (such as Saint John), as well as in details like the *Dextera Domini* or the seven-eyed lamb of the Apocalypse (Rev. 5:6) on the vault, doesn't extend to the whole of the decoration in the apse and certainly not to the schematic painting in the left lateral apse. However, thanks to the fragments recently recovered and preserved *in situ* we can complete the iconography of the intrados of the arch of the presbytery, with the offering of Cain and Abel and Abel's death by Cain's hand, narrated with the skill of the great master of the apse, and the story of Poor Lazarus and the Rich Man.

On December 11th, 1123, the day after the consecration of Sant Climent, the Bishop of Roda consecrated the church of Santa Maria de Taüll. It's obvious at a glance that although the artists had access to a similar iconographic and ornamental repertory, whoever did Santa Maria was less skilled in the art of painting. In addition, at least three teams worked on the decoration here. One did the central apse, presided by a *Maiestas Mariae*; a second decorated the right lateral apse, which is of excellent quality and very like the paintings of Santa Cruz de Maderuelo (Soria), now in the Museo del Prado; and a third did the cruder decoration all over the nave and aisles, columns and counter-façade. We don't know if it was all finished in time for the consecration, though from the unity of the iconographic programme we can deduce that the work was divided up amongst the teams from the start so as to get the church ready as soon as possible. But what really stands out about the building is the fact that it is the only one whose decoration has survived almost complete, and not just in the apse. This helps understand the importance of the way the images are distributed around the church according to the significance and the function of the different parts of the building. The right aisle, a space set aside for the faithful, is used to explain the mystery of the Incarnation, with the story of Herod, the Wise Men and the Epiphany, or the Revelation to Zachariah in the Temple, the birth of his son John the Baptist (Lk. 1:5-20) and his naming (Lk. 1:62-64). The space reserved for the baptistery, between the tower and the façade, has its walls decorated with the struggle between David and Goliath, a metaphorical image of the good Christian overcoming Evil, and with a Hell full of terrible punishments, as Baptism frees us of Original Sin and makes us renounce Satan. Finally, the counter-façade is decorated with the Last Judgement, in which a Christ in Majesty (now lost), come to judge the living and the dead, is accompanied by a following of angels (Mt. 25:31), amongst which the angel carrying the Cross of triumph over death stands out. At the bottom, on the right, is the Psychostasis, or Weighing of Souls, with Saint Michael holding the scales, and on the left the souls being hurled into the eternal fire of the damned (Mt. 25, 41).

The cycle of Santa Maria de Taüll is undoubtedly a rare example of the educational function of images, derived from the Gregorian Reform. In this case, the images are intended for the congregation of a humble parish church in the Pyrenees, which explains the simple resort to ecclesiological metaphors like the columns, the support for the

49. GINESTARRE: APSE.
Mural paintings from the apse of the church of Santa Maria de Ginestarre.
In the vault, the Maiestas Domini *surrounded by the symbols of the four evangelists and in the central register, the twelve apostles with the Virgin holding the chalice.*
Second half of the 12th century.
580 × 365 × 250 cm.
MNAC/MAC 15971

50. GINESTARRE: DETAIL.
Detail of the legs of Mark's symbol, from the decoration in the vault of Santa Maria de Ginestarre

49

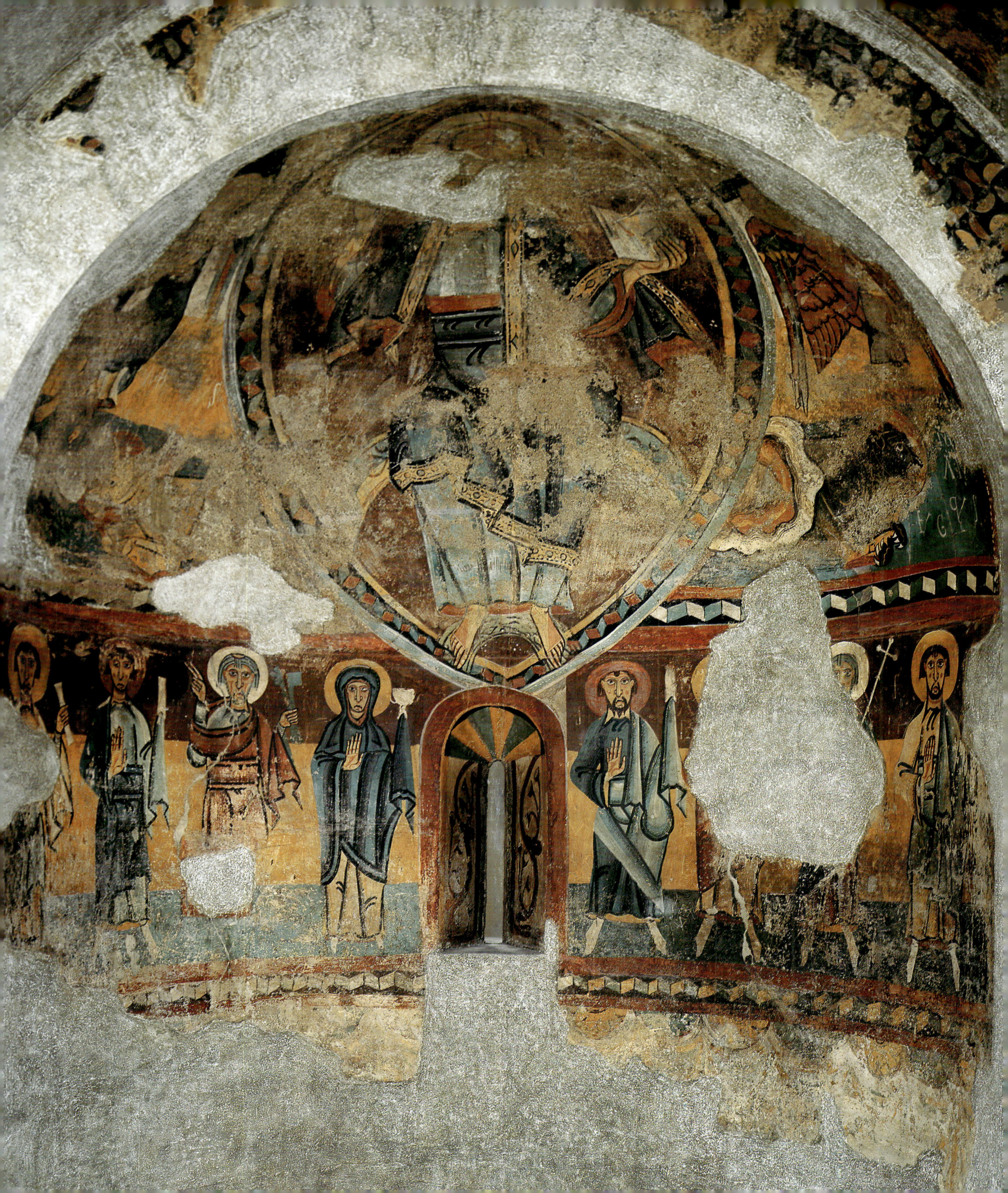

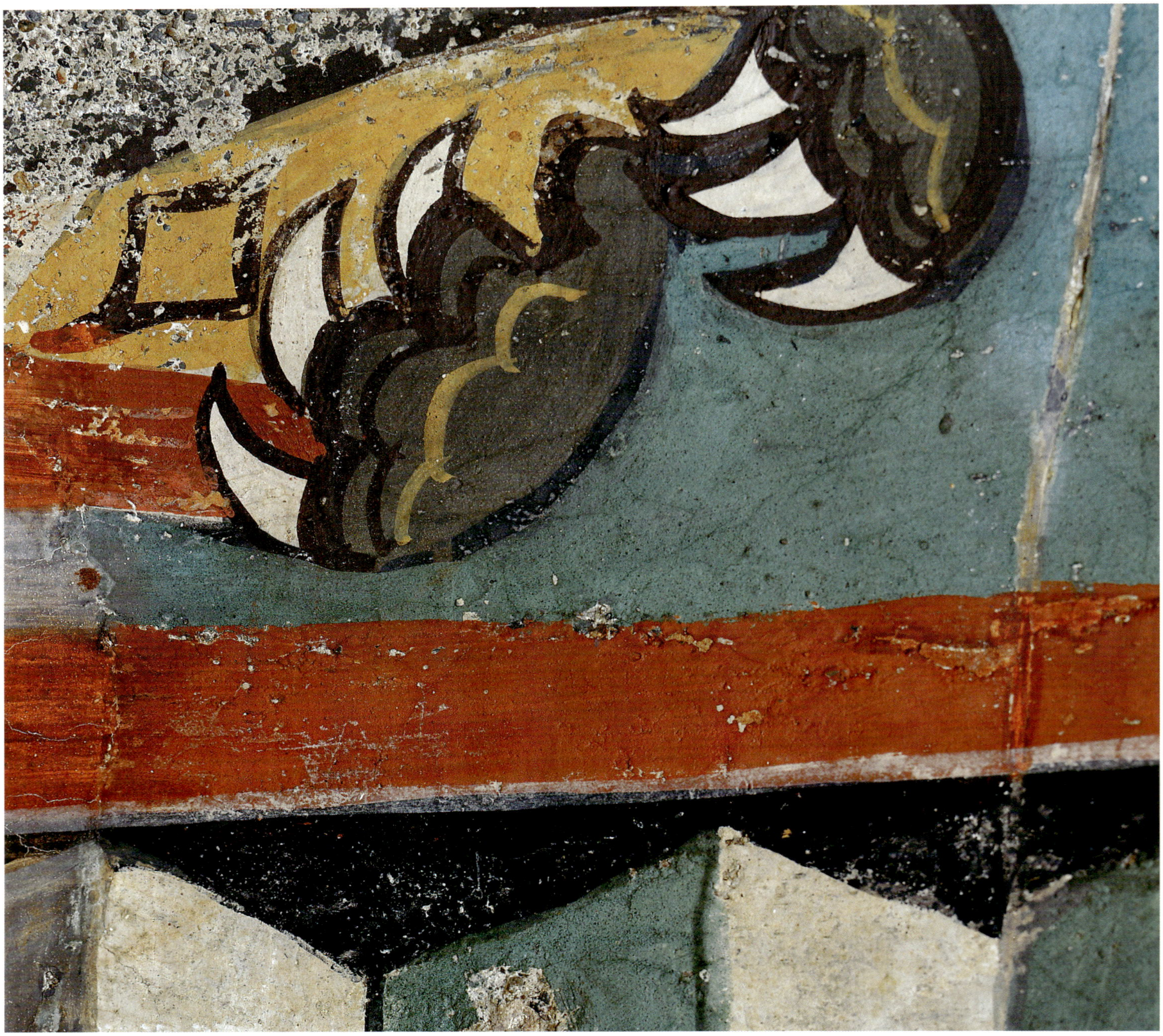

50 51

church, which are decorated with images of bishop saints like Saint Nicholas, a model of the honest prelate, or Pope Saint Clement. Similarly, the emphasis on the folk festival of the Epiphany, with warm touches like the representation of the Magi with their names or the twofold depiction of the star of Bethlehem in the apse, and the emphasis on the prophets announcing the coming of the Messiah, like Zachariah (Lk. 1:78-79), Isaiah or Ezekiel (on the intrados of the baptistery arch), seem to evoke the liturgical plays performed in those days on Christmas Eve, like the *Officium Stellae* or the *Ordo Prophetarum*, which were intended to reveal to the common people the mystery of the Incarnation.

Another series of painted apses from churches in the former bishopric of La Seu d'Urgell speak for the persistence of a technique and an approach to mural decoration in

51. Sant Pau d'Esterri de Cardós.
Detail of the mural paintings in the apse of Sant Pau d'Esterri de Cardós.
Next to the vault, the figure of the Maiestas Domini *with the symbols of the evangelists, a seraphim, a cherub and the archangels Gabriel and Michael. In the central register, Saint Paul, Saint John the Evangelist, Saint Bartholomew and Saint Thomas.*
Second half of the 12th century
610 × 430 × 370 cm. MNAC/MAC 15970

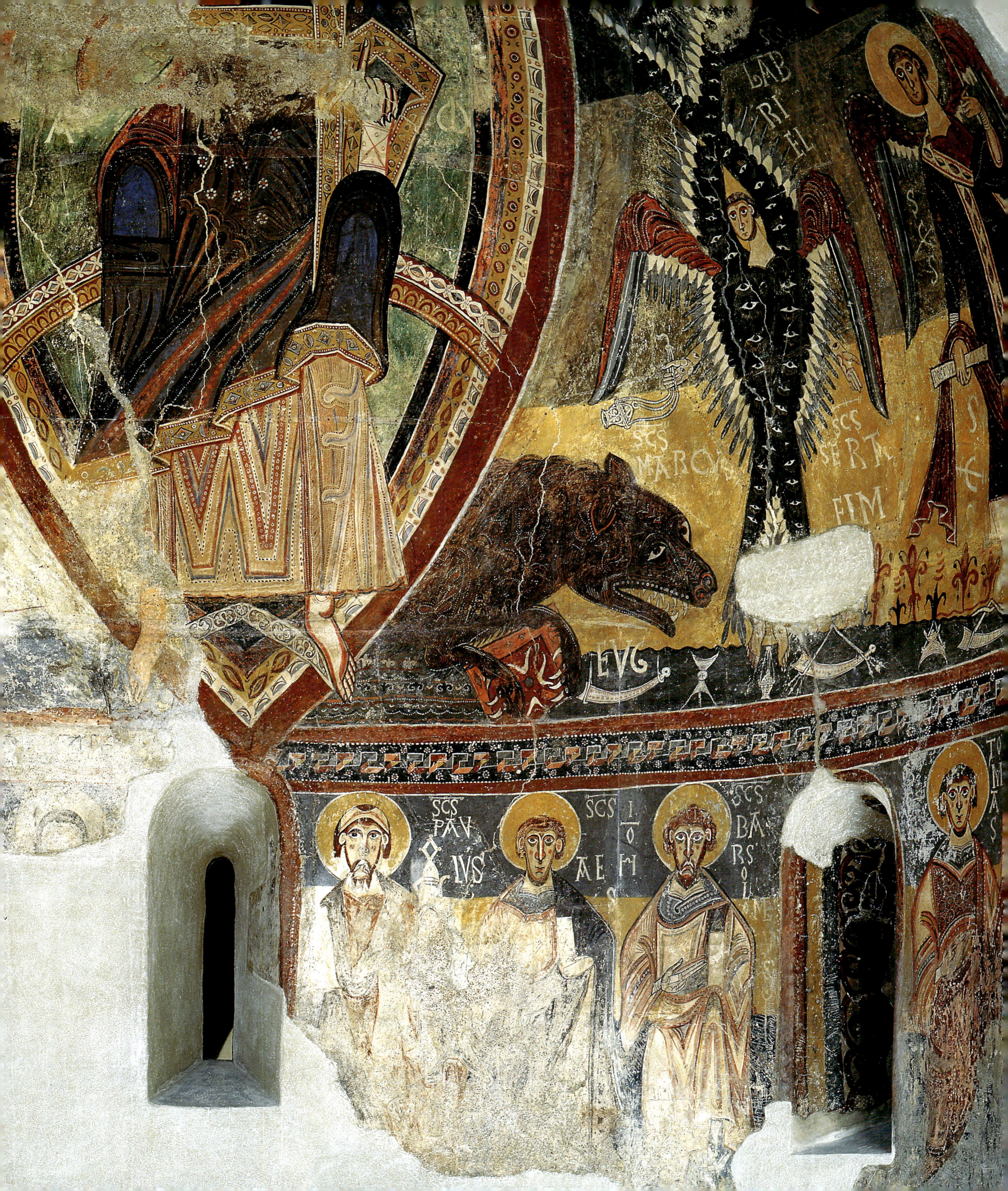

the second half of the twelfth century derived from prior experience of the 'Pedret Circle', though with an extreme, crude simplification of the illusionism that characterised it. With certain variations, the cycles of Santa Maria de Ginestarre, Sant Pau d'Esterri de Cardós, Santa Maria d'Estaon and Sant Miquel d'Engolasters repeat a tripartite scheme. The upper register is occupied by Christ in Majesty surrounded by the Tetramorph and accompanied by his heavenly following (Archangels, the Seraphim and the Cherub); the middle register is occupied by the Apostles, which sometimes includes the Virgin with a chalice (Ginestarre, Estaon), while the lower register imitates curtains, which sometimes, as in Estaon, are decorated with scenes of Psychomachy, in which a hunter captures a wild boar with the help of his bloodhound and a net. Finally, the powerful liturgical meaning of some of these programmes is clear, with chalices, censers and horns included on the frieze dividing the first and second registers in Esterri de Cardós or the varied representation of virgin saints (Eulalia, Lucy, Agnes) in the middle level at Estaon.

Of all these groups from the diocese of La Seu d'Urgell, that of Sant Pere de Sorpe, dated in the mid-twelfth century, stands out for the quality of its pictures as it preserves the illusionist tradition of the 'Pedret Circle', to which it adds the trends in ornamentation found in the central apse of Santa Maria de Taüll. What's more, in this case, fortunately, the decoration on the walls of the nave has been preserved, with an interesting display of New Testament scenes on the Gospel side (Annunciation, Nativity, Crucifixion) and a hint at an Old Testament cycle on the Epistle side (Rivers of Paradise). This was common in the great Romanesque pictorial programmes (Sant'Angelo in Formis) evoking the decoration of Saint Peter's in the Vatican. The iconography stands out for its loyalty to the Byzantine repertory, which can be seen in the way the Nativity is arranged in registers, with the Bathing of Christ by the midwives at the bottom, and in the presence of the spy behind the curtains at the moment of the Annunciation while Mary weaves the temple veil. Similarly, our attention is drawn to the marked ecclesiological content of the subjects on the Gospel side on the inside of the pre-apsidal arch. At the top, Mary ('S(AN)C(T)A MARIA') with the Child on her lap ('(R)EX') appears enthroned in the foreground against a backdrop formed by two trees, the leafy tree of the New Law and the drier one, in the form of a *menorah* or branching candelabrum, of the Old Law, a reference to the metaphor of the Virgin as the new Ark of the Covenant already present in Àneu. At the bottom, another image of the Church appears, probably that of the call to the first disciples, Peter ('PETRV(S)') and Andrew ('ANDREA(S)'), fishermen on the Sea of Galilee, to follow. What better image to vindicate a return to the Church's Early Christian beginnings, since the humble boat flies the standard with the Chrismon or Labarum of Constantine?

Finally, a curious profane cycle, at the bottom, probably inspired in the iconography of the Zodiac, with Gemini ('GEMINI'), Cancer ('CRANC'), Sagittarius and a mysterious Elephant, suggests possible access to illustrated astronomical miscellanea, like the one in Ms. 19 in the Biblioteca Nacional de Madrid. This manuscript, produced in Ripoll in about 1134, includes technical recipes which would explain the application of metal leaf on the *suppedaneum* on the Cross. From the scheme and composition of this Crucifix we can attribute it to the same master who did the one in Estaon (Museu Diocesà de la Seu d'Urgell).

This long, diverse and fruitful venture into Romanesque painting in Catalonia couldn't end in a collection like the MNAC's without a grand finale. This is provided by the

52. ESTAON: DETAIL OF THE CENTRAL REGISTER.
The Baptism of Christ, from the decoration of the central register of the apse of the church of Santa Eulàlia d'Estaon. Middle of the 12th century.
MNAC/MAC 5969

53. ESTAON: DETAIL OF THE CENTRAL REGISTER.
Saint Anne and Saint Lucy, from the decoration of the central register of the apse of the church of Santa Eulàlia d'Estaon. Middle of the 12th century.

52

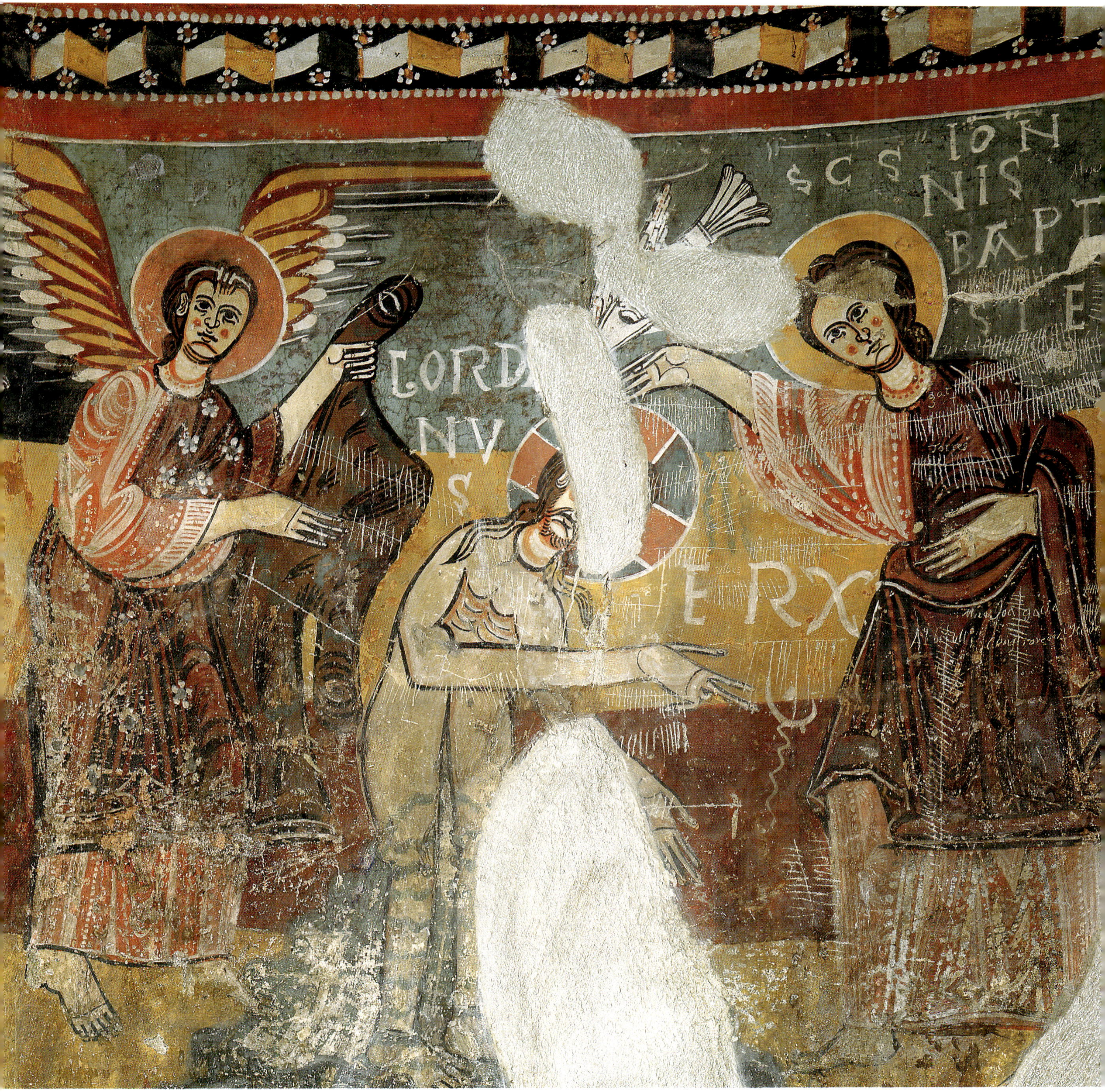
SCS ION
NIS
BAPT
CORD
NV
S
ERX

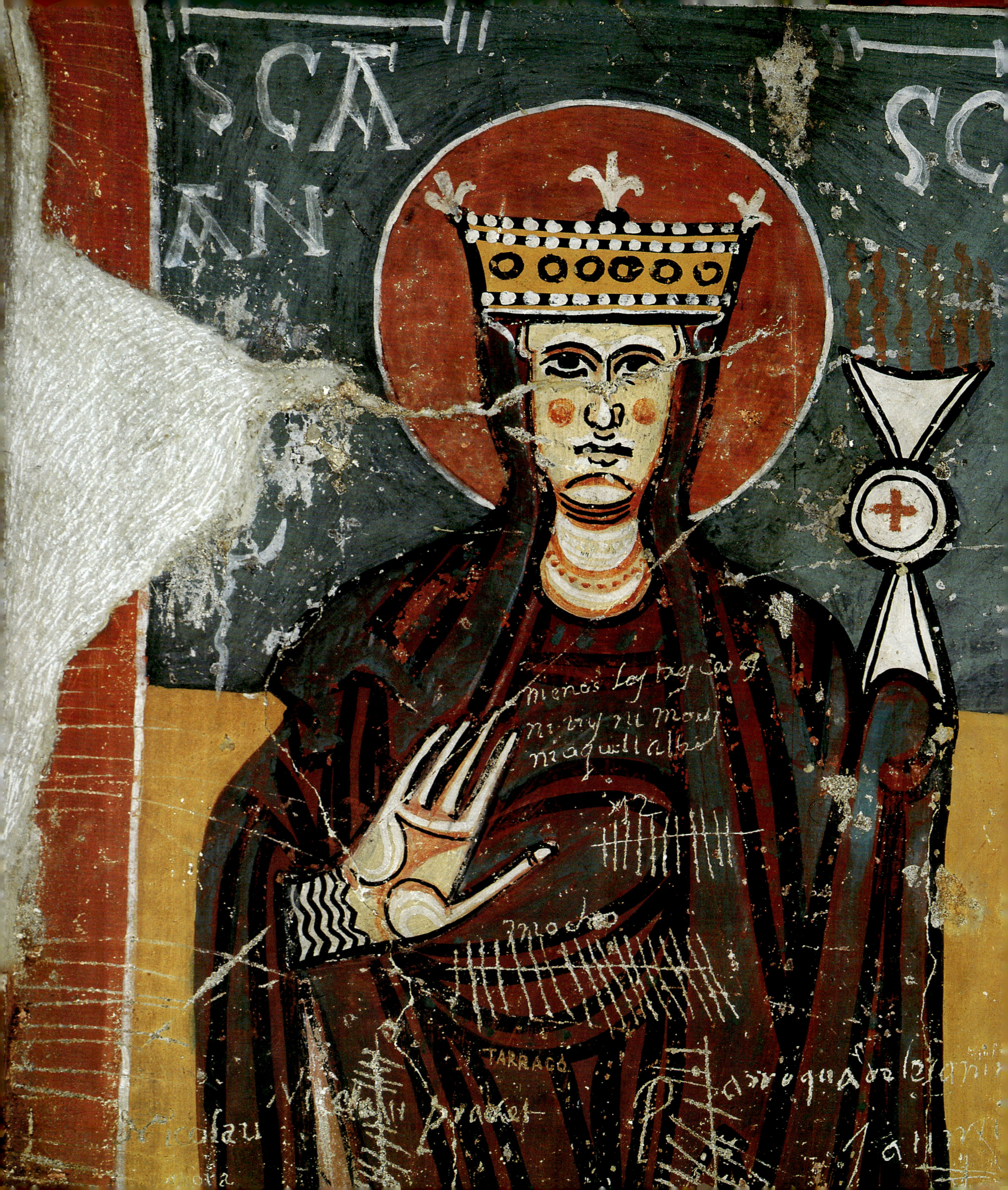
SCA
AN
SC
TARRAGO

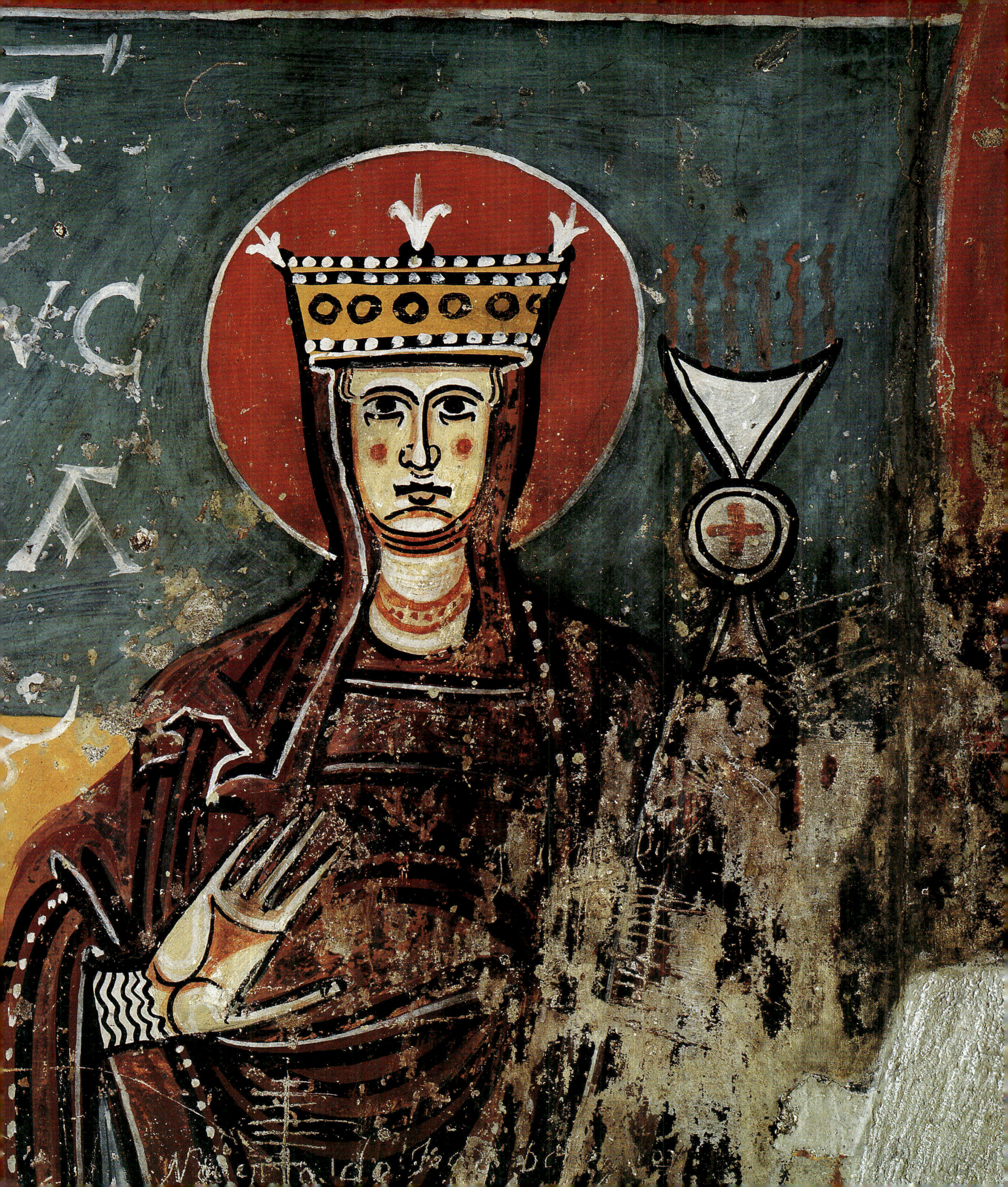

emergence at the end of the twelfth century of a great international style, known as 1200 Art, which took hold in the art then taking shape in the courts of Europe, from the Mediterranean to the Atlantic, and which is characterised by a powerful imprint from Komnenian Byzantine art, which brought a virtuous naturalism to the old Romanesque style. The causes of this renewal can be found in the assimilation of the 'art of the Crusaders', heightened in 1187 by the fall of Jerusalem to Saladin and the defeat of the Third Crusade, with the subsequent migration of models from East to West. In addition, the seizure of Constantinople in 1204 favoured the arrival in the West of a large number of relics, objects and even artists. The catalysts for this revolutionary artistic venture were the Latin Kingdom of Jerusalem (and its successor in Acre), Cyprus, Sicily, the Holy Roman Empire and the Anglo-Norman domains of Henry II and Leonora Plantagenet and their children, and it also had powerful repercussions in the kingdoms of the Iberian Peninsula. Leon and Galicia, under Ferdinand II (1157-1188) and Alfonso IX (1188-1230), Castile, under Alfonso VIII (1158-1214), and the Crown of Aragon, under Alfonso the Chaste (1164-1196) and Peter the Catholic (1196-1213), joined this new adventure and played an active part in it.

In the case of Aragon, the paintings in the chapter house of the monastery of Santa Maria in Sigena (Huesca) are considered one of the masterpieces of this European international style. Unfortunately, the monastery was burned down in 1936, at the beginning of the Spanish Civil War, causing irreparable damage. To be precise, the magnificent Mudejar coffered ceiling of the chapter house was burned and many of the murals decorating the building were lost, on top of which the colours of the surviving fragments were permanently altered. The paintings on the arches were removed that same year by a team of specialists from Barcelona who transferred them to cloth and restored them. Thanks to photographs taken before the fire, it was possible to complete those fragments that had been destroyed.

The pictorial programme combined scenes from the Old and New Testaments. Those from the New Testament covered the walls of the room in a series which, from north to south, summed up the story of the Salvation, from the Incarnation to the Anastasis. Meanwhile, the spandrels of the diaphragm arches are devoted to a cycle from the Old Testament, dominated by scenes from Genesis that cover two complete arches while the other three contain episodes referring to Noah, Abraham, Moses and David. These paintings, along with the plants and animals depicted in the centre of the arches, are the ones that most resemble the Anglo-Norman miniature. In fact, the style here has been directly associated with the workshop of the Master of the Morgan Leaf from the Winchester Bible (1160-1171). Recently, though, it has also been shown to be related to the 'Anglo-Catalan Psalter', made in Canterbury at the end of the twelfth century (Paris, BN, ms. Lat. 8846). This may have reached the Crown of Aragon in about 1200, thus influencing not only Sigena but also the course of the new style in this area.

To combine the two cycles of the Old and New Testaments, Christ's ancestors are depicted on the intrados of the arches, following the genealogies of Matthew and Luke. Originally there were up to seventy portraits, or fourteen per arch. Although a parallel has been drawn between these and the cycle of stained glass in Canterbury cathedral (1178-1207), certain features of these portraits, such as the fact that they are busts framed in a

54. ENGOLASTERS: APSE.
Mural paintings from the apse of Sant Miquel d'Engolasters (Andorra). In the vault, the Maiestas Domini; *below, two angels hold the symbols of evangelists Luke and Mark; at the top on the left the archangel Michael triumphs over the dragon, and on the right the eagle, symbol of the evangelist John.*
Last third of the 12th century
360 × 305 × 195 cm
MNAC/MAC 15972

55. SORPE: ANNUNCIATION.
The Annunciation, from the decoration of the Gospel wall of the church of Sant Pere de Sorpe.
Middle of the 12th century
670 × 664 × 896 cm
MNAC/MAC 113144

56. SORPE: CRUCIFIXION.
The Crucifixion with the Virgin, Longinus, Stephaton and the skull of Adam, from the decoration of the Gospel wall in the church of Sant Pere de Sorpe

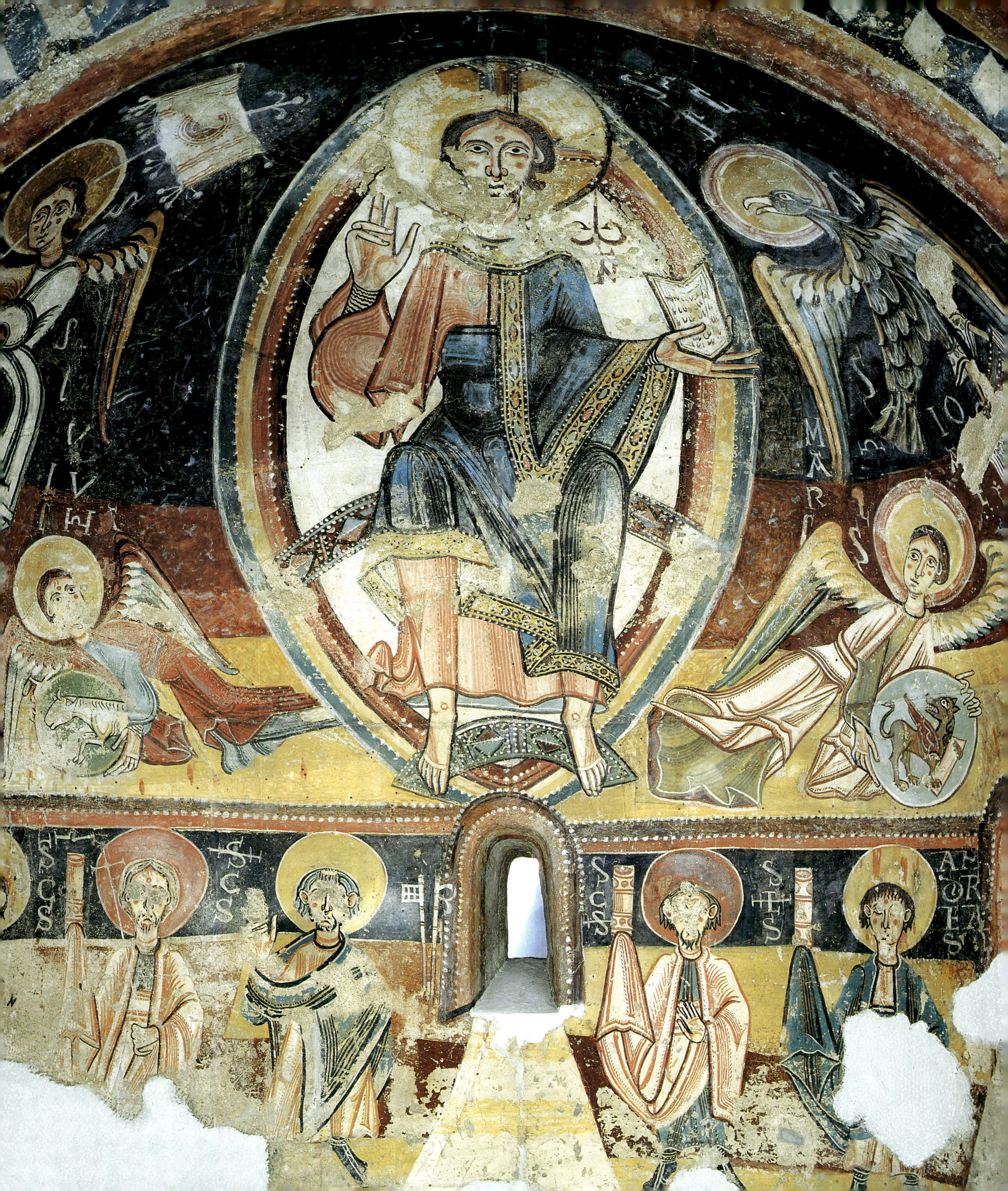

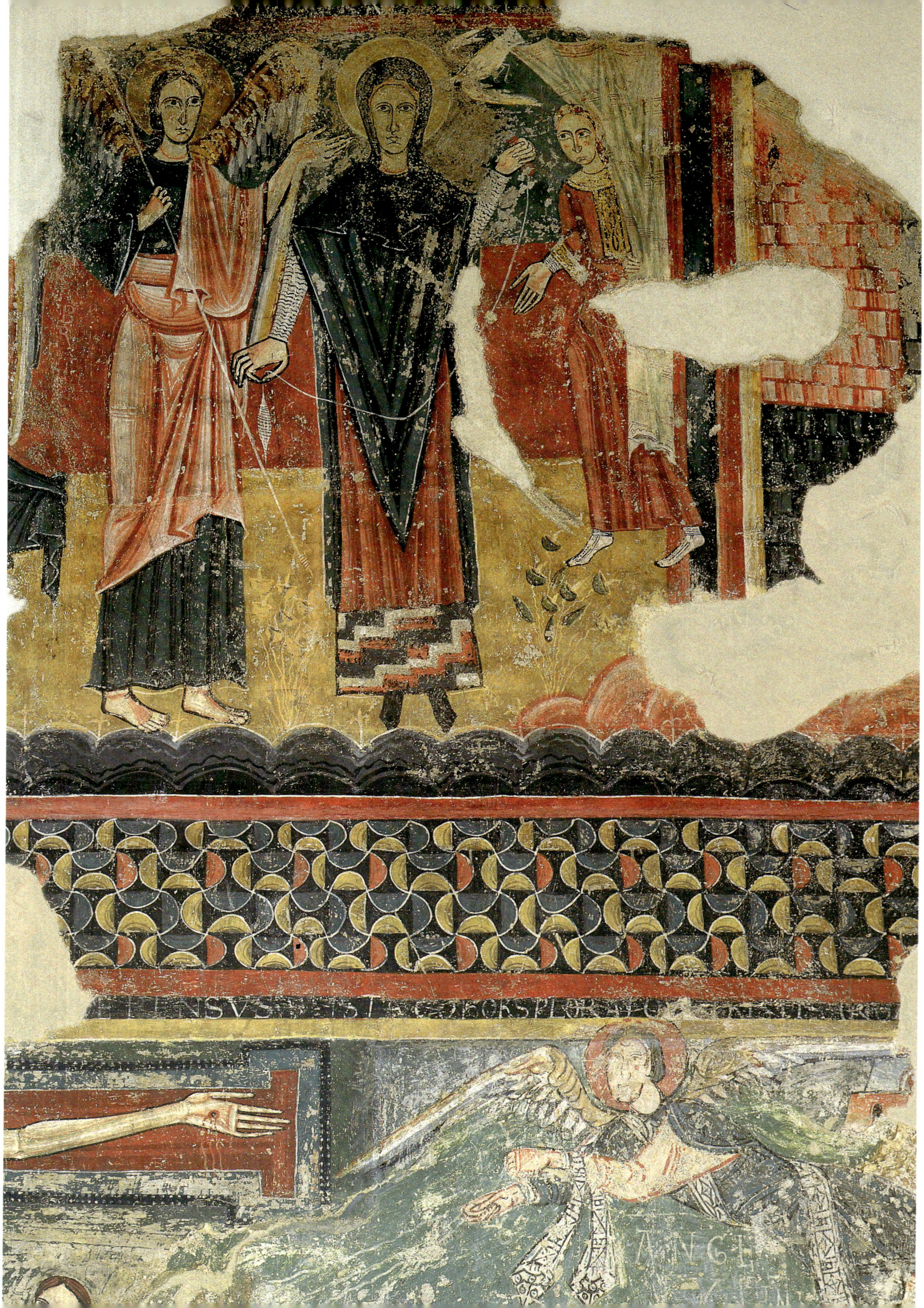

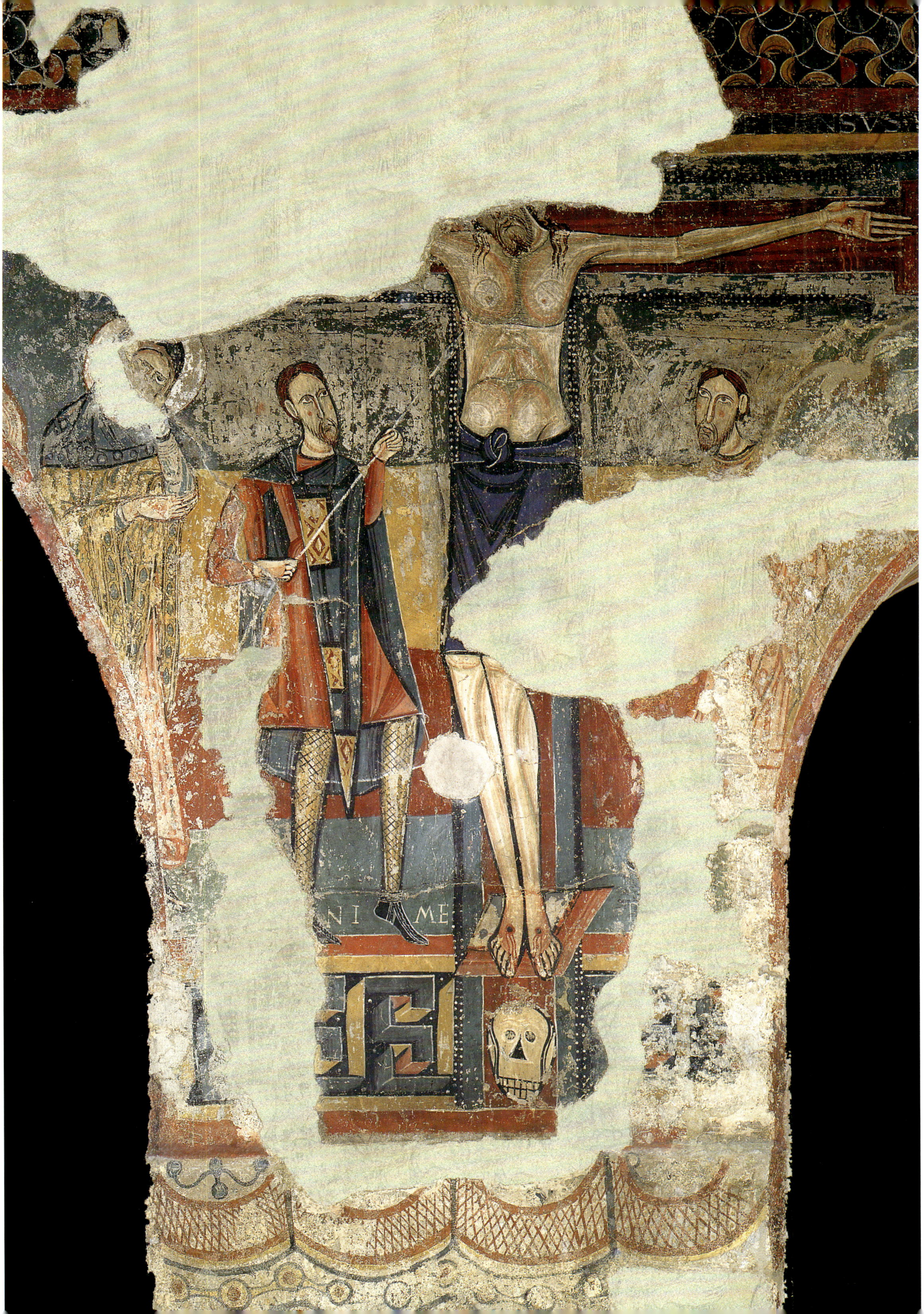

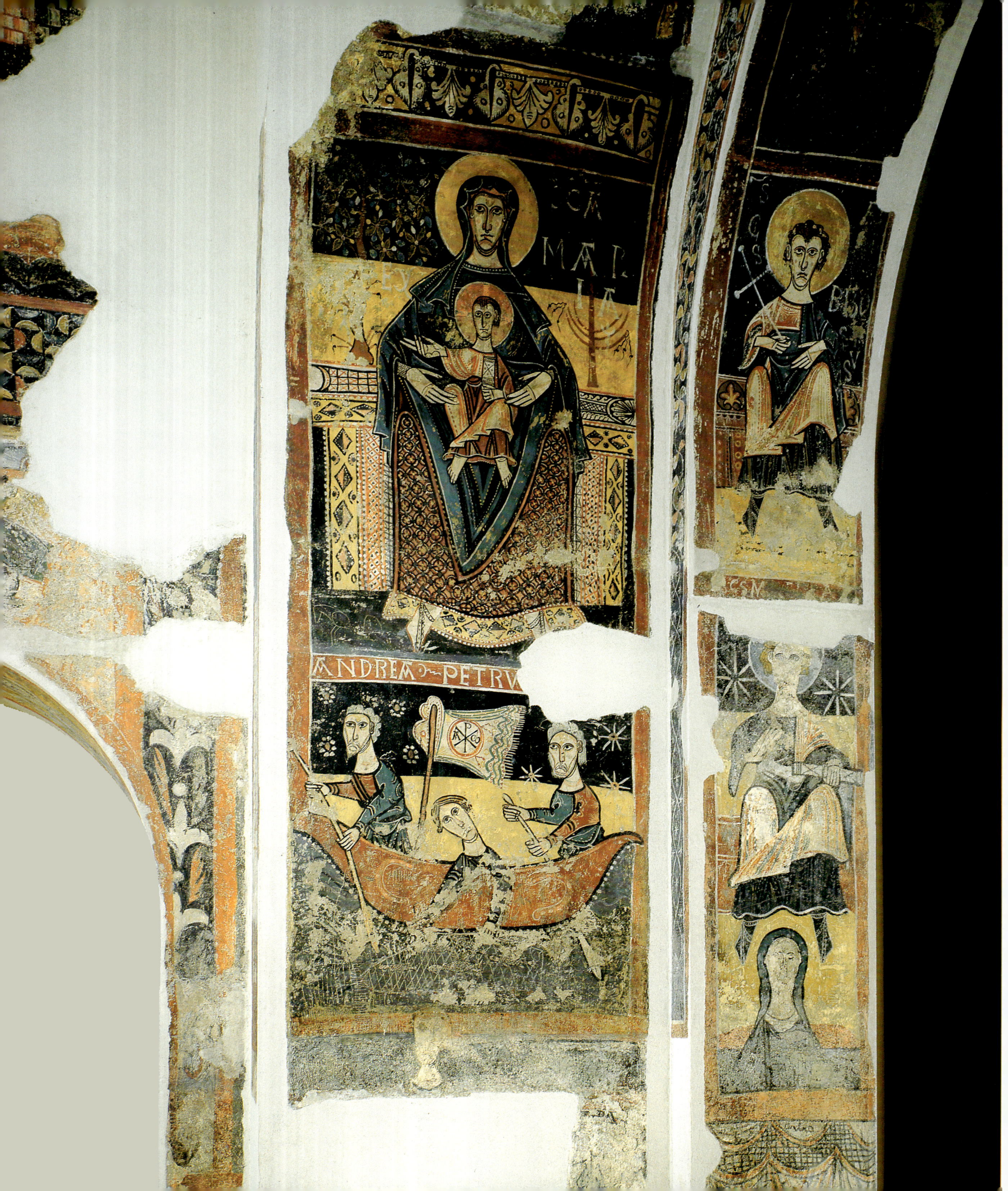
MAR IA
ANDREM PETRV

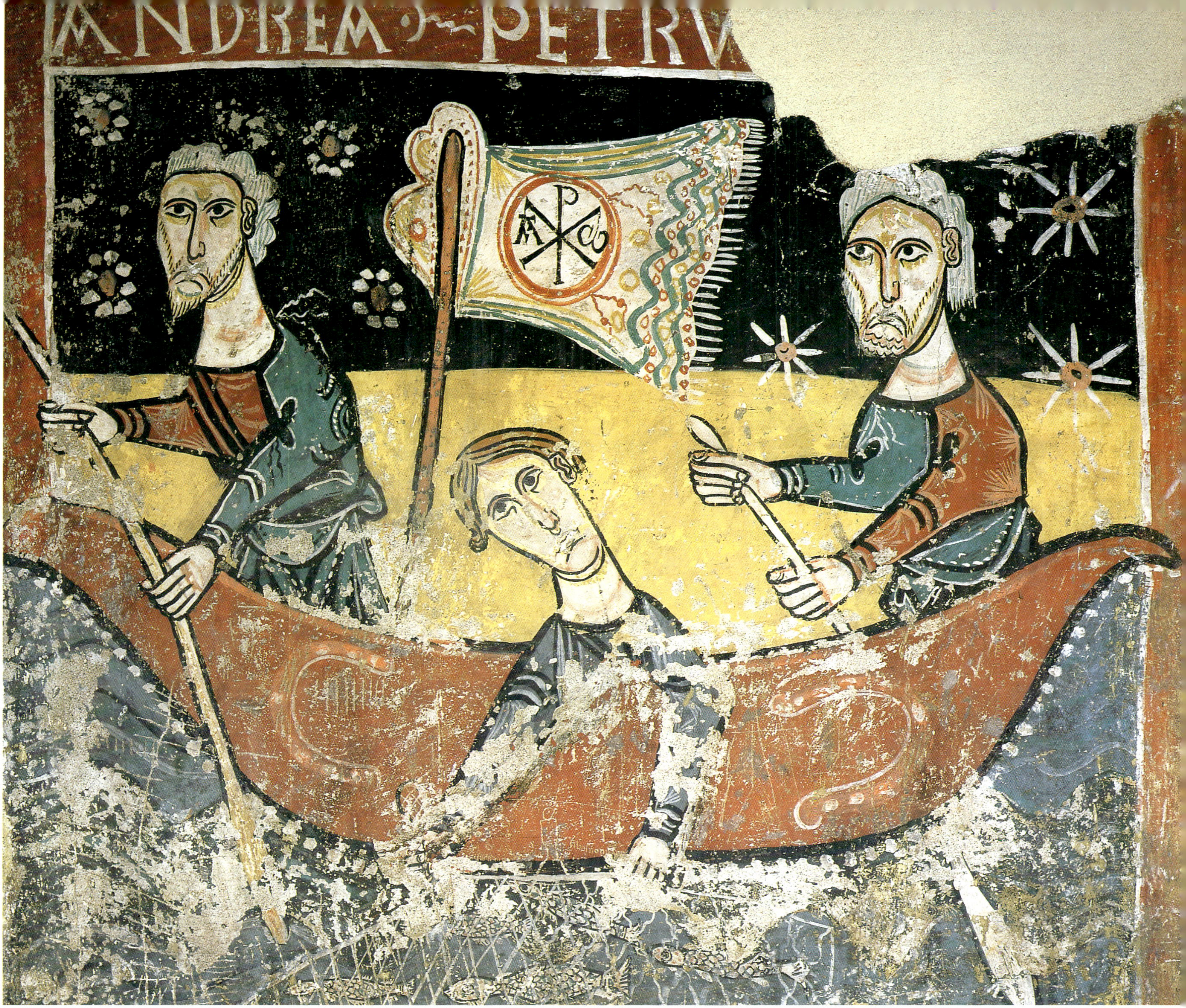

57-58. SORPE:
MAIESTAS MARIAE AND THE BOAT OF THE CHURCH.
Maiestas Mariae and the boat of the Church, from the decoration of the presbytery arches of the church of Sant Pere de Sorpe

rectangle and were originally embellished with metallic elements, lead me to think they are influenced by Komnenian Byzantine art, either via the Sicilian mosaics in the Palatine Chapel in Palermo or via the church of Santa Maria in Monreale, and either via miniatures or via icon painting. Unfortunately, the loss of colour makes it impossible to appreciate the original bright, iridescent tones that were characteristic of these works. Our only knowledge of them comes from the paintings on the arch leading to the cloister (which was shut off at the time of the fire) and from the watercolours painted *in situ* by Valentín Carderera (1866) and by the pupils of Lluís Domènech i Montaner (1918).

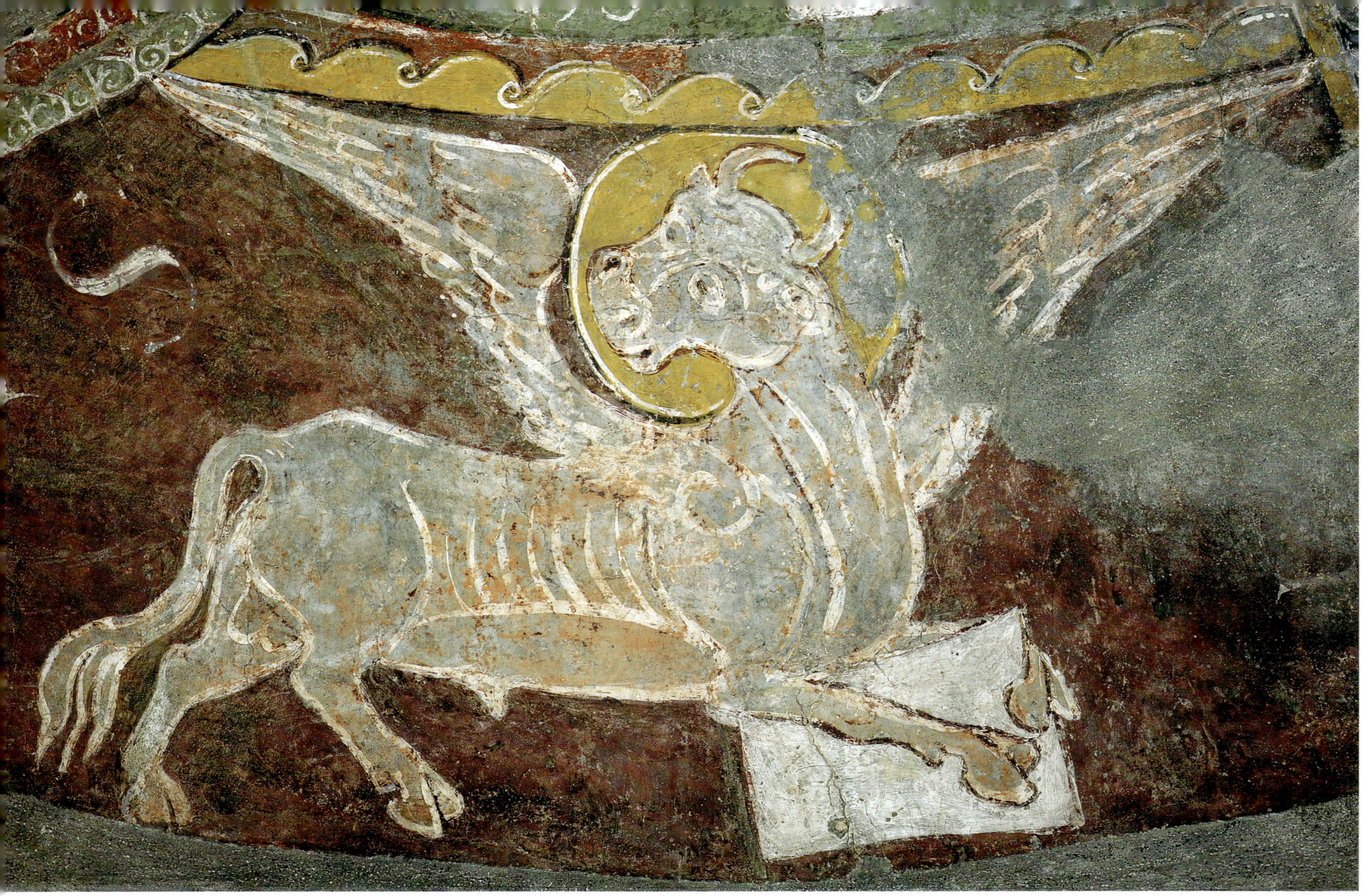

59

59. Sant Esteve de Andorra.
Detail of the symbol of the evangelist Luke on the north small apse of the church of Sant Esteve de Andorra la Vella.
1200-1210
MNAC/MAC 35711

The obvious palatine nature of the building is undoubtedly due to royal patronage by Queen Sancha, founder in 1188 of this female monastery for nuns of the Hospitaller Order of Saint John of Jerusalem. Following the death of her husband, Alfonso the Chaste, in 1196, she withdrew here until her death in 1208, which is precisely the date the church was dedicated. It therefore seems probable that the paintings in the chapter house were done during the period the queen stayed there, when the monastery was still a royal pantheon and a place of withdrawal for princesses.

The paintings from the Torre del Tesoro at the Benedictine monastery of San Pedro de Arlanza (Burgos), whose remains are scattered between the MNAC, The Cloisters (New York) and the Fogg Art Museum in Harvard (Cambridge, Massachusetts), are also steeped in that same palatial air. These fragments once decorated a palatine room with windows located in the chapter house and decorated with animals, mostly mythical creatures, fabulous beats like the griffin, the undisputed guardian of treasures. This repertory, probably inspired in Anglo-Norman Bestiaries of the same time, had a heraldic air in Arlanza which could be seen in the representation of the lion or in the inclusion of castles, the symbol *par excellence* of the Crown of Castile. In fact, the iconographic programme in the chapter house is probably connected with the veneration in Arlanza of the mythical founder of the Castilian dynasty, Count Fernán González. From the style of the paintings, they can be dated to the first decades of the thirteenth century, as they show nu-

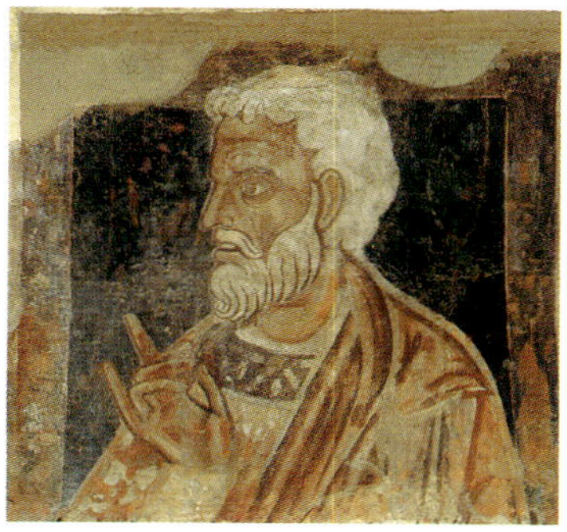

60

60. SIGENA: DETAIL.
AN ANCESTOR OF CHRIST (RESÀ),
from the mural decoration on the intradoses of the arches in the chapter house of the nunnery of Santa María de Sigena (Huesca) 1196-1208

61. SANTA CATERINA DE LA SEU D'URGELL.
The dispute and arrest of Saint Catherine from the decoration in the central register of the old Saint Catherine's Chapel in the cathedral of La Seu d'Urgell. Middle of the 13th century 165 × 180 cm MNAC/MAC 214241

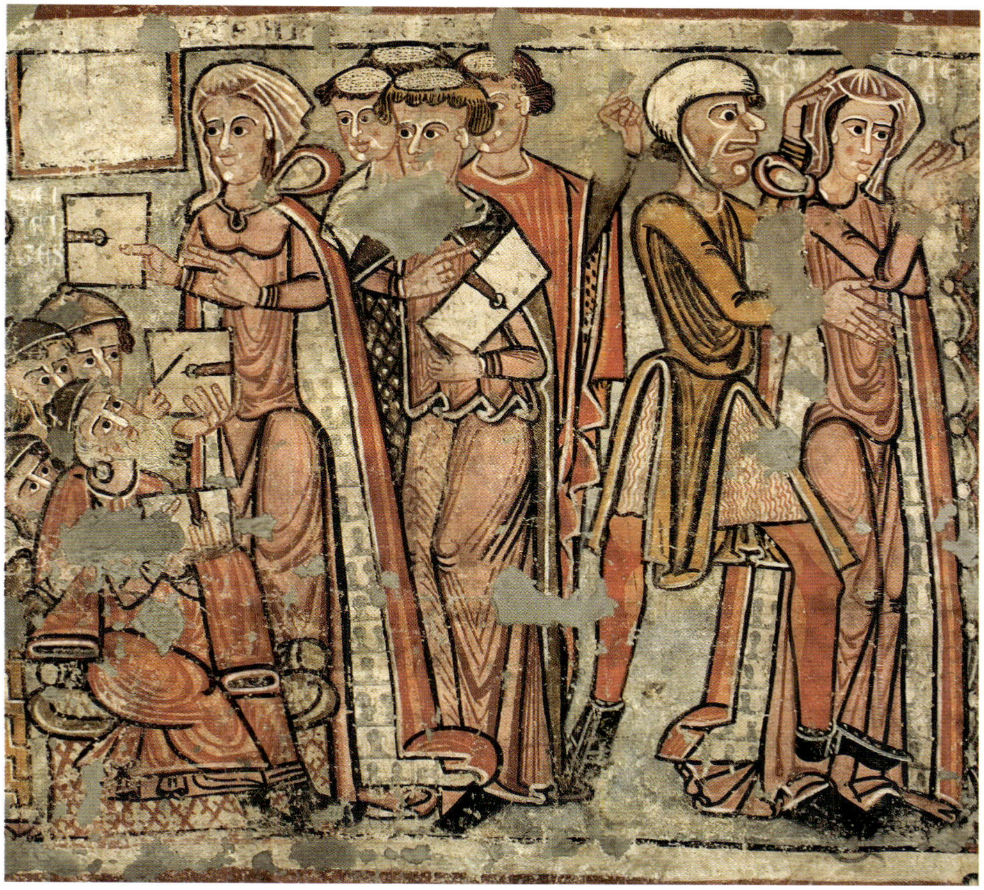

61

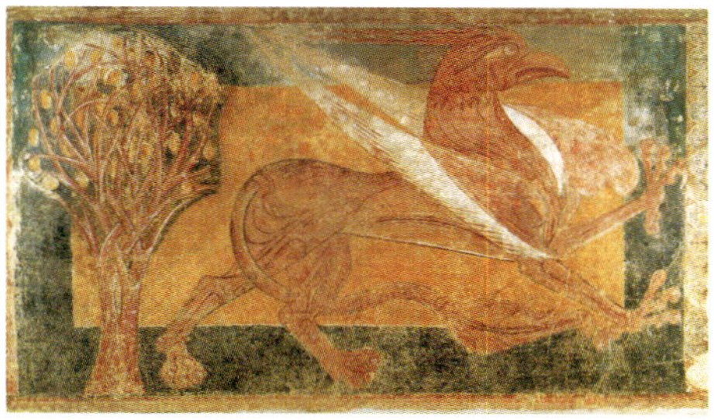

62

62. SAN PEDRO DE ARLANZA:
GRIFFIN AND THE TREE OF LIFE.
The griffin and the tree of life that decorated the walls of the first floor of the Tower of the Treasure of the monastery of San Pedro de Arlanza (Burgos). Around 1210 MNAC/MAC 40142

merous similarities with the miniature of Alfonso IX in Tumbo A of Santiago Cathedral, painted between 1211 and 1216.

In Catalonia the 1200 style also played an important role, which in the case of mural painting seems to have been concentrated once again in the diocese of La Seu d'Urgell. The church of Sant Esteve d'Andorra, which in those days belonged to this diocese, was decorated with an extensive Christological cycle characterised by the presence of complex background architecture and a figurative composition marked by steely clothing, an articulate gestural language and a tendency to expressionism and caricature in the faces. The work therefore resorts to formulas characteristic of the Byzantine miniature previously interpreted in the West, showing great similarities with the style of the School of Salzburg. It is tentatively dated to the first years of the thirteenth century, as its painted panel version would be in the 'Master of Lluçà', active in the first third of the thirteenth century. This painter is also characterised by figures with large heads presented in three-quarter view with faces picked out with flesh tones and with characteristic flat clothing, almost like a negative, as though incised (*muldenfandenstil*). An example of the merger between these two late Romanesque trends in 1200 art can be seen in a recent acquisition by the MNAC, the paintings from the former chapel of Santa Caterina in La Seu d'Urgell, possibly done between 1230 and 1257 under Bishop Ponç de Vilamur. In them the saint disputes with the pagan philosophers, showing great dialectical skills, and finally convinces them. A perfect image to announce the arrival of the grand age of the universities and Gothic.

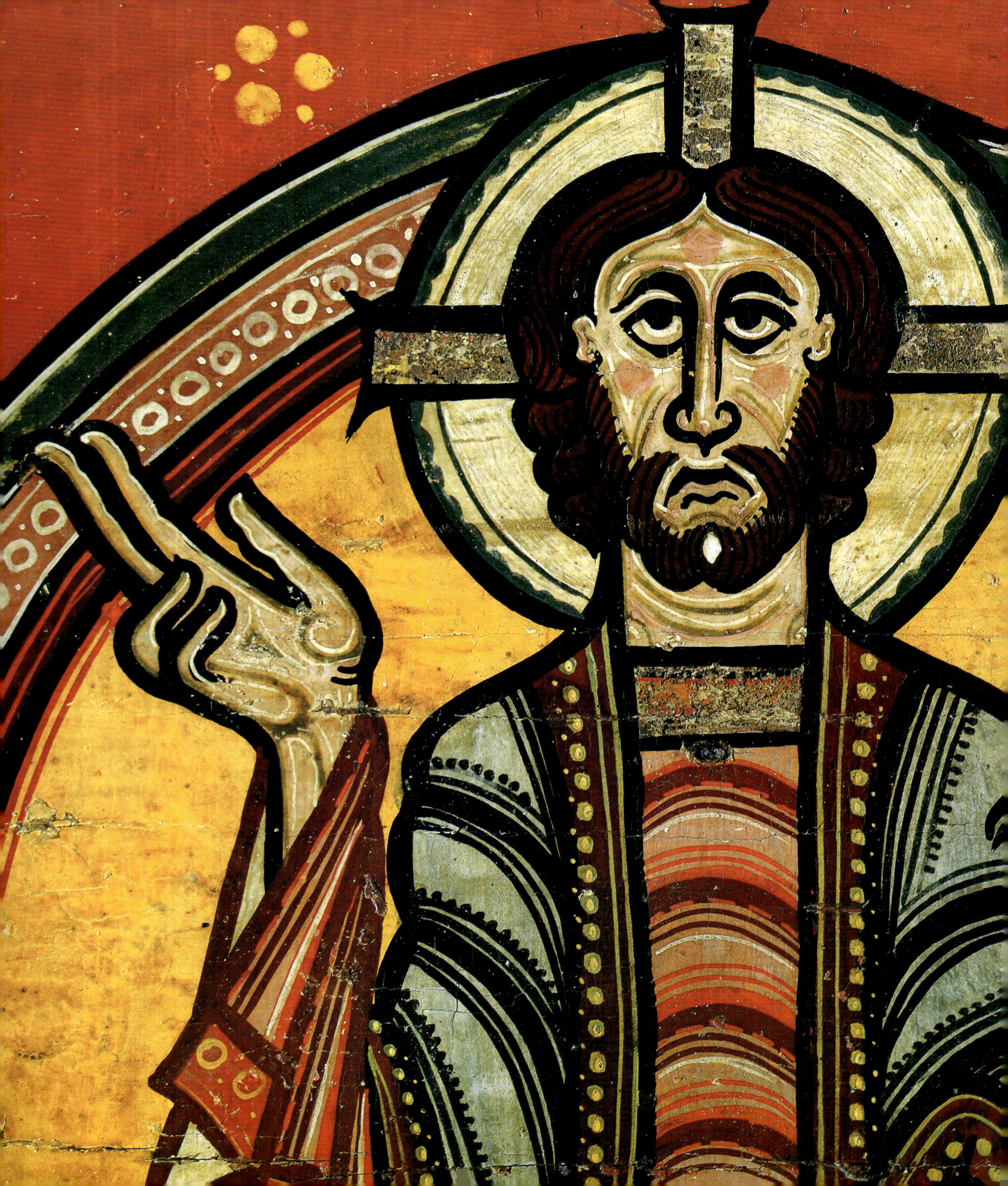

Panel Painting

Manuel Castiñeiras

63-64. Altar Frontal of La Seu d'Urgell or of the Apostles.
Altar frontal from La Seu d'Urgell.
In the centre: Maiestas Domini; *in the side compartments, the apostles in two groups of six. Second quarter of the 12th century*
Tempera on wood. 102 × 151 cm
MNAC/MAC 15803

Discovery and valuation: from the retrospective exhibitions to the Museum

The Romanesque section of the Museu Nacional d'Art de Catalunya contains the largest and oldest collection in Europe of altar frontals, canopies and painted beams. Of all these items, the most representative group is undoubtedly that of the altar frontals or altar panels, painted during the twelfth and thirteenth centuries, most of which come from what is known as *Catalunya Vella* (Old Catalonia). The number of works (twenty-nine), the format and the range of techniques and iconography make this not just the most comprehensive collection in Catalonia, which has other outstanding collections in the Museu Episcopal de Vic and the Museu de Lleida Diocesà i Comarcal, for example, but also in Europe. In fact, though it's true that Norway has a rich heritage consisting of thirty-one painted altar frontals divided between museums in Oslo (Universitetes Oldsaksamling) and Bergen (Bergen Museum), these are from later dates, between 1250 and 1350, and are therefore classed as 'Gothic'. Besides Switzerland (painted ceiling of zillis), only central Italy has an important collection of

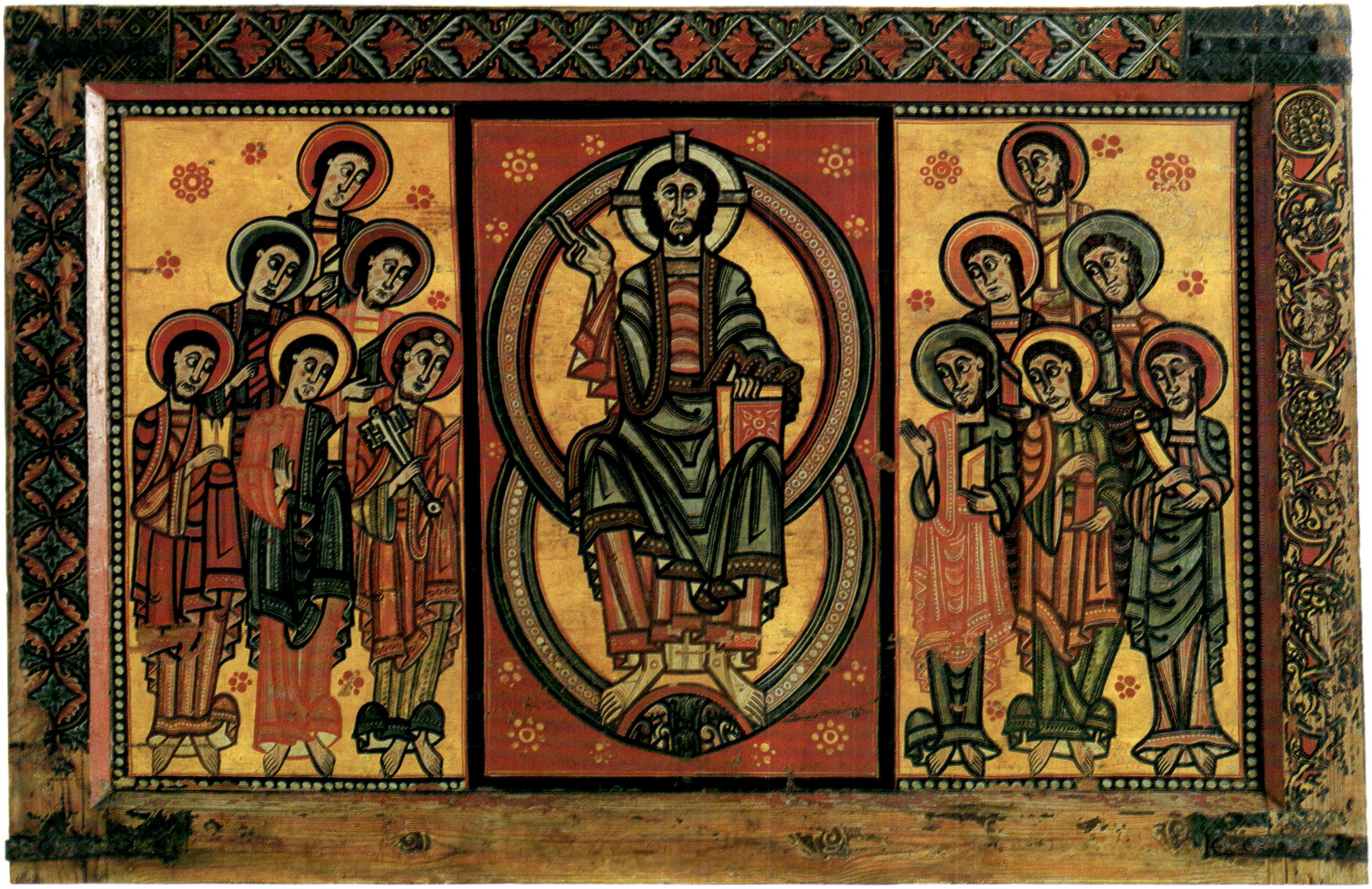

63 64

panel paintings done in the twelfth century, though the main formats here are different: the gigantic painted crosses from Tuscany that used to be placed over the *tramezzo* or entrance to the presbytery area, and the panels, diptychs or tabernacles in Rome and Lazio, which originally stood on the altars or hung on columns or on the iconostasis. In fact, in Italy, to find the painted wood altar frontals that are so widespread in Catalonia from the first half of the twelfth century, we have to turn to once again to later work such as the Berardenga antependium, painted in 1215 and kept at the Pinacoteca Nazionale in Siena.

Altar frontals were the objects that drew most attention in the formative period of the Romanesque art collections of the museums in Vic and Barcelona at the end of the nineteenth century. In 1868 the *Circol Literari de Vic* organised the *Exposición Arqueológica-Artística*, at which the altar frontal from Santa Margarida de Vilaseca was exhibited for the very first time. This was followed up by the work of Josep Morgades, Bishop of Vic, the driving force behind the restoration of the Romanesque monastery of Santa Maria de Ripoll (Girona) between 1886 and 1893. Morgades gathered a representative group of *antependia* from the parishes in his diocese, which went to form the main body of the Romanesque collection at the future Museu Episcopal de Vic (1891). Alongside this, during the 1880s two exhibitions were held in Barcelona in which Romanesque altar frontals played an important part. The first, in 1882, *Álbum de detalles artísticos y plástico-decorativos de la Edad Media*, organised by the Sociedad Artístico-Arqueológico Barcelonesa, had reproductions of three altar frontals (Espinelves, Santa Margarida de Vila-seca and Coll), complete with commentaries, which subsequently entered the collection at the Museu Episcopal de Vic (MEV, n. 7, 5, 3). It also presented the *Esquius Altar Frontal*, which at that time belonged to Mr Barnola and in 1958 was acquired by the Museo de Arte de Cataluña (MNAC/MAC 65502) as part of the Santiago Espona bequest. At the second event, the Universal Exhibition of 1888, the researcher Josep Puiggarí produced the first *catalogue raisonné* of these items, in which he included minute iconographic descriptions along with interesting chronological details. This was just before these works began to enter Catalan museums on a large scale. By 1891, most of the panels included in the catalogue formed part of the recently inaugurated Museu Episcopal de Vic. That same year, the Museu Municipal de Belles Arts was set up in the Palau de Belles Arts, the arts pavilion built for the Universal Exhibition. The new museum exhibited the *Ix Altar Frontal*, a work purchased in 1889, which, especially during the first years of the twentieth century, was followed by a large number of panel paintings, like the altar frontals from Avià (1903), Urgell (1905), Mosoll (1906), Alós d'Isil (1907), Esterri de Cardós, Baltarga and Farrera (1911), the *Tavèrnoles Canopy* (1906) and the *Beam of the Passion* (1907).

The exceptional nature of the collection soon aroused the interest of scholars and researchers in Catalonia and abroad, who tended to give very early dates in the eleventh century to what they considered to be the first examples (Puigbó, Ix, Urgell and Dosmunts). Alongside the pioneering work of J. Puiggarí and the catalogues of the Museu Episcopal de Vic (1893) and the Museu de Belles Arts de Barcelona (1906), we have the studies by Josep Gudiol (1904), Antonio Muñoz (1907), Salvador

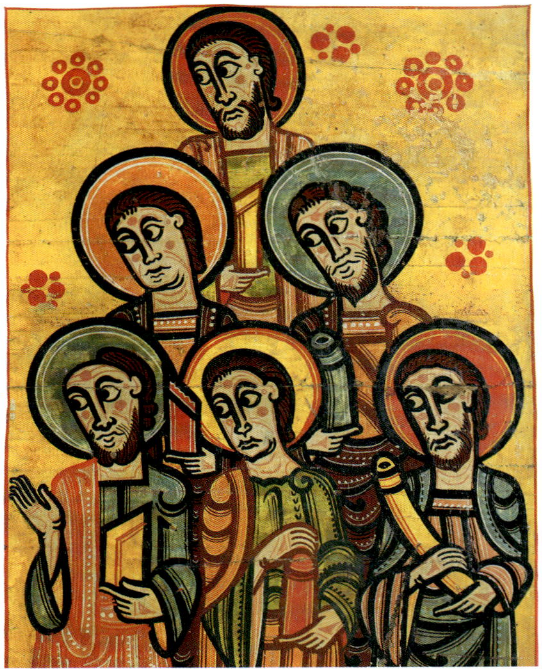

65

65. Details of the Altar Frontal of La Seu d'Urgell or of the Apostles. *Detail of the face, of the cruciferous halo with traces of golden glaze and of the hand of the* Maiestas Domini *from the Altar Frontal of La Seu d'Urgell or of the Apostles.*

Sanpere y Miquel (1908) and, in particular, the *catalogue raisonné* of Romanesque and Gothic art of the old Museu de Belles Arts de Barcelona by Raimon Casellas (c. 1910), which was never published. However, attention soon began to shift away from Romanesque altar frontals in response to renewed interest in architecture and the recently discovered mural painting. The ambitious publications of the recently set up Institut d'Estudis Catalans (1907), *Arquitectura romànica a Catalunya* (1907-1918), by Josep Puig i Cadafalch, and *Pintures murals catalanes* (1907-1921) by Josep Pijoan, are an example of the direction in which historical and artistic research was now focussing its attention. What's more, as we saw in the previous chapter, the removal of the apse paintings between 1919 and 1923 and their transportation to Barcelona for installation in the Parc de la Ciutadella (since 1915 the site of the old Museo de Bellas Artes, which was now called the Museu d'Art i Arqueologia) undoubtedly represented the culmination of this new monumental view of Romanesque. From that moment, the mural painting technique was to attract the attention of researchers like no other, as a result of which Sant Climent de Taüll was to become the undisputed masterpiece of Catalan medieval art.

In all fairness though, the interest in panel painting didn't disappear entirely during the twenties, as that was when the altar frontals of Sant Romà de Vila (1922) and of Durro (1923) entered the Museum. Even so, so far as the historiography is concerned, there was a certain paralysis as regards the earliest studies. Publications by the Director of the Museu d'Art i Arqueologia, Joaquim Folch i Torres (1924, 1956), and by the curator in Vic, Josep Gudiol i Cunill (1927), which belonged to the historiographic moment when a chronology was established for the great artistic landmarks of twelfth-century Catalan Romanesque (the paintings from Taüll, the Ripoll portal or the storied cloisters, for example), nevertheless still defended an early date for some examples of panel painting (in particular the altar frontals from Puigbó, Ix, Urgell and Dosmunts). These they placed in the second half of the eleventh century, along the lines laid down by J. Puiggarí and S. Sanpere y Miquel and partly confirmed by R. Casellas. We shouldn't therefore be surprised at their insistence on connecting this artistic technique with eleventh-century metalwork or the small number of comparisons they drew with the main sequence of Romanesque mural painting or of monumental sculpture.

The revolution in research into Catalan panel painting came from the American historian W.W.S. Cook, who between 1923 and 1929, in a series of articles published in the magazine *The Art Bulletin*, returned the dates of the oldest examples to the twelfth century. In his opinion, the *Puigbó Altar Frontal* and the *Ribes Canopy* had been done in the second quarter of this century; the altar frontals of La Seu d'Urgell and of Ix, in the middle of the century, and the altar frontals from Esquius and Dosmunts during the second half. This new chronological table, based largely on a comparison with the monumental art of the time, in which the work of renovation on the abbey of Ripoll played an important part, provided the ideal point of reference for a better understanding of the circumstances in which Catalan panel painting had originated.

66

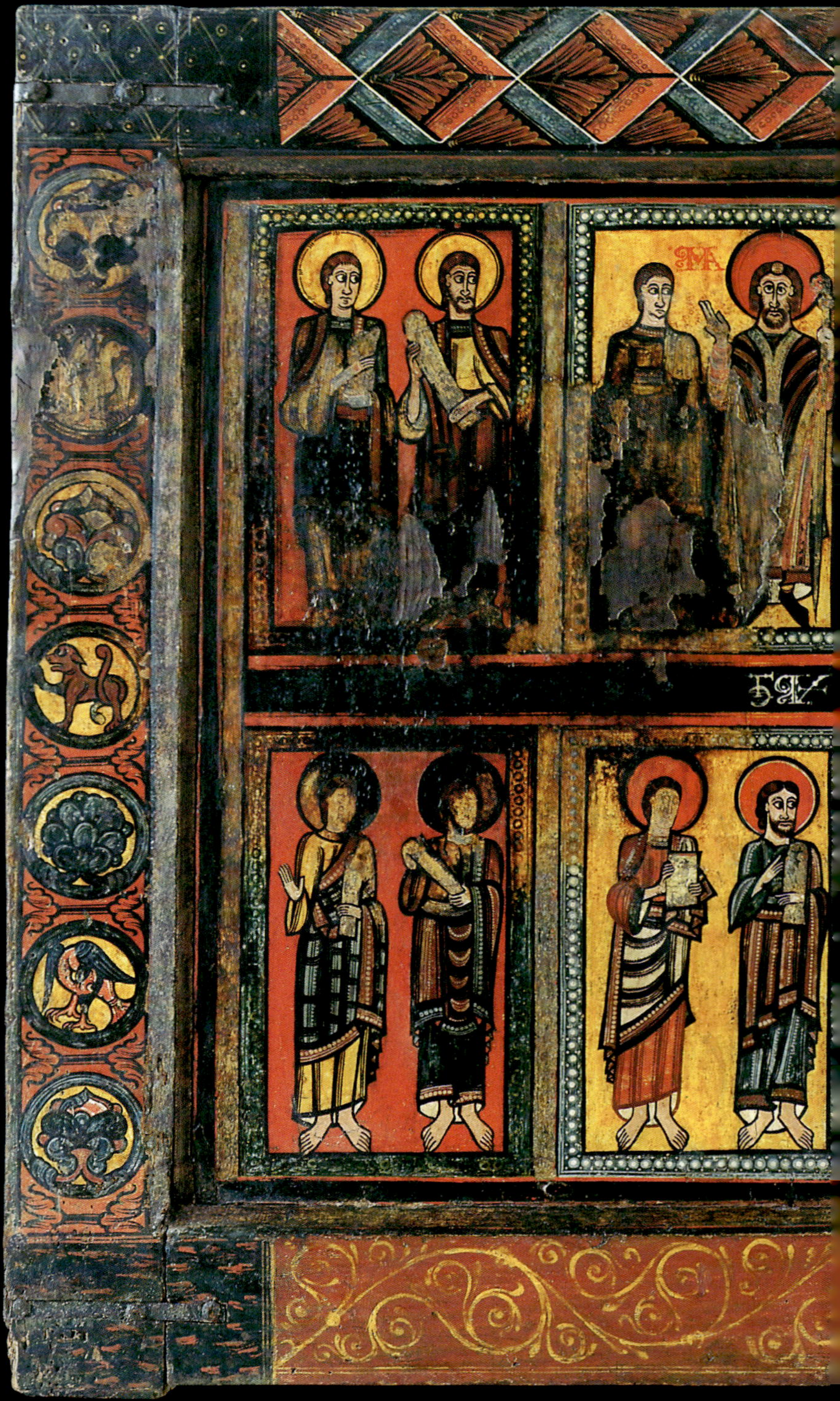

66. ALTAR FRONTAL FROM IX.
Altar frontal called "from Ix".
In the centre, the Maiestas Domini.
In the top left-hand compartment,
two apostles, in a first box, and Saint Martin
as a bishop accompanied by the cathecumen
resurrected, in the second. In the top right-hand
compartment, Saint Peter and another apostle
in a first box, and Saint Martin cutting
his cape in two to give it to a poor man, in
the second. In the bottom left- and right-hand
compartments, four pairs of apostles
in the corresponding boxes.
Second quarter of the 12th century.
Tempera on wood
From the church of Sant Martí d'Ix
92 × 157 cm
MNAC/MAC 15803

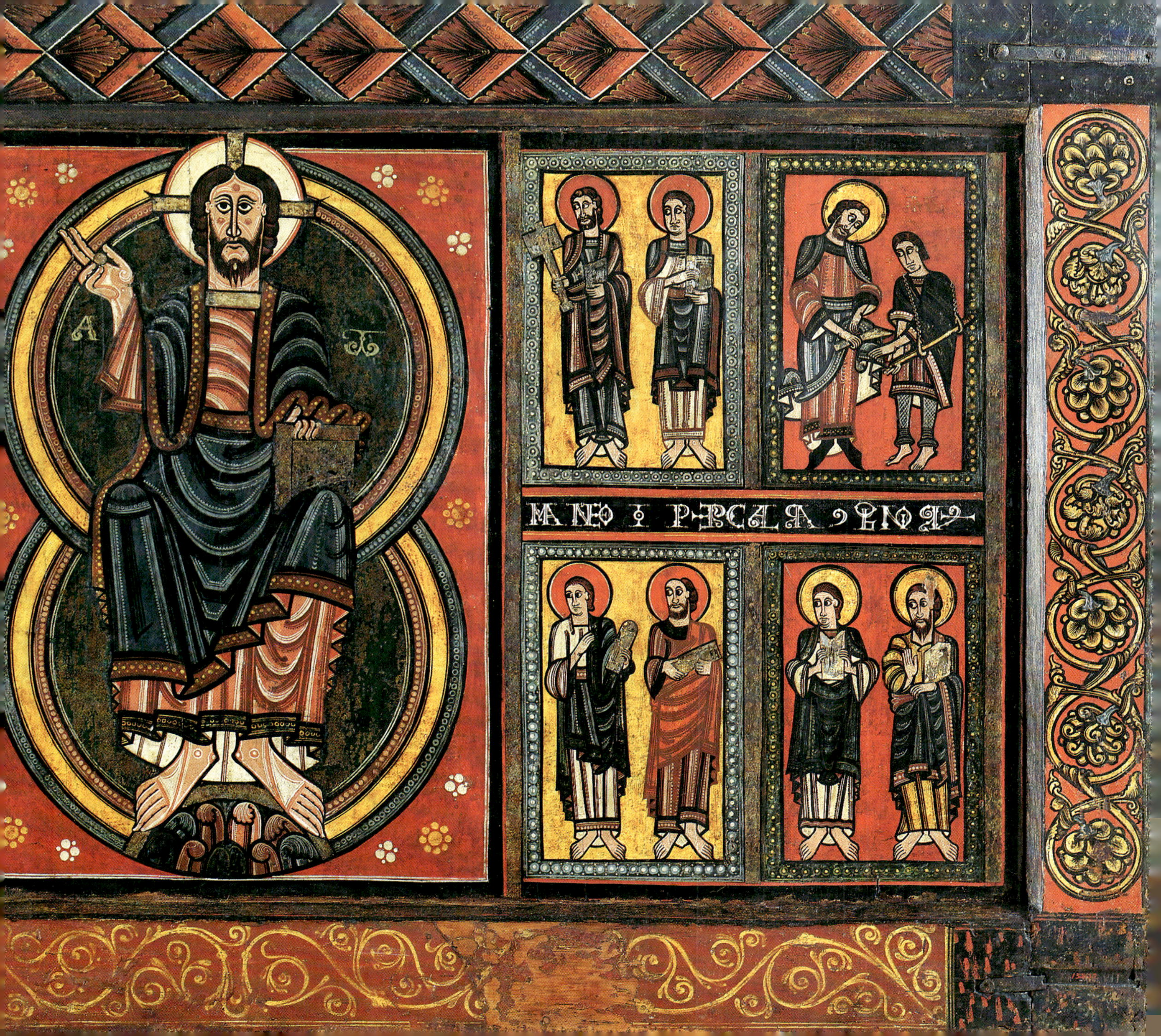

It has traditionally been considered that the origin of the first *antependia* painted in Catalonia lay in the imitation of eleventh-century metalwork altar frontals. According to this hypothesis, making these furnishings from wood was intended as a way of providing rural churches with a 'cheap' version of the precious metalwork which documents tell us decorated the great Catalan abbeys and cathedrals of the eleventh century. In fact, there are accounts of altars with silver canopies and with frontals composed of sumptuous gold-plated and silver-plated elements decorated with enamel figures making up complete narrative cycles. Unfortunately, not a trace has reached us from this period and the only way it can be reconstructed is through descriptions in altar inventories or consecration records and the possible comparisons that can be drawn with similar early medieval works in Italy or France.

Three panels and a metalwork altar canopy are described on the high altar of the monastery church of Santa Maria de Ripoll in the treasury inventory of 1047, drawn up following the death of Abbot Oliba. These ornaments were probably commissioned by Oliba for the consecration of the church in 1032. The principle panel or altar frontal was covered in gold and had precious stones and sixteen enamels, and there were also two smaller panels covered in silver that were probably used to decorate the sides of the high altar. All of this was framed by a spectacular altar canopy, with columns and top covered in silver. But perhaps the case that best illustrates the wealth of metalwork altars in Catalonia is the high altar of Girona cathedral, a church dedicated by Bishop Pere in 1038 at an event attended by Oliba, Bishop of Vic and Abbot of Ripoll. According to the consecration records, the Countess Ermessenda (*c.* 975-1058), sister of the Girona prelate and widow of Ramón Borrell II, Count of Barcelona, donated an enormous quantity of gold (300 *uncias*) for the construction of a gold panel. From the description made by J. Villanueva at the beginning of the nineteenth century, we know that this gold panel was presided by a central oval with the Virgin Mary, surrounded by the four Evangelists, in enamel and *tituli*, as well as thirty-two compartments in *cloisonné* enamel with the life of Christ. The panel, richly adorned with encrusted stones, was divided into bands and at the foot of the oval and the central mandorla of the Virgin had the names of its patrons: *'Ermensindis'* and *'Gisla cometissa fieri jussit'*. While the first was simply carved on a stone, the second surrounded the enamel with the seated portrait of the Countess Guisla de Lluçà (d. 1079), second wife of Berenguer Ramon I (d. 1035), son of Ermessenda. Guisla probably carried out his wish of offering a gold altar frontal to Girona cathedral, together with her mother-in-law, between 1038, the date it was consecrated, and 1041, the year Ramon Berenguer I came of age. This work, which was progressively enriched during the twelfth and fourteenth centuries with more encrusted stones and three more silver panels with figures to enclose the remaining sides of the high altar, survived until 1809.

The absence of material remains of these altars doesn't allow any further details. Nevertheless, the great importance given them by Catalan artistic historiography as the origin and forerunners of the twelfth-century painted altar frontals is in my opinion exaggerated. In fact, the Catalan panel painting of the first half of the twelfth century

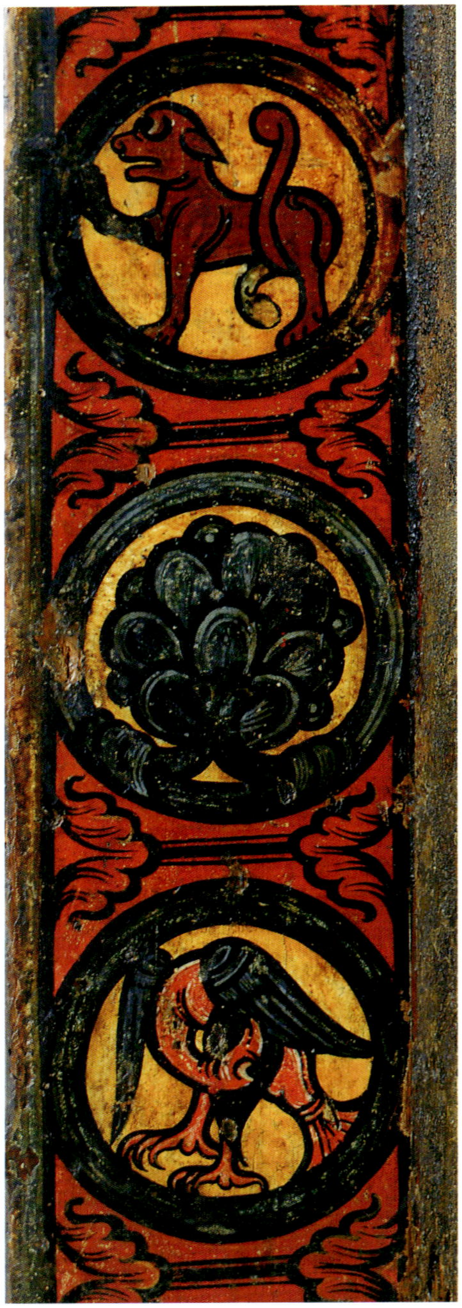

67

67. LEFT-HAND SIDE BORDER OF THE ALTAR FRONTAL FROM IX.
Left-hand side border with animalistic and floral decoration of the altar frontal from Ix.

68. COMPARTMENT OF THE ALTAR FRONTAL FROM IX.
Saint Martin cutting his cape in two to give it to a poor man, a scene on the altar frontal from Ix.

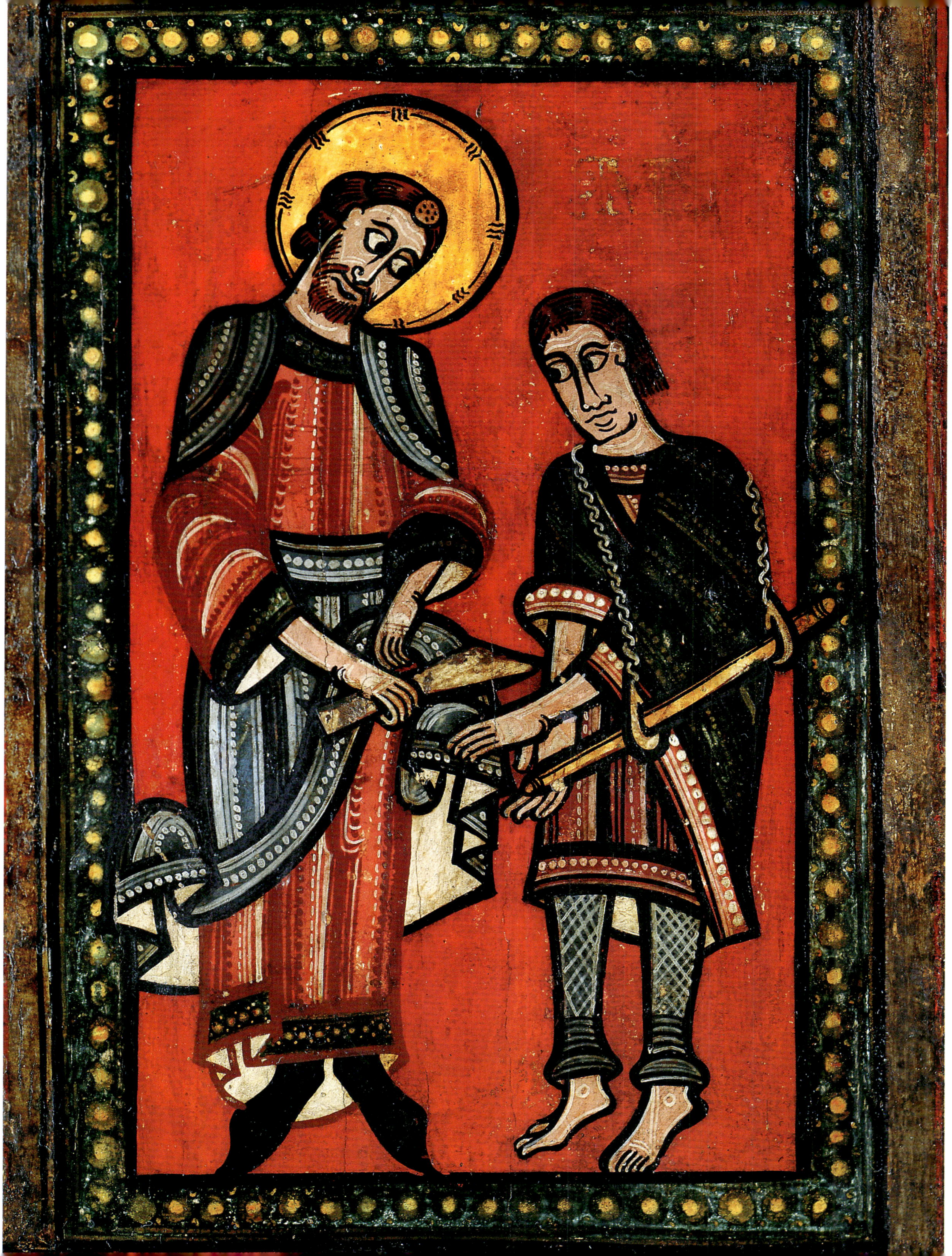

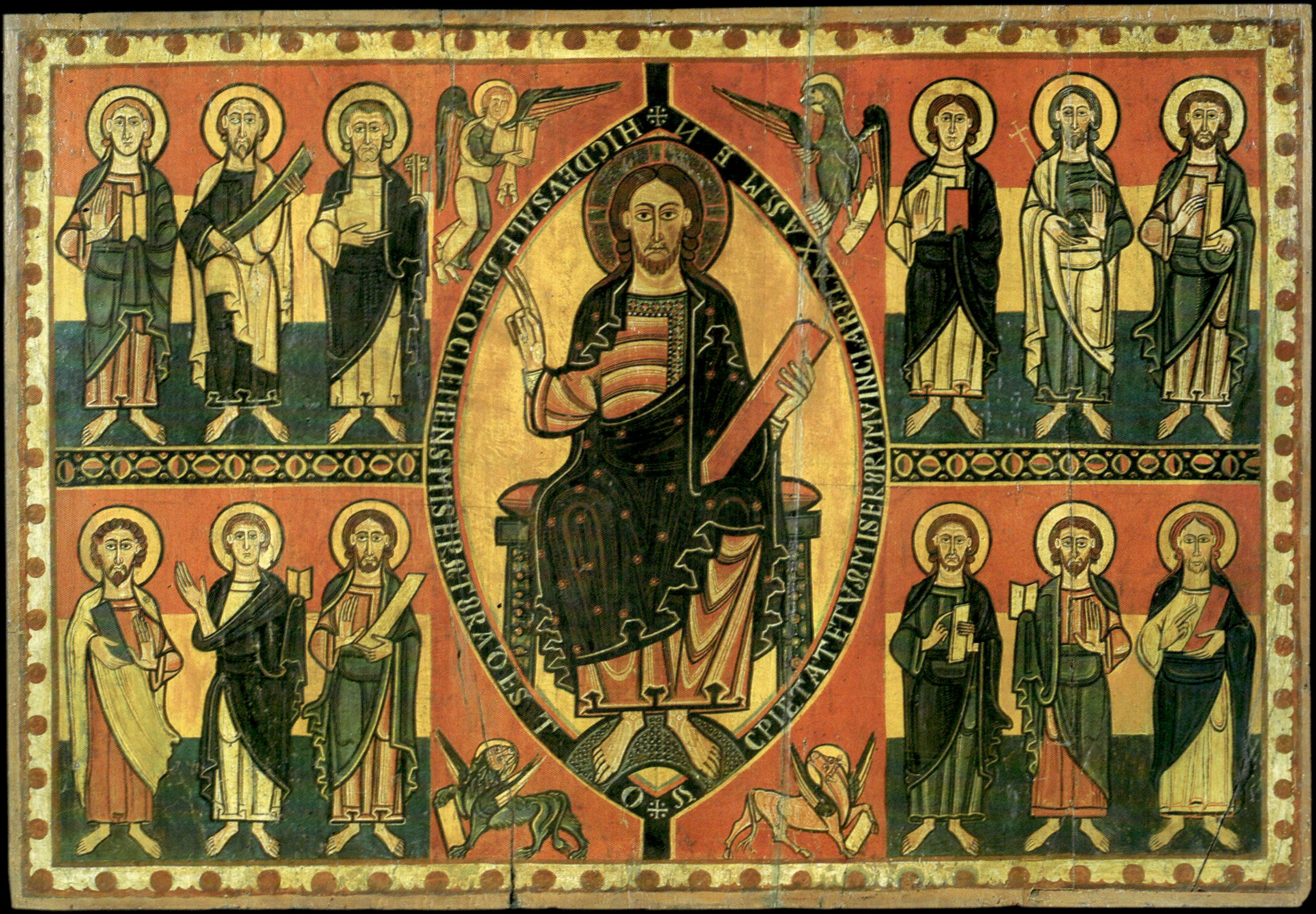

69

70

69. Panel from Esquius.
Panel called "from Esquius".
In the centre, the Maiestas Domini,
surrounded by the symbols of the four evangelists. In the side compartments, four groups of three apostles.
Second quarter of the 12th century
Tempera on wood
96 × 132 cm
MNAC/MAC 65502

70. Detail of Esquius.
Detail of the Maiestas Domini *from the panel called "from Esquius".*

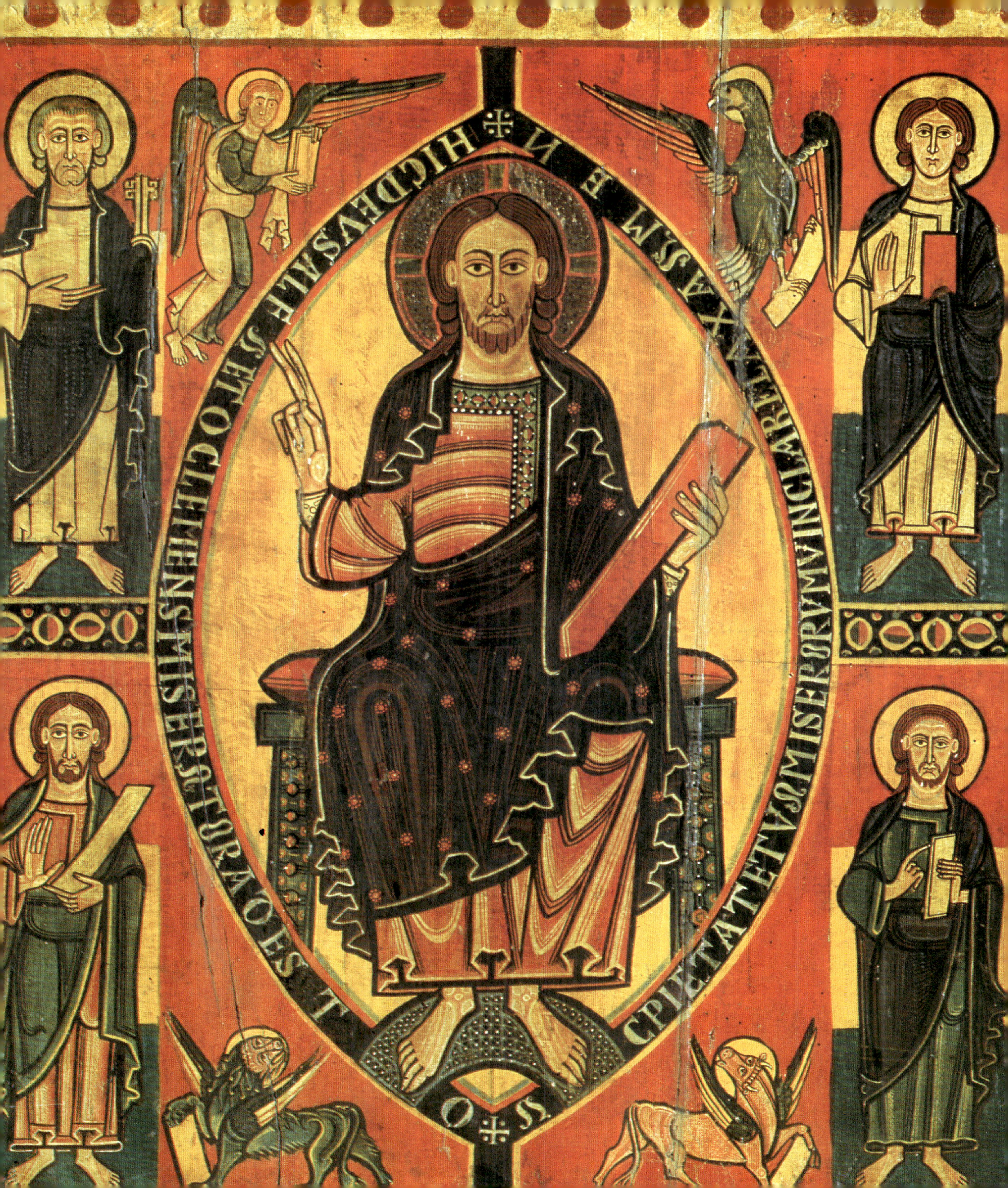

71

71. Altar Frontal of Saint Quiricus and Saint Julitta from Durro.
Altar frontal from Durro. In the centre, Saint Quiricus and Saint Julitta. On the right-hand side, Saint Julitta lacerated with nails and swords. On the left, Saint Julitta disembowelled with the aid of a saw and finally mother and son in a pot of boiling water.
Middle of the 12th century
Tempera on wood.
From the hermitage of Sant Quirze and Santa Julita de Durro (Alta Ribagorça)
100 × 120 cm
MNAC/MAC 15809

72. Durro: detail.
Martyrdom of Saint Julitta with a saw

73. Durro: detail.
Martyrdom of Saint Julitta with nails

74. Durro: detail.
Saint Julitta and Saint Quiricus in the pot of boiling water

75. Durro: detail.
Martyrdom of Saint Julitta with swords

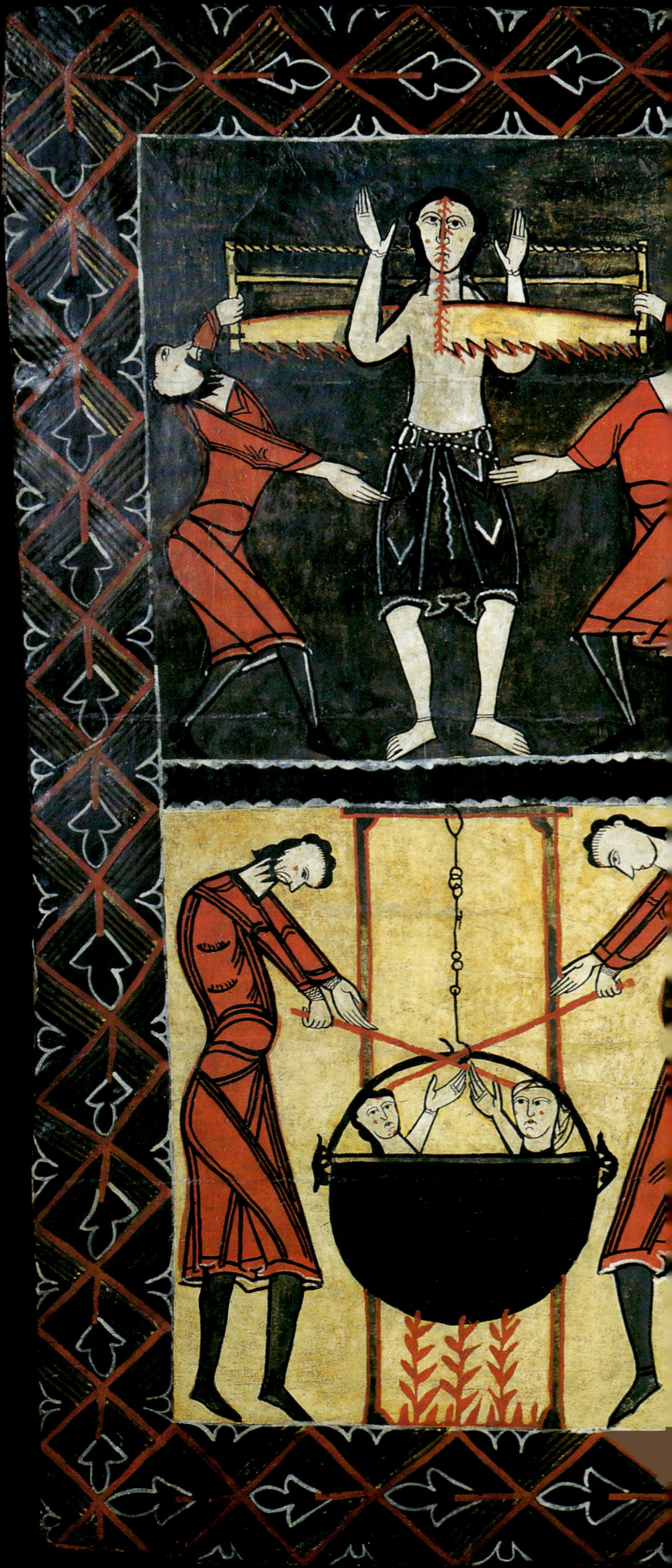

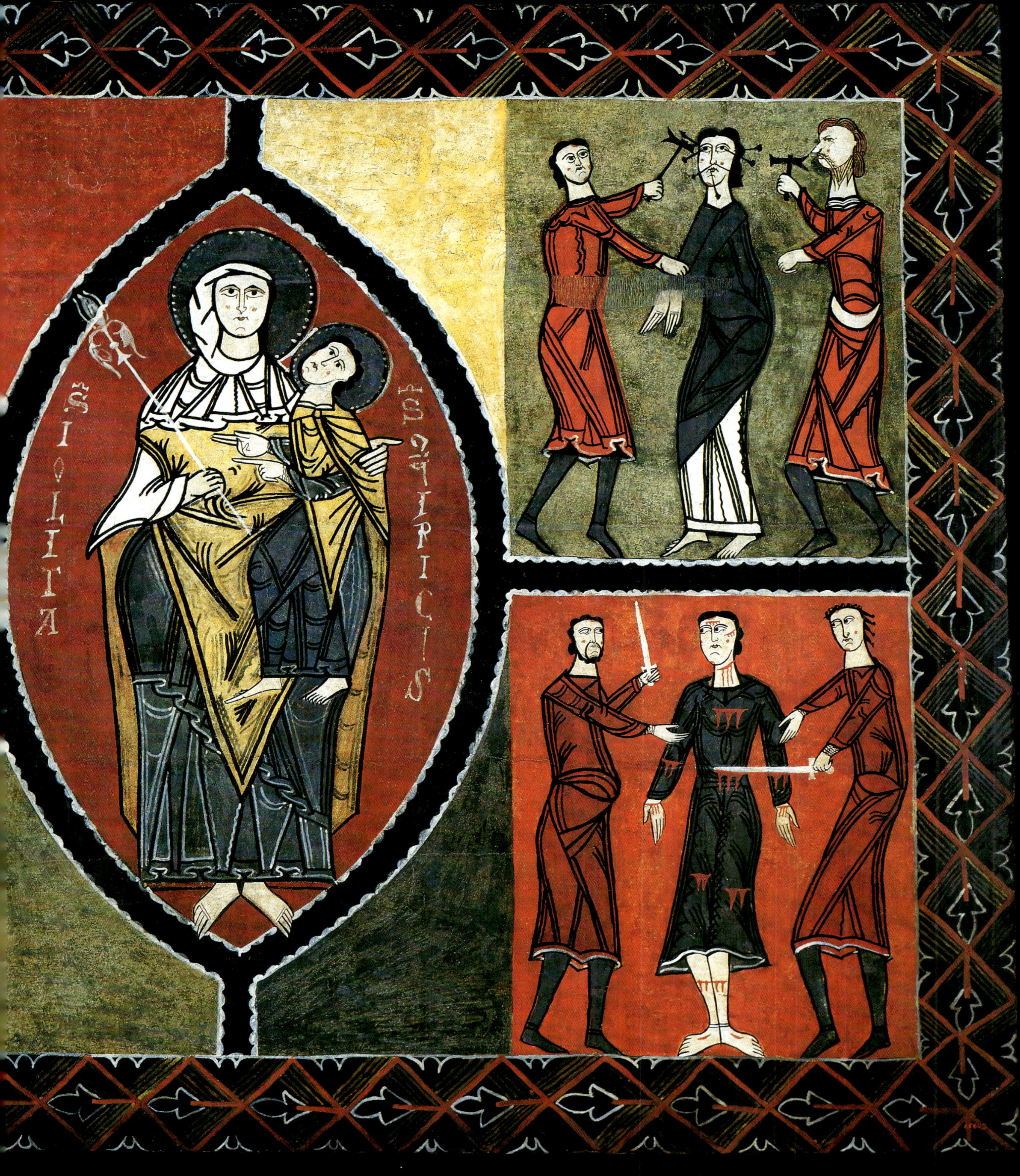

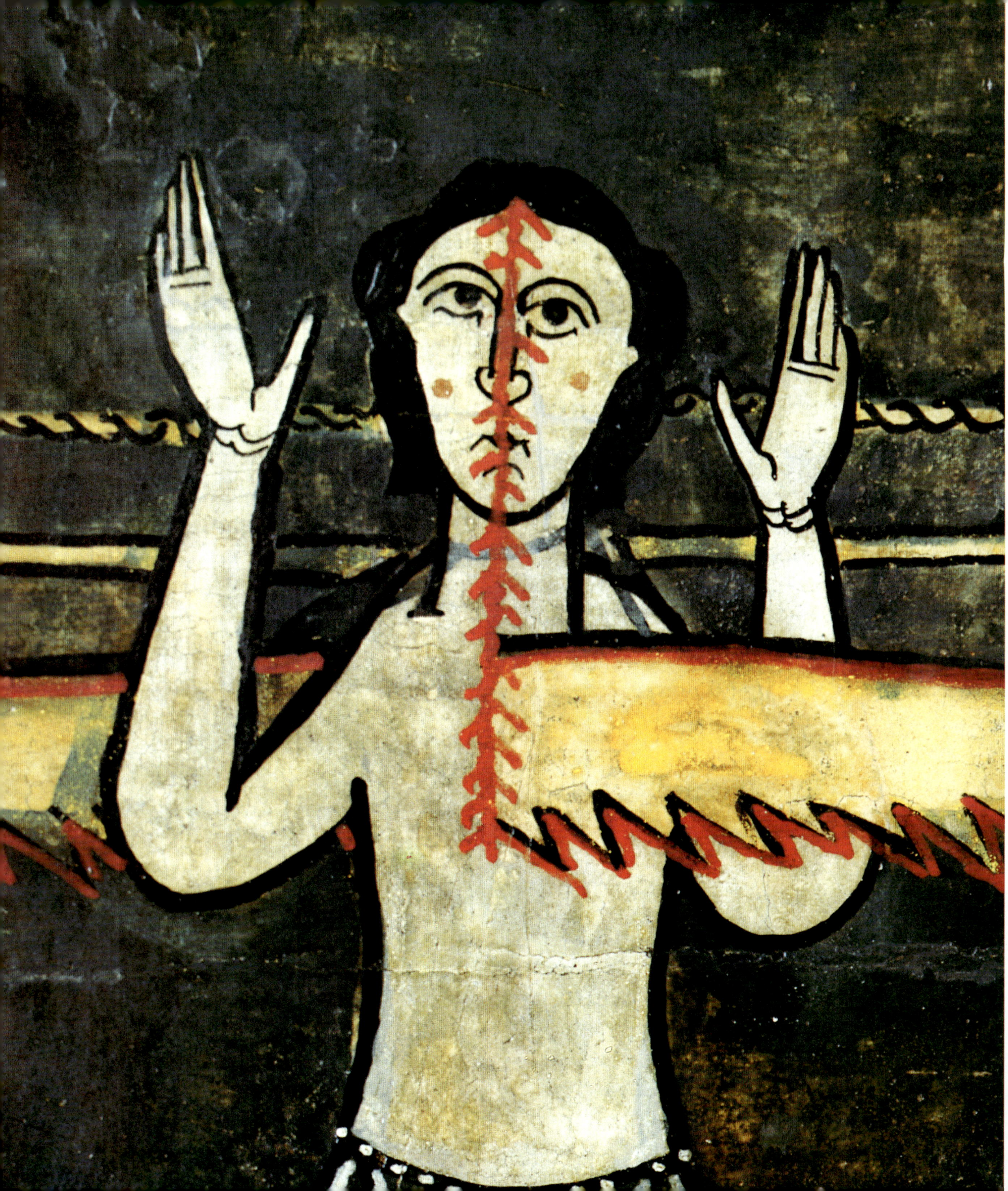

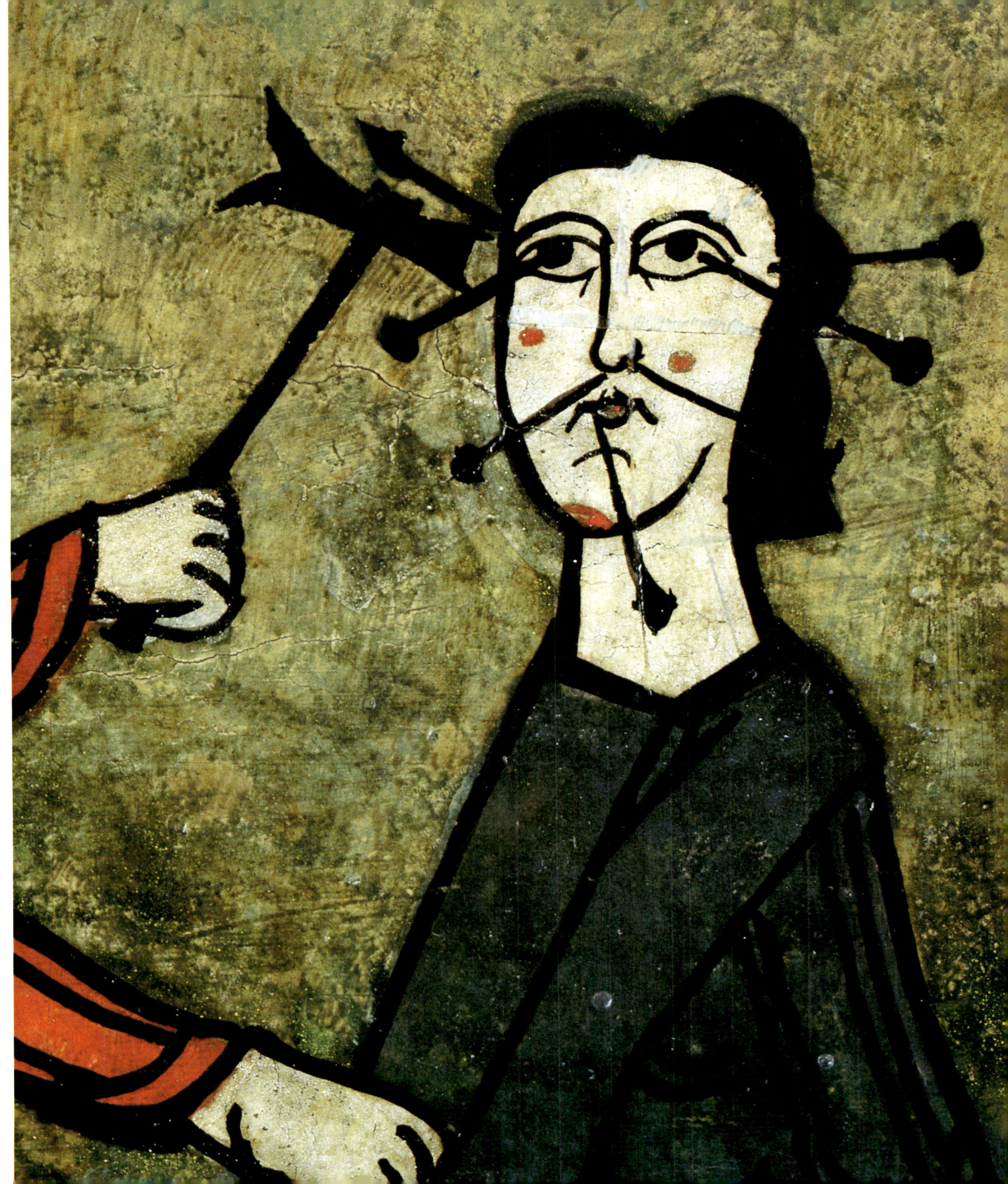

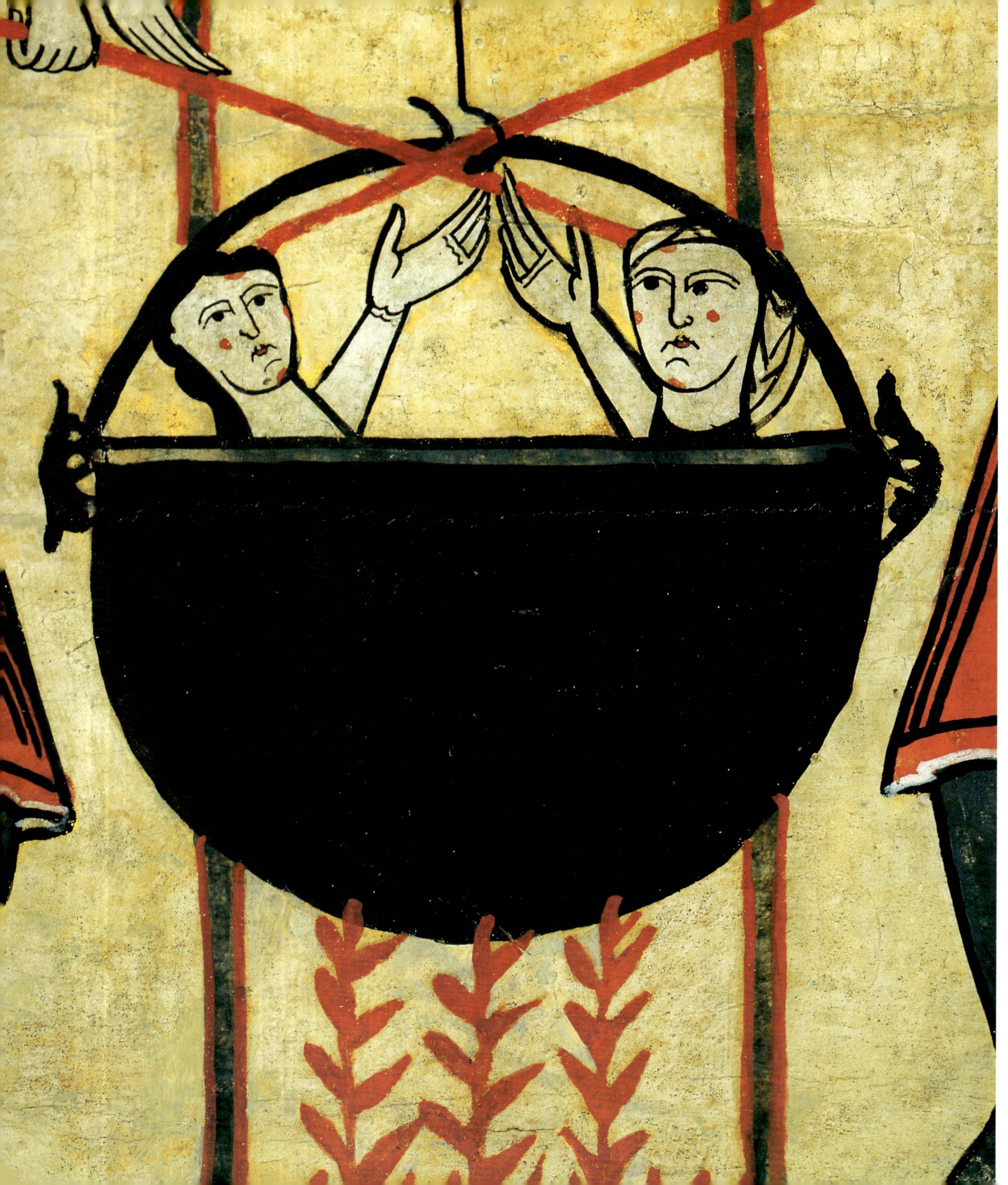

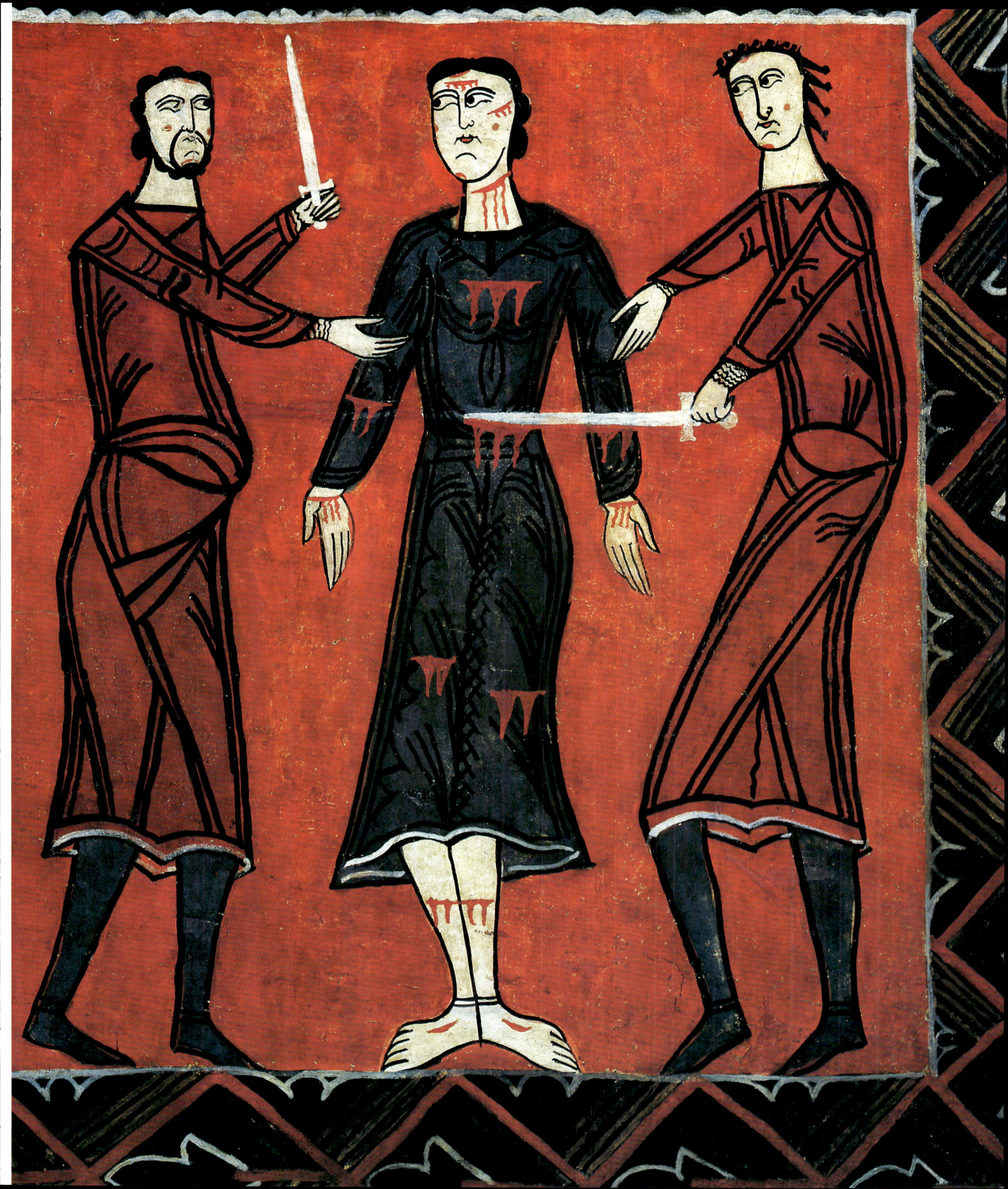

(Urgell, Ix, Puigbó, Esquius) is too far removed from metalwork formulas, as it shows no trace of the compositions with numerous small frames in *cloisonné* enamel containing scenes from the Life of Christ or of the cross-and-lozenge arrangement in bands. On the contrary, originally, the Catalan painted altar frontals of the first half of the twelfth century (except in the case of Puigbó) showed a tendency to concentrate on a single Theophanic image, like the Ascension (Urgell) or the Second Coming (Esquius). In addition, none of the existing examples preserves any kind of portrait or inscription alluding to the patron, unlike what we find in examples of eleventh-century metalwork. The repeated absence of these elements in panel painting is explained by the fact that wood was a cheap medium intended mainly for use in small churches and therefore never seen as a lay 'donation' so much as a liturgical furnishing supplied to rural churches by the 'anonymous' workshops in the episcopal see or monasteries, whose churches did have magnificent metalwork altars. On the other hand, the monumental arts in Catalonia, both in sculpture and in mural painting, incorporated portraits of their lay benefactors in their extensive iconographic series, as in the case of the Countess Llúcia de Pallars ('(LUC)IA CONMITESA') in the central apse of Sant Pere del Burgal or the possible Counts of Besalú, Bernat Tallaferro and his son Guillem, who appear on the right of the Ripoll portal.

In addition, thanks to the analyses of the altar frontals of La Seu d'Urgell, Ix and Esquius, it has been possible in recent years to get a better understanding of the technique used by these early painters and their more than obvious links with the practice of miniature painting, as described in the treatises of Heraclius (tenth/twelfth century) or of the monk Theophilus (twelfth century). This has cast doubt over the established belief that this tradition had its origin in metalwork. In general, the figurative compositions on these panels come closer to the pages of an illuminated book than to the metalworker's craft. In addition, the technique used, tempera, and the figurative and ornamental compositions seem to be highly dependant on illuminated models. In fact, to find a real imitation amongst Catalan altar frontals of the *repoussés*, *cabochons* and enamels of metalwork we have to turn to works from the second half of the twelfth century like the Planès Altar Frontal.

Building and decorating these painted panels was an arduous and complex task. First of all, the wooden medium had to be prepared. It was normally made up of several planks placed side by side, glued edge to edge and joined together with round dowels. In some examples, however, the surface of the medium has a cloth covering glued to it (Planès) or the joins are strengthened with glued pieces of parchment (*Ribes Canopy, Avià Altar Frontal*). The whole was framed in a wooden structure made up of four pieces, which were joined together in the same way as described above, though in some cases, as in Urgell and Ix, they might be strengthened with wrought-iron corner pieces. Similarly, the structure was usually reinforced with crossbeams on the back attached with wrought-iron nails. The wood used for building them was usually Scots pine (*Pinus sylvestris*) (Urgell, Ix), a tree to be found in some Pyrenean valleys, black pine (*Pinus nigra*) (Planès, Tost Panel), which is common in Catalonia, or poplar.

Two layers of plaster were applied to the support, as described by Cennino Cennini: the bottom layer, of *gesso grosso*, a compound of calcium with an earthy consistency, the top one, of *gesso sotile*, which after treatment becomes as soft as silk. The

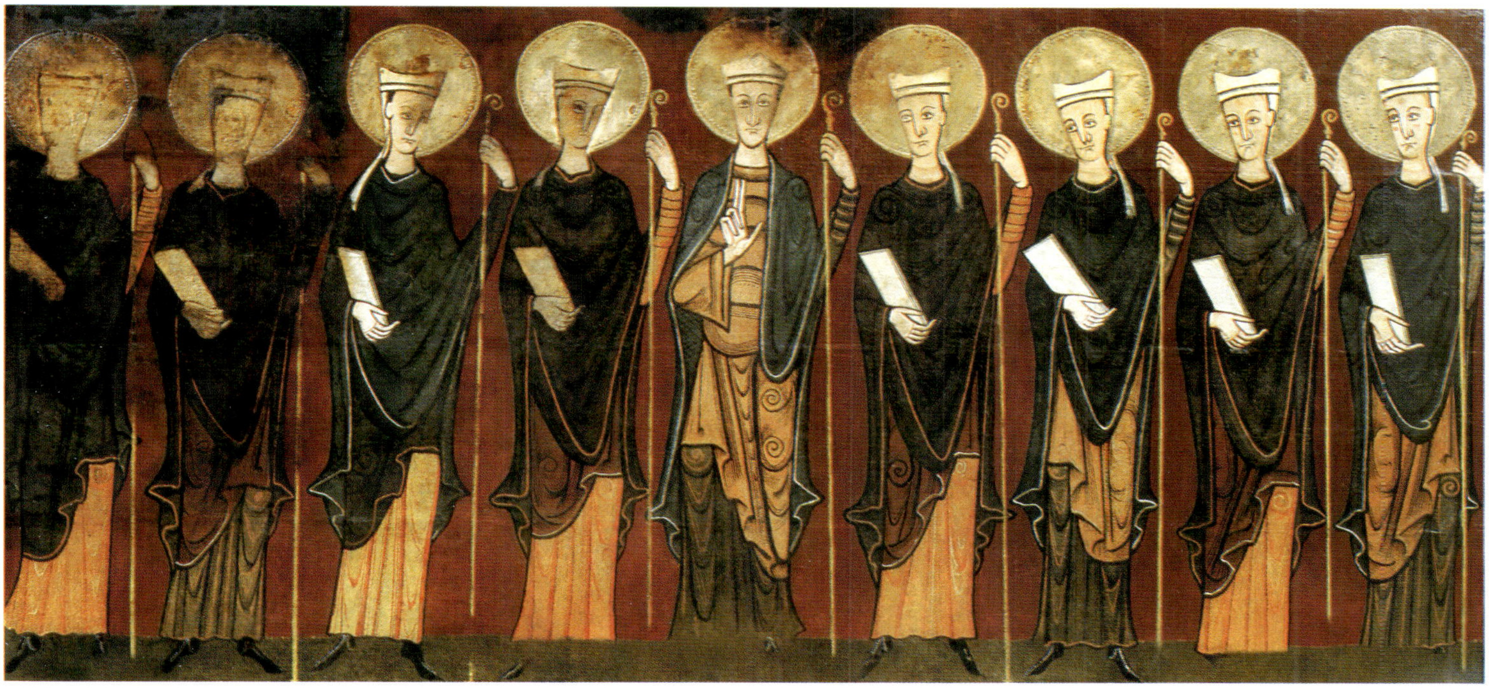

76

76. ALTAR FRONTAL FROM TAVÈRNOLES. *Altar frontal called "from Tavèrnoles". Second half of the 12th century Tempera on wood. From the church of Sant Serni de Tavèrnoles (Alt Urgell) 118 × 218 cm MNAC/MAC 15786*

77-78. DETAIL OF THE FRONTAL FROM TAVÈRNOLES. *Side panel of the frontal from Tavèrnoles showing Saint Martin of Tours.*

composition is cut into this layer, as can still be see in the *Sant Romà de Vila Altar Frontal* and in the panel from the *Tost Canopy*, or else the outline of the preliminary drawing was simply stencilled onto it, as in the case of the *Planès Altar Frontal*. Then the tempera pigments were applied with an organic binder, generally consisting of egg yolk. However, analysis of the oldest panels (Urgell, Ix and Esquius) has shown the use of another protein binder of animal origin that is difficult to identify. It is very probably *charavella* glue, which according to Cennino Cennini was made from boiling soft animal skin, like muzzle, hooves and viscera, or even from parchment.

As far as pigments are concerned, these are mainly of inorganic origin, though the presence of plant lacquers for blues and reds is evidenced at the beginning of the thirteenth century, specifically in the *Tost Canopy* and the *Mosoll Altar Frontal*, both produced in the workshop in La Seu d'Urgell with a powerful Byzantine imprint of 1200 art. In an initial phase, painters made use of inorganic pigments, typical of the recipe books for miniatures, therefore creating a palette rich in bright colours like yellow, red and blue-green, as in the case of the *Seu d'Urgell Altar Frontal*. These colours are characteristic of illuminated manuscripts. It has in fact been possible to identify the use of expensive, finely ground pigments typical of this technique, such as orpiment (arsenic sulphide) for the yellows and cinnabar for the reds. Cinnabar was combined with lead white (hydrocerussite) for the flesh tones, while for clothing it was mixed with red lead (minium) over a coarser layer of iron oxide (haematites) (Ix, Esquius, Planès). For blue, Pyrenean aerinite was used (Urgell, Ix) and exceptionally lapis lazuli (Esquius), while green was made by mixing or overlaying aerinite and orpiment (Urgell, Ix, Planès, Tost). Overlaying pigments to obtain a particular colour is common, especially with navy blue, which to imitate the effect of lapis lazuli is applied over a layer of carbon black (Planès,

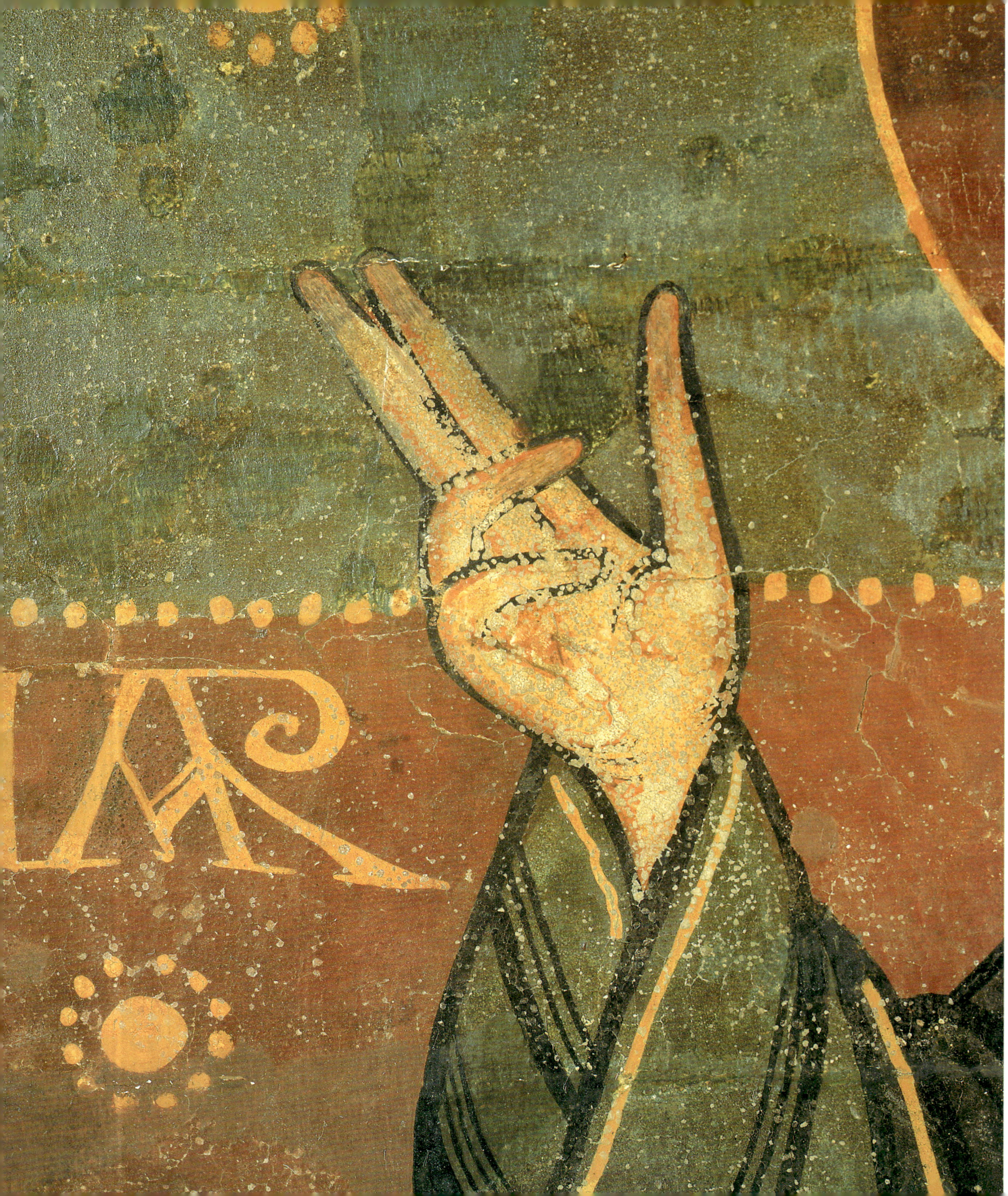

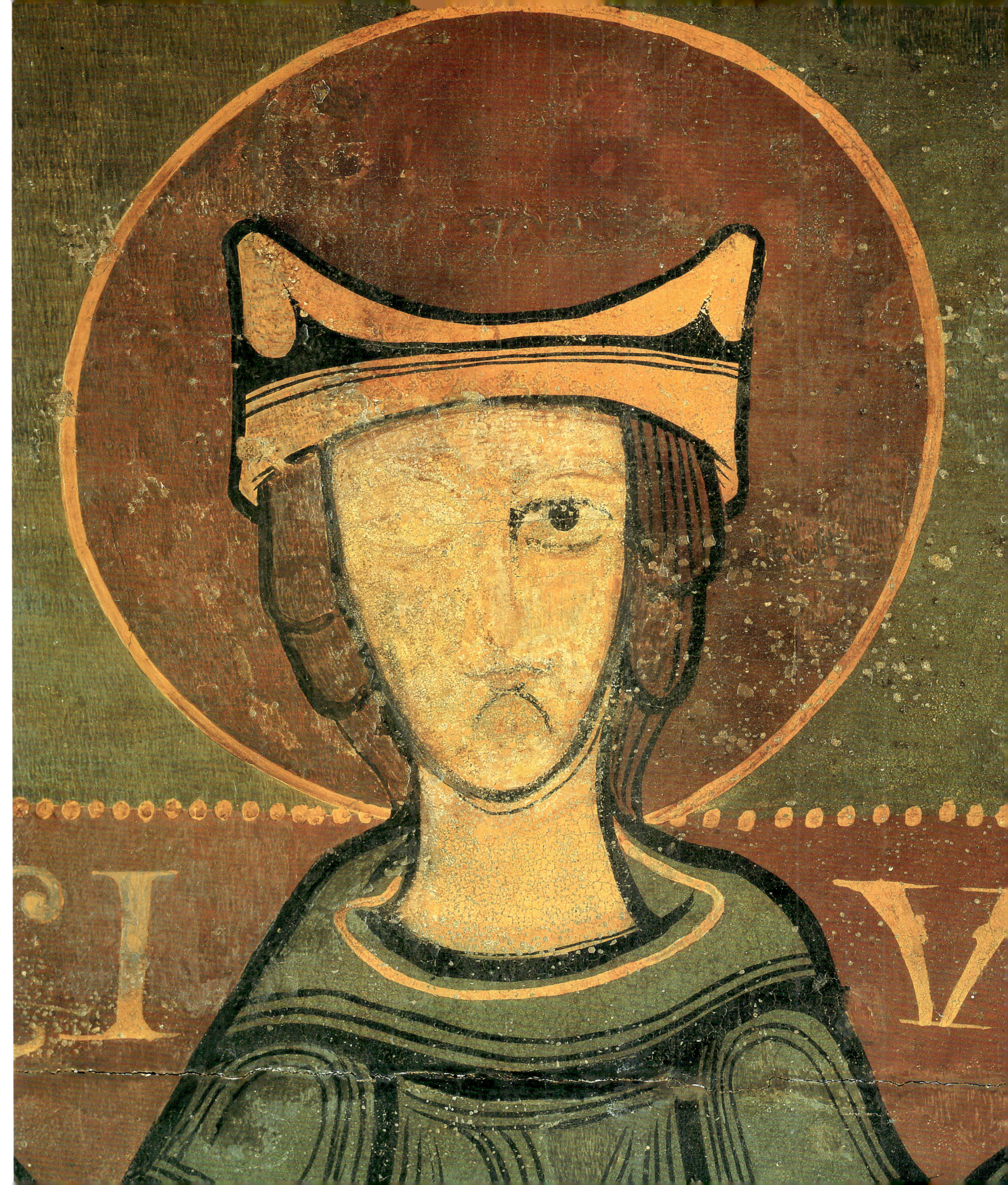

Tost). I might add that many of these recipes were to be found in the chapters on figurative illuminations in the best-known professional treatises, like Heraclius or Theophilus.

Equally indicative of familiarity with these recipes, in particular of what the contemporary Theophilus called translucent painting, is the application of varnished tin-plating to ennoble certain parts. Incipient use of this technique is made in the earliest painted panels in Urgell, on the cross of Christ's nimbus; in Ix, on the cross in the nimbus and on Christ's globe, in the attributes of the Apostles (Peter's keys, books and scrolls), in the scenes of Saint Martin (the knife cutting the poor man's cape, the bishop's crosier in the scene in which he resurrects the catechumen); and in Esquius, where remains of plaster relief (*pastigilia*) can be seen in Christ's crossed nimbus, over which the sheet of varnished tin would have been placed.

This gilt varnish technique, known as *colradura* in Catalan or *deauratio facilis* in Latin, is described in the recipes in an anonymous manuscript made in 1134 in the monastery of Santa Maria de Ripoll (Madrid, Biblioteca Nacional, Ms. 19). Its sophisticated systematic use over the whole of the surface of the panel was to become a characteristic of Catalan Romanesque, illustrated in the altar frontals of Planès (Ripollès), Alós d'Isil, Ginestarre (The Cloisters, New York) and Esterri de Cardós. This formula was intended to all effects and for the first time to systematically imitate the relief (human figures, plant decoration and *cabuchon*) and the shininess of metalwork, specifically of the fashionable Limoges enamels of the time. However, the process could vary. While in Planès the plaster figures are first made in a mould and then applied to the surface to be painted, in the other altar frontals the *pastiglia* method predominated. Here the hot plaster was applied over the surface and then modelled with a palette knife before being covered with tin plating coloured with varnish.

The fact that artists had access to the different books of recipes and their obvious debt to the tradition of the miniatures suggest that the earliest masters of panel painting worked under the wing of the great ecclesiastic centres like Ripoll, Vic or Urgell, whose institutions, being the repository of the necessary technical knowledge, oversaw their work and training. These workshops, probably located in the actual cathedral or monastery buildings, supplied the humble parishes of the diocese or of the territory of the abbey with the liturgical furnishings that ensured ornate worship and helped spread the dogma. They were clearly 'cheap' objects when compared with the magnificence of the great metalwork altars of these production centres, but they were sufficiently 'sightly' to contribute to the aesthetic of the Christian mystery of the Incarnation.

Consequently, although we don't know if the artists were ecclesiastics or laymen, everything suggests, with all due caution, that in the early days they were *clericus* trained in abbeys and cathedrals. Remember that in the case of Tuscany, production of these liturgical furnishings of painted panels, with a purely religious nature and function, also relied on a knowledge of sophisticated technical recipes and traditional work in illumination, which is why their production has always been attributed to mythical artist monks. One example is the famous crucifix in Sarzana cathedral (La Spezia, Liguria, Italy), signed in 1138 in leonine hexameters by the painter and man of letters Guglielmus, who is always assumed to have had an ecclesiastical background. At the same time, we mustn't forget that the production of these 'sacred' panels has always been

79

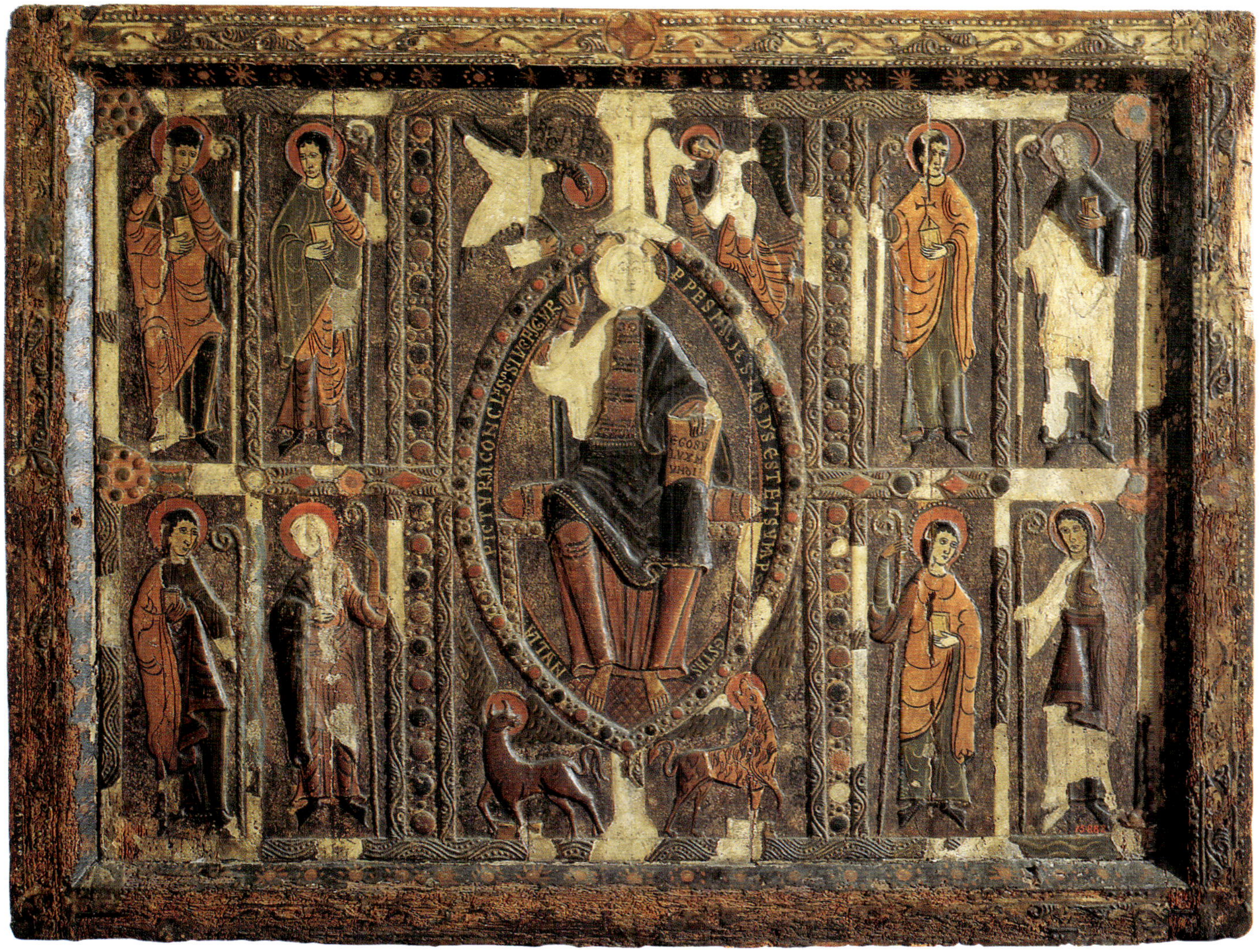

79. Altar Frontal from Planès.
Frontal from Sant Marcel de Planès de Rigalt (Ripollès).
Second half of the 12th century
Tempera, with plaster reliefs and golden glazed sheets of tin
92 × 120 cm
MNAC/MAC 15882

coloured with an unmistakably pious and 'religious' sense. While the famous monk and painter of icons of Mount Athos invoked the Virgin Mary *Hodegetria* and the Evangelist Saint Luke before starting work, Cennino Cennini himself reminds us in chapter 104 of his *Craftsman's Handbook* that the painter of panels is also under the obligation to pray before starting work:

> 'We begin panel painting in the name of the Holy Trinity, ever invoking its name and that of the glorious Virgin Mary'.

Similarly, the master painters of the panels of Ix, Esquius and Planès also show a mastery of Latin rhetoric, adding inscriptions to their images painted in beautiful calligraphy, as though they had trained in a monastic or cathedral school. In Ix, a Latin inscription referring to Saint Martin, the titular saint of the church and the subject of

80

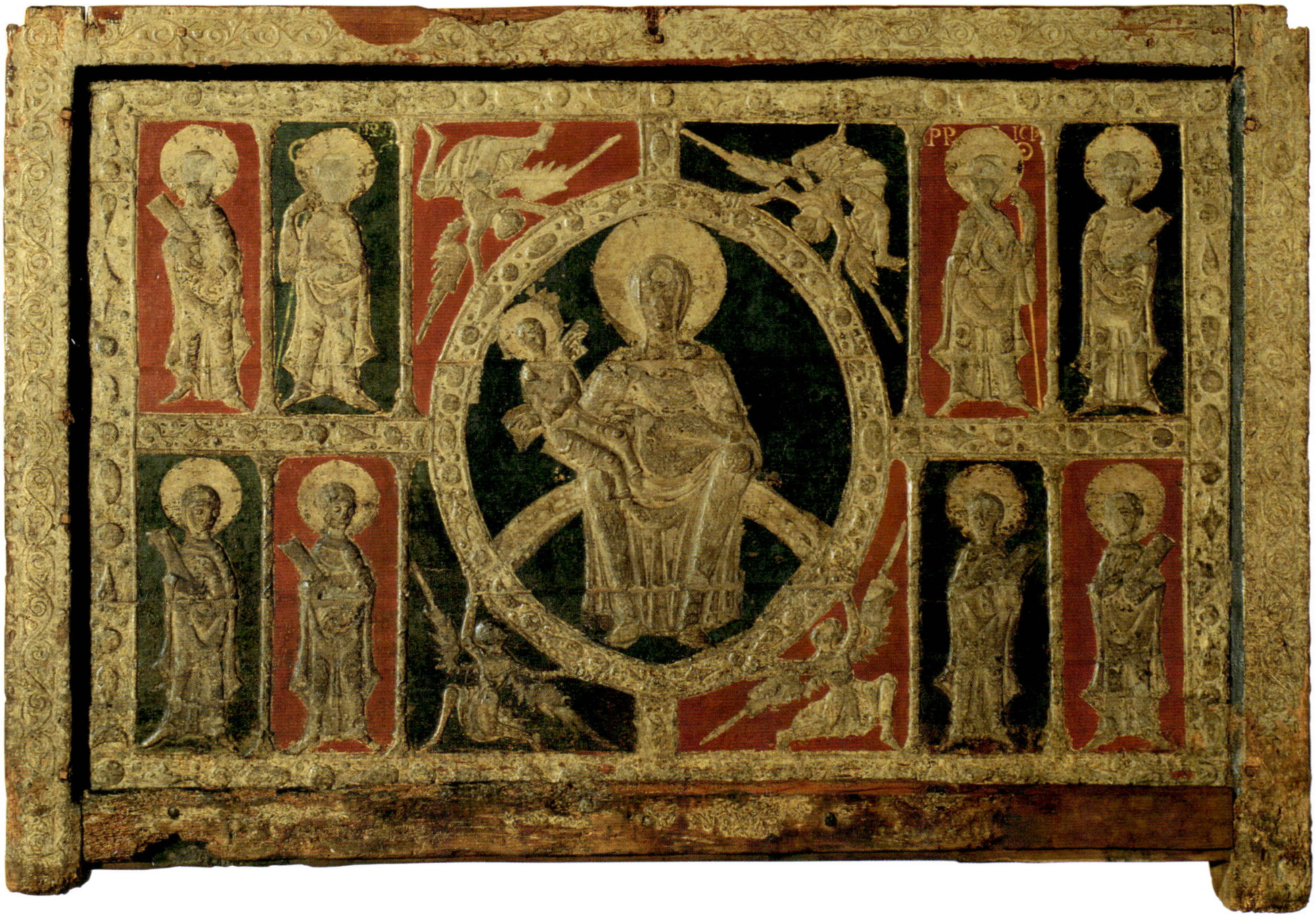

80. Altar Frontal from Alòs d'Isil.
Altar Frontal from Alòs d'Isil.
First quarter of the 13th century
Plaster reliefs and golden glazed sheets of tin
106 × 161 cm
MNAC/MAC 15834

two scenes from the altar frontal, ran right across both sides of the central image: 'SOL ET LVX SANCTORVM/MANEO IN PRECLARA ET BONORVM'. The bulbous lines of the lettering bring to mind the characteristic calligraphy of *Chrysography*, or writing in gold, whose recipes are to be found in none other but the miscellaneous manuscript of Ripoll from 1134. For its part, the pleading tone of the writing in the mandorla of the Christ in Majesty on the Esquius Panel also seems to have come from a bookish monastery culture:

> '+HIC DEVS ALFA ET O(mega) CLEMENS MISERATOR ADESTO/ + AC PIETATE TVA MISERORVM VINCLA RELAXA AMEN' (This is the God of the Alpha and of the Omega. Come, with your mercy and loosen the chains of the afflicted. Amen).

Finally, the disturbing Neoplatonic content of the inscription that can be read in Christ's mandorla in the *Planès Altar Frontal* once again suggests these humble

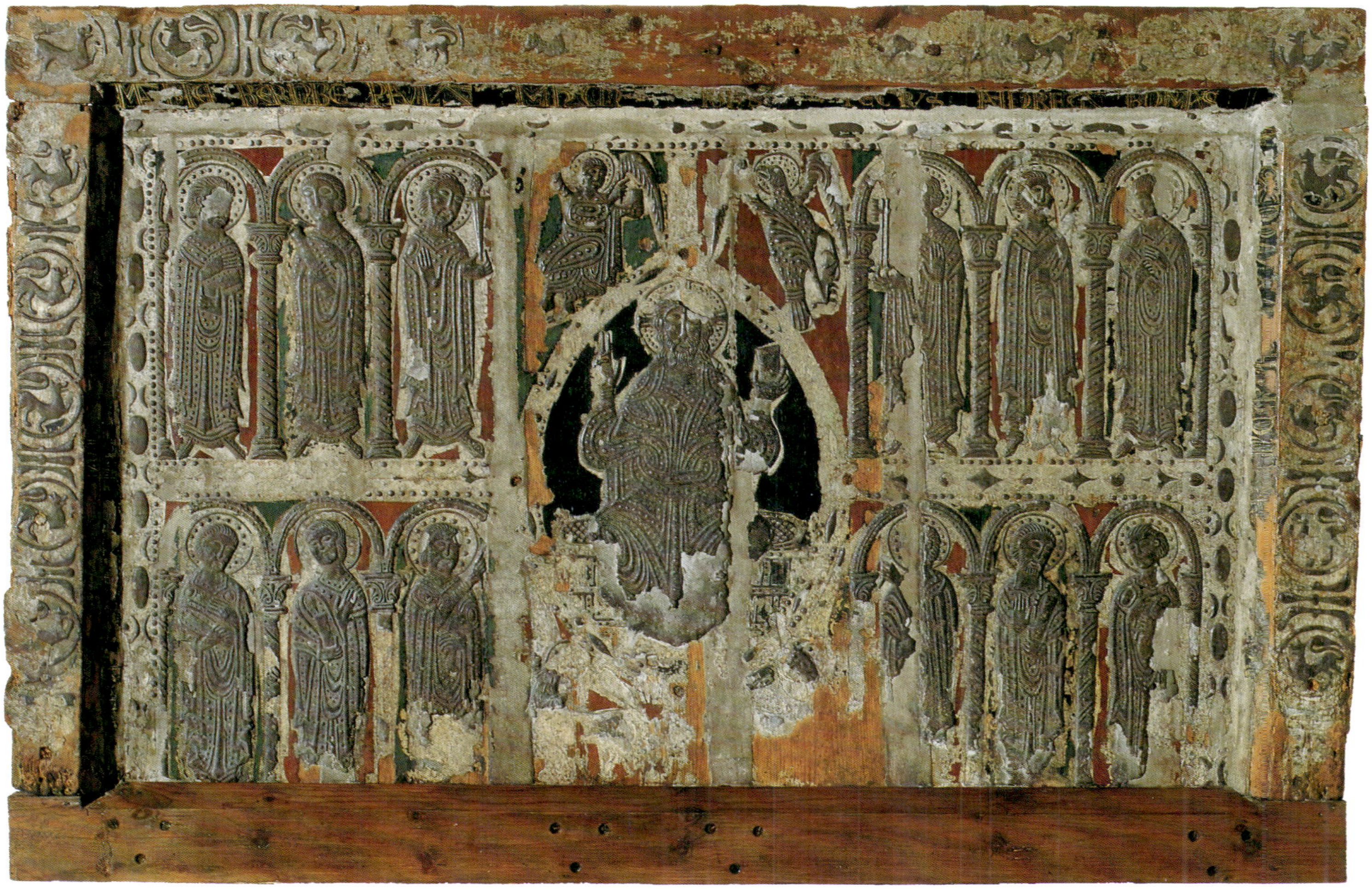

81

81. ALTAR FRONTAL FROM ESTERRI DE CARDÓS.
Altar Frontal from
Sant Pau d'Esterri de Cardós.
1225 (according to the inscription)
Plaster reliefs and golden glazed sheets of tin
108 × 161 cm
MNAC/MAC 15970

masters of panel painting were familiar with monastic culture, which probably provided their training:

> 'NVLLA PICTURA CONCLVSA SIVE FIGVRA PERPES, MAGESTAS D(ivinitati)S EST ET SVMMA POTESTAS' (No finished painting or figure is like the perpetuity, the majesty and the utmost power of God).

In the previous chapter a possible background was suggested for the painter in Catalonia, whose artistic apprenticeship might have started with the practice of panel painting and gradually led up to the execution of mural paintings. One thing seems to confirm this. The appearance of the panel painting technique on the Catalan art scene in the 1120s (Urgell, Ix, Puigbó, Ribes) seems to coincide with a revolution in its monumental pictorial tradition: the Master of Sant Climent de Taüll. His work breaks entirely with the illusionism of the Master of Pedret's Circle, as it is called, and seems to ignore the lessons of this mural tradition and opt for novel experiments, both in com-

82

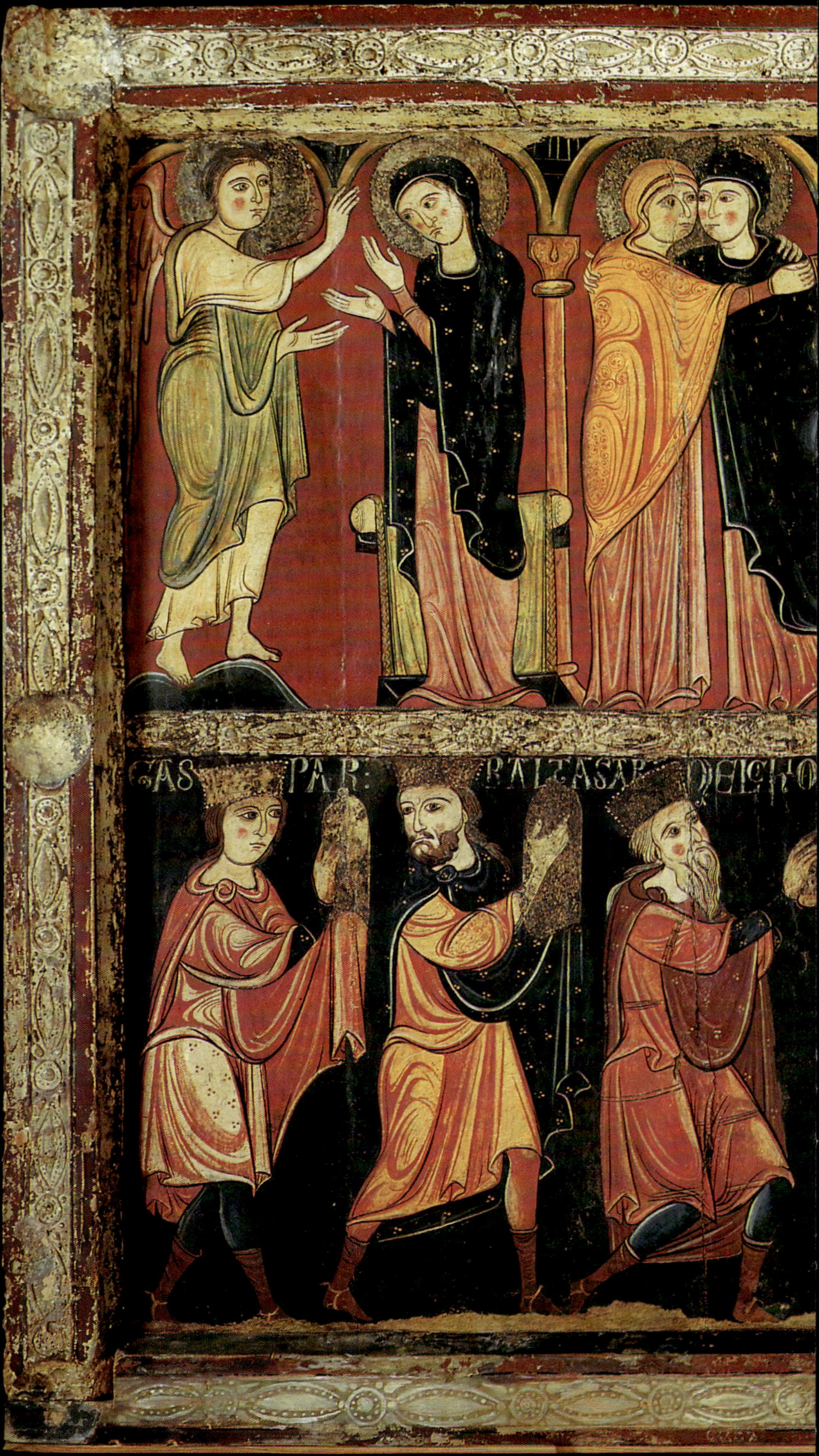

82. Altar Frontal from Avià.
Altar frontal from Avià. In the centre: the Maiestas Mariae.
In the top left-hand compartment, the Annunciation and the Visitation.
In the top right-hand compartment, the Nativity.
In the bottom right-hand compartment, the Epiphany.
In the bottom left-hand compartment, the Presentation in the Temple
Around 1200
Tempera on wood with golden glazed stucco reliefs
From the church of Santa Maria d'Avià
105 × 176 cm
MNAC/MAC 15784

83. Detail of a compartment of the Frontal from Avià.
Detail of the Annunciation and the Visitation from the frontal from Avià.

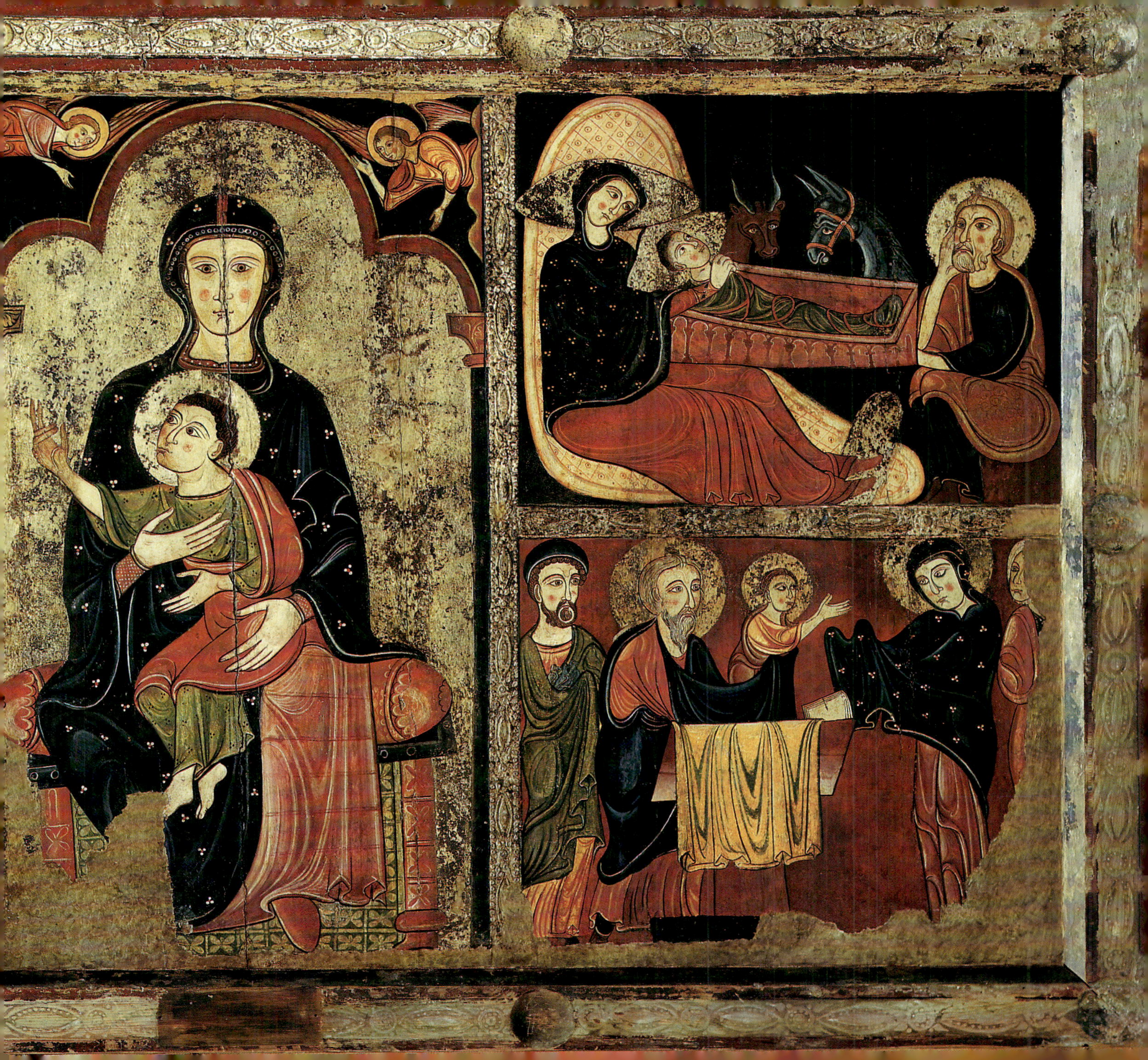

position and in the use of colour. These bring him closer in line with the aesthetic of the emerging panel painting and therefore suggest a common apprenticeship and the exchange of recipes between the two techniques. All of this would explain the marked ornamental feel, the excessive black outlining and the superimposed layers to achieve certain colours, as in the blue cloak.

Finally, we mustn't forget that Catalan painted panels, like Byzantine icons, underwent a special ritual blessing. The Byzantine *Acolouthia* consisted in a ceremony in which the icon was anointed on the altar and a prayer was recited so that divine grace would descend on it. The work was left there for forty days. The *benedictio tabulae*, whose formula in Catalonia is preserved in the *Pontifical de Vic*, made sacred objects of the panels as though they were the new tablets of the law of Moses:

'*Suplices tibi Domine Deus omnipotens pater preces effundimus, ut metalli hujus expoliata matherias supernis sacrifiis imbuendam ipsa tua dotare sanctificationis ubertat digneris, qui condam scripsit lapideis legem in tabulis*' (Oh Lord, Almighty Father, we beseech you to accept our prayers, that he who engraved the stone tablets may see fit to endow this panel with his abundant sanctity so that it may be ready and anointed for the heavenly sacrifices).

We know very little about their liturgical function, apart from their obvious use as altar decoration and therefore an ornament for the site of the Eucharist. I am in no doubt that many of their commonest iconographic themes, like the Ascension or the Incarnation of Christ, are related to the ritual of Eucharistic consecration and the mystery of transubstantiation. Their fine state of conservation makes it quite likely that for most of the year they were covered by the precious cloths or canopies that always appear in the inventories of Catalan altars, which were removed or left in place according to the liturgy and the annual cycle of feasts. An old photograph of the high altar of Sant Climent de Taüll taken by Domènech i Montaner in 1904 shows the altar table covered with a cloth. The same sort of thing can still be seen today in the parish church of Orellà, where the bottom of the altar has a recess covered with a cloth where the magnificent *Orellà Altar Frontal* used to be placed. In fact, in Norway, where an important corpus of wooden *antependia* from the thirteenth to fourteenth centuries has been preserved, there are accounts of these liturgical furnishings being exhibited in public only for important feasts and spending the rest of the year covered under precious cloths, the case of the gold altar frontal in Trondheim cathedral. Similarly, the magnificent *Pala d'Oro* on the high altar of Saint Mark's Basilica in Venice was also covered most of the year with the *Pala Feriale*, or weekday altarpiece.

This suggests the possibility that the role of these images was centred on certain feasts during the liturgical year. In fact, in Catalonia there are plenty of panels with Christmas subject matter (Espinelves, Mosoll, Avià), Easter content (altar frontals of Sant Climent de Taüll and Sagàs in the Museu Episcopal de Vic) or simply of a hagiographic nature relating to the titular saint of the church (Saint Martin in Ix, Saint Quiricus and Saint Julitta in Durro, Saint Andrew in Baltarga, Saint Andrew in Sagás, Saint Martin in Gia), where one glimpses a reference to the liturgical and para-liturgical functions relating to these feasts.

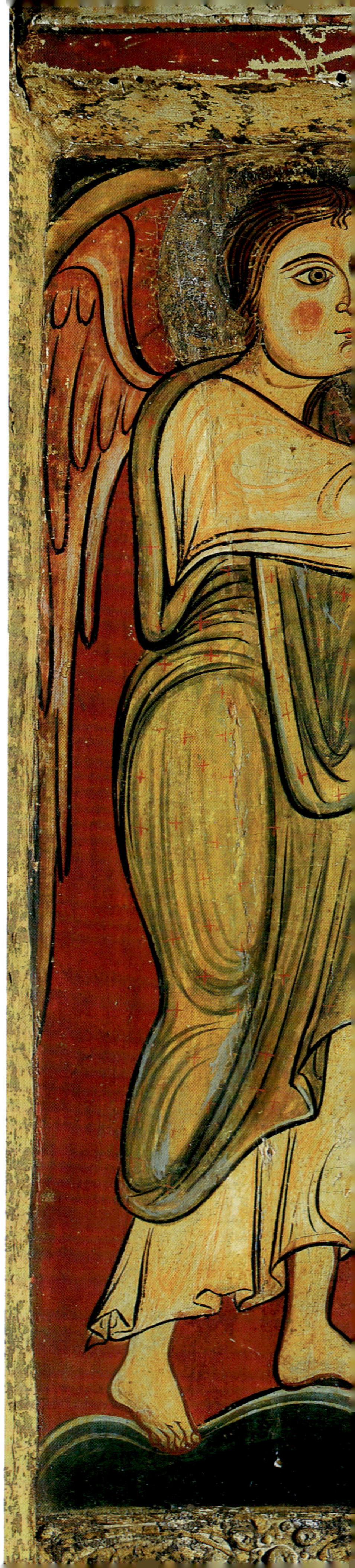

83

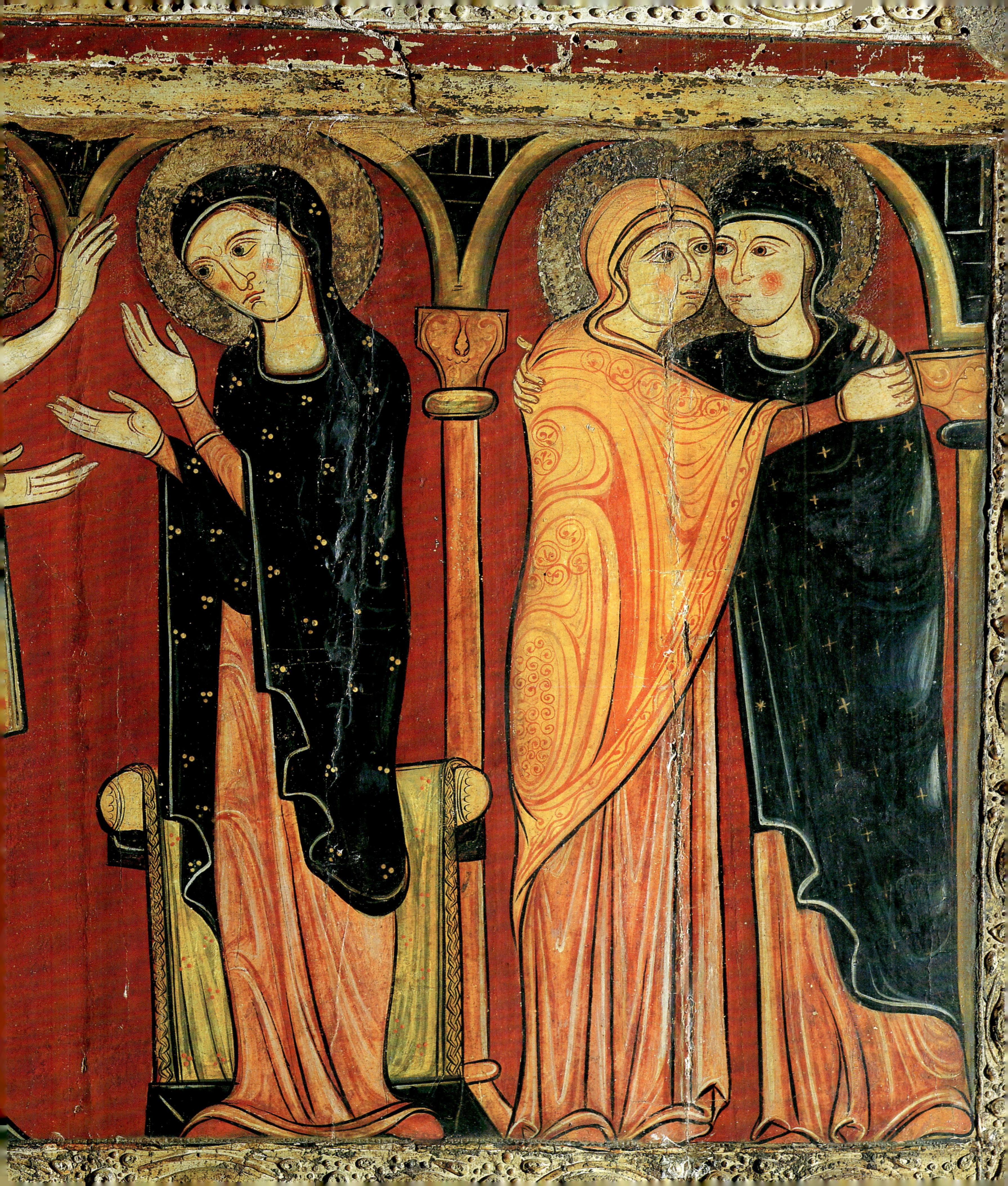

For want of dates or artists' names, except for the brief inscription on the altar frontal of Esterri de Cardós ('AB INCARNATIONE CHRISTI MCCXXV') or the signature on the frontal of Gia ('IO(HANNE)S PINTOR ME FECIT'), the most successful method for tracing the panorama and development of Catalan panel painting has been to pinpoint local pictorial workshops in which individual techniques, styles and chronologies can be singled out. The table established by W.W.S. Cook has survived to our day with minor changes, although it requires in-depth revision in the light of the latest research.

For the twelfth century the idea is that there were three large workshops connected respectively with the cathedrals of Urgell and Vic and the monastery of Ripoll. Urgell is credited with the altar frontals of Urgell, Ix, Tavèrnoles, Martinet and Durro, Ripoll with the canopy of Ribes de Freser, the Esquius Panel and the altar frontals of Puigbó, Llanars, Planès, Sagàs and the side panels of Mataplana, all of which came from the territory of the former monastery, and finally Vic is attributed the altar frontals of Sant Martí de Sescorts, Coll, Sant Llorenç Dosmunts and Espinelves. This rich outlook for the twelfth century may need to be adjusted because, as we shall see later, the predominance and the imprint of the models from the abbey of Ripoll are clearly visible in the altar frontals of Urgell, Ix, Martinet, Durro and Espinelves.

In about 1200 there was a renewal in the production of panel painting, which took the form of a Byzantinism of its own which we call '1200 art'. The altar frontals of Avià, Baltarga, Orellà, Lluçà (Museu Episcopal de Vic), Sant Martí (The Walters Art Gallery), Rotgers (Museu Episcopal de Vic) and Angostrina, the beam of the Passion and the Cardet beam all show this new international style to different degrees. To them were added, according to Cook, in the course of the thirteenth century, a Pyrenean group with a 'folk' interpretation of the new Byzantine formulas, consisting of Mosoll, Farrera de Pallars, Sant Romà de Vila and the beam from Sant Miquel de Cruïlles (Museu d'Art de Girona). Alongside this, there was the workshop in Lleida, characterised by the relief technique using plaster, tin-plate and gilt varnish, which produced the altar frontals of Esterri de Cardós, Alós d'Isil, Ginestarre, Cardet, Rigatell (Betesa), Tresserra, Sant Pere de Boí, Gia, Estet and Sant Climent de Taüll. This division into three main groups—Byzantinist, Pyrenean and Lleida—is obviously based mainly on stylistic considerations and not on a precise knowledge of the working of the supposed workshops in the area. In fact, as we shall see, during this long thirteenth century the workshop at La Seu d'Urgell (not included in Cook's divisions) seems to have grown in importance due to the need for furnishings in its diocese. Thus Mosoll, Esterri de Cardós, Ginestarre, the canopies of Tost and Tavèrnoles and the panels of Orós are works more closely related amongst themselves than it might seem at first sight.

Whatever the case, the group of panels at the MNAC from the second quarter of the twelfth century (Urgell, Ix and Esquius) show three characteristics: a marked debt to models from miniatures, a formal interpretation of those repertories that reflects what was happening in monumental sculpture and, finally, a Benedictine visionary tone in the way the subject matter is formulated. The altar frontal from La Seu d'Urgell is perhaps the one that best sums this tendency up. The composition is divided into three

84. DETAIL OF A COMPARTMENT OF THE FRONTAL FROM AVIÀ.
Detail of the Virgin with the Child from the frontal from Avià 84

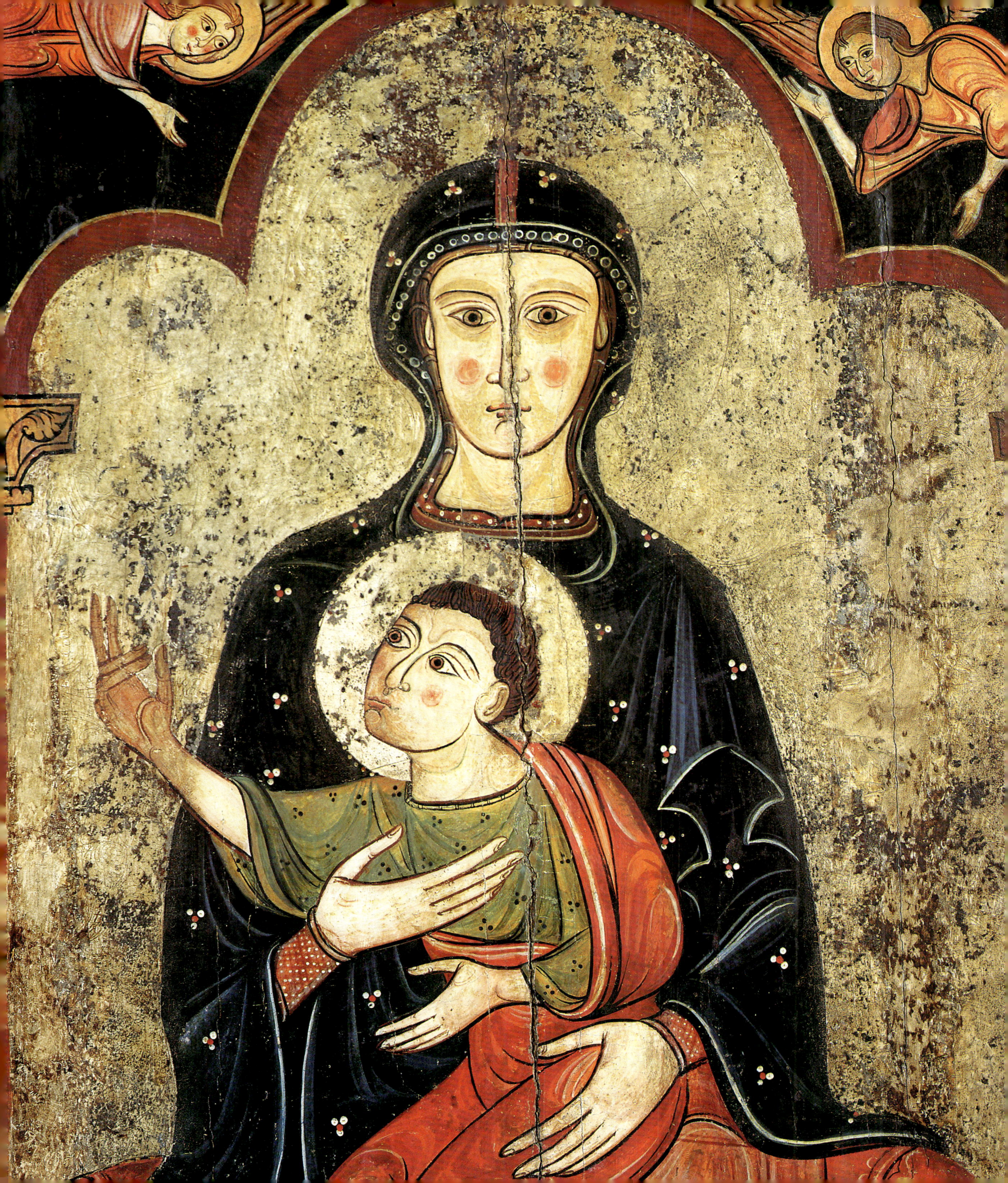

85

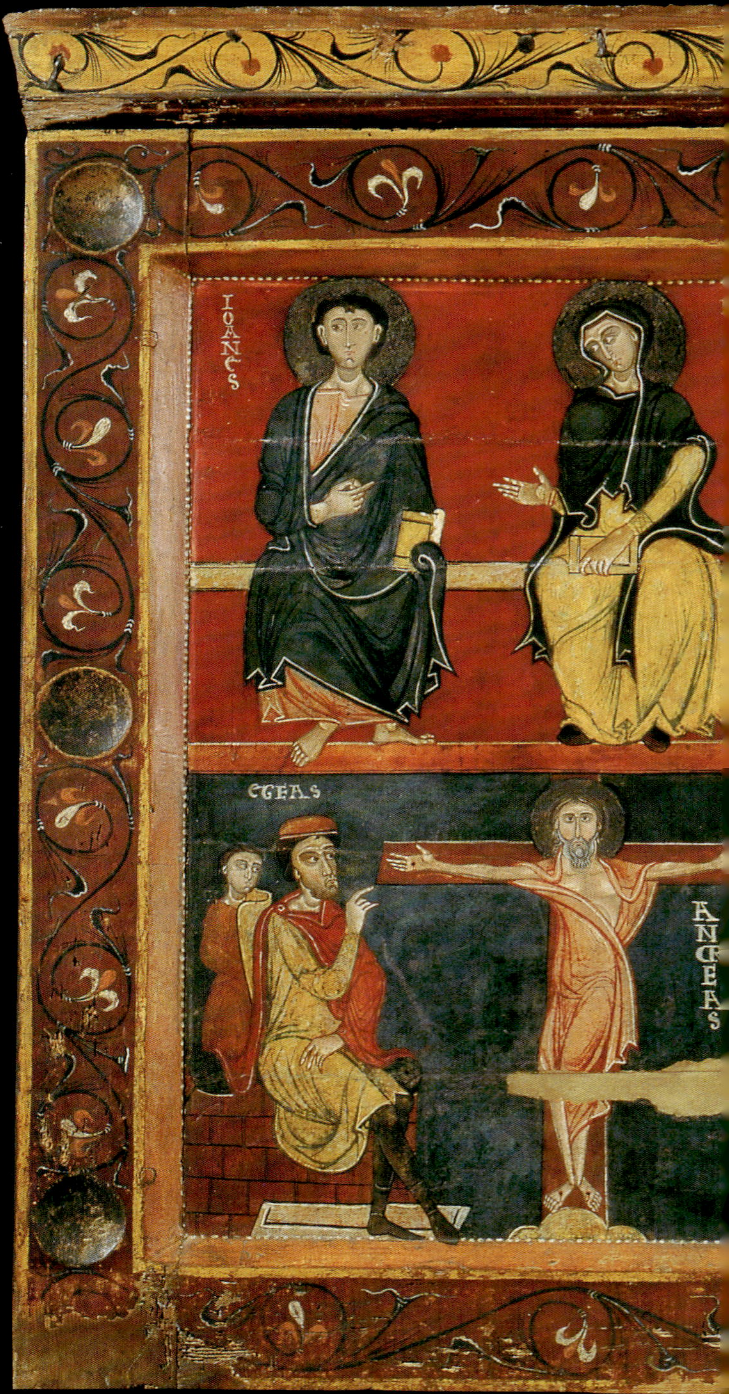

85. ALTAR FRONTAL FROM BALTARGA.
In the centre, the figure of Christ blessing surrounded by the symbols of the four evangelists.
In the top left-hand compartment, Saint John and the Virgin.
In the top right-hand compartment, Saint Andrew and Saint James.
In the bottom left-hand compartment, the martyrdom of Saint Andrew before the Proconsul Egeas.
In the bottom right-hand compartment, Saint Philip and Saint Thomas.
Around 1200
Tempera on wood
From the church of Sant Andreu de Baltarga (Baixa Cerdanya)
94 × 165 cm
MNAC/MAC 15804

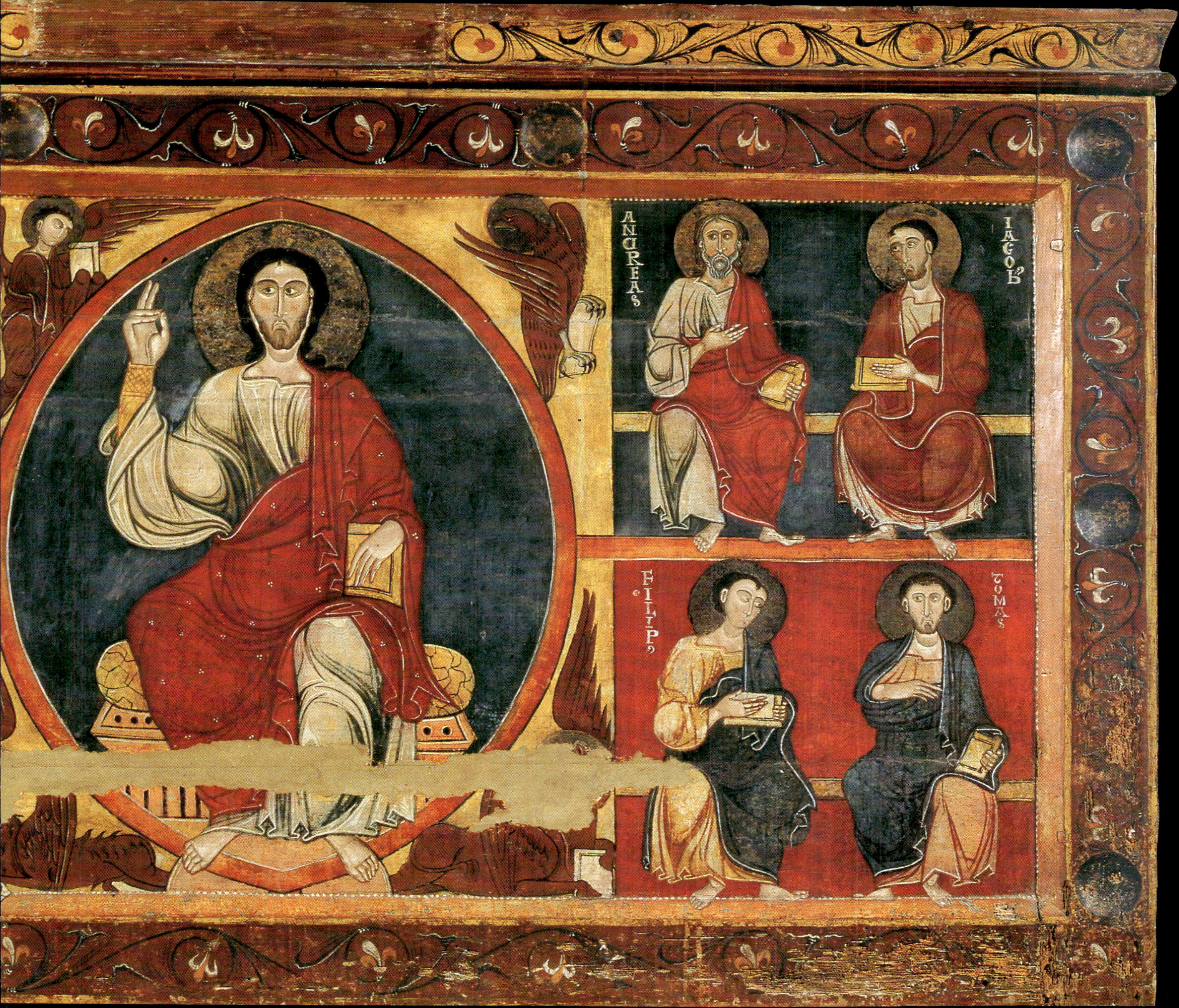
ANDREAS
IACOB
FILIP
TOMAS

rectangular compartments. In the centre, a frontally seated Christ against a double mandorla blesses with his right hand and holds a book in the other, while groups of Apostles stand on either side, slightly turned three-quarters, gesturing and accompanied by their attributes (Peter's key, books and scrolls), their heads forming a pyramidal composition. The scene is an Ascension reduced to its essential elements (Christ and the Apostles), deliberately omitting other motifs (the Announcing Angels, the Virgin or the angels carrying Jesus up to heaven in a mandorla) that normally appear in biblical illustrations derived from the Syrio-Palestinian tradition, like the Ripoll Bible. A very similar composition to the one in Urgell, specifically a Syrio-Palestinian Ascension adapted to the monumental format of an apse, can be found in the paintings from the church of San Pietro di Crepacore (Torre Santa Susanna, Apulia) (late ninth to early tenth century), in which the Apostles are arranged in the same pyramidal compositions. In addition, the choice of an Ascension as the central theme of an altar frontal is perfectly suited to the location, as it was there, on the altar, that the sacrament of the Eucharist took place, through which Christ's triumph over death with the subsequent Resurrection and Ascension into heaven was evoked during the mass. Whoever chose the image had a perfect knowledge of the canon of the Divine Office and of the image's possibilities during the Easter rites, in which ornaments were covered with dark cloths during Holy Thursday and uncovered on Holy Saturday.

Furthermore, from the point of view of iconography and composition, both Christ's double mandorla (also present in Ix) and the pyramidal composition of the Apostles in Urgell have precedents in the Catalan miniatures of the eleventh century which the master seems to be familiar with, specifically the illuminated page known as the *Crist Mestre* in the Museu Episcopal de Vic (MEV 7822) (1060-1080). It's nevertheless true that in both Urgell and Ix the excessive rigidity of the clothing, which looks very stiff, seems to be a result of adapting old schemes from the Catalan miniature to the monumental format, which was mandatory in the 1120s and 1130s. We must therefore take it that this master was contemporary with the paintings of Sant Climent de Taüll (1123), the portal of Saint-Pierre de Moissac or the portal of Santa Maria de Ripoll (1134-1150). The two altar frontals could therefore perfectly well be placed in the second quarter of the twelfth century, since in the very archivolts of the portal at Santa Maria de Ripoll we find the same ornamental repertory of dogs, birds and flowers as on the left border of the frame of the *Ix Altar Frontal*.

For its part, the Sant Martí d'*Ix Altar Frontal* (Cerdanya) has always been attributed to the Urgell workshop and specifically to the same master as that of La Seu d'Urgell, something which has also been confirmed by technical analyses of the two works, as we saw. Nevertheless, Ix shows certain special iconographic features worth mentioning. First of all, the composition has been multiplied: although Christ in Majesty in a double mandorla is maintained in the centre, the sides of the altar frontal have been divided up into eight squares (four on either side) to house the Apostles in pairs and include two hagiographic scenes relating to the life of the titular saint of the church. Thus on the left Saint Martin of Tours appears with his bishop's crosier '(MAR(TINUS)' in the act of blessing a disciple, while on the right the saint cuts off a piece of his cloak for a beggar (MAR(TINUS)). This is undoubtedly an exaltation of

86. ALTAR FRONTAL FROM MOSOLL.
In the top register, from left to right, Caspar, Balthasar and Melchior, the Virgin with the Child, Saint Joseph and the Visitation. In the bottom register, from left to right, the Annunciation, the Presentation of Christ in the Temple with Joseph, Mary and Simeon and, finally, the Dormition of the Virgin.
First third of the 13th century
Tempera on wood and golden glazed stucco reliefs
From the church of Santa Maria de Mosoll, Das (Baixa Cerdanya)
100 × 168 cm
MNAC/MAC 15788

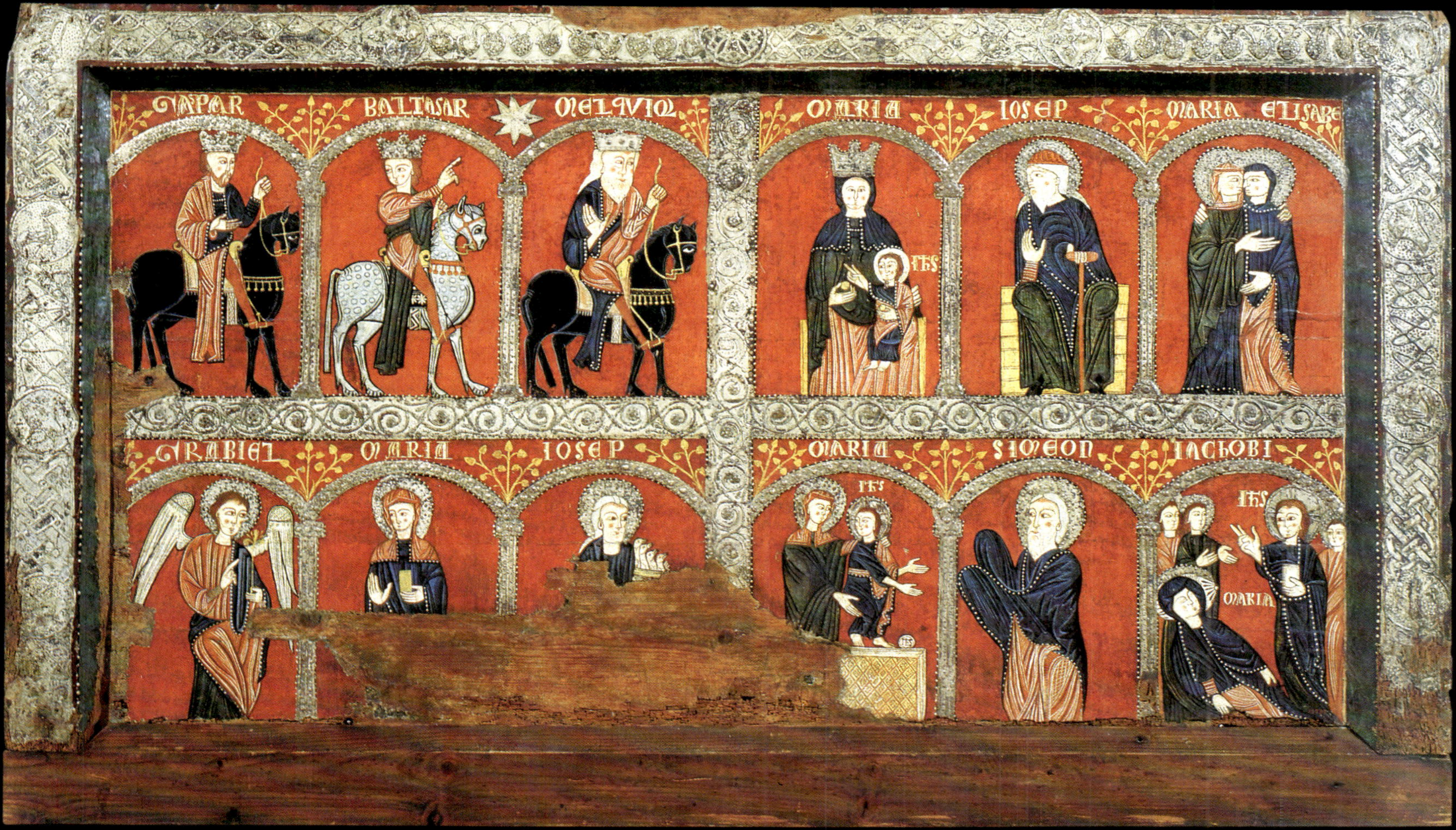

86

the virtues of a saint who had been worshipped in Catalonia since Carolingian times and whose iconography was to be highly successful on altar frontals (Tavèrnoles, Alós d'Isil, Gia). Furthermore, an attractive inscription in Latin referring to Saint Martin runs on either side of the central image ('SOL ET LVX SANCTORVM/MANEO IN PRECLARA ET BONORVM') with lettering like that of *Chrysography*, writing in gold, which looks like the work of a painter and man of letters trained in a monastic or cathedral school. Unfortunately, the text on the left has only been partly preserved due to what seems to be a burn, clearly visible in the oldest photographs of the item. Could this have been a consequence of the violent Cathar uprising instigated by

Arnau, Viscount of Castellbó, and Ramon Roger, Count of Foix, that affected most of the *comarca* of Alt Urgell in the year 1196? According to accounts, during the revolt armed groups under their command entered the churches and destroyed the altar ornaments. Thanks to a report on the damage drawn up between 1241 and 1251, we know that in the case of Ix the assailants profaned the church and took various books and liturgical objects. Perhaps during the looting they tried to set fire to the altar frontal, as the Cathars were especially opposed to this sort of ornament, above all when it was used for worshipping saints. This could well be the reason for the mysterious burn on the panel.

The possible central role of the monastery of Santa Maria de Ripoll in the training of some of these early masters of Catalan panel painting is corroborated by what is known as the *Esquius Panel*, which was probably made in this monastery's workshop in the second quarter of the twelfth century. There are still doubts today as to the work's provenance; the location of Esquius has never been identified but it could be the Castle of Montesquiu, in the north of the *comarca* of Osona. It's function, too, is unclear. The format is smaller than that of the altar frontals from Urgell and this fact, along with the absence of a frame, its lightness and the presence of an inscription in Christ's mandorla intended to be read from below, all suggest that it might, as in Ribes, have come from a ceiling-canopy and was therefore originally placed over the altar.

87. Beam of the Passion.
Between 1196 and 1220
Tempera on wood
20.5 × 233.5 cm
MNAC/MAC 15833

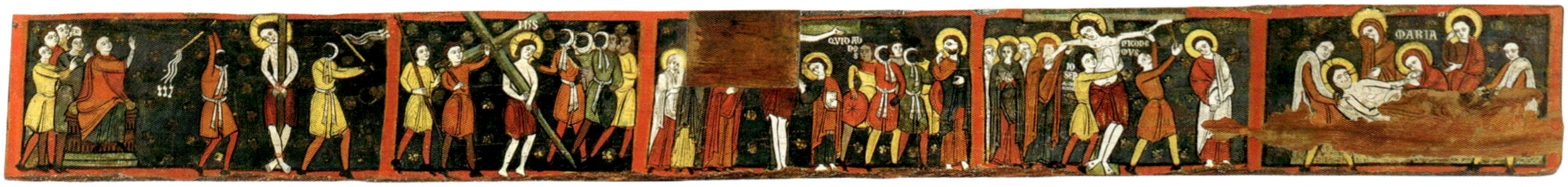

87

From an iconographic point of view, the panel is the oldest example of a Theophanic representation that was to be highly successful in Catalan Romanesque. In it the central area is filled with Christ in Majesty with the Tetramorph, accompanied on either side by the Apostles depicted in two registers (Esterri de Cardós, Farrera de Pallars, Sant Romà de Vila, etc.). In Esquius, as though it were an illuminated work, extremely expensive pigments usually found in miniatures have been used, finely ground and in large quantities: orpiment for the yellow, cinnabar for the red and lapis lazuli for the blue. In addition, the Tetramorph, with the yellow nimbuses, is highly reminiscent of the miniatures at the beginning of the codex of the Epistles of Saint Paul made in the abbey of Ripoll in about 1130. We must bear in mind that in the years following work began on the monumental west façade of the monastery church (1134-1150), which shows many stylistic and iconographic similarities with panel painting in this area. In addition, the background of bands of colour (green, yellow and red) behind the Esquius Apostles seems to repeat formulas from mural painting, specifically the central apses in the churches in Taüll.

In the second half of the twelfth century panel painting began to diversify in its approach, technical resources and subject matter. On one hand, then, as we see in the *Altar Frontal of Saint Quiricus and Saint Julitta of Durro* (Vall de Boí, Alta Ribagorça) the hagiographic cycles begin to be strengthened so that the saint and her son, also a mar-

88. Altar Canopy from Tost.
Central panel of the altar canopy from Sant Martí de Tost.
Maiestas Domini *surrounded by the symbols of the four evangelists.*
Around 1220
Tempera on wood
177 × 175 cm
MNAC/MAC 3905

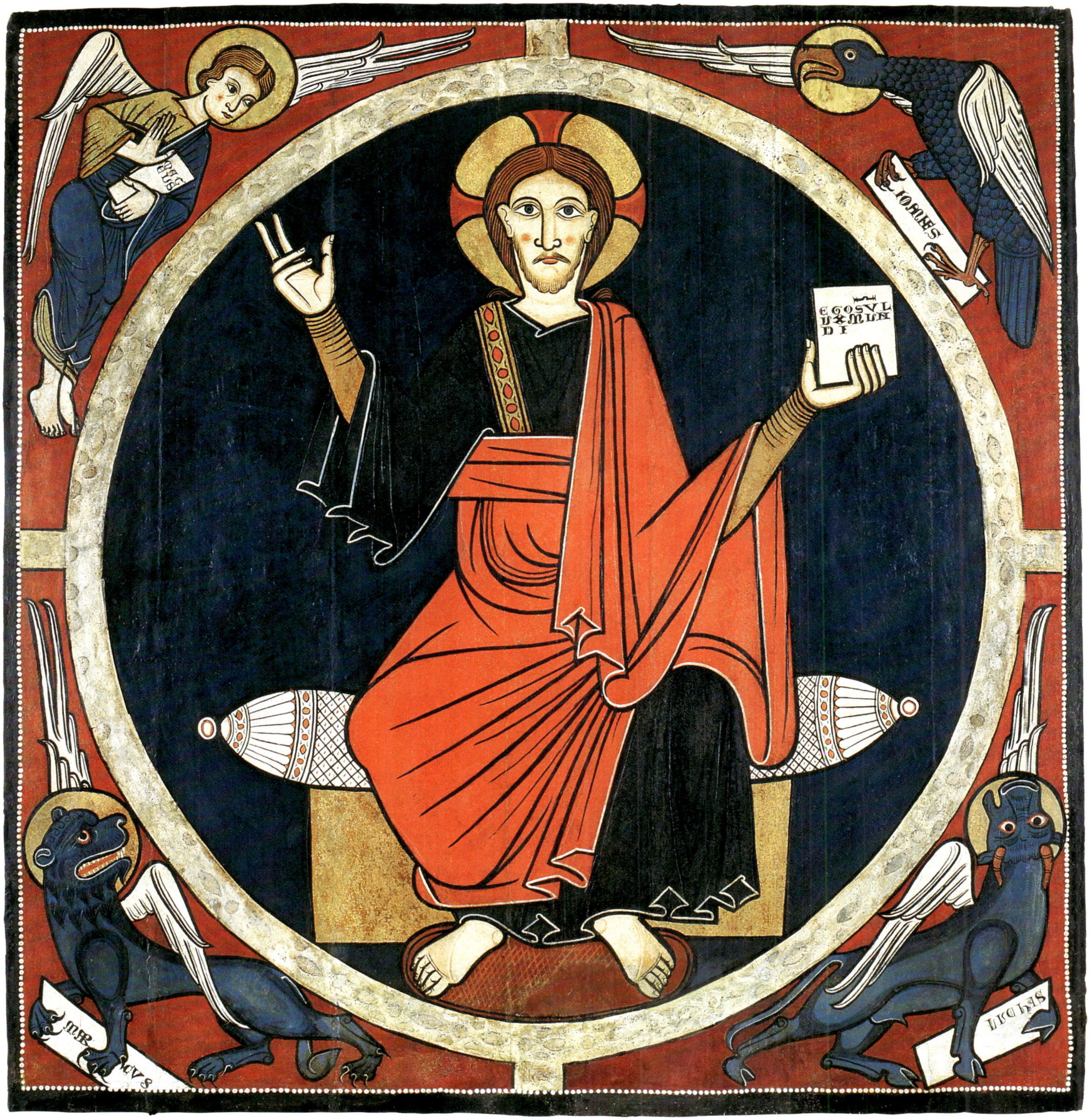

88

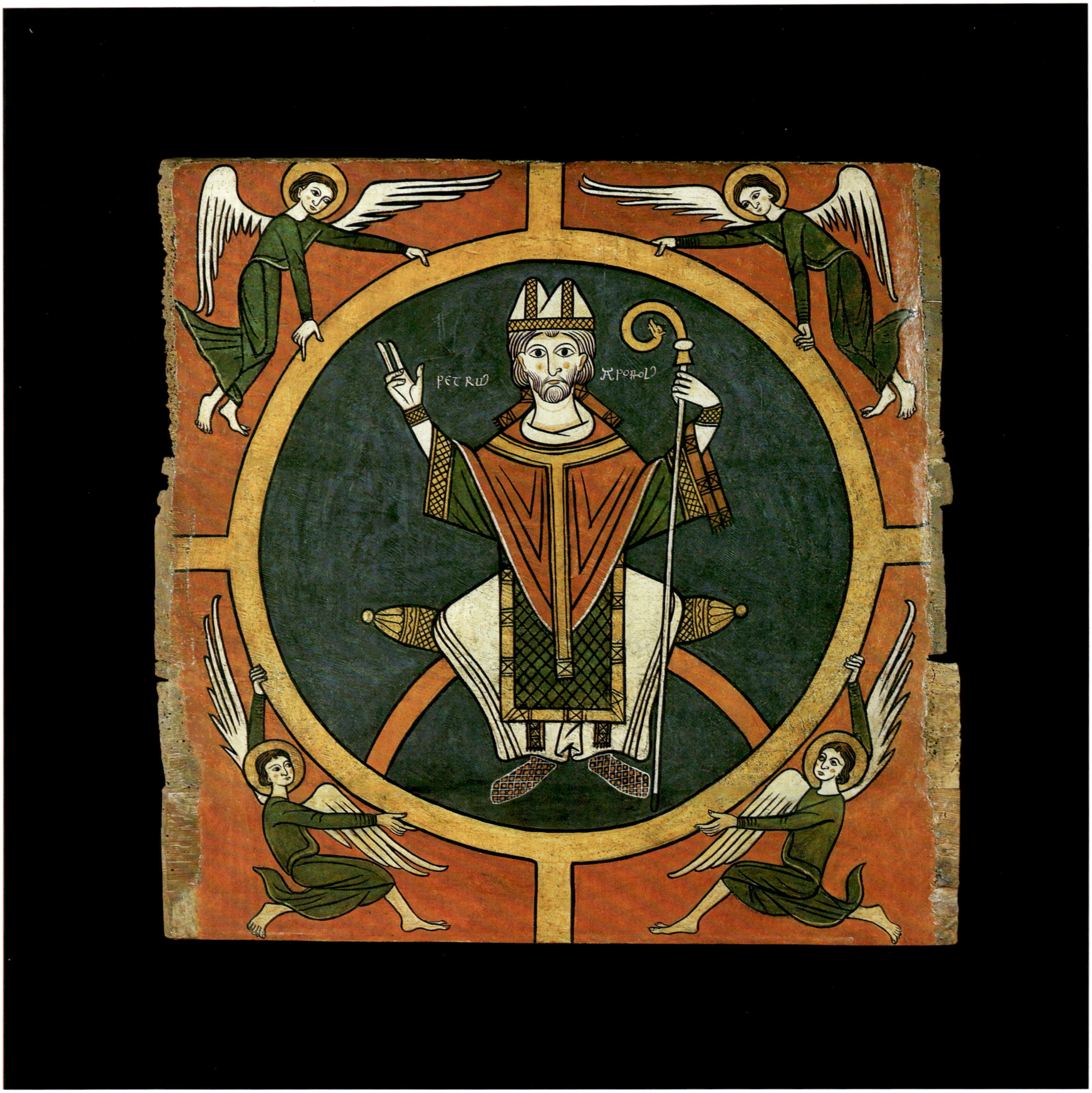

89

89-90. ALTAR PANELS FROM SANT PERE D'ORÓS.
Side (?) panels from the altar of Sant Pere d'Orós depicting Saint Peter and Saint Paul surrounded by angels.
1120-1240
Tempera on wood. 80 × 80 cm
From the church of Sant Pere d'Orós (Pallars Sobirà). MNAC/MAC 3906, 3907

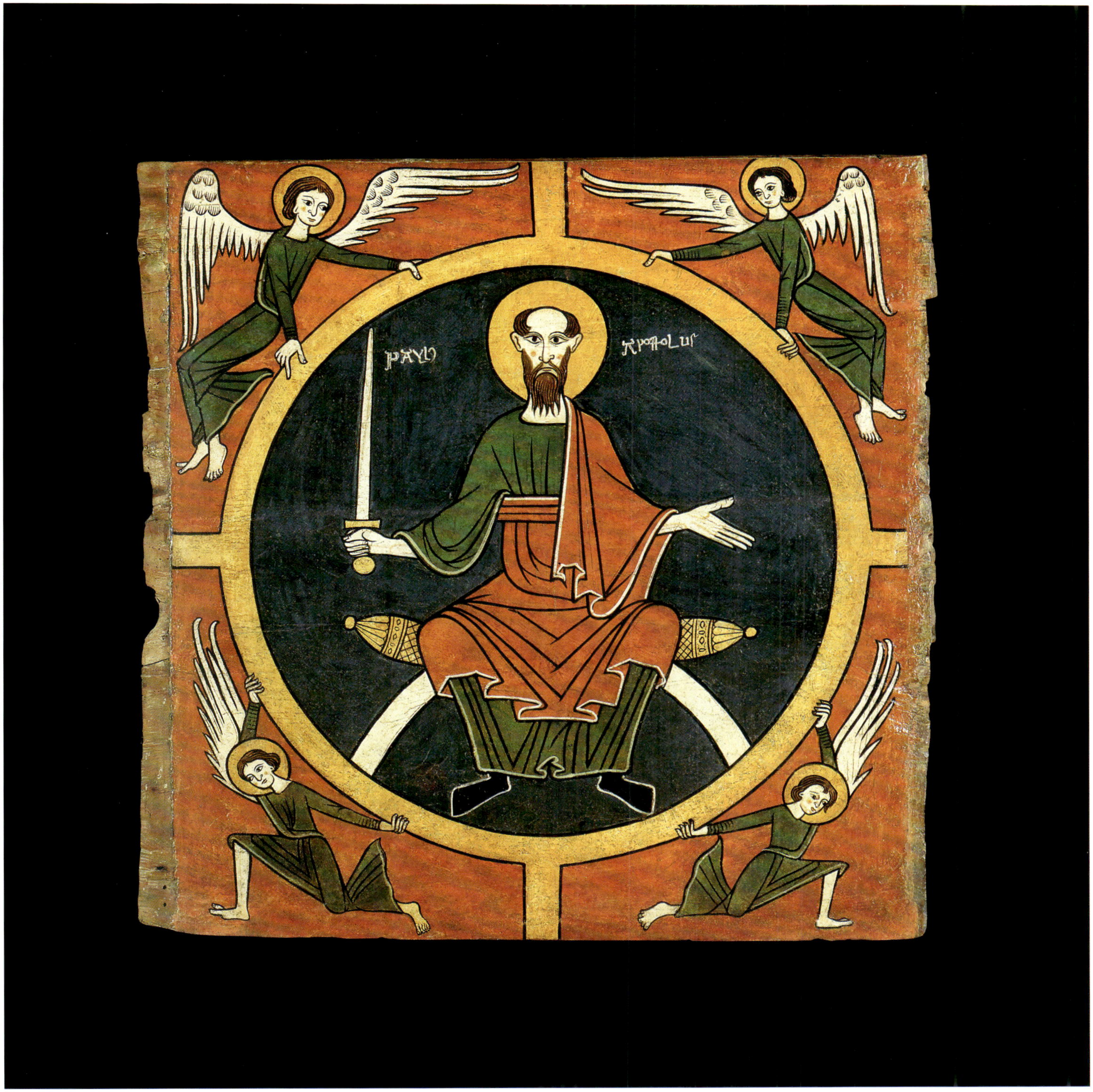

90

tyr, occupy the central mandorla as though this were the Virgin in Majesty in an apse. Four scenes depict the brutal martyrdom of Saint Julitta, whose body is lacerated by swords and nails, before being skinned alive and then boiled with her child in a cauldron. To judge from the use of bright coloured backgrounds and certain highly caricaturish, naïve folk features of the figures, the style seems to derive from that of the workshop of Santa Maria de Taüll, which worked on the walls of the south aisle, the baptistery and the counter-façade of the Last Judgement. The altar frontal could therefore have been done in the mid-twelfth century, there in the Vall de Boí, following the pattern of this workshop. In fact, as M. Guardia points out, the composition of the cruel scene in which the saint is sawn in half by two executioners is modelled on one in the Book of Prophets in the Bible of Rodes (Death of Isaiah, vol. III, f. 2v), whose repertory, remember, was known to the muralists of Sant Joan de Boí.

What's more, very probably during the second half of the twelfth century, an official image circulating in the diocese of La Seu d'Urgell showed bishop saints with crosiers, following the model in the minutes of the Council of Jaca, as A. Orriols points out. In the case of the altar table of the monastery of Sant Serni de Tavèrnoles, the altar frontal is taken up by nine bishop saints presided by the titular saint of the church, Saturninus, evangeliser of Gaul, while the sides are occupied by two more bishop saints, Saint Martin of Tours and his successor in the see, Saint Bricius. Echoes of the presence of this episcopal model in the diocese of Urgell, which is possibly inspired in a lost work from the cathedral, can be found in the altar frontals of Sant Marcel de Planès and Sant Lliser d'Alós d'Isil, where eight bishops appear with their crosiers, though in the latter two of them have been conveniently identified, as in Tavèrnoles, as Saint Martin and Saint Bricius.

Remember that Planès, a church that depended on the monastery of Ripoll but was located in the diocese of Urgell, was a pioneer in the new technique in altar frontals of tin-plated relief figures with gilt varnish. During the first third of the thirteenth century these figures were gradually perfected and became highly successful in the area of the bishopric of Urgell (Esterri de Cardós, Ginestarre, Alós d'Isil). In the case of Alós d'Isil there is an obvious influence from the Byzantine models that arrived via the Mediterranean around the year 1200. The innovative dialogue established by the Virgin Mary in the central mandorla when she points to the child and touches his right knee as he turns towards her brings to mind the Byzantine iconography of the Virgin *DEXIO KRATOUSA*. This image was very widespread in the Komnenian period as a frontispiece for Gospel books representing the Incarnation of the Logos (Kiev Gospel, A 25) and soon became the icon of the Incarnation (*Mater tou logou*). It can be seen in the icon in the early-thirteenth-century church of Panagia Theoskepasti in Paphos (Cyprus), where the nimbus furthermore is decorated with an ornamented stucco relief, which was to be common in Catalan altar frontals after 1200.

A new period then began in Catalonia with a marked Byzantine imprint, whose models have been amply discussed. Some authors, such as Rosa Alcoy, defend an intermediate transmission of these models via the Anglo-Norman miniature, especially for the altar frontal of Santa Maria d'Avià, where the influence of models derived from the Bury St. Edmunds Bible, the Winchester Psalter or Eadwine's Psalter seems obvious. Others prefer to leave the way open for a direct contribution by the Eastern Mediterranean to the

91. Toses and Sant Romà de Vila.
Altar canopy from Sant Cristòfol in Toses (Ripollès). On the spandrels, the prophets Daniel and Jeremiah and, on the frame, clypeus with imaginary animals.
First third of 13th century
Tempera on wood
488 × 238 × 216 cm
MNAC/MAC 4523-4525
The altar canopy covers the altar table of Sant Romà de Vila (Encamp, Andorra).
First half of the 13th century
Tempera on wood, with plaster reliefs
113 × 125 × 91 cm
MNAC/MAC 15875

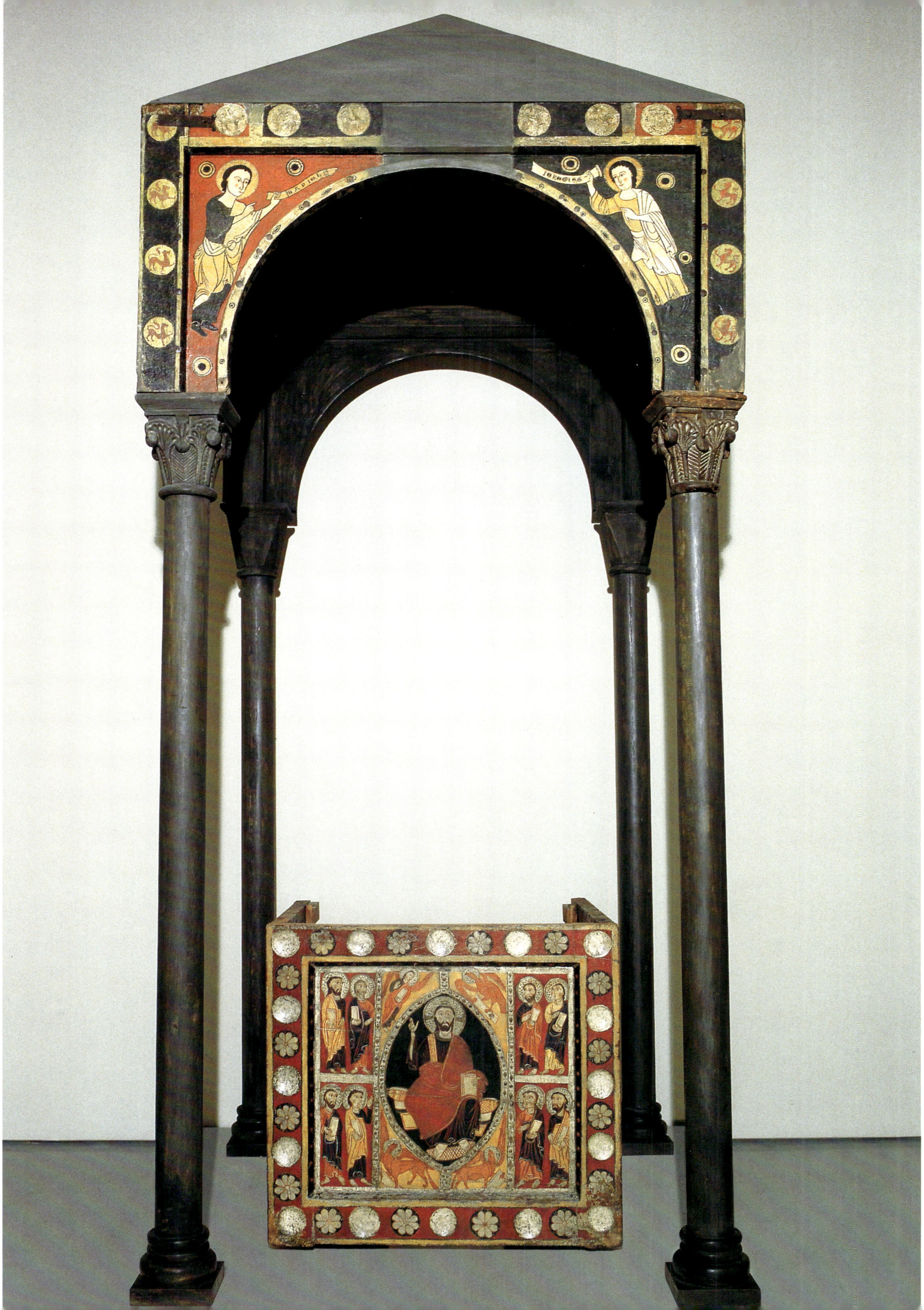

West coinciding with the fall of Jerusalem at the hands of Saladin in 1187 and the capture of Constantinople by the Crusaders in 1204.

In the case of Avià, certain losses and abusive restorations have profoundly changed its original appearance. The central image of the seated Virgin and Child in the centre of the panel is set against a gilt-varnished background brought to life with plant motifs, possibly imitating the look of the silver-plating in twelfth-century Byzantine icons, like the famous Virgin of Vladimir, which artists in Cyprus had imitated at the beginning of the thirteenth century with the *pastiglia* technique. Similarly, certain iconographic details in Avià, like the representation of Mary as the *Hodegetria*, with two angels at the top, is reminiscent of the Marian representations of the Cypriot church of Lagoudera (1192). In addition, in these Cypriot frescoes, painted by Byzantine artists after the establishment on the island of the Frankish Lusignan dynasty, we find the same iridescent colours that appear in the altar frontal of Sant Andreu de Baltarga (Baixa Cerdanya). This magnificent work, which doesn't seem to be by a local artist, shows a series of typically Byzantine features. The fine, elongated, translucent faces of the central Christ and of the Virgin and the Apostles on the lateral registers point directly to formulas in Konmenian painting (Santa Maria delle Cerrate, Apulia, Italia). Even the variety of types of faces on the Apostles brings to mind Byzantine sketchbooks of the time (Oxford, Magdalen College, ms. gr. 3). Finally, the lock of hair on Christ's left is a direct reference to the face on the Holy Tile (*Keramion*), or the imprint on the Veronica of Christ, whose cult then passed from Byzantium to the West. The panel also includes a scene of the martyrdom of the titular saint of the church, Andrew, before the proconsul Aegeas.

In dating Avià and Baltarga and all the group most directly related with these panels (the *Orellà Altar Frontal* and the one from Sant Genís les Fonts, now destroyed, signed by one *Magister Alexander*), we have to consider a moment no earlier than 1200. In fact, the church in Baltarga was looted in 1196 by troops under the Viscount of Castellbó and the Count of Foix at the height of the Albigensian revolt, so the manufacture of a new altar ornament would coincide with the policy undertaken by the bishopric of Urgell in the first third of the thirteenth century of redecorating rural churches that had been burned.

In this same context (the affirmation of the dogma of the Eucharist with respect to the elevation of the host during consecration and to the real presence of the blood of Christ, something the Cathars denied) a series of iconographic altar programmes were elaborated to illustrate the Incarnation. This is the case of the altar frontal of Santa Maria de Mosoll (Cerdanya), where there is a cycle of Christ's Childhood and the Life of Mary against a red background that alludes to the blood of the sacrifice. This idea of the physical presence of Christ in the Eucharist is made even more explicit in the scene of the Presentation at the Temple, in which the Child Jesus is lifted onto the altar next to the representation of a host, metaphorically following the precepts of the Fourth Lateran Council, which recommended raising the host during the mass (1215). In the second half of the twelfth century there was also an extensive series of writings with the miracle of the apparition of the Child Jesus during the Eucharistic celebration, which can be connected with the original lifting of Christ the child onto the altar in the Temple beside a host. This assertion of the dogma is repeated in another of the churches profaned in 1196 during the Albigensian revolt, Santa Maria de Mosoll. Finally, remember that the *Avià Altar Frontal*,

92. DETAIL OF A COMPARTMENT OF THE ALTAR FRONTAL OF THE ARCHANGELS.
The archangels Raphael and Gabriel carry the soul of a dead man to heaven. Scene from the Altar Frontal of the Archangels

94. DETAIL OF A COMPARTMENT OF THE ALTAR FRONTAL OF THE ARCHANGELS.
Detail of the devil in the psychostasis on the Altar Frontal of the Archangels

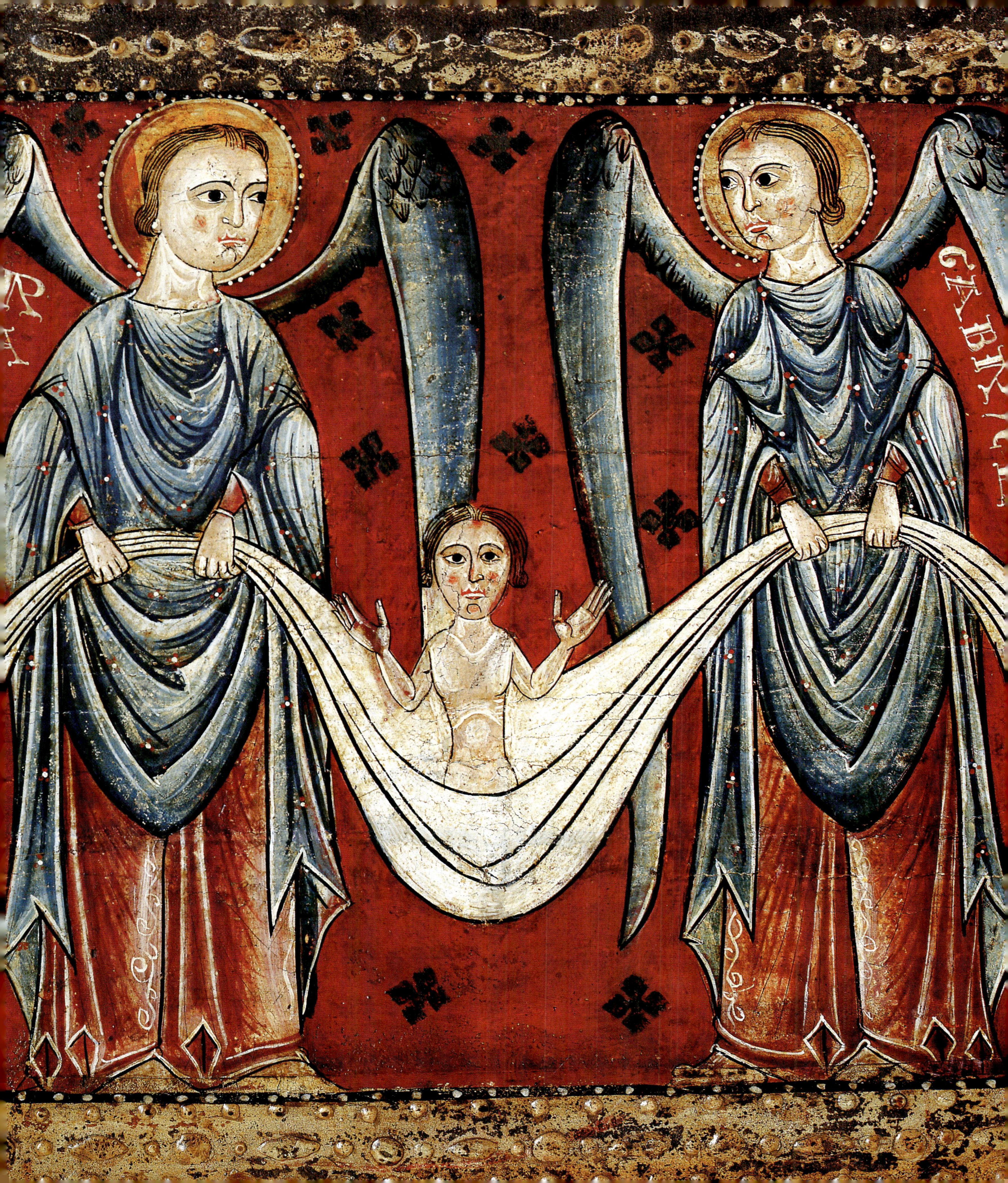

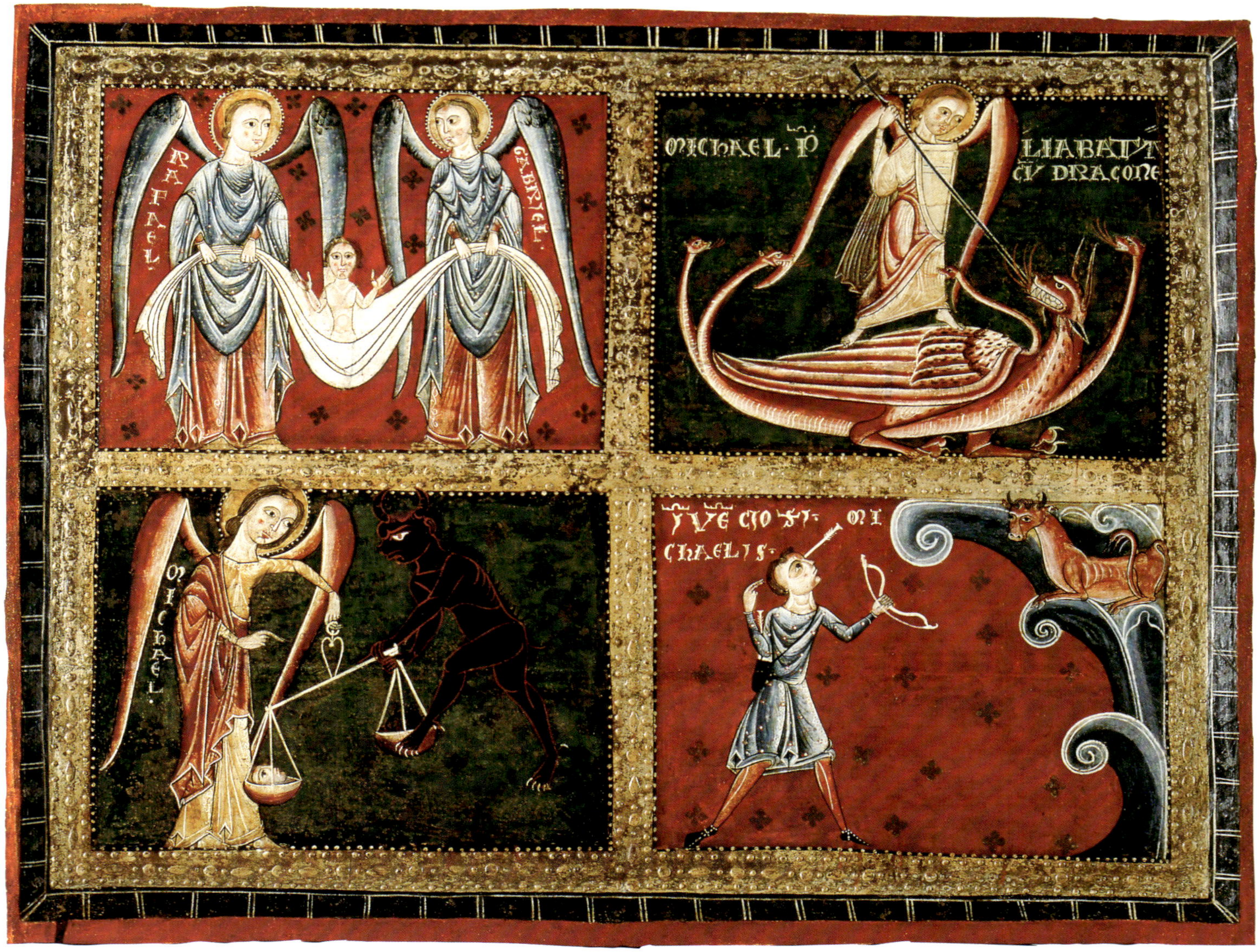

93 94

which is also dedicated to the Incarnation, resorted to red using an original formula consisting in painting the hand of the Child Jesus red. We mustn't forget, though, that all of this also has a definite background in folk tradition: at Christmas, in Catalan churches, red candles were given out which were known as candles of the Magi and which symbolised the Incarnation.

Other items in the collection speak for the long, eventful journey of art in thirteenth-century Catalonia, revealing the full wealth of types of liturgical furnishings in Catalonia. The *Beam of the Passion*, as it's called, attributed to the chief miniaturist of the *Liber Feudorum Maior* (1196-1220), shows a familiarity with the English miniature of the second half of the twelfth century. The content is organised in six scenes—the Flagellation, the Road to Calvary, the Crucifixion, the Descent from the Cross, the Deposition in the Tomb and the *Visitatio Sepulchri*—and includes the curious figures of executioners with Negroid features and turbans, as though they were Muslims. It's quite possible the work was originally part of a ceiling-canopy type of structure, or else it was simply a beam at the entrance to the altar, like the *epistyles* of the Byzantine *temploi*, which were also decorated with scenes of liturgical feasts.

93. Altar frontal of the Archangels.
In the top left-hand compartment, archangels Raphael and Gabriel carry the soul of a dead man to heaven.
In the top right-hand compartment, Saint Michael fights the dragon.
In the bottom left-hand compartment, the psychostasis, Saint Michael weighing the souls. In the bottom right-hand compartment, the miracle of Mount Gargano.
Between 1220 and 1250
Tempera on wood, with plaster reliefs with golden glaze
106 × 127 cm
MNAC/MAC 3913

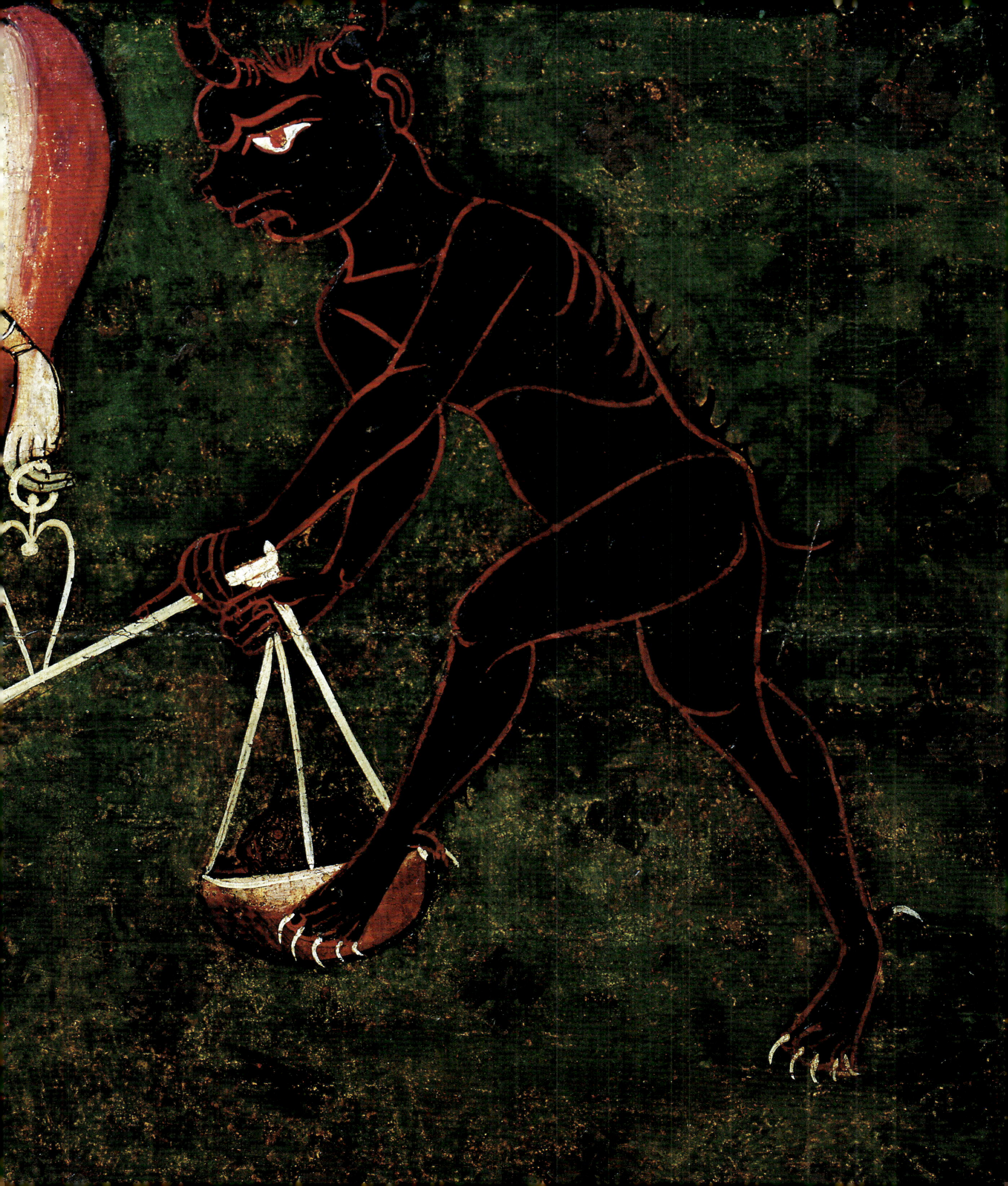

The canopies of Sant Martí de Tost (*c.* 1220) and Sant Serni de Tavèrnoles (mid-thirteenth century) are possibly the most spectacular examples of the distinctive Catalan ceiling-canopy: an aerial structure located over the altar in an apse, half-way between a tabernacle and a wooden ceiling. Its purpose was to underline the presence and the sacred nature of the altar table, like a triumphant, Theophanic iconographic programme, with subjects like the Second Coming (Tost) or the Ascension into heaven (Tavèrnoles). In the case of Tost, while the quality of the firm drawing and the delicate choice of colours ties in with the models from 1200 art that reached the Crown of Aragon via Sigena, the iconographic repertory shows a particular familiarity with the Bestiaries of the time, an echo of which could be glimpsed in Sigena. Thus the way in which the Lion, the symbol of Saint Mark, is represented on the panel, and the medallions with scenes of Psychomachy on the front beam, kept at the Museu Episcopal de Vic, are not unlike the repertories of the English bestiaries of 1200, which are also apparent in the decoration of the Cardet Beam. The spread of these models in the diocese of Urgell is more than obvious. There are medallions with fantastic animals on the *Toses altar Canopy* (Ripollès), which bring to mind the ones on the front beam of Tost or the panels from Sant Pere d'Orós (Pallars Sobirà), whose representations of Saint Peter and Saint Paul *in cathedra*, enclosed in a mandorla and supported by angels, are half-way between the style of Tost and that of the *Tavèrnoles altar Canopy*.

Finally, two thirteenth-century works illustrate the creative force with which panel painting took root in the Catalan artistic tradition and how painted panels served increasingly to express devotion to local cults: the *Altar Frontal of the Archangels* and the *Altar Frontal of Sant Martí de Gia*. The first, although its provenance is not known to us, must be related to a chapel dedicated to Saint Michael, as it depicts a cycle of four scenes. The first scene, at the bottom right, contains the miracle of Monte Gargano, the origin of the cult of Saint Michael, while the rest illustrate the Archangel's powers and functions: fighting and overcoming the Dragon, a symbol of Evil, with his spear, weighing the souls (Psychostasis) and finally, his *psychopomp* companions, Gabriel and Raphael, transporting the souls to heaven. From the point of view of style, this item shares with the paintings of Sant Pau de Casserres (Berguedà) the sweeter, more delicate version in the Lluçà cycle, for which reason Rosa Alcoy places it between 1225 and 1250.

As for the *Altar Frontal of Sant Martí de Gia* (Alta Ribagorça), executed in the second half of the thirteenth century, along with examples like the ones from Santa Maria de Rigatell and Sant Pere de Boí, this piece illustrates the survival in the *comarca* of Ribagorça of the technique of tin-plated plaster reliefs with gilt varnish, with a more than obvious presence of Gothic formulas. In it, an enthroned Saint Martin presides the central compartment while the lateral scenes narrate the best-known episodes from his life and miracles: the sharing of his cape with the poor man, the Saint Martin's Mass with the miracle of the sleeves, the resurrection of the two young girls and the apparition to the saint of the Madonna and Child and finally the last moment of his life when, on his death bed, he rejects the Devil's approaches. At the inside bottom of the frame can be read the signature 'IOH(ANNE)S PINTOR ME FECIT' (John the painter made me), thereby beginning the new Gothic age of panel painters, with names and biographies.

95. ALTAR FRONTAL FROM GIA.
*In the centre, Saint Martin as a bishop.
In the top left-hand compartment,
Saint Martin cutting his cape in two to give
it to the poor man. In the top right-hand
compartment, Saint Martin's Mass.
In the bottom left-hand compartment,
the miracle of the resurrection of the two
ladies and the figure of the Virgin of the Milk.
In the bottom right-hand compartment,
Saint Martin repudiates the Devil on his
deathbed. Second half of the 13th century
Tempera on wood. From the church
of Sant Martí de Gia (Huesca)
99 × 145 cm
MNAC/MAC 3902*

95

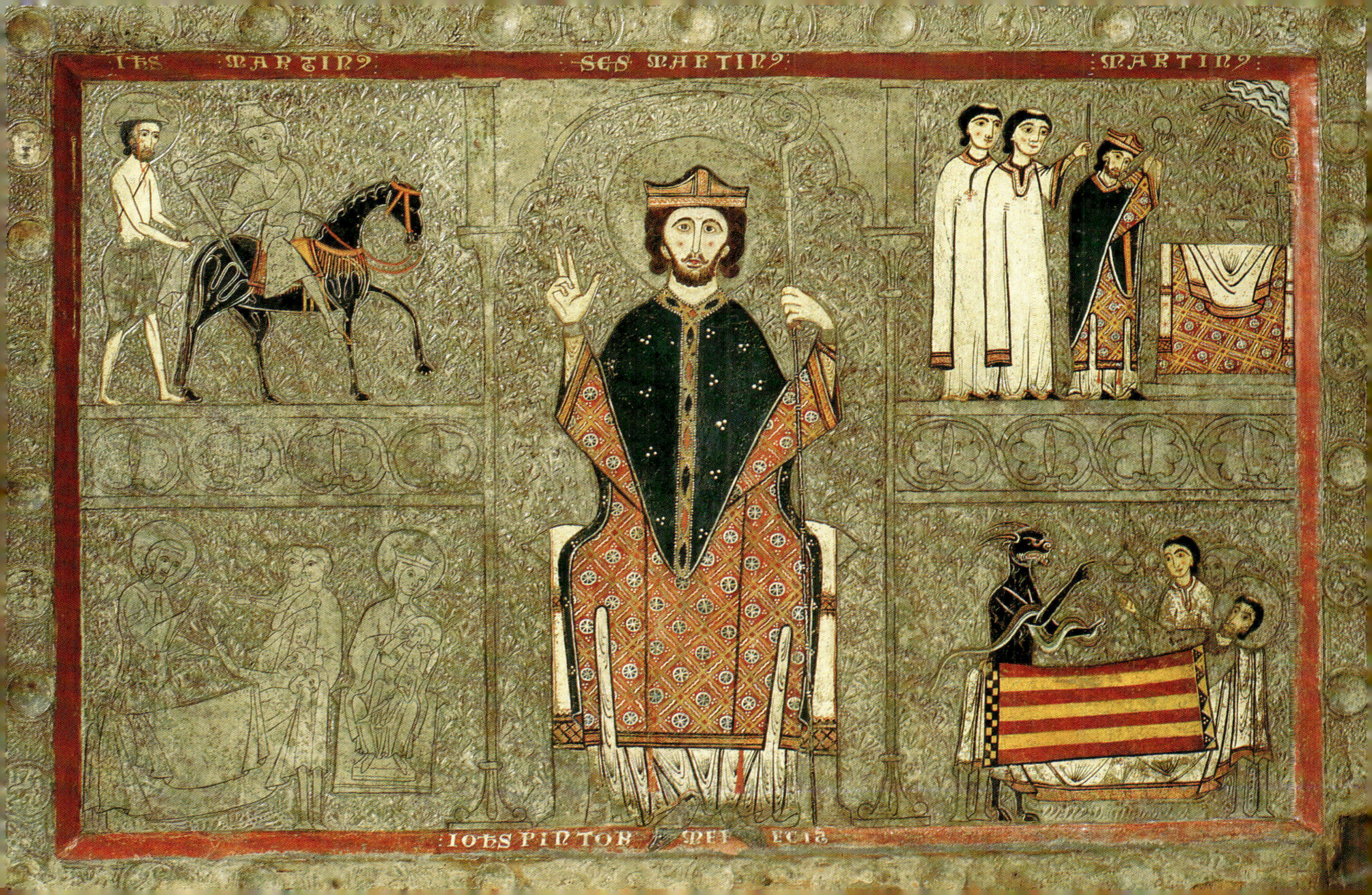
IHS MARTIN9
SCS MARTIN9
MARTIN9
IOHS PINTOR ME F ECIT

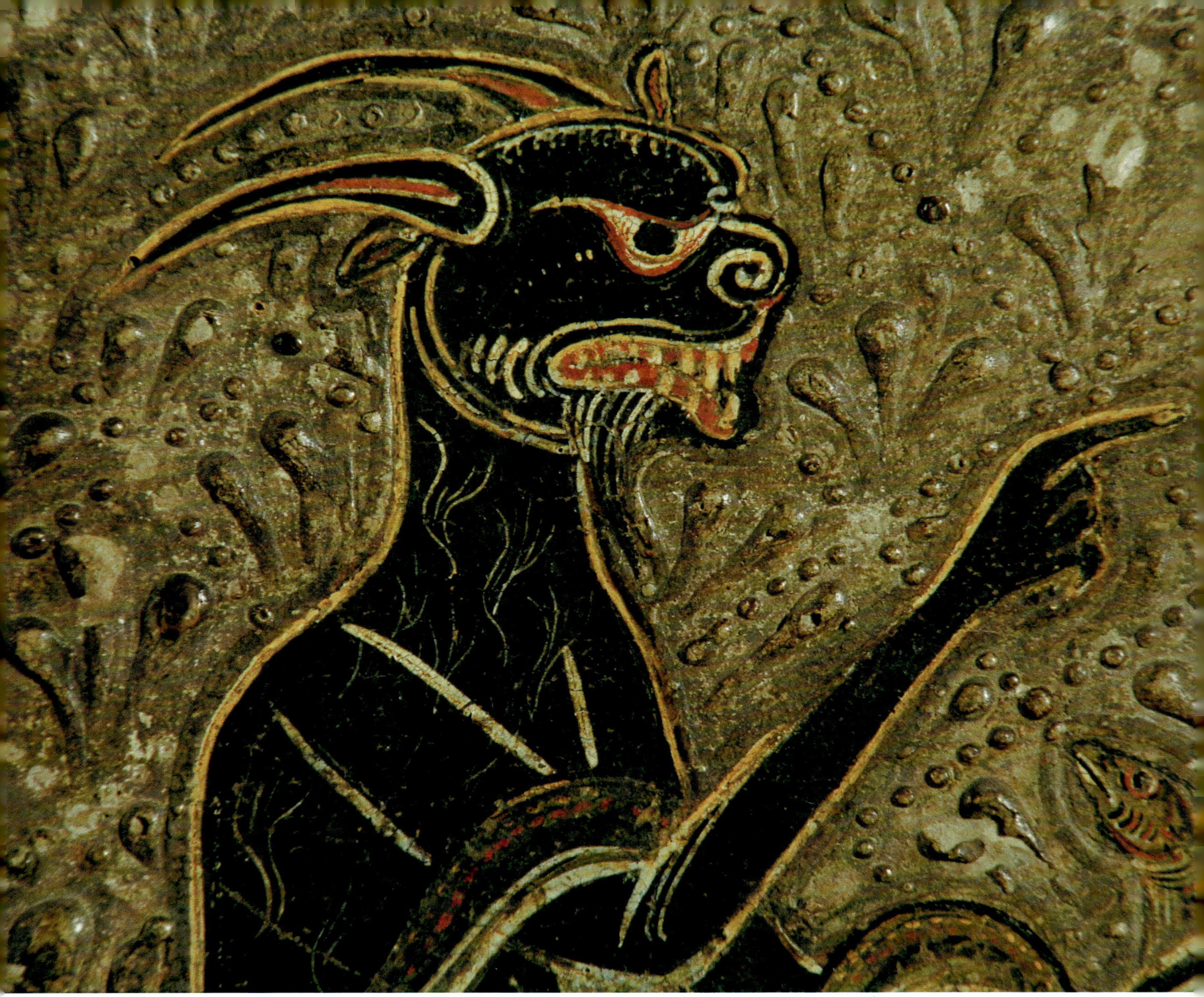

96

97

96. DETAIL OF THE ALTAR FRONTAL OF GIA.
Detail of the Devil from the scene of the death of Saint Martin on the altar frontal from Sant Martí de Gia.

97. ALTAR FRONTAL FROM RIGATELL.
In the centre, the Virgin of the Milk;
in the top compartment, the Annunciation,
and in the one on the right, the Nativity.
In the bottom compartment, the Epiphany and
the Announcement to the Shepherds.
Second half of the 13th century
Tempera on wood with plaster reliefs
104.6 × 112 cm
From the Virgin of Rigatell sanctuary (Alta Ribagorça)
MNAC/MAC/MAC 35701

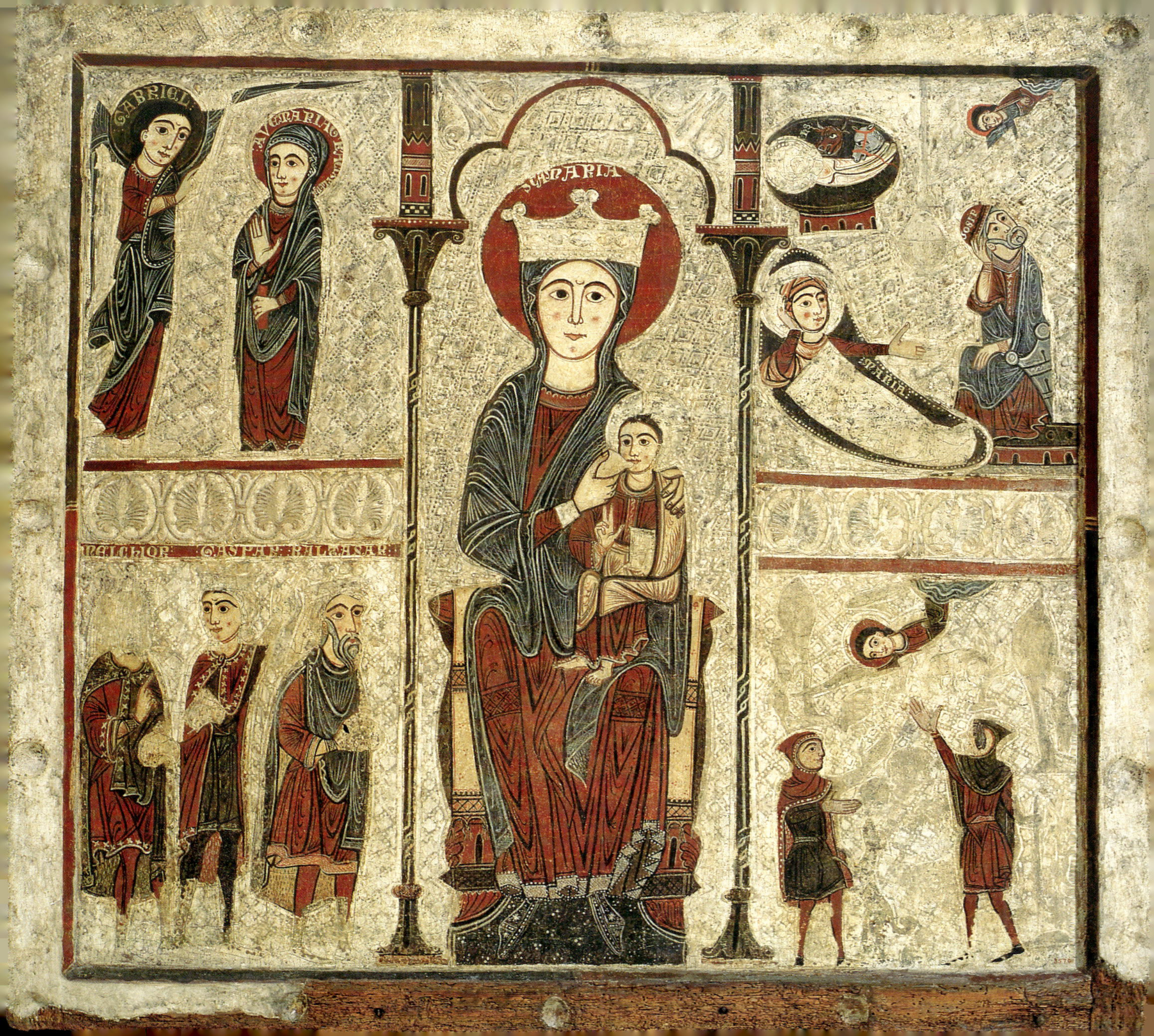

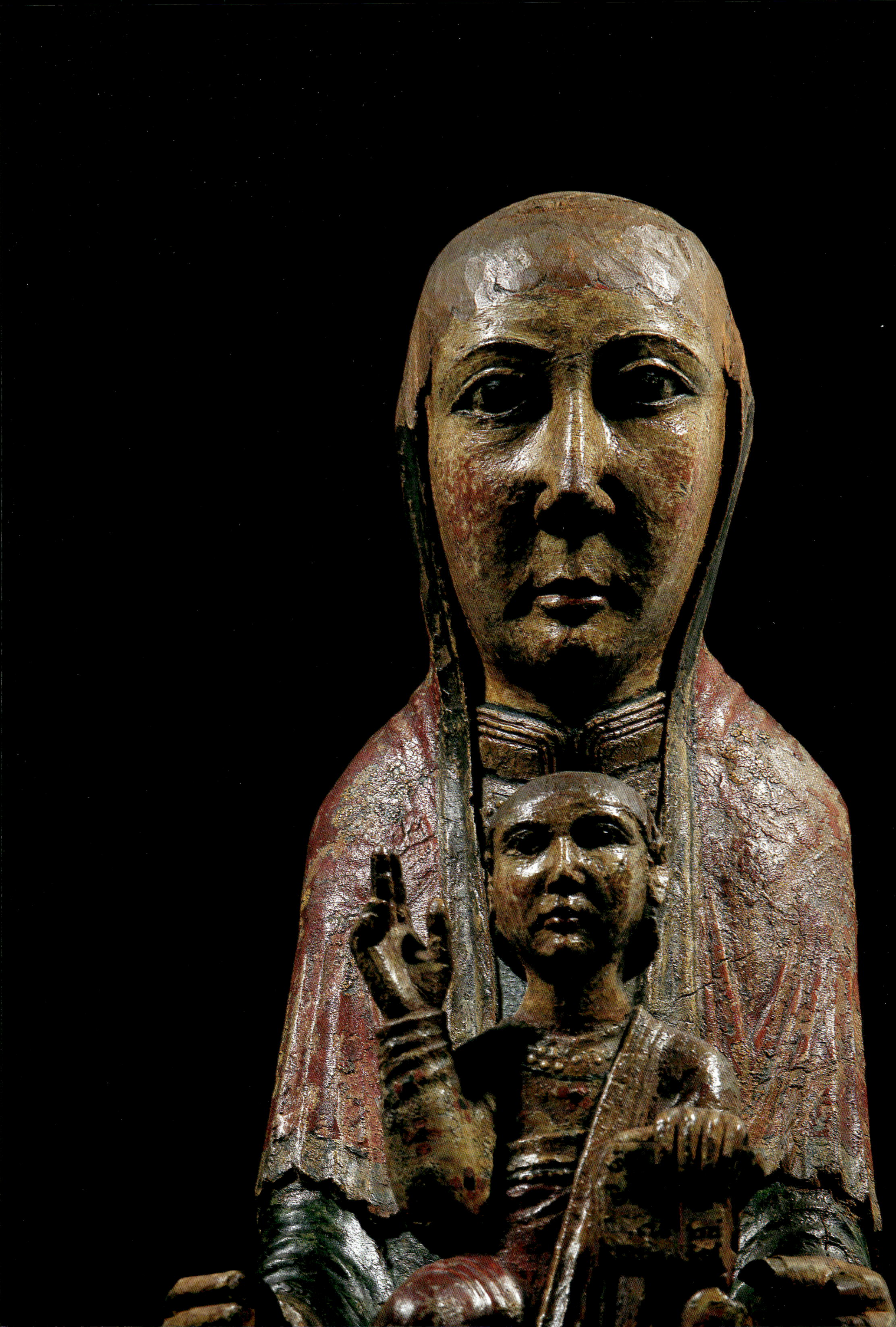

Wood Carving

Jordi Camps

The MNAC's collection of polychrome wood carvings shows a remarkable range of types and includes a series of masterpieces in the history of the Romanesque. The work gathered to date is largely the result of efforts by Catalan and Barcelona institutions with a feeling for the artistic and cultural heritage, who from the end of the nineteenth century took an interest in this kind of work.

The collection and its history

Over and above the traditional interest in religious images as objects of veneration, appreciation for wood carvings was aroused at the end of the nineteenth century, both from the scientific point of view and in the art market. From that moment, alongside the publication of the first scientific studies by Jean-Auguste Brutails on the Roussillon and by Gudiol i Cunill with his *Nocions d'Arqueologia Sagrada Catalana*, first published in 1902, the first works of this type arrived at the Museum. It's a revealing fact that at the Universal Exhibition of 1888 a Crucifix belonging to the Museu Episcopal de Vic, specifically the one from Les Planes d'Hostoles, should have been compared with objects kept in churches, like those in Caldes de Montbui or Beget. Today the situation is almost the other way round, as more of these objects are kept in museums and private collections than in their original buildings.

Although some images, like the Christ of Sant Cugat del Vallès, already formed part of the old collections in the museums that were the basis for today's MNAC, the first important acquisitions took place during the first decade of the twentieth century, as a result of expeditions and negotiations in the Pyrenees. This is the case of the *1147 Christ* and the *Organyà Majesty* in 1906 and of the *Tragó de Noguera Calvary* in 1912. In 1914 the *Batlló Majesty* was donated to the Barcelona Provincial Corporation, since which time it has become one of the highlights of the Museum's Romanesque section. Other works are the result of the acquisition of private collections. With the purchase of the Plandiura collection in 1932, a large number of carvings entered the Museum, amongst them two from the Erill la Vall Descent (the remaining five had been in Vic since 1911) and the four figures from the Santa Maria de Taüll Descent. Later, the Espona bequest in 1958 meant a significant new influx of works, including a new masterpiece for the collection, the *Virgin from Ger*. Since then the collection has been gradually enriched with other statues that have entered the Museum on permanent loan, such as the *Christ from Cubells*, in 1985, or the *Virgin of Sant Joan Despí*, in 2003.

The collection of polychrome wood carvings exhibited at the MNAC is therefore a faithful reflection of the importance and the quality of twelfth-century and thirteenth-century wood carving in Catalonia, as well as a cross-section of the different types and styles. Classifying and dating these works has been a challenging task for art historians as direct references to the images and altar furnishings are few and far between and items can very rarely be dated exactly. Furthermore, a large number of the surviving works have reached us outside their original context and much transformed as a result of successive adaptations and restorations at different times or simply due to wear and tear. So far, they have been attributed to hypothetical workshops and

98. Detail of the Virgin of Ger.
Second half of the 12th century.
Woodcarving polychromed in tempera
52.5 × 20.5 × 14.5 cm
From the church of Santa Coloma de Ger
(Baixa Cerdanya)
MNAC/MAC 65503

dated on the basis of their geographical distribution and of an analysis of the historical links between production centres and of stylistic and iconographic comparison, the same as in the production of painting on wood (altar frontals, baldachin panels, etc.). Thus it seems very likely that there were workshops in large monasteries and cathedrals, like Ripoll, Vic, Girona and La Seu d'Urgell, amongst others. Studies of techniques and materials being carried out at the MNAC on some of these simply painted or carved pieces provide further evidence for the existence of these workshops, as described earlier.

The technique and its applications

The uses of polychrome wood carvings extend to a variety of types and images around the altar as well as to church seating. As far as the images are concerned, broadly speaking these fall into the three usual types in Romanesque in general, with particularities we shall deal with in due course. The most common are the Madonna and Child, the Crucifixes, with the variant known as the Calvary, and the group scenes of the Descent from the Cross, without forgetting certain examples of Christ in Majesty (or Saviour) and figures of saints. As regards the elements applied to the altar, there are several examples of frontals, while small altarpieces also begin to appear, in the form of small constructions or as a forerunner of what would later be the predella. In addition, we mustn't forget that some canopies also had carved elements. Finally, seating has also survived, in the form of both benches and chairs.

The work of carving needs to be understood from the moment the pieces of wood it will be made from are acquired to the completion of its polychrome decoration. In Catalonia, the most commonly used types of wood include poplar, walnut, pine and several species of fruit tree, as we can deduce from the analyses being done on minute samples taken from the images. For the MNAC's *Batlló Majesty*, for example, walnut, willow, elm and oak wood were used for the different parts of the crucifix, including the cross. Generally speaking, the basic core of the image was made from a single piece, though in the crucifixes the head, some of the limbs and other complementary elements were sometimes carved from other pieces. In the case of the Virgins, the Child was almost always made from a separate block. There are even cases of images in which, on account of their size, two or more pieces have been used just for the actual body, as in the carving of *Mary from the Durro Descent (MNAC)*. The different pieces were fitted together using wooden dowels, which can often still be seen under the polychromy. One or two preliminary layers of plaster preceded the application of colour, which sometimes involved overlaying different colours to achieve a range of effects, showing a clear knowledge of the treatises on techniques of the time. This knowledge can also be observed in use of imported pigments (cinnabar for the red, lapis lazuli for the blue, etc.) alongside others the workshops could obtain locally. Apart from the use of colour, remember that, like the altar furnishings, some parts were given relief decoration, worked in plaster coated with metals, as we can see in the seat of the *Virgin from Ger* (MNAC) or the crowns of some images. We mustn't forget that some items were

99. Virgin.
13th century
Woodcarving polychromed in tempera
54 × 16 × 17.5 cm
Provenance unknown
MNAC/MAC 3921

100. Virgin of Covet
Second half of the 12th century
Woodcarving polychromed in tempera
83 × 31 × 24 cm
From the church of Santa Maria de Covet (Pallars Jussà)
MNAC/MAC 4395

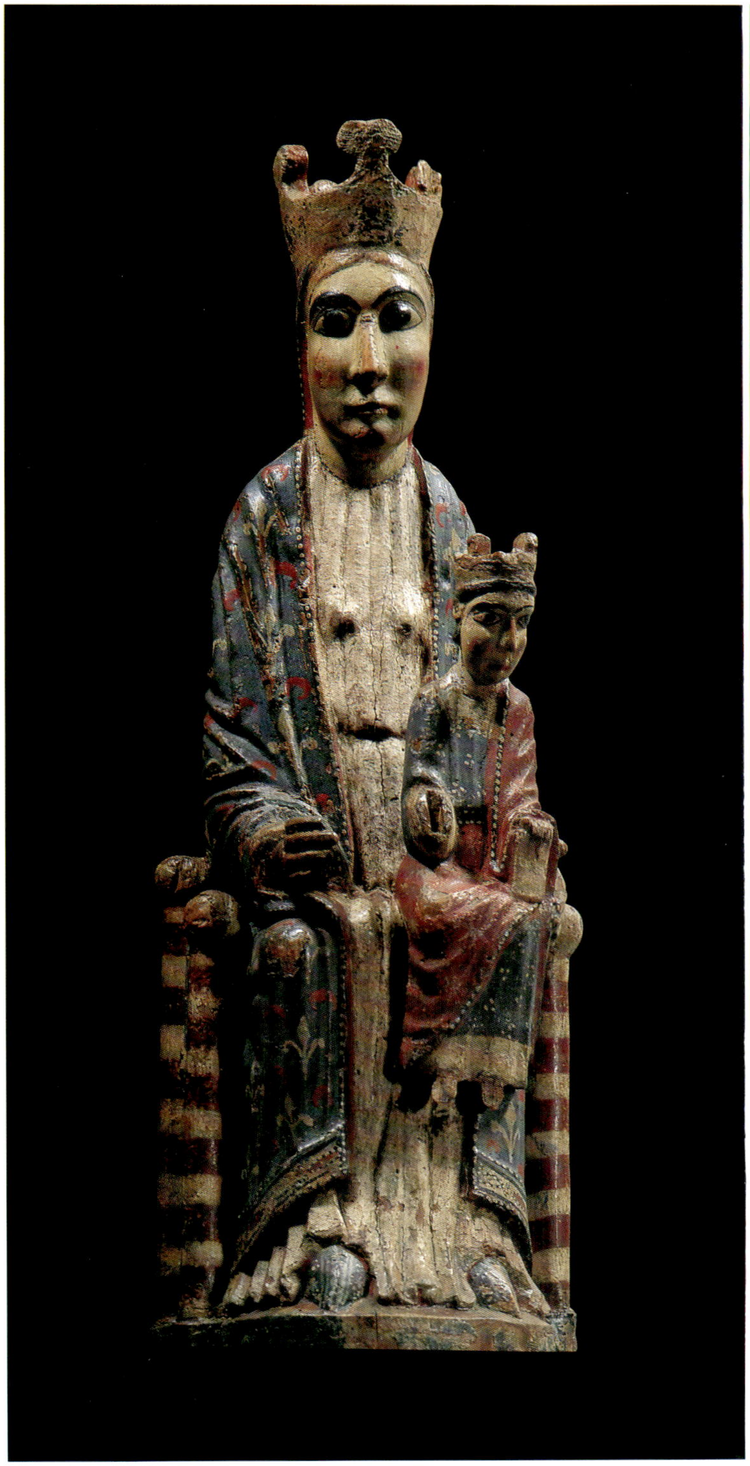

99

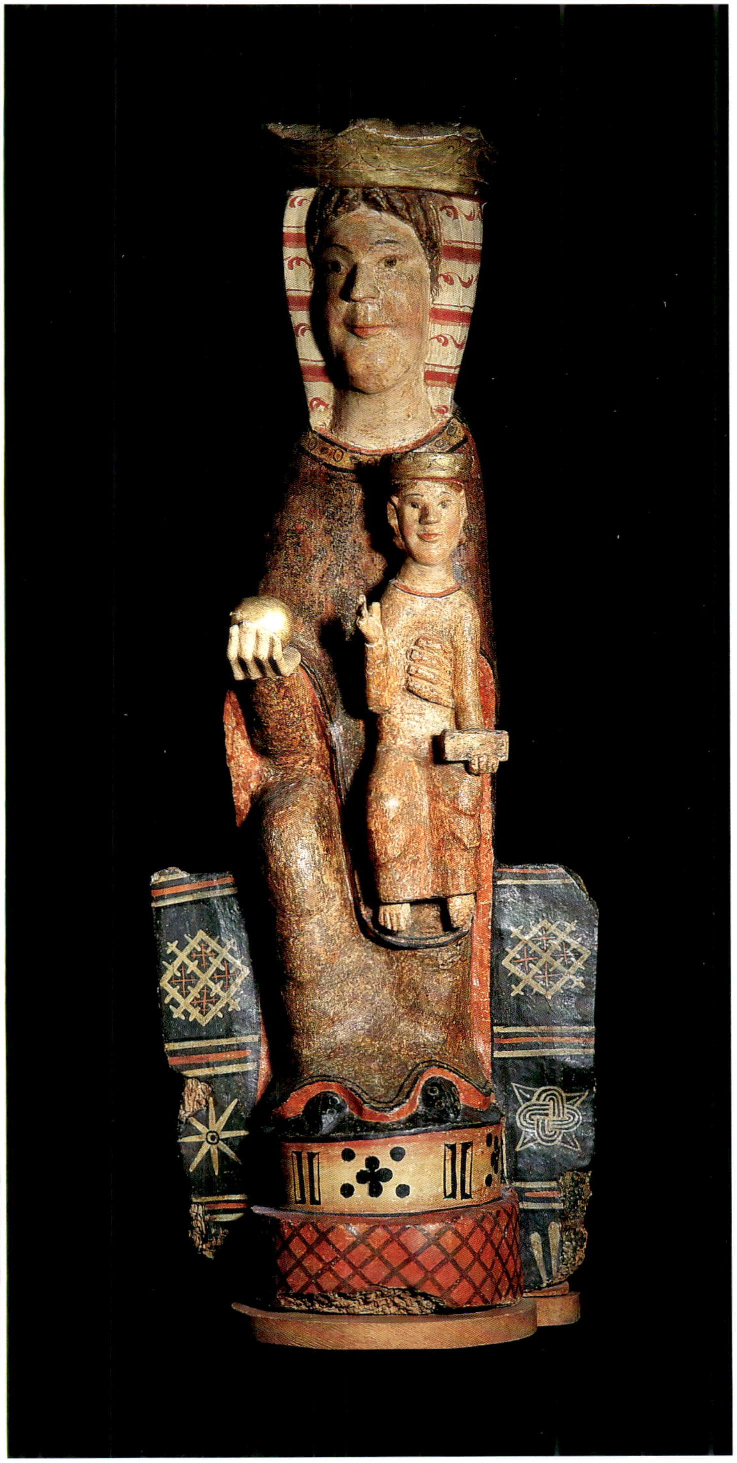

100

completely coated in precious metal, as in the case of the silver-plated Virgin in Girona cathedral and the ones in Tuir and Plandogau, which are lead-plated or tin-plated.

However, in the course of their long history these wooden carvings have had alterations made to them, been reworked and seen successive repainting, so that very often their original appearance has changed significantly.

Images of the Madonna

Images of the Madonna and Child, sometimes known as *marededéus* in Catalan (Mothers of God), make up a great variety of styles and iconographies, especially bearing in mind the number of specimens that have survived. In general, they are groups characterised by their basically frontal composition. Mary is seated on a throne, or on a simpler seat, looking towards the observer with a hieratic pose, while the Child is on Mary's lap, often in the centre, sometimes to one side, also looking forward, making the gesture of blessing with his right hand and holding a book in his left. The clothing varies according to the group and the period, between the presence of the veil in the case of Mary and various forms of mantle and the tunic in both figures. In this composition marked by its frontality and by the absence of any gestural connection between the two characters, Mary appears as the *Sedes Sapientiae*, the Throne of Wisdom, of Christ. Being the Throne, she takes precedence over the Child, whose figure, which is almost always depicted as an adult making the gesture of blessing and showing the book he holds in his left hand, corresponds to that of the sovereign in keeping with his majesty. He also takes on the sense of a priest, which once again relates to Mary as the personification of the Church.

These examples were frequent throughout the Romanesque period in Europe. Amongst the oldest examples mentioned is the gold-plated Virgin of Clermont-Ferrand cathedral (Auvergne), made by Adelelmus in 946. The image has now been lost, but is known to us from a late tenth-century or early eleventh-century illustration. In fact, one of the most unusual and uniform series of Romanesque Madonnas was produced in the Auvergne region.

The image of the *Virgin from Ger* (Cerdanya) is one of the examples in which the technical quality is highest and the composition is characteristic of the type described here. In this case, Mary is seated on a simple bench, while the Child appears seated in the middle. Originally, the two figures must each have had their corresponding wooden crown, the same as other example of this type, which must have been replaced later with metal crowns, as a result of which irregularities can be seen on the top of the heads. The delicate work of the folds in the clothing and in Mary's facial features make this an exceptional piece, the star product of a workshop that turned out a large number of items in Cerdanya. It must have been made in the last third of the twelfth century. The *Virgin of Ix* and the *Virgin of Bastanist*, now lost, are included in this group. We don't know the origin of this workshop, but there are some very suggestive analogies between the Ger carving and an angel that must have been part of a group scene from Cologne (Germany) of the Three Maries at the Tomb (Berlin, Staatliche Museen

101. Virgin. Detail.
Its compositional traits show a clear rigidity, despite being ahead of its time
MNAC/MAC 3921

101

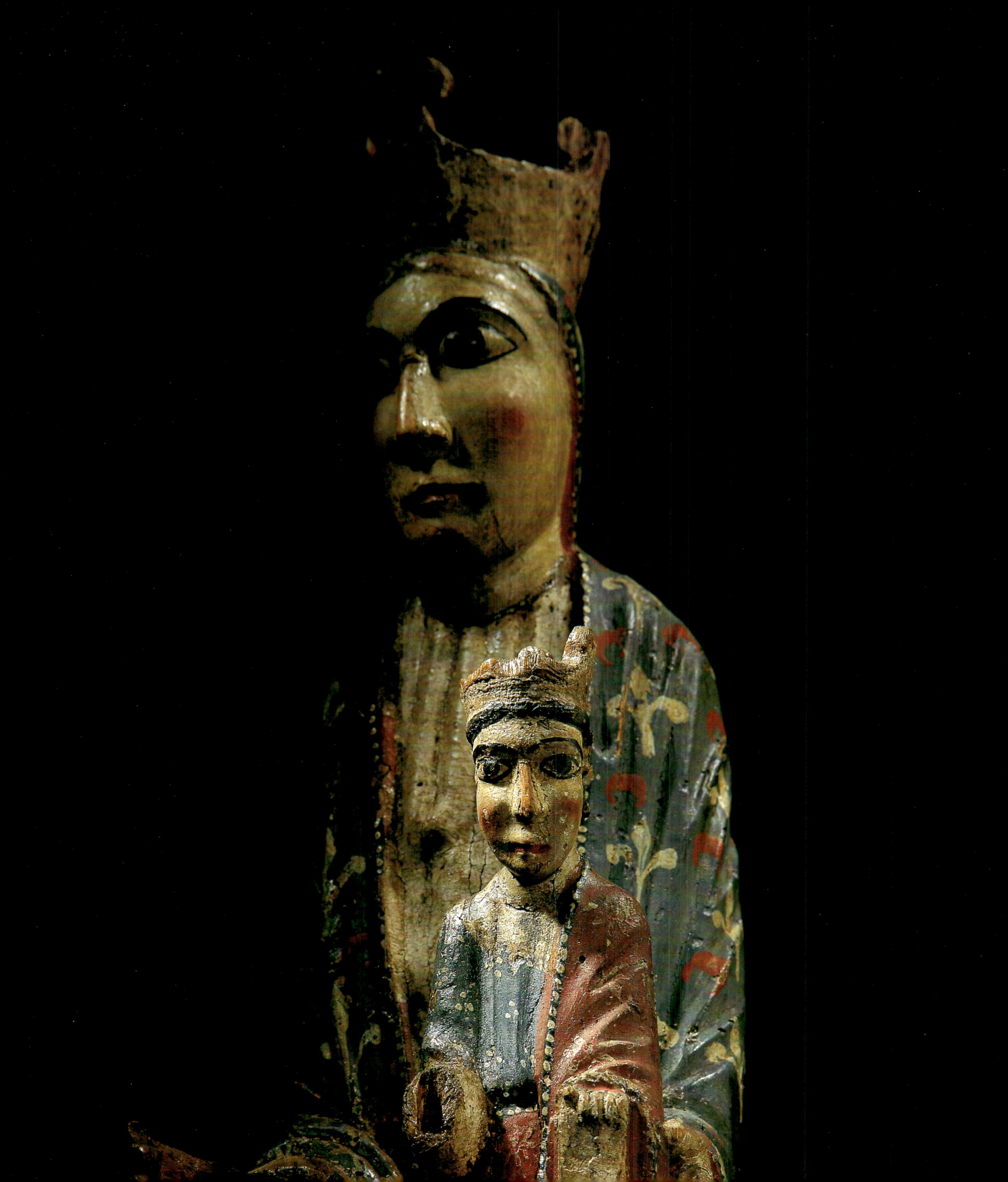

Preussischer Kulturbesitz). These analogies point to the use of very similar technical and stylistic resources based on general formulas or else to a single sculptor or workshop for both carvings. From the point of view of technique, there are plaster reliefs on the front of the bench, the same as we find in other examples from Occitania.

The study of the *Virgin from Ger* provides another interesting aspect related to the history of images for veneration and the developments they have been through over the course of time. Photographs from the first decades of the twentieth century show the image with the figure of the child in a different position from the original, sitting not in the middle but on Mary's left knee, while the position of both figures' hands was also changed. Another surprising fact is that there seems to be no polychromy on Mary's uncovered lap, which might indicate that the item was clothed. Soon afterwards, in a subsequent restoration before it entered the Museum, the work was returned to the original composition as we see it today.

The examples of carved Madonnas kept at the Museum reflect the variety of types that developed in Catalonia and Spain in general during the twelfth and thirteenth centuries. While the *Virgin from Ger* reflects a type of composition that is very closed and withdrawn, there are other examples that are characterised by greater monumentality. This is the case of the *Virgin of Gósol*, in which the figure of Mary seems to carry more weight within the whole and appears seated on a throne. It's also interesting to remember that during his visit to Gósol in 1906 Picasso had a chance to see this image, which at the beginning of the twentieth century must still have been in the church there. It has been suggested that its features are visible in some portraits of Fernande Olivier and in the picture *Woman with Loaves*, painted in Gósol in 1906. This would make the image another element in the primitive influences in the development of Picasso's art, something already documented in the case of African masks or Iberian sculpture.

Some images are composed as groups characterised by a certain monumentality, with a more majestic presentation, often of a greater size, without abandoning the approach marked by frontality and a hieratic air. This is the case of several examples such as the Virgin of All (MNAC) and the Virgin of Sant Martí Sarroca (Alt Penedès), now lost. To some extent this is also the approach used in a Madonna of unknown, probably Catalan origin (MNAC/MAC 3923). It has preserved significant remains of polychromy, especially the blue and red of the clothing on the figures of Mary and the Child, and remains of the preliminary layer of plaster and of cloth, which was used for fixing the pieces of wood. All these examples could date from around 1200.

Hispanic images are represented by a Madonna (MNAC 3924) which is thought to be of Castilian or Leonese origin, though for the time being we can't be more precise. While the composition corresponds broadly to the concept of Mary as the *Sedes Sapientiae*, it has a predominantly monumental nature and the features and clothing are lighter. The work obviously had polychromy, so that its present aspect is radically different from that of the original. The dynamism of the bottom of Mary's tunic points to a later date, after 1200, and shows significant parallels with European examples, especially from the North of France, England and Germany in the first third of the thirteenth century. This work has also been shown to have points in common with the

102. VIRGIN.
First half of the 13th century
Woodcarving with traces of polychrome tempera
80 × 30 × 22 cm
Probably from Castile
MNAC/MAC 3924

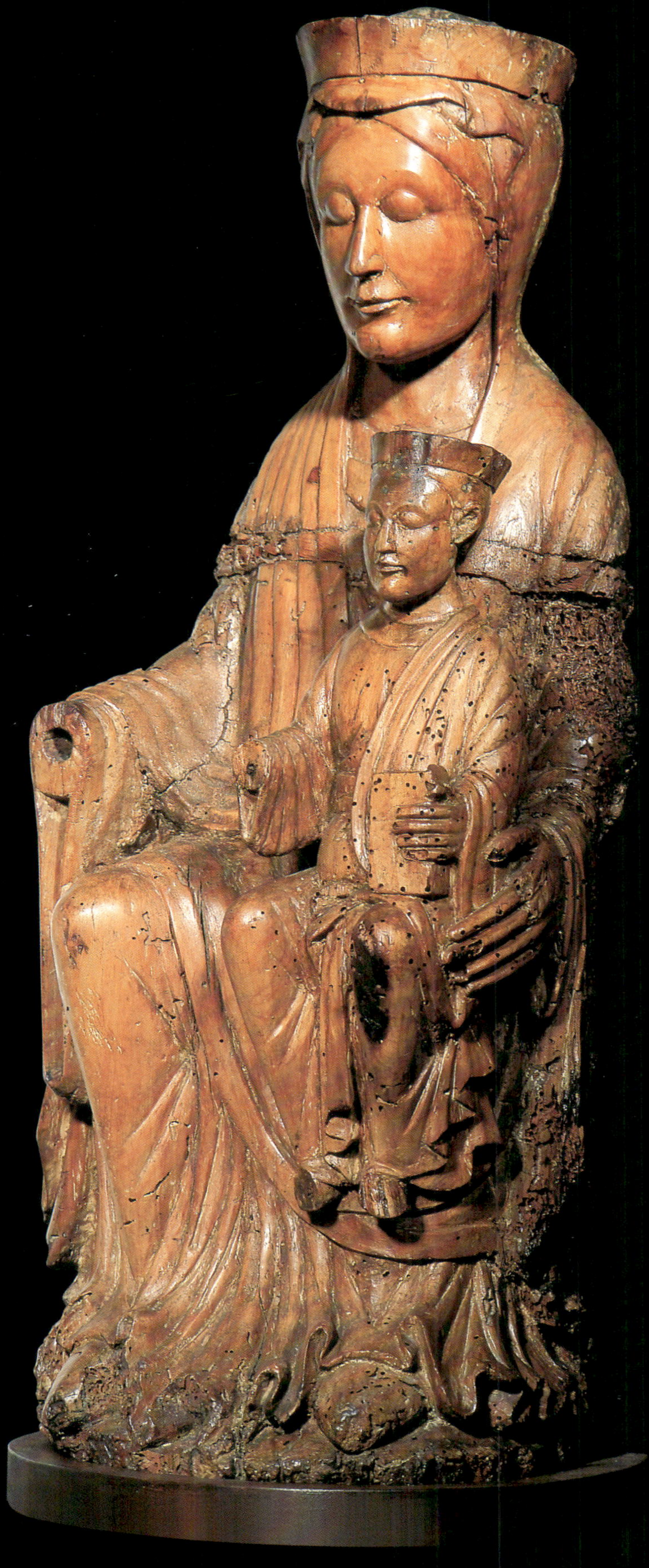

monumental stone carving in Castilian sites around 1200, like the relief in the cloister at Silos dedicated to the Virgin. In this respect, the image is an example of the parallels to be found between different sculptural techniques.

Some of the works were by sculptors who were more limited technically and who produced what have been classed as 'folk' items. The compositional scheme they follow and their attributes are common from the twelfth century, presenting Mary as the *Sedes Sapientiae*, but in many cases they belong to much later dates, even outside the chronological limits for the Romanesque. This is the case of the surprising *Virgin of Covet*, in which the carving is simpler and coarser and whose unusual headgear places it amongst a series of items from the Lleida area dated around 1300, the same as the Virgin of El Puig de Meià (Noguera) or a work from Val d'Aran (Francisco Godia Collection).

These images have rarely come down to us in their original context, which makes it difficult to reconstruct their position on the altar. Nevertheless, many of them belonged in a larger context and were placed in small constructions and accompanied by other images or scenes, often combining other techniques. There is plenty of evidence in Catalonia to imagine them often set in *edicles*, small architectural structures after the fashion of a tabernacle or baldachin, as could be seen in Sant Martí d'Envalls (Angostrina, Cerdanya), where the Madonna and Child were at the centre of a composition that had two painted side panels containing the Annunciation and the Visitation. Another important *edicle* was the one now lost from San Martí Sarroca, of which some of the panels have survived, with carvings on them (MNAC), which must have represented the Annunciation to Mary and the Adoration of the Magi. We cannot therefore rule out the possibility that some images that have reached us as isolated items formed part of works like the ones mentioned and were placed on the altar, near the back. Other thirteenth-century examples foreshadow forms of altarpiece or of what later would be the predellas of the great Gothic altarpieces.

Apart from being placed in a privileged position in the church as an object of veneration, we must remember that images of Mary were attributed with miracles that drew the faithful and increased their prestige and their following. This was the case of the Virgin of Montserrat. In 1218, James I, Count of Barcelona and King of Aragon, in response to the miracles attributed to the image, granted immunity to pilgrims visiting it. In fact, accounts of healings and donations were frequent from the last quarter of the twelfth century. As regards the dark or black colouring that is a feature of this famous image today, this is not the same as its original flesh tones, a fact that was demonstrated by the analyses carried out in 2001. The same goes for the so-called 'black Madonnas' made in the twelfth and thirteenth centuries. The present appearance of some of these examples could be the result of gradual darkening caused by the smoke from the candles or alterations in some of the materials used for painting them, like the lead in the white flesh tones. Returning to the Madonna of Montserrat, it seems that in the sixteenth century it was repainted in brown and in a further restoration in the nineteenth century it was given a coat of black paint.

They were often also used to hold relics, as in the case of the Virgin of Sant Cugat del Vallès (Museu de Terrassa). Restoration work in 1989 brought to light a hidden reliquary with various relics in the back of the head, along with a document referring to the consecration of the image in 1218. This made it possible to date the work with an accuracy that is unusual for this type of object. But the purpose of these carvings could go beyond their permanent presence close to the church altar, and they can also be seen as movable objects. It's known that the images also took part in processions, according to the festivities of the liturgical year, and they could also be used in performances of liturgical plays. In this case, a particularly important drama in the Middle Ages was the *Officium Stellae*, during the feast of the Epiphany, when three priests dressed as the Magi paid tribute and gave offerings to the image of the Madonna. In Ripoll, some of these forms of theatre must have been familiar since the tenth or eleventh centuries, as a codex from this time includes directions for the three Magi.

Crucifixes

Images of Christ on the Cross, alone or as part of larger groups, are the other commonest type in churches. In Catalonia, a quite remarkable number and variety have survived, represented in the MNAC's collections by emblematic works. As regards the crucifixes, there are two very widespread types which are, basically, Christ in Majesty (*Christus triumphans*) and the suffering Christ (*Christus patiens*). Later we shall look at the few items we call 'Calvaries', where the crucifix is accompanied on either side by the figures of Mary and John, and which should perhaps include some examples which until now have been considered simply crucifixes. Finally, we mustn't forget the group scenes of the Descent from the Cross, which, as we shall see, make up a very special series in the Middle Ages and contain elements that are also related to the components of the Crucifix and the Calvary.

Apparently the two forms of Christ in Majesty and Christ Suffering developed during the Romanesque period alongside one another. At any rate, there are no conclusive signs to date that one came before the other. The earliest examples appeared during the second third of the twelfth century and there were still very significant examples in the thirteenth century. There is, on the other hand, a certain geographical differentiation, as most of the carvings of Christ Triumphant have survived in the north-east, while the suffering Christ appears clearly in the north-west and in the area around Lleida.

103. Batlló Majesty.
Middle of the 12th century
Woodcarving polychromed in tempera
94 × 96 × 17 cm (Christ)
156 × 120 × 4 cm (Cross)
From La Garrotxa
MNAC/MAC 15937

104. Detail of the Batlló Majesty.
The features of the head combine the planes and angles of the surfaces with very precise carving in the details.

The *Batlló Majesty* is an emblematic example of Christ in Majesty, also called *Majestats* ('Majesties') in Catalonia. Christ appears dressed in a richly decorated tunic, in imitation of Byzantine fabrics, and holds his arms out horizontally in a stiff, solemn stance, reinforced by having his eyes open, symbolising the triumph of Christ over death. It perfectly illustrates the idea of *Christus triumphans*, of which a very prestigious prototype is known to us, the *Volto Santo* of Lucca cathedral in Tuscany. According to legend, this famous image in wood had been carved by Christ's disciple Nicodemus and arrived from the Orient in the eighth century. It may in fact be a carving from the end of the eleventh century or even later, whose following extended during the Romanesque period and has survived to our own day. It's quite possible that

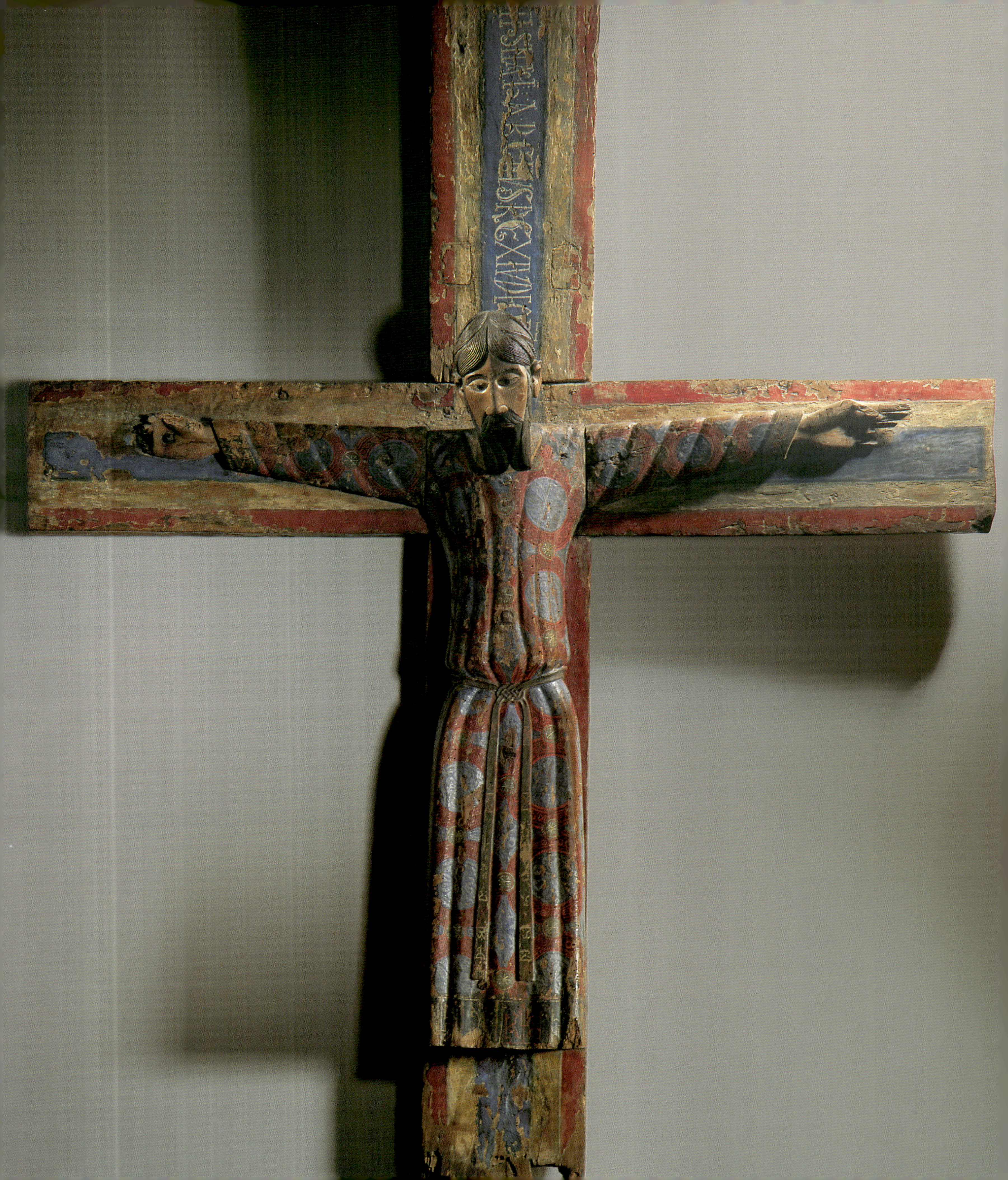

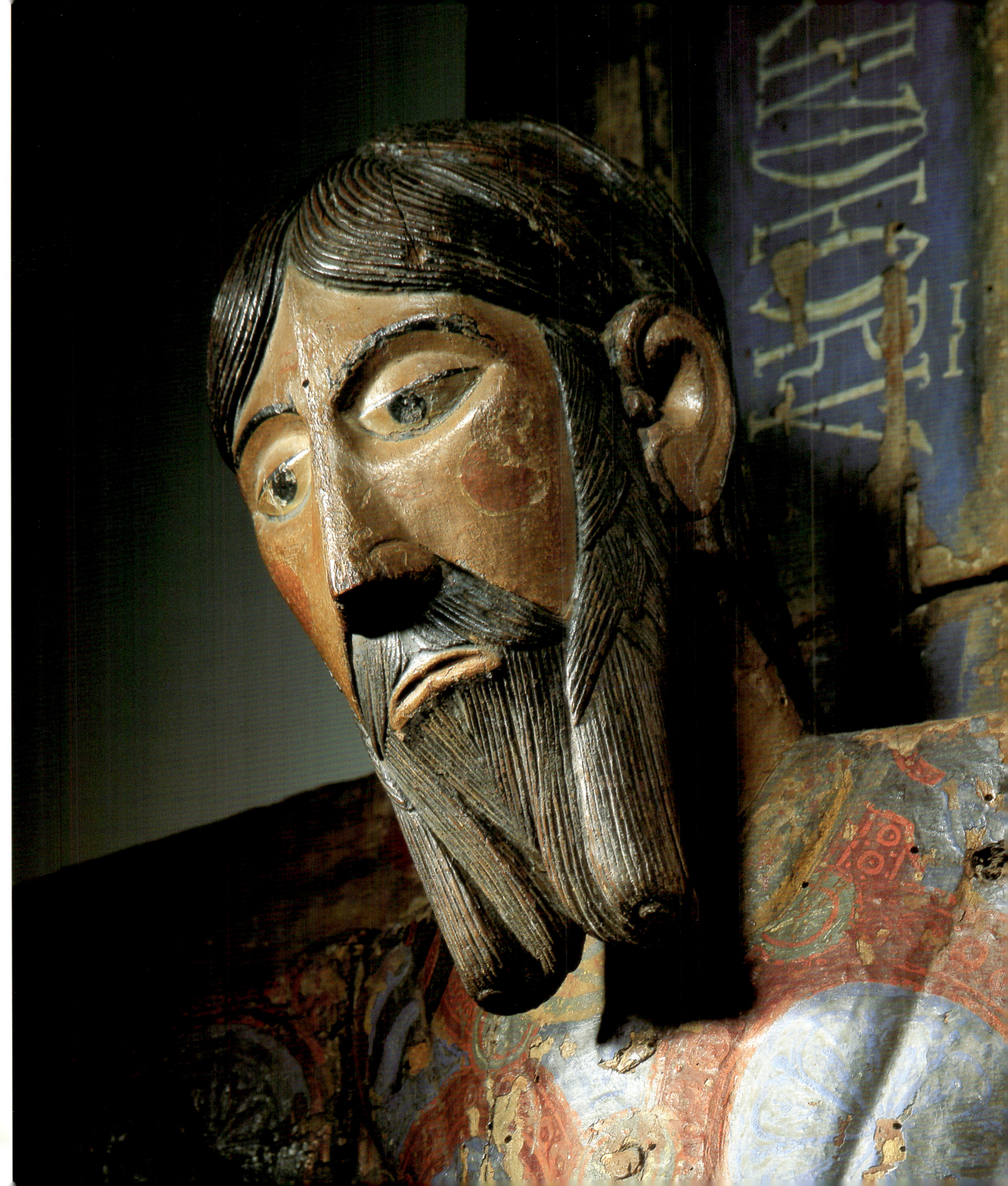

the cult spread from Tuscany to other regions. In fact, in Catalonia, other works like the Majesty of Caldes or that of Beget, which are still worshipped in their churches, show the survival of a cult that must have developed during the Romanesque and that in modern times is reflected in the words of the *Goigs*, traditional rhymes that were sung in honour of Mary, of Christ or of the saints, and which it seems already existed in the fourteenth century. As regards Catalan examples, we mustn't forget there are accounts that hint at the worship of images of the crucifix with connotations that might even suggest a link to the Eastern Mediterranean. One case is the cult of the miraculous Christ of Beirut. There are accounts of the celebration of the *Passio imaginis Christi* ('the Passion of our Lord and Saviour who was crucified in Beirut') in Girona in the tenth century, while similar celebrations are documented in Ripoll and Vic in the eleventh century. It is nevertheless risky to draw a direct connection between these eleventh-century accounts and the twelfth-century sculptures.

The *Batlló Majesty* has preserved a large part of its original polychromy, both on the figure and on the cross. There are also remains on the back, which makes us think it was visible from all angles, which also goes for other important examples like the Majesty of Sant Joan les Fonts and that of Cruïlles (kept at the Museu d'Art de Girona). The analysis of samples of the image carried out during 2007 speaks for a knowledge of the techniques of the time, with a clever overlaying of coats of paint, as well as the use of pigments like cinnabar for certain areas of red and of lapis lazuli for those in blue. These were expensive materials that were not easy to get hold of during the twelfth century. All of this suggests the work came from a powerful workshop and was intended for an important site, and although its exact origin isn't known to us, the fact that it was purchased from an antiquarian in Olot suggests a production centre between Ripoll and Besalú. Analysis of other aspects of the work, like the inscriptions and the crosses that appear on the back, could help pinpoint the church it was originally intended for. We mustn't forget that some of the key examples came from this area, like the Beget Majesty.

Along with the *Batlló Majesty*, the MNAC keeps other carvings of the same sort, such as the Majesty of Éller (Cerdanya) and the *Organyà Majesty*. The latter seems to be related to works that appeared in the area of the Bishopric of Urgell and marks one of the Western limits to the presence of Romanesque Christs in Majesty in Catalonia.

The second type, as we saw, is the *Christus patiens*. One of the prime examples is known as the *1147 Christ*, although it has come down to us without its polychromy. It features a composition with inclined arms, the semi-naked body dressed in the *perizonium* and the head steeply inclined. the facial features aren't given the somewhat geometrical and inexpressive treatment of the Majesties, but are harder, with the cheekbones more clearly marked. These features are characteristic of the suffering Christ, which reflects the human component of his death and also connects with a long tradition going back to the Early Middle Ages. Many representations in ivories and manuscripts from the Carolingian and Ottonid worlds show this variant, which in the monumental format is at its most impressive in the *Gero Cross* in Cologne, dated to about 960-980.

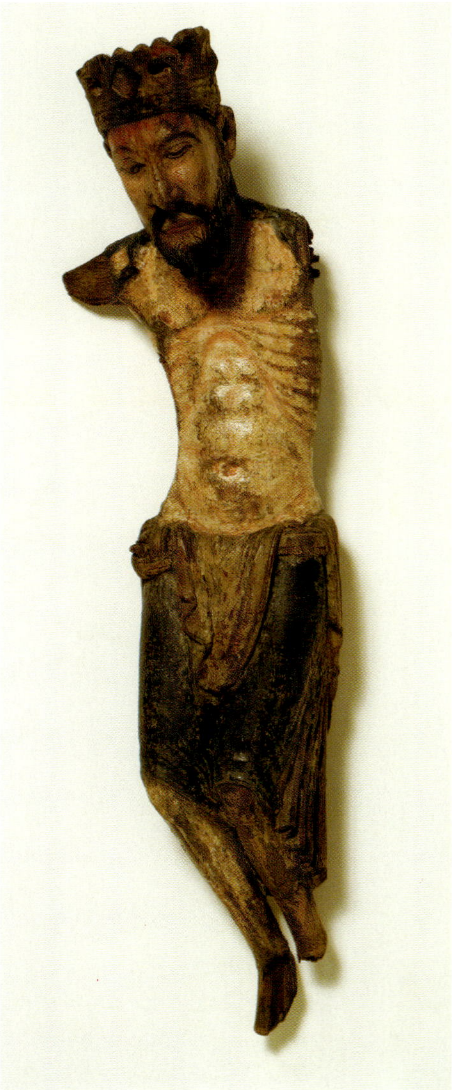

105

105. Christ of Cubells.
13th century
Woodcarving polychromed in tempera
67 × 19 × 14.2 cm
From the church of La Mare de Déu
in Cubells Castle (Noguera)
MNAC/MAC 122672

106. Detail of the Christ of 1147.
Consecrated in 1147
Woodcarving with traces of
polychrome tempera
100 × 91 × 16 cm (Christ)
187 × 118 × 4.5 cm (Cross)
From the bishopric of Urgell
MNAC/MAC 15950

10

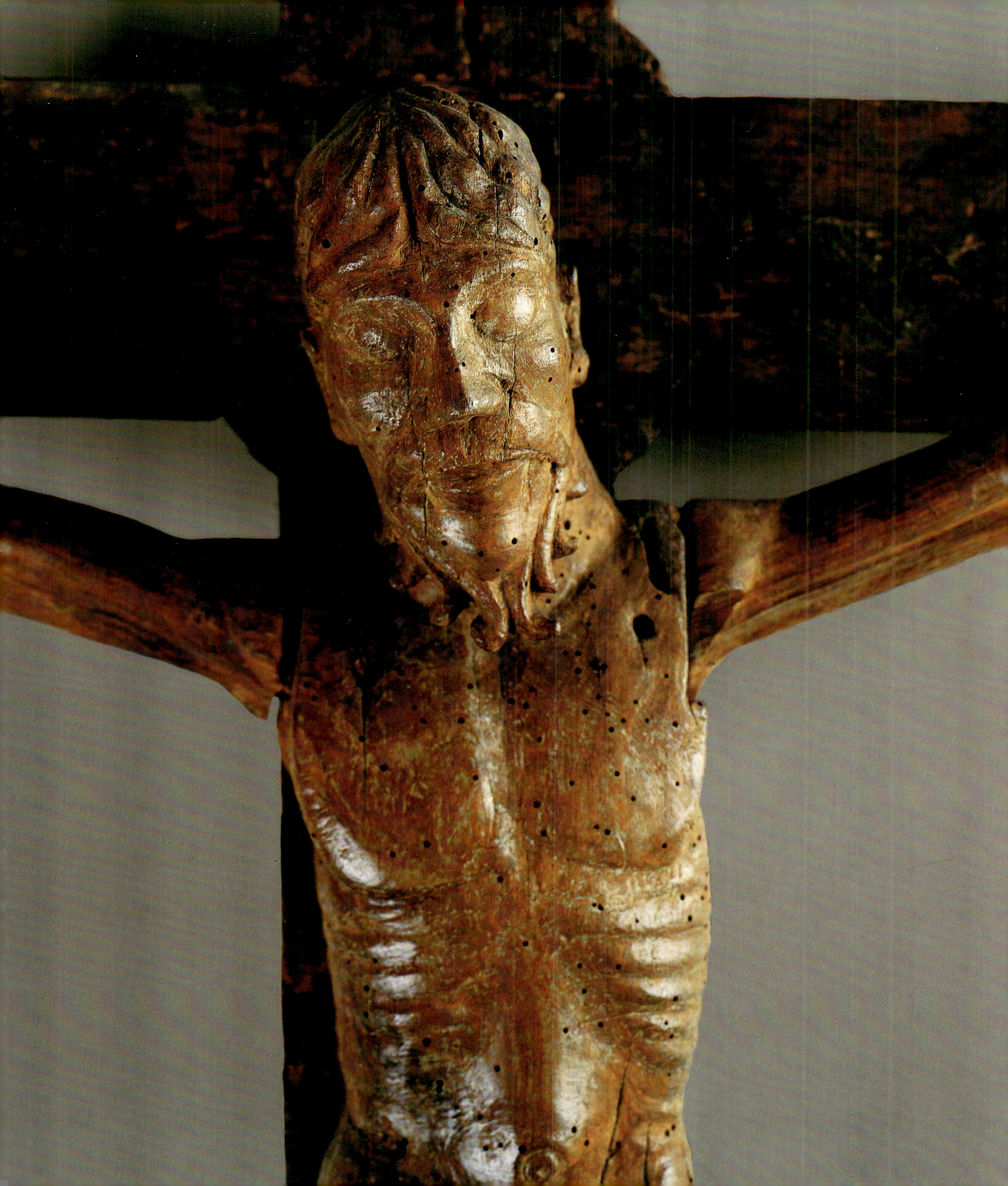

The *1147 Christ* is undoubtedly one of the most outstanding carvings in the MNAC's collections, not only for its quality and representativeness, but also because of the information it provides on the role of these images. While it was being restored in 1952, a reliquary was discovered in the back of the figure of Christ, with a series of packets of relics wrapped in Andalusian fabrics (now kept at the Museu Tèxtil i d'Indumentària de Barcelona), as well as two fragments of parchment. One of these contained the date of consecration of the work, 1147, which is where the image gets its name, as it provides a very precise reference for dating it. This is exceptional as there are only two other works that can be dated in Catalonia, the *Virgin of Sant Cugat del Vallès* (1218) and the *Descent from the Cross from Sant Joan de les Abadesses* (1251). But over and above this valuable reference, the importance of the work lies in the fact that it was a reliquary.

Apart from this item, undoubtedly connected with the area around La Seu d'Urgell, there is a series of examples of the suffering Christ that are located around the city of Lleida. Amongst them, another outstanding example is the *Cubells Christ* (Noguera). Although badly damaged and without its cross, in this case what stands out is the painstakingly refined treatment of the facial features, the hair and beard and the *perizonium*, while the base of the crown must have been fitted with precious stones, to judge from the lozenge-shaped hollows. In this respect, this is another example in which certain aspects of the wood carving bring to mind, or try to imitate, the qualities of plated images using precious metals. In some cases they are late examples, in which the crucified Christ has his feet crossed and nailed with a single nail, unlike earlier ones. This treatment can also be seen in a case from Ripoll, the *Sant Pere de Ripoll Crucifix* (MNAC), which can be dated to the second half of the thirteenth century.

The 'Calvaries'

The image of Christ crucified was sometimes accompanied by the figures of Mary and Saint John in smaller applied carvings on the ends of the horizontal bar of the cross, with Adam resuscitating at the base and other characters. Generally speaking, this type has been given the name 'Calvary'. One of the most outstanding Catalan examples is the Tragó de Noguera Calvary. With a cross covered in shoots, like an image of the tree of life (which relates the tree of Original Sin with the idea of redemption), it shows Mary and John identified by the corresponding inscriptions. At the base there are remains of the figure of Adam emerging from the grave and of the hole for the dowel it must have been fixed with. The presence of Adam is related to the belief that Christ was crucified in the same place, Golgotha, where Adam was buried, so that Christ represents the new Adam, who through his death redeemed the sin he had committed. The back of the work is also decorated, as is customary in other crucifixes, with the image of the *Agnus Dei*. There are very few examples of applied carving in Catalonia, but from the thirteenth century a more monumental format began to develop, with the two side figures presented independently, at the same level as Christ, as we see in Spanish works like those at Castiliscar (Aragon) and Sant Antolín de Toques (Galicia) and others of the

107. Detail of the Calvary called of Tragó de Noguera.
Work on the head that tends to schematization is visible.
Second half of the 13th century
Woodcarving polychromed in tempera
60 × 55.5 × 13.5 cm (Christ)
148 × 81 × 9 cm (Cross)
MNAC/MAC 15887

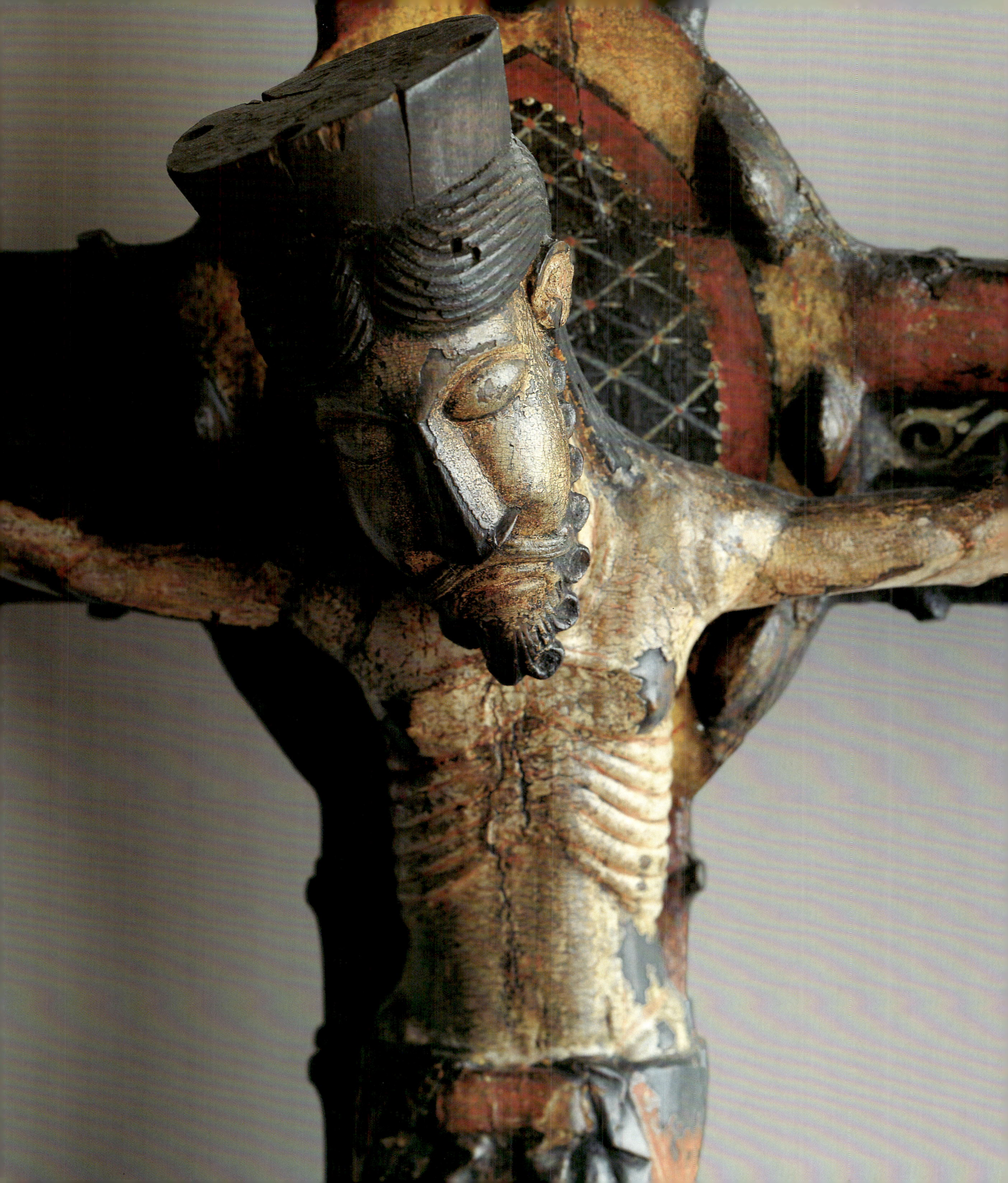

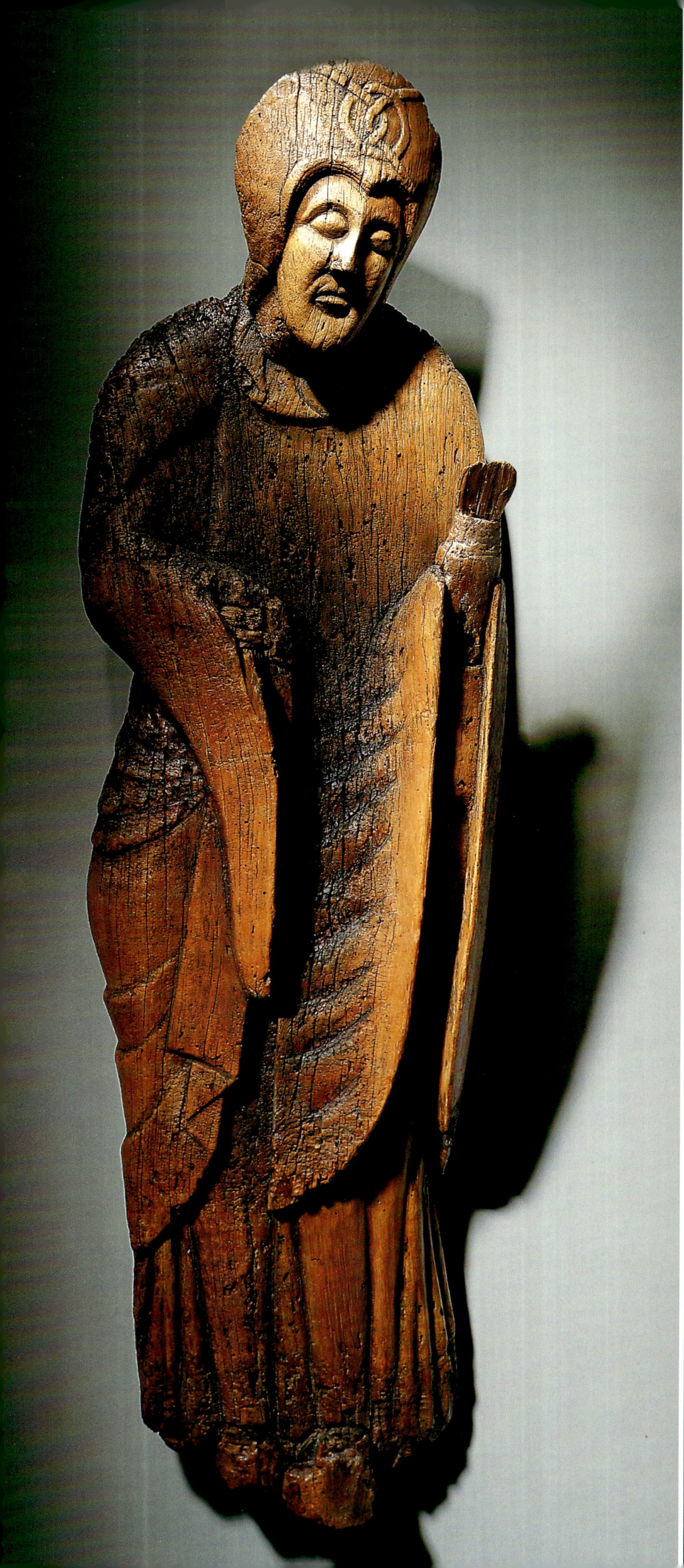
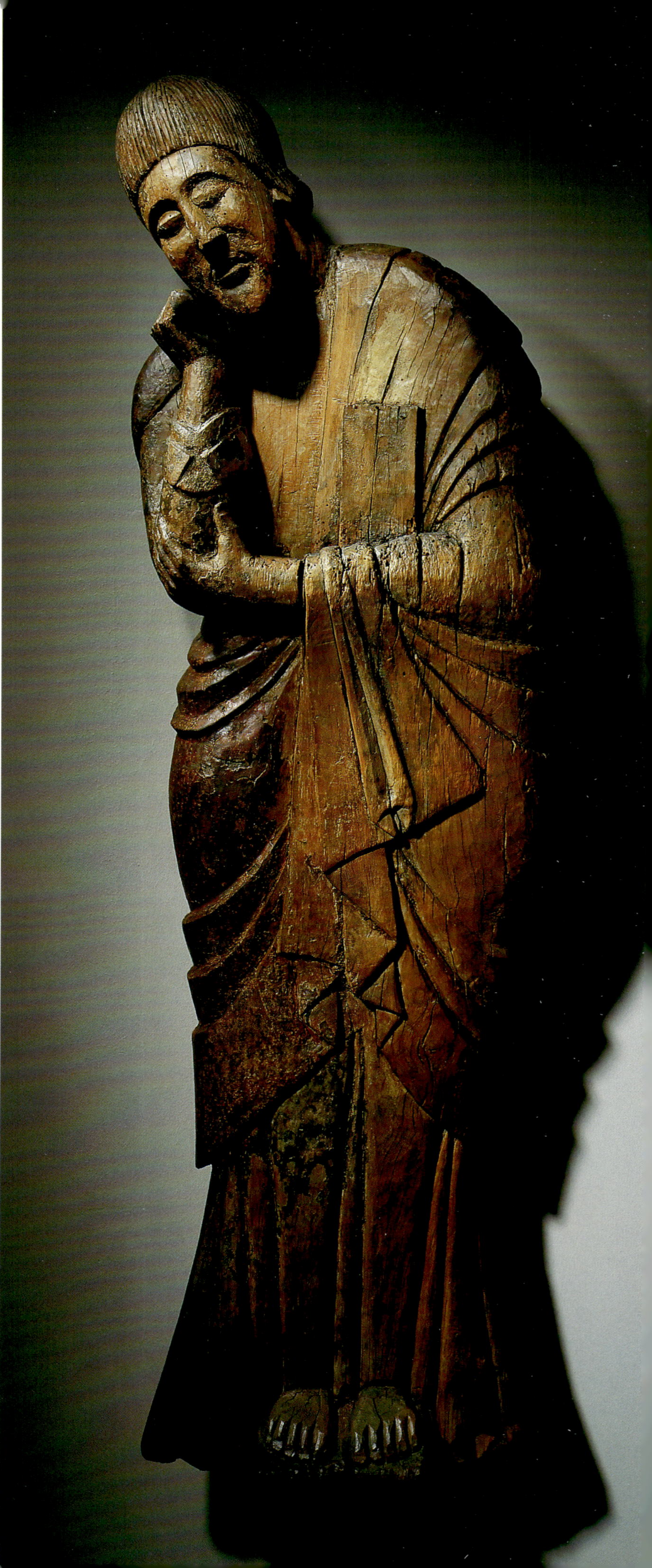

time. Similarly, the two approaches are seen on the gold and silver altar crosses or on book covers. On book covers, in fact, the figures of Mary and Saint John are depicted at the same height as Christ crucified and of a size closer to his.

But apart from the examples with applied carvings,there are a large number of carved crucifixes, especially of the suffering type, that showed the figures of Mary and John strictly painted at the ends of the horizontal arms of the cross, as well as others on the front and back. One of the most remarkable cases is the Salardú Christ (Val d'Aran), preserved *in situ*, in which restoration work made it possible to appreciate the painted decoration on the cross, which amongst others includes the figures of Mary and John, combined with the carving of Christ.

The group scenes of the Descent from the Cross

One of the most original types in Catalonia is that of the group scenes representing the Descent from the Cross, which reached a certain monumentality in the church. Amongst those preserved, the ones from the Vall de Boí stand out, with their total of seven characters, unlike the other examples known in Europe and, especially, in Central Italy. Only one other example, the *Descent from the Cross from Sant Joan de les Abadesses*, dated 1251, has a composition like the ones from Ribagorça.

The *Erill la Vall Descent* is the most complete work in this magnificent series, having preserved the seven carvings making it up, which means we can define the iconographic and stylistic features of the Vall de Boí series. Its discovery in modern times took place in the framework of the famous scientific expedition organised by the Institut d'Estudis Catalans in the summer of 1907. It was eloquently recorded in the photographs by Adolf Mas, which show the works soon after being found abandoned in a closed-off section of the church porch. Later, in 1911, five of the carvings were purchased by the Museu Episcopal de Vic, while the remaining two, those of Mary and Saint John, after forming part of the Plandiura collection, entered the Museu d'Art de Catalunya, as it was then called, in 1932.

They have all of them always been prominently exhibited in their respective museums and have been gathered together on various occasions. The seven carvings are worked in wood and originally had polychrome decoration. They make up a totally coordinated, dramatically posed group of almost life-size figures, but adapted to the architectural setting they were to be placed in. The figure of Christ is at the centre of the group, with his head bowed, his semi-naked body clothed with the *perizonium*. On his right (the observer's left), Joseph of Arimathea makes the gesture of holding up Christ's body and his left hand is visible on Christ's ribcage, forming part of the same block of wood. On the other side is Nicodemus, who is depicted unnailing Christ's left hand. Maintaining a more or less symmetrical scheme, this group is flanked by the figures of Mary and Saint John, the first holding Christ's right arm, now freed, while the second holds the book as an attribute and expresses his grief through the gesture of touching his cheek with his hand. Finally, at either end are the two crucified thieves, Dismas and Gestas. The various figures have lost most of the polychromy that covered them,

108. The Virgin and Saint John from the Descent from the Cross of Erill la Vall. *The five remaining carved figures (Christ, Joseph of Arimathea, Nicodemus and the two thieves) are kept in the Museu Episcopal de Vic. Second half of the 12th century Woodcarvings with traces of polychrome tempera 144 × 40 × 21 cm From the church of Santa Eulàlia d'Erill la Vall (Boí Valley, Alta Ribagorça) MNAC/MAC 3917/3918*

109-110. Details of the Virgin and Saint John from Erill. *The figures have lost almost all their polychromy, and thus their original appearance was very different from the current one*

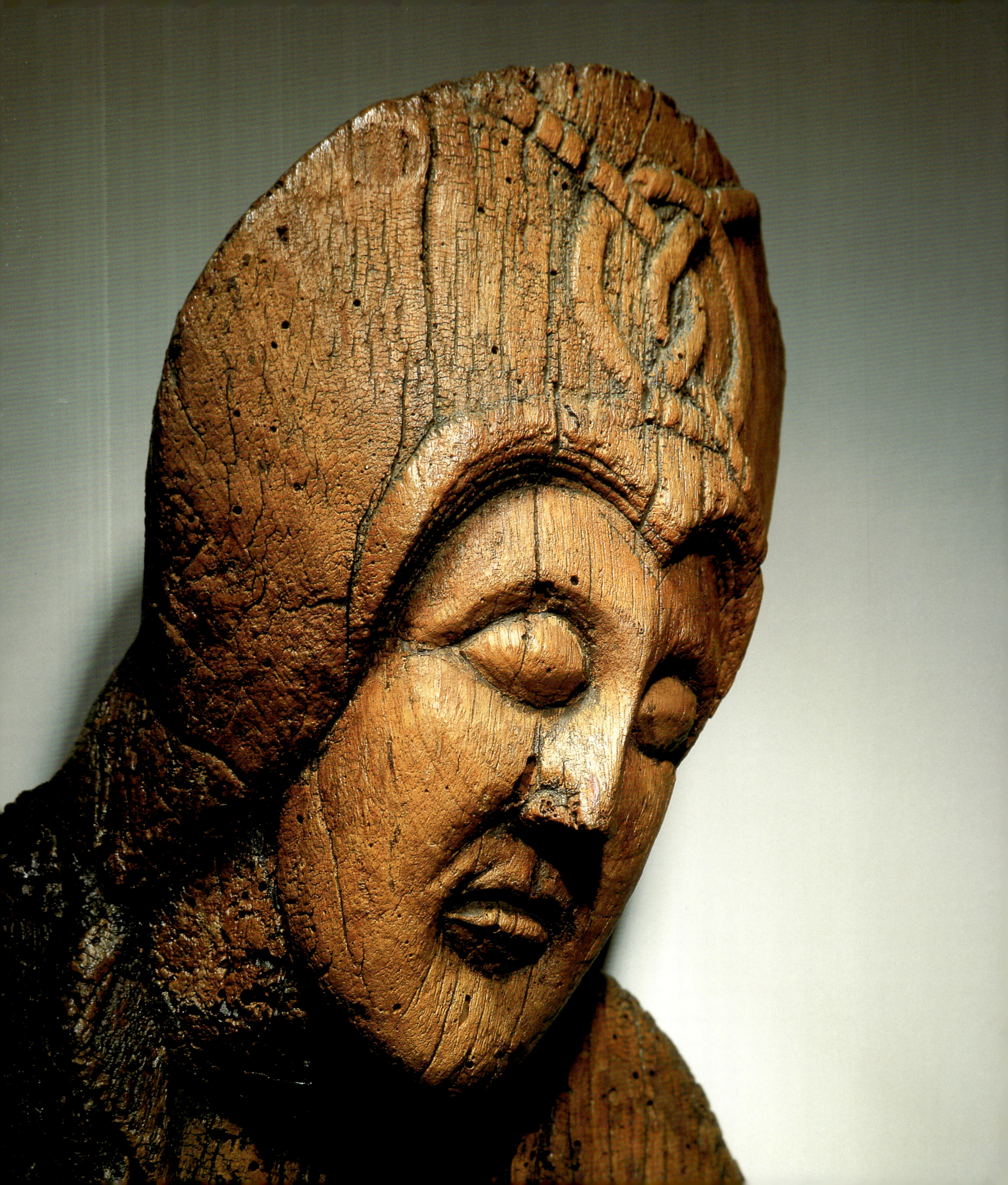

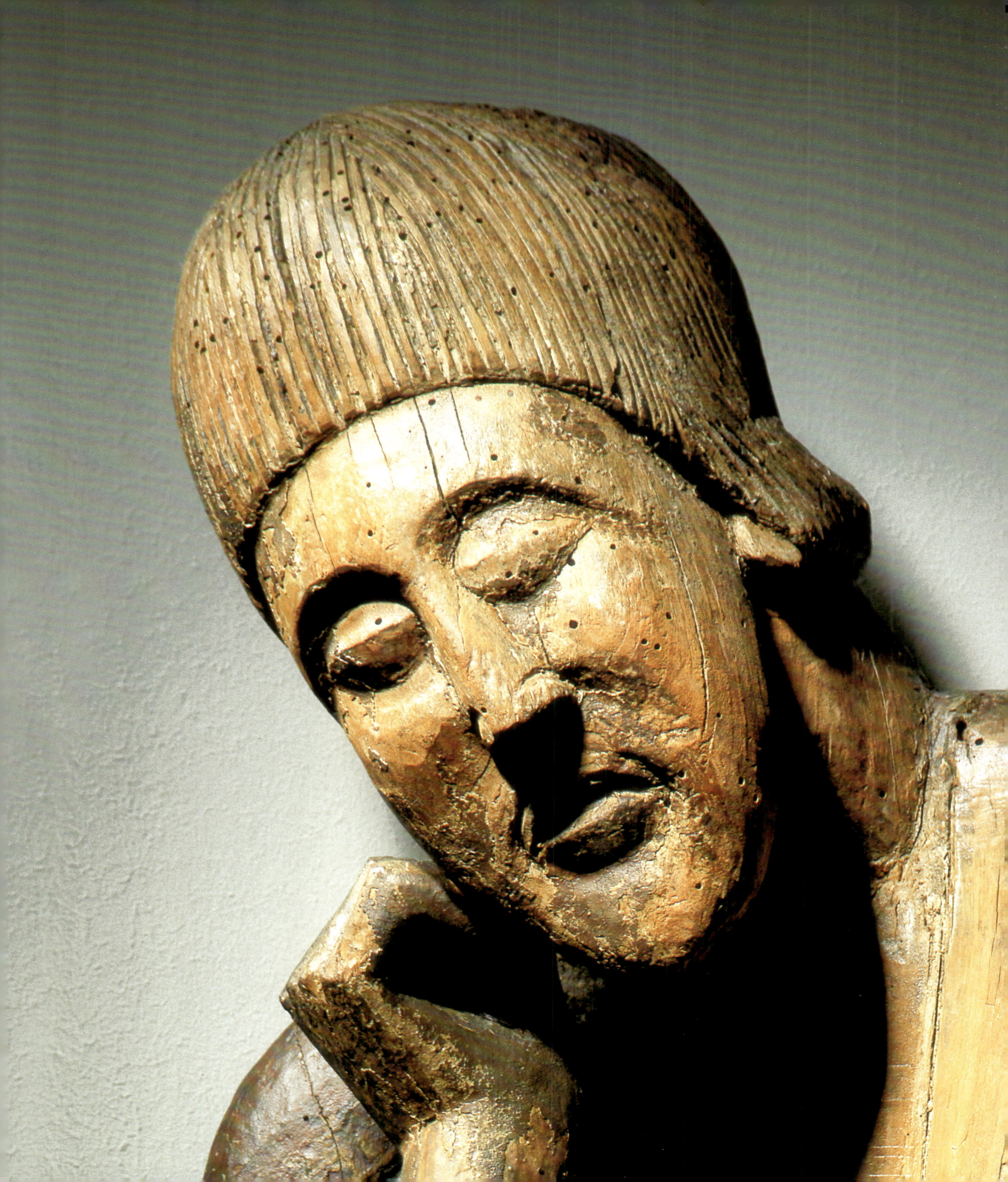

and only the figure of Saint John preserves considerable remains of red in the area of the mantle. Also gone are the pieces of wood that formed the crosses as well as several of the figures' limbs.

One of the aspects that has most concerned researchers is the placement of these groups in the church and their purpose. The fact that at the bottom of some carvings there are remains of dovetails or pegs show that the group was arranged up high, with the figures attached to a wooden structure, a beam like the one from the church in Cardet (MNAC). It has therefore been thought that they might have been placed under the entrance arch to the presbytery, as the reproduction set up in the church of Erill la Vall during the restoration work done between 1994 and 1997 set out to demonstrate. But other possible locations also need to be considered. In Sant Joan de les Abadesses, in the Ripoll area, it seems the group was placed in the chapel of Santa Maria, possibly behind the altar and clearly visible. In larger buildings than the ones in the Vall de Boí, some groups are also known to have stood on the wall of the choir, as we see in the Cistercian monastery of Las Huelgas, in Burgos, though the Descent there is later than the ones that concern us.

In fact, the presence of these monumental group scenes of the Descent of Christ from the Cross must be related to the cycle of the Passion and its liturgy. The episode is very briefly told in the Gospel texts, referring to Joseph of Arimethea's request to Pilate to take the body of Christ down and bury it. The Descents can only have been important as part of the liturgical celebrations surrounding the death of Christ, so it's even possible, in view of their size and the space they took up, that they were only on show and visible during these celebrations. However, the presence of these groups in certain points in the Pyrenees has also been explained in the light of the Church's propaganda struggle against the Cathar heresy. Insistence on the idea of Christ's suffering, with its human side, would reinforce the idea that Christ died on the Cross, which was refuted by the Cathars.

As I say, the presence of the two thieves, Dismas and Gestas, is unusual in that they don't appear in other sculptural representations of the Descent from the Cross, except for the one from Sant Joan de les Abadesses, in a different area to that of Ribagorça and dated 1251. It might be thought that these groups reflect a tradition of including the thieves in representations of the Descent with a large cast of characters, as we see in Catalonia in examples of eleventh-century and twelfth-century illustrated manuscripts or in the paintings in the cloister of Sant Pere de Rodes (eleventh century). On the other hand, though, their presence could be due to their use in liturgical theatre performances of other episodes concerned with Calvary.

From a technical and stylistic point of view, the Erill group is one of the masterpieces of Romanesque sculpture in Catalonia and is so representative it has given its name to a hypothetical workshop credited with other similar works, including the Durro and Taüll Descents. Another culminating point is in the figures of Mary and Saint John, with the slender bodies achieved by curving the bottom half and the rhythmic treatment of the folds in the clothing. However, what is probably the key work in this series is not in the Vall de Boí; this is the Mijaran Christ, currently kept in the parish church in Vielha, which was once part of another Descent of a very

111. THE VIRGIN FROM THE DESCENT FROM THE CROSS OF DURRO.
Second half of the 12th century
Woodcarving with traces of polychrome tempera
189 × 51 × 23 cm
From the Mary's Nativity church in Durro (Boí Valley, Alta Ribagorça)
MNAC/MAC 15895

111

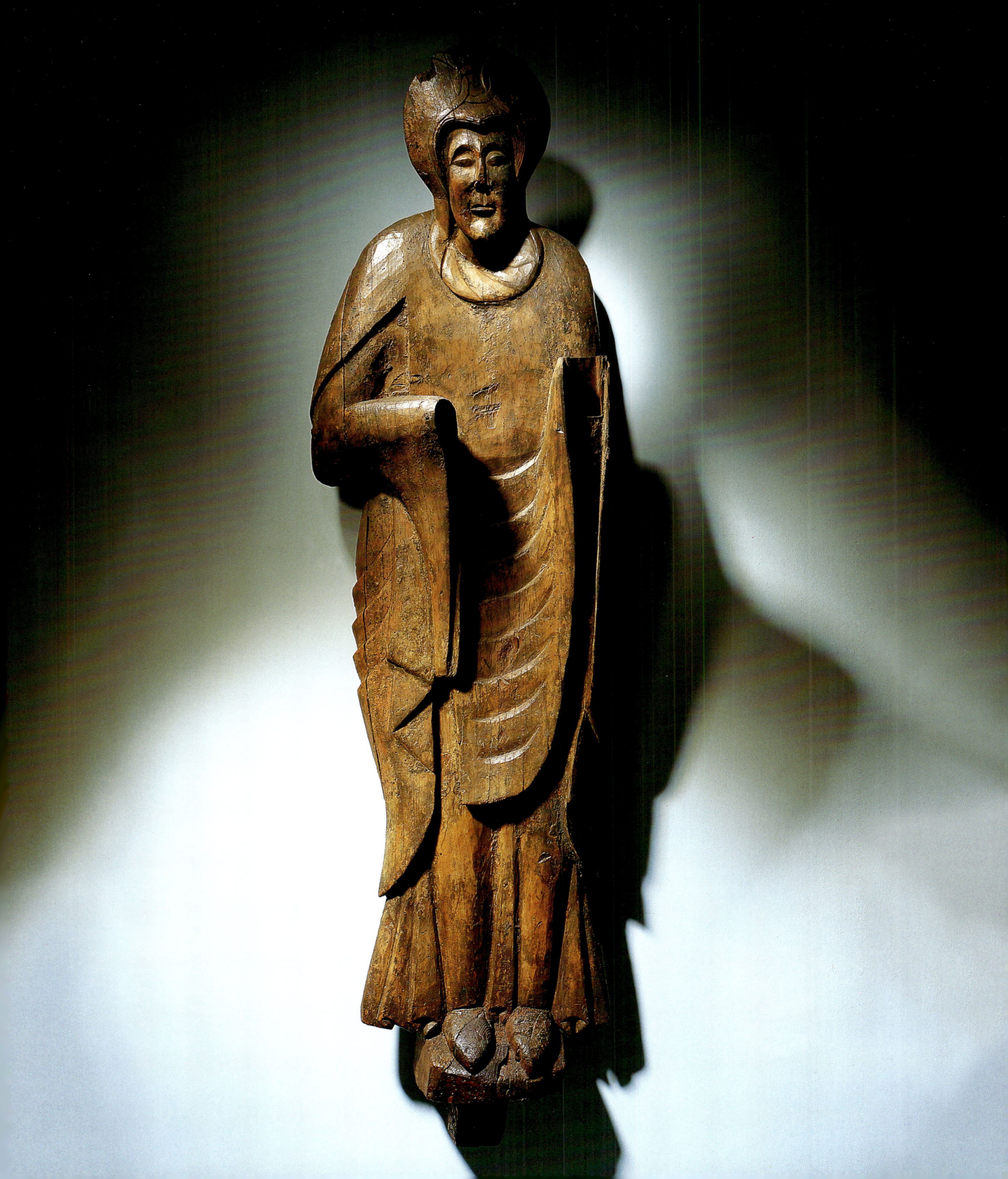

monumental type. The modelling of the head and the taste for detail in the hair, beard, etc. seem to have provided a reference for the works from the Vall de Boí, with their simpler, more schematic surfaces. The works that best connect with the Aranese Christ are the two carvings of the Maries that must have formed part of a group scene of the Three Maries at the Tomb, originally from Santa Maria de Taüll (Fogg Art Museum in Cambridge, Massachussets, United States, and Musée national du Moyen Age, Paris). This group obviously opens the way to another type of monumental group of images, also linked to liturgical theatre and to the veneration of the Holy Sepulchre. Remember that there are accounts of the existence in Vic of the drama of the three Maries at the tomb, the *Quem queritis*, in the eleventh century.

Returning to the *Erill la Vall Descent*, another important issue is that of the date and consequently of the series it belongs to. Some authors have placed it in the first decades of the twelfth century, on the basis of the similarity between the headgear on the figures of Mary in the apse of Sant Climent de Taüll (about 1123) and those in the Descents, bur the corporeity of the figures and the dramatic sense of the composition lead me to think the group belongs to a later moment in the twelfth century, not before 1150. We must also remember that there are clear signs of the survival of similar stylistic treatments during the thirteenth century.

In the church of La Nativitat de Maria in Durro there used to be another group, larger than the one in Erill. The figures of Christ and Mary were reported in 1907. The first disappeared in 1936 and today can only be viewed in old photographs, while the second was purchased by the Barcelona museum in 1922. To these two figures are added the various fragments of the image of Nicodemus, discovered during restoration work done in the church during the years 2000 to 2002 and discovered in the brickwork behind the Altarpiece of the Holy Christ. It seems the composition of the group must have been the same as the one from Erill la Vall, with seven characters. To judge from the size of the figure of Mary, it was clearly bigger than the one from Erill la Vall, from which it appears that it followed a model or formula establishing a series of iconographic and stylistic features that were then adapted to the needs of each commission.

The general composition and style of the work, then, coincide with those of other groups of the same type from the Vall de Boí, which stylistically are grouped around a workshop that has been named Erill, which gave rise to a very particular stylistic approach. Amongst the most characteristic features of this group is the tendency to schematise anatomical features, as we see in Christ's ribcage or in his facial features. It's worth stressing that the hard, austere appearance of each of the images would have been softened by the polychromy applied to them and, very possibly, by the theatrical effect of the group as a whole.

The third group we know of is the one from Santa Maria de Taüll, of which enough carvings have survived to reconstruct a scene similar to the ones from Erill and Durro described above. The images are those of Christ, Joseph of Arimathea, the Virgin and one of the two thieves, so the ones missing are therefore those of Nicodemus, Saint John and the other thief. With the group's new installation in the Museum, presented in 2005, a tighter composition can be exhibited, with the characters

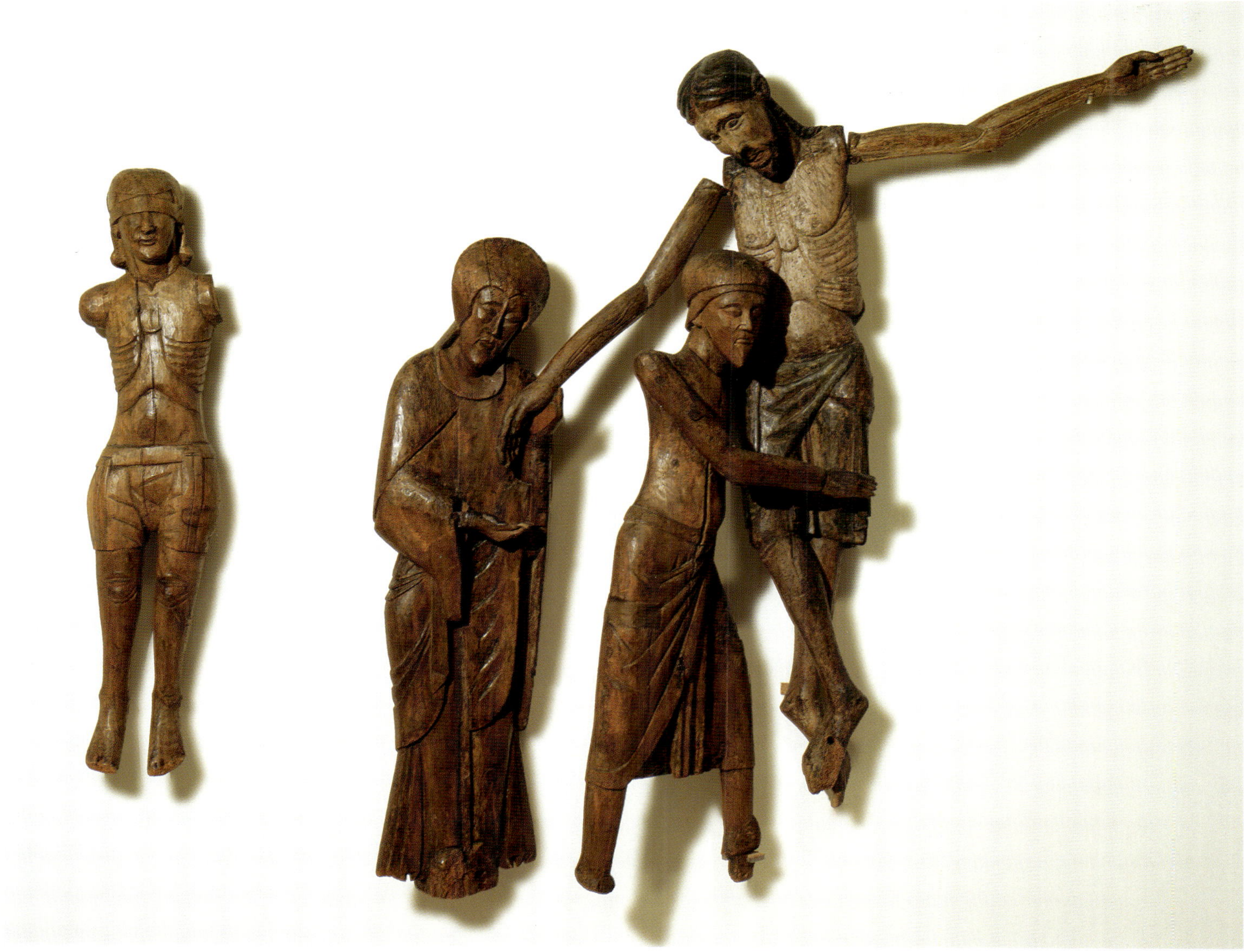

112

112. Figures from the Descent from the Cross of Santa Maria de Taüll.
Late 12th century
Woodcarvings with traces of polychrome tempera
100 × 20 × 15 cm
110 × 29 × 17 cm
103 × 38 × 29 cm
122 × 168 × 22 cm
From the church of Santa Maria de Taüll (Boí Valley, Alta Ribagorça)
MNAC/MAC 3915

far more closely related amongst themselves through their gestures. Joseph of Arimethea's body directly supports the Christ crucified, and Mary, next to him, holds Christ's right arm in her left hand while with the other she must have gathered Christ's blood in a vessel that has now been lost.

The group also belongs to the series of carvings from the workshop that produced the other Descents from the Cross and also other types of image such as Crucifixes, as we deduce from the analogies to be found in the composition and iconography as well as on a stylistic level. However, the *Santa Maria de Taüll Descent* can be distinguished from the others by the figure of Christ, first of all because its feet were crossed and were fixed to the cross, which has not survived, by a single nail, and secondly because its arms are articulated thanks to metal rings attached to the torso. These two details are both clear signs that this image can be dated no earlier than the second half of the thirteenth century. Furthermore, there are remains oif polychromy to be seen and facial features which heighten the dramatic effect of the image, suggesting that the work was used and reused centuries later. This group's interest lies

113

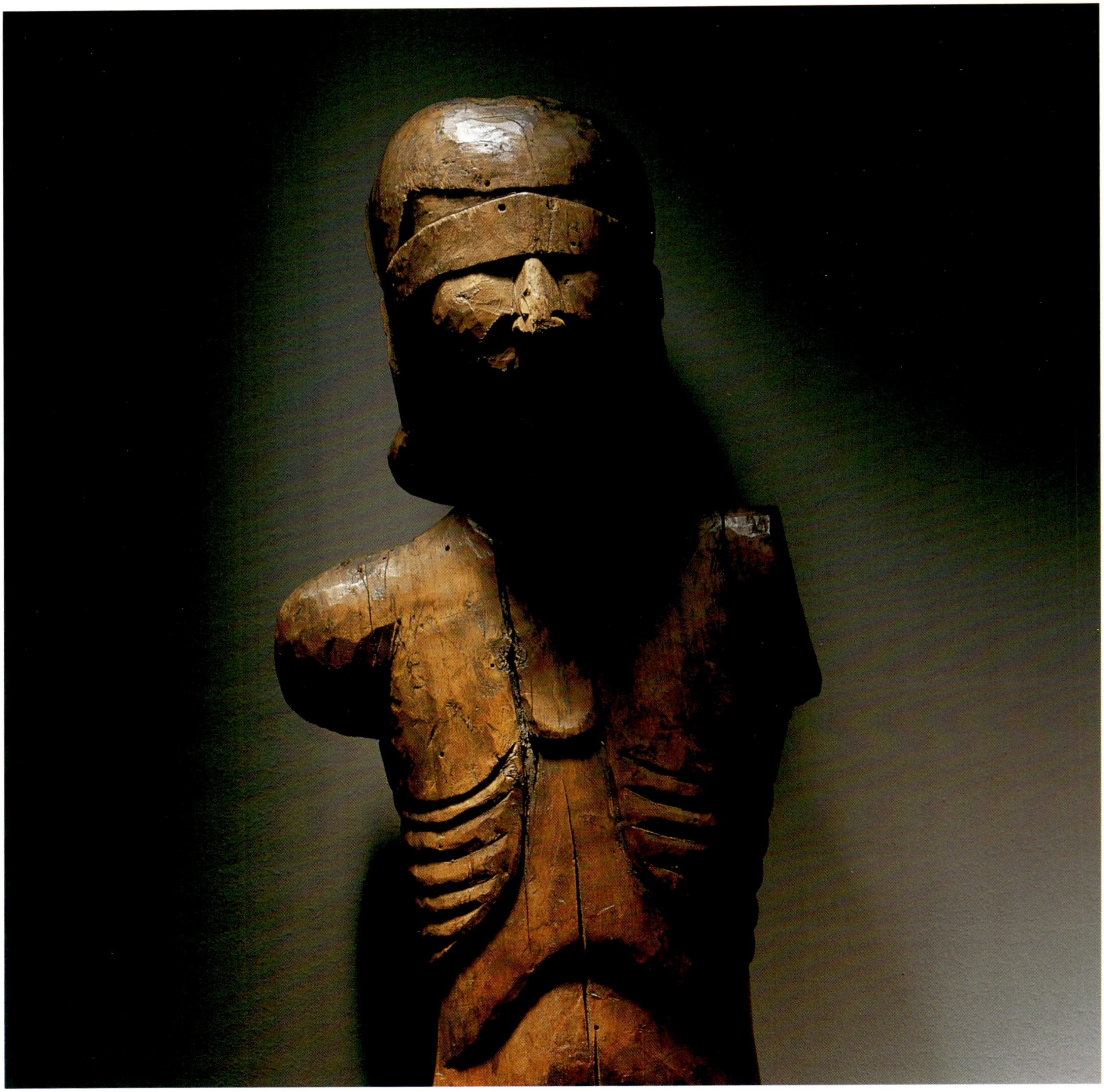

113-114. DETAILS OF THE FIGURES OF A THIEF AND THE CHRIST FROM THE DESCENT FROM THE CROSS OF SANTA MARIA DE TAÜLL.
The figure of the thief has its eyes covered. The features of the figure of Christ, with its mouth open and the expression of suffering, seem to correspond to restoration work on the group carried out after the Romanesque period.

11

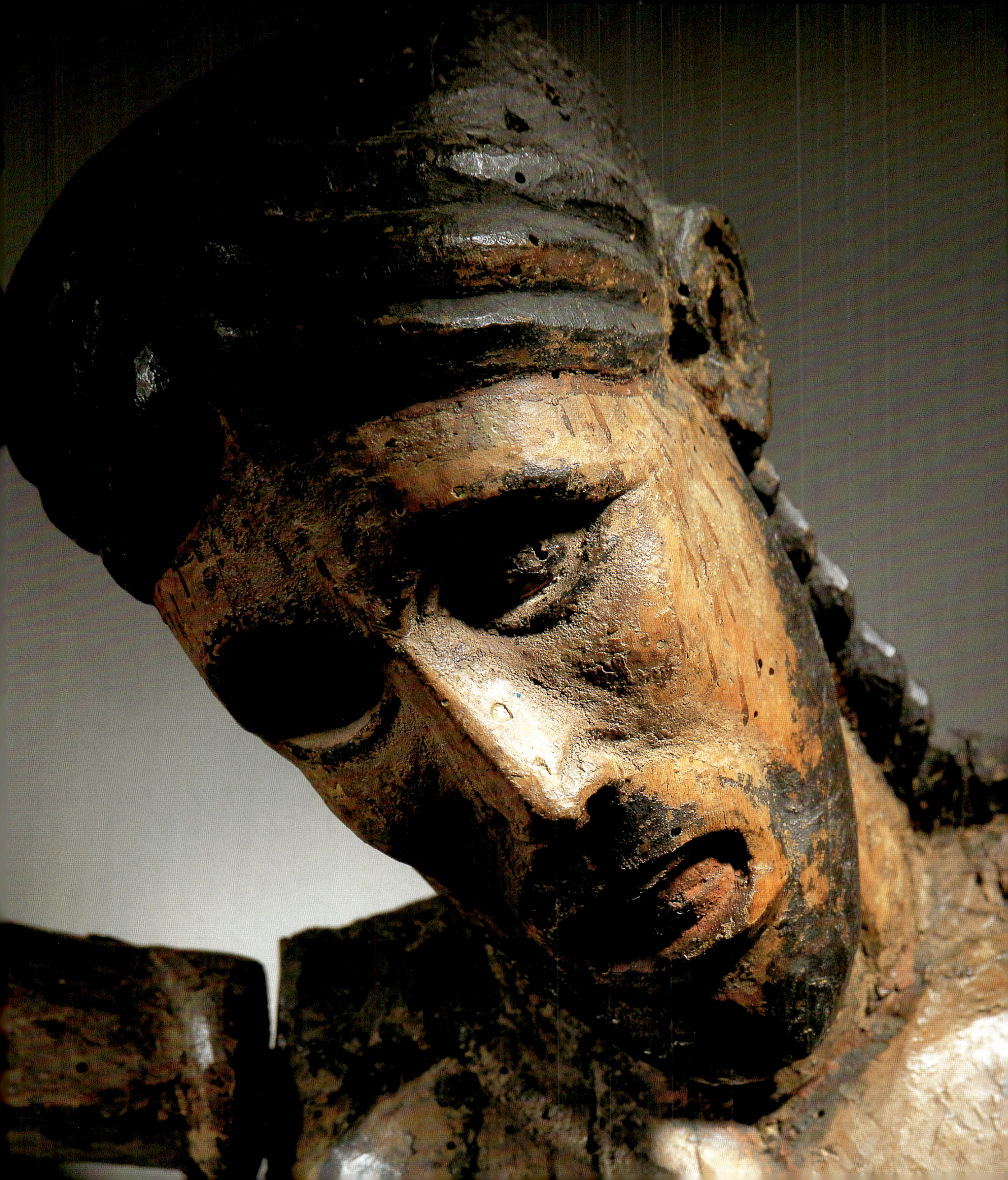

in the possible continuity in the production of Descents from the Cross at later dates than that of the Erill la Vall and Durro groups and in the persistence of stylistic approaches adopted in the twelfth century well into the thirteenth century. But it's also likely that the Christ was rebuilt to adapt it to new liturgical necessities or for some other reason that is not clear to us now.

Altar furnishings and church seating

Although most twelfth-century and thirteenth-century altar frontals and altar tables that have survived in Catalonia had panels painted in tempera, there is a series of examples in which the figures were present as applied carvings on the panels, following the usual repertories and compositions of other cases. It's difficult to explain this choice of technical approach, in which sculpture clearly plays a central role, which furthermore is to be found around very important centres with a high production, like Ripoll, which is where one of these pieces came from (Museu Episcopal de Vic).

If we look at the surviving examples, another centre that resorted to this technical approach was in the Vall de Boí, the origin of another remarkable work, the *Altar Frontal from Santa Maria de Taüll*. The general composition of the work follows that of the strictly painted frontals, with the *Maiestas Domini* presiding it in the central register, originally accompanied by the symbols of the Evangelists, now lost. The figures of the Apostles are arranged on either side, each one inscribed in an arch. The painstaking work in the treatment of the folds in the clothing and the variety of the characters' gestures and stances has been compared to works of sculpture in stone. This work also provides very interesting information about its own history, clearly reflecting the treatments and changes works of art can go through in the course of time. The frontal was repainted in the sixteenth century, as is revealed by the remains of an inscription at the top of the frame which reads, 'FOC PINTAT EN 1579' ('I WAS PAINTED IN 1579'). Changes were probably made in the composition at the same time, replacing one of the images with a Saint John from a Calvary now lost of the Tragó de Noguera type. This carving appears in the first photographs taken of the work when it was discovered in 1907 and is also kept at the Museu Nacional d'Art de Catalunya. More recently, there was a restoration in 1924, signed on the frame of the frontal itself, which involved changes in the positions of some of the carvings and the loss of much of the polychromy mentioned in the sixteenth century.

There is also a frontal from the Vall de Boí which is sometimes thought to have come from Santa Eulàlia d'Erill la Vall. It is currently dismantled and kept at an unknown location and can only be studied from old photographs. In the same sphere of Ribagorça there are further testimonies to the importance of this type of work. One of these is the Bibils frontal, with an iconography similar to that of Taüll, some parts of which are kept at the MNAC, and the other is the Buira frontal (Museu de Lleida Diocesà i Comarcal). Some images of Christ in Majesty or of the Madonna and Child that were not too thick might also have been attached to altar panels, as in the case

115
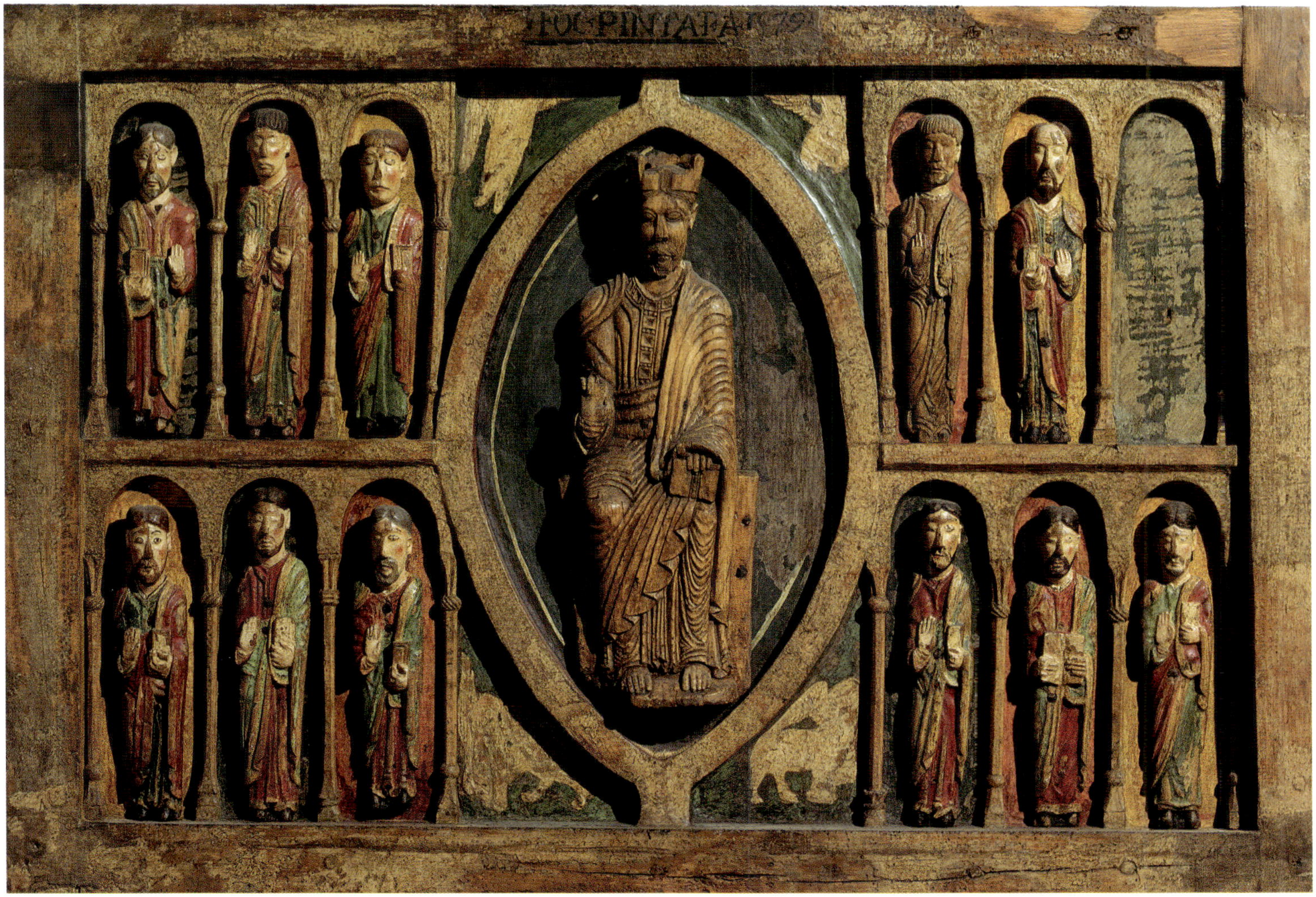

115. ALTAR FRONTAL FROM SANTA MARIA DE TAÜLL.
Around 1200 (repainted in 1579)
Woodcarvings polychromed in tempera
135 × 98 cm
From the church of Santa Maria de Taüll
(Boí Valley, Alta Ribagorça)
MNAC/MAC 3904

of an item from Aragon, the *Basarán Christ* (MNAC), at the ends of which can be seen the holes for the dowels with which the item must have been applied to the supporting panel.

In fact, applied sculptures in wood can include other types of object, like the capitals and other details of baldachins. This is illustrated by a capital of unknown origin reused to make the Toses Baldachin. Similarly, it's important to bear in mind the seats and other church furnishings that have not survived. Amongst the most outstanding work is the faldstool in the cathedral at Roda d'Isàvena, carved in boxwood and painstakingly decorated with plant and geometrical motifs that bring to mind metal working, and others of a marked traditional nature that use highly simplified motifs and are difficult to date, like the *Sant Climent de Taüll Bench* (MNAC).

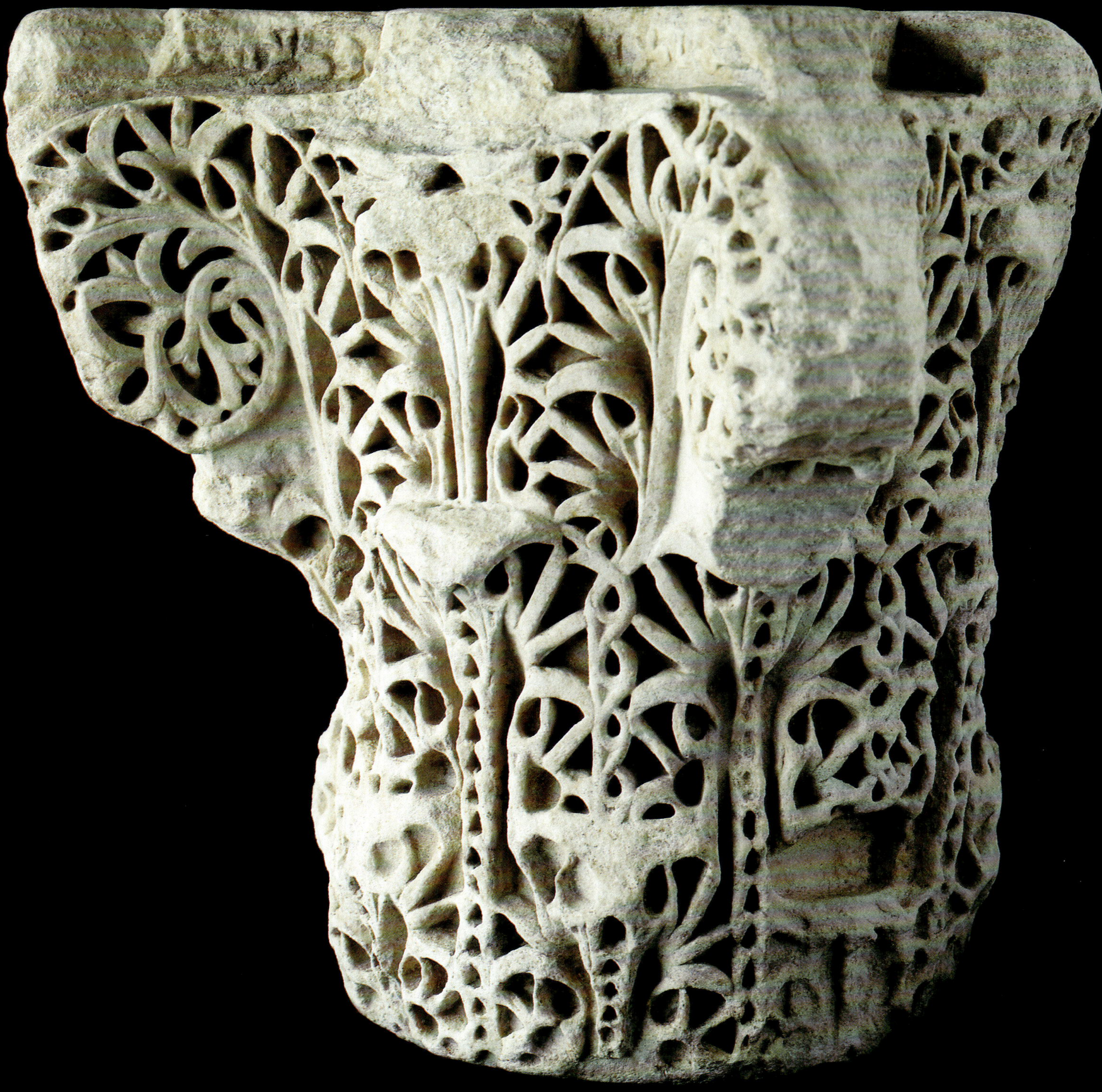

Stone Sculpture

Jordi Camps

The MNAC's sculpture collection contains an interesting collection of objects carved in stone in a timeframe ranging from the end of Antiquity (fifth to sixth centuries) to the Romanesque period (eleventh to thirteenth centuries). Taken together it gives a clear picture of the part played by the architectural sculpture of the Early Middle Ages and the Romanesque period, applied to portals, cloisters and various points in the interiors of churches, monasteries and cathedrals. Most of the exhibits are of Catalan origin and illustrate some of the centres, workshops and trends involved in Romanesque sculpture in Catalonia, along with their general evolution. Included are examples of eleventh-century Catalan sculpture and of some of the workshops that best represent the monumental sculpture of the twelfth century, such as Ripoll and Besalú, and items from sites in Barcelona belonging to the last decades of the twelfth century and to the thirteenth century. Outside the Catalan context, there is one outstanding group of items from tenth-century and eleventh-century Al-Andalus, amongst them some from Cordoba, which reflect the splendour of the Hispano-Muslim world.

The initial basis for the MNAC's collection of stone carving was the collection in Barcelona's old 'Museo Provincial de Antigüedades', which for years had been housed in the chapel of Santa Àgata, gradually growing in size. It contained items of architectural sculpture (especially capitals) recovered from abandoned religious buildings and saved from destruction during Barcelona's nineteenth-century urban reforms. Many of these objects are therefore already mentioned in the catalogue published by Elías de Molins in 1888. Some of the exhibits later entered the museum in La Ciutadella, amongst them the capitals that must have been located as a result of the research programmes at the beginning of the twentieth century. These included capitals from the cloister of Sant Serni de Tavèrnoles in 1906 and—one of the few items that are not Catalan—a capital decorated with interlaced patterns, now considered to be from the Languedoc artistic sphere. Later there were other significant additions, such as the series of items from the castle church in Camarasa, which had formed part of the exhibition 'El Arte en España' in the framework of the 1929 International Exhibition, and especially with the acquisition of the Plandiura collection in 1932. In the course of the second half of the twentieth century the collection was gradually built up with other occasional additions. Amongst the most important of these were the Andalusian capitals that came from donations by private organisations and antiquarians during the 1970s and 1980s, or the group of capitals from Santa Maria de Besalú, thanks to the transfer in lieu of tax from the Godia collection in 1994. More recently, two capitals from the Jaume Juan i Arnal collection were donated in 2000, probably from the cloister of the monastery of Sant Serni de Tavèrnoles, which completed the group of items acquired at the beginning of the twentieth century.

The period from the fourth to eighth centuries includes the stages that mark Late Antiquity, with the changes in the Roman World and the crisis of the Western Empire. Within this framework we can observe how compositional schemes and technical resources obey different principles to those of the classical world, even though many elements survive. On the Iberian Peninsula, this stage coincides largely with the rule of the Visigoths, heirs to the Hispano-Roman world. From this period, for example, is a bevel-carved relief from the former basilica in Barcelona which can be dated to the sec-

116. Andalusian caliphal capital from the alcázar of Córdoba.
Around 964-965
(according to the inscription from the time of Caliph Al-Hakam II)
Marble. 41 × 36 × 36 cm
From the alcázar of Córdoba
MNAC/MAC 122001

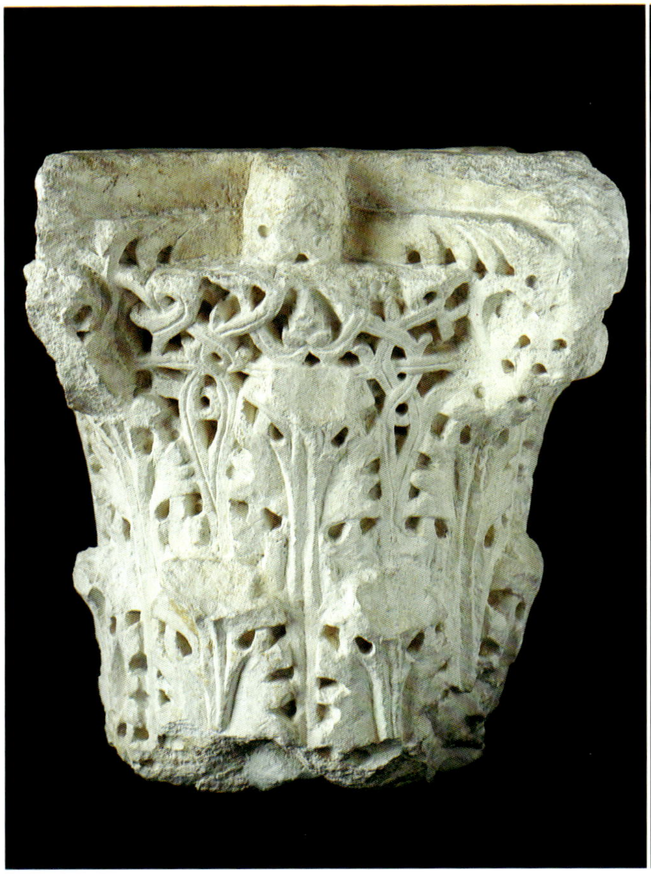
117

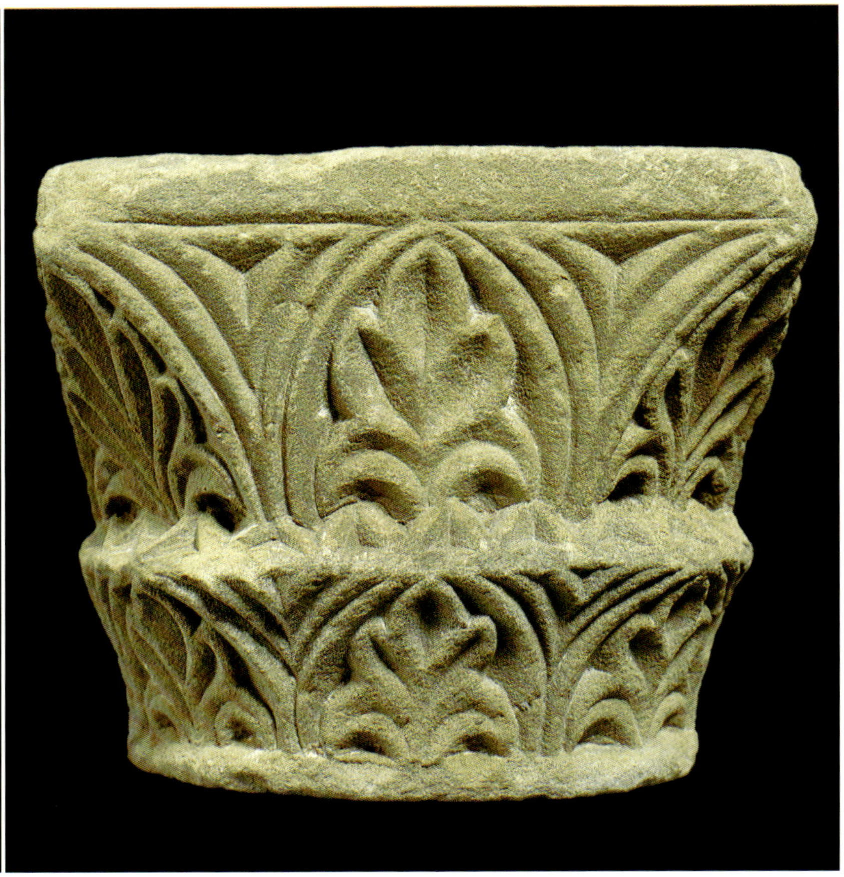
118

ond half of the sixth century. This technical resource makes use of the two planes and is based on chiaroscuro effects.

The Early Middle Ages in the Iberian Peninsula were marked by the splendour of the arts of the emirate and caliphate of Cordoba, basically the ninth and tenth centuries and the beginning of the eleventh. Examples of its architectural sculpture can be seen at the MNAC. One of them, a capital worked in white marble, has a pattern derived from the Corinthian capital, with two rows of acanthus leaves, carved in flat relief but with a design that hints at a naturalistic approach. The caulicoles are joined at the top of the capital by means of interlaced stalks. This work belongs to the period of the emirate and can be dated to about the first third of the tenth century, and therefore illustrates the survival of formulas from Antiquity, a characteristic of the early stages of Islamic art in general. Different circumstances are reflected in another item, one of the most outstanding Andalusian items kept at the MNAC, which probably comes from the Alcázar in Cordoba. Its composition is still related to that of Roman Corinthian and Composite capitals, with three crowns of acanthus leaves and large volutes, while there is a tendency towards more stylised forms in the treatment of the motifs and to chiaroscuro effects. The inscription that runs along the sides of the abacus dates the work to the time of the Caliph Al-Hakam II (AD 961-976, 350-366 AH), as it includes

117. ANDALUSIAN CAPITAL FROM THE EMIRO-CALIPHAL PERIOD.
First third of the 10th century
Marble. 28 × 23 × 24 cm
From Córdoba
MNAC/MAC 122673

118. CAPITAL FROM SANT PERE D'ÀGER.
11th century
Stone. 30 × 33 × 37 cm
From the crypt of the old collegiate church of Sant Pere d'Àger (Noguera)
MNAC/MAC 24002

119 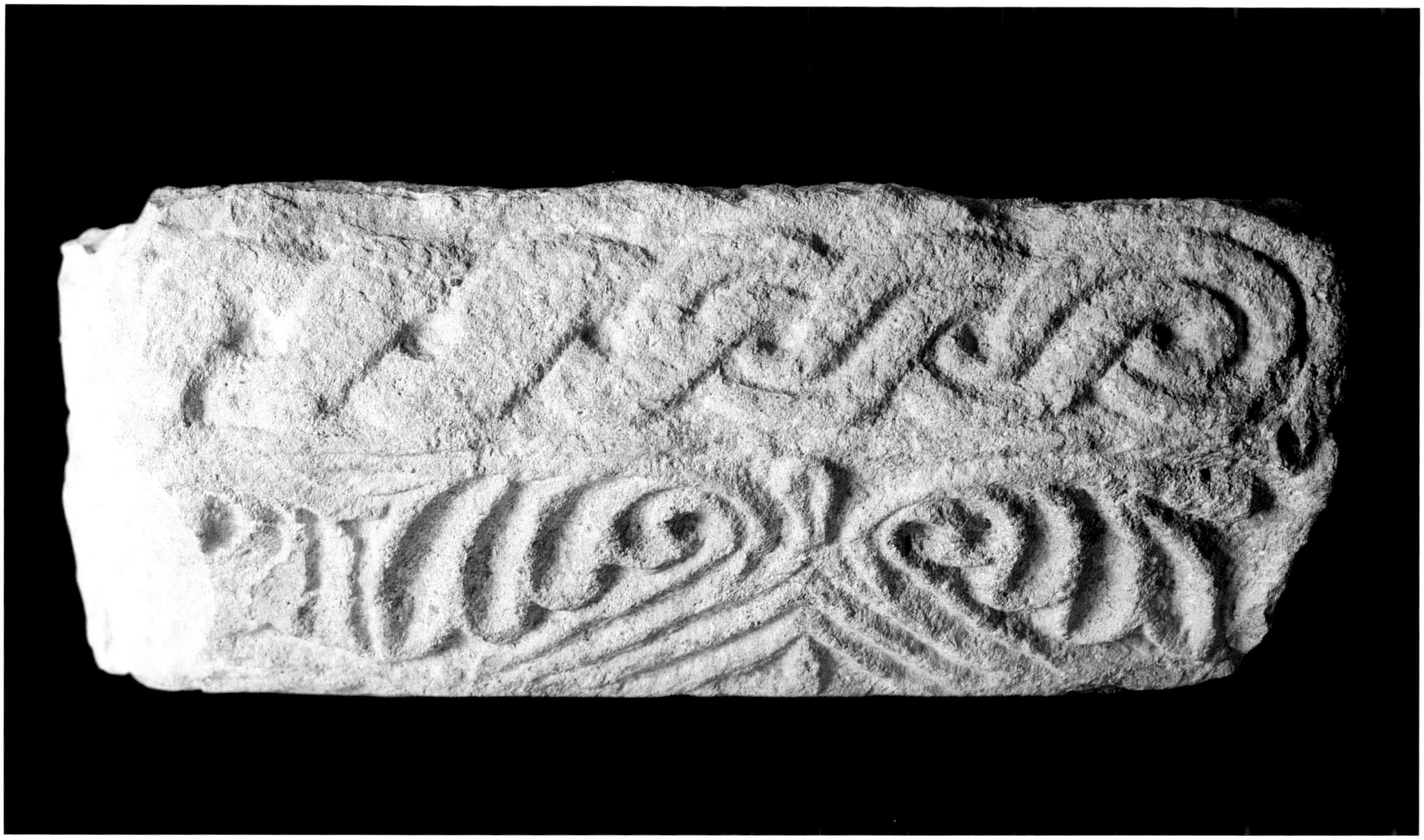

119. IMPOST FROM BARCELONA CATHEDRAL. *11th century* *Stone. 27.5 × 70 × 43 cm* *From the Romanesque cathedral of Barcelona* MNAC/MAC 14397

references to him. This item therefore belongs to one of the most brilliant periods in the art of the Caliphate of Cordoba, a time of exceptional works like the most lavish enlargement of the mosque in Cordoba, with the rich mosaics of Byzantine origin in the most sacred area (the *mihrab*) and the construction of the palatine city of Madinat al-Zahra.

During the same period, the situation in Catalonia is one of modest early constructions which have either not survived or else must have contained very few decorative elements. The first examples of a certain monumentality begin after 1000 with the construction of the first great cathedrals and monasteries. One of the most significant trends can be seen in the production of the figurative programmes on the Roussillonese lintels of Sant Genís de Fontanes and Sant Andreu de Sureda and on the façade of Sant Pere de Rodes, of which only the large window has survived. In these cases and in others, the carving is flat, on two planes and bevelled, and also resorts to highly characteristic geometrical and plant patterns based on palmettes and half-palmettes and rich in chiaroscuro effects. This type of relief, whose technique was related to the late Roman world and which also had ties to Byzantine sculpture, was to become highly characteristic of, though not exclusive to, eleventh-century Catalonia.

There are two clear examples of this type in the Museum. One is the capital and impost from the crypt of the church of Sant Pere d'Àger, which are largely covered with plant decoration of palmettes and half-palmettes. This work has been associated with the Viscount of Àger, Arnau Mir de Tost (d. 1072), and could belong to the central decades of the eleventh century. Next there are two imposts from Barcelona cathedral (consecrated in 1058), which must have formed part of the decoration on the pillars, like the ones kept at the Museu d'Història de la Ciutat de Barcelona. These are therefore important testimonies to Barcelona's Romanesque cathedral, lost with the construction of the new Gothic cathedral, beginning at the end of the thirteenth century.

The widespread use of architectural carving applied to façades, portals, cloisters, etc., and perfectly integrated in the building is something that began in Europe around the last quarter of the eleventh century. There was a return to sculpture seen as a three-dimensional component with a strong sense of volume and modelling, accompanied by the appearance of figurative and storied subject matter in every sphere. There are illustrative testimonies of this in the monuments in the north of the Iberian Peninsula (from Santiago de Compostela to Jaca), from Languedoc (Saint-Sernin in Toulouse), and in the North of Italy (such as Modena cathedral). It's thought that in Catalonia this renewal arrived slightly later than in these large centres, probably from the second quarter of the twelfth century, and in the main cases through the influence of foreign centres. From this date on, great eleventh-century centres like the monasteries of Ripoll, Cuixà or Sant Pere de Rodes or the cathedrals of Vic and Girona, amongst others, were the object of important changes, with the addition of new spaces and portals and construction or renovation of cloisters, accompanied by changes in the liturgical furnishings.

The models provided by repertories going back to Antiquity played a decisive role in the recovery of the sense of volume in Romanesque sculpture. In the Catalan sphere, this fact can be seen most clearly in the production centring on the 'Master of Cabestany'. This anonymous sculptor, whose work has also been traced in Languedoc and Tuscany, worked on important sites like the portal of Sant Pere de Rodes, the church of Sant Pere de Galligans (Girona) and the tympanum of the Roussillonese church of Cabestany, from which the artist gets his name. The surviving works reflect a knowledge and study of the resources provided by ancient and especially early Christian sarcophagi, like the reused examples kept in the presbytery of the church of Sant Feliu in Girona.

Another aspect of this connection with the ancient world is the survival of compositional schemes derived from the Corinthian capital. In Catalonia, one of the groups that best reflects this are the capitals in the church of Santa Maria de Besalú. The two levels of acanthus leaves and the volutes have a well-developed volume that shows a debt to ancient capitals and a certain relationship with centres in Mediterranean Languedoc and Provence, with which some Catalan centres maintained important ties. What's more, in this case it's quite possible that there was a tendency to a rather austere decoration characteristic of the canonical church of Saint-Ruf in Avignon (Provence), on which Santa Maria de Besalú had depended since the eleventh century. However, the fact that the repertories and the decorative tendency seem to coincide in no way imply a direct connection between the two workshops. Santa Maria, which has been partly preserved while some of the material has been scattered, must have been built towards the second third of the twelfth century. All together the picture is one of a relative cultural and artistic homogeneity in the Western Mediterranean regions, all of which are

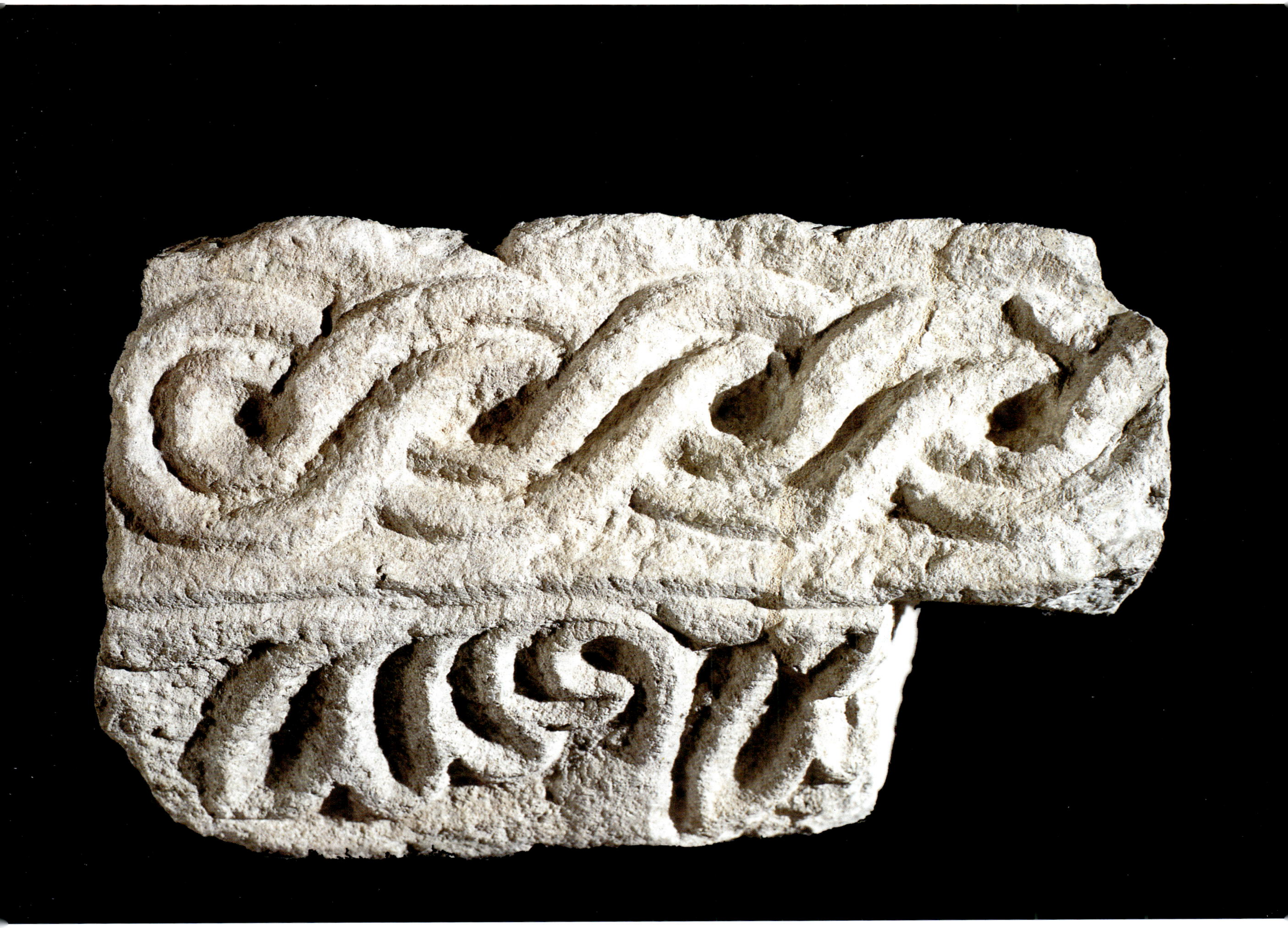

120

120. IMPOST FROM BARCELONA CATHEDRAL
11th century
Stone. 27.5 × 40 × 43 cm
From the Romanesque cathedral of Barcelona
MNAC/MAC 14398

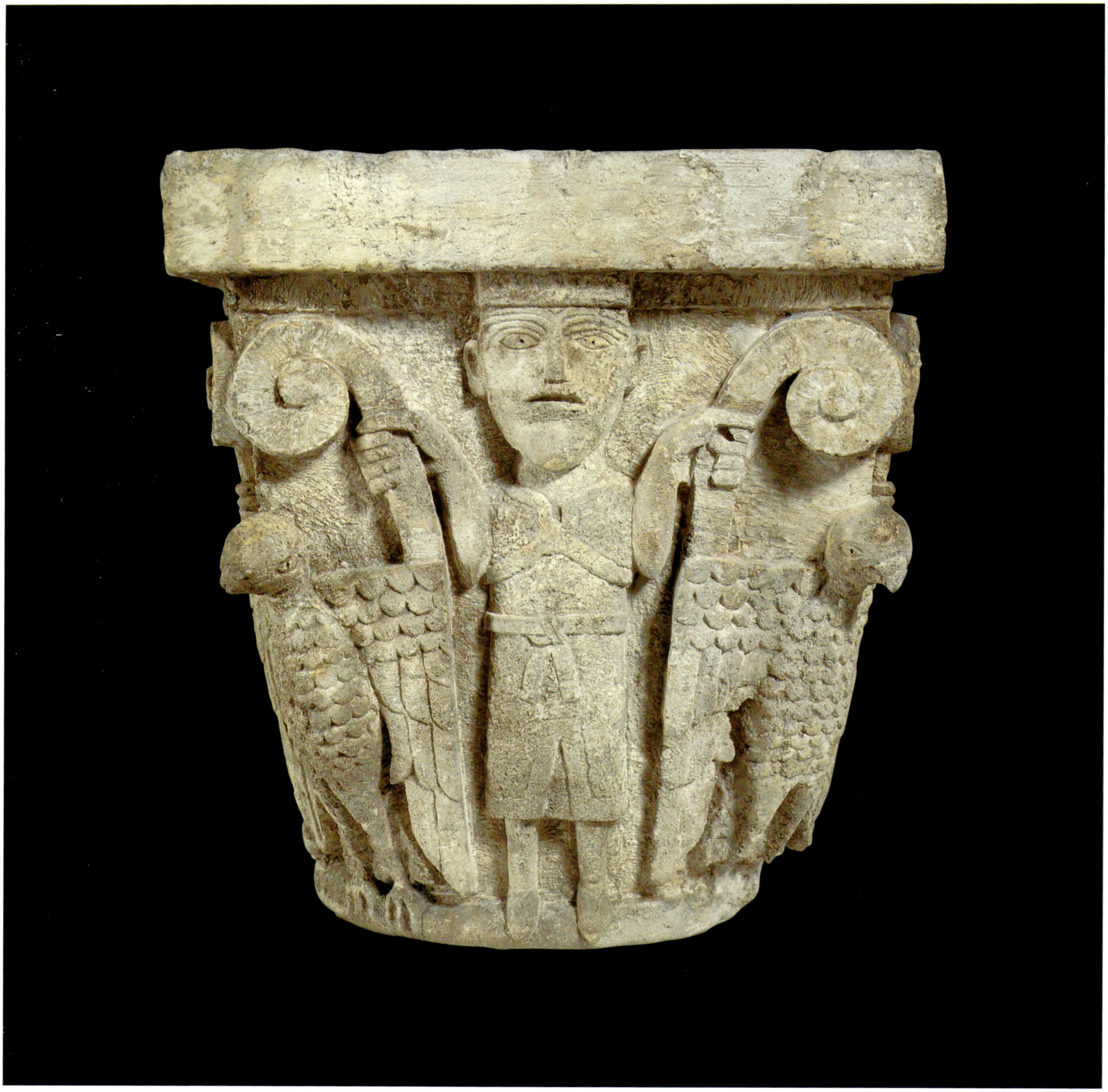

121

121-122. Capitals from Santa Maria in Besalú.
Between 1137 and 1167/1171
Stone. 64 × 55 × 56 cm; 63 × 56.5 × 56.5 cm
From the canonical church of Santa Maria de Besalú (Garrotxa)
MNAC/MAC 200688/200689

123. Detail of a Corinthian-style capital from Santa Maria de Besalú.
This detail shows the survival of the use, during the Romanesque period, of technical and decorative formulae related to the ancient Roman world

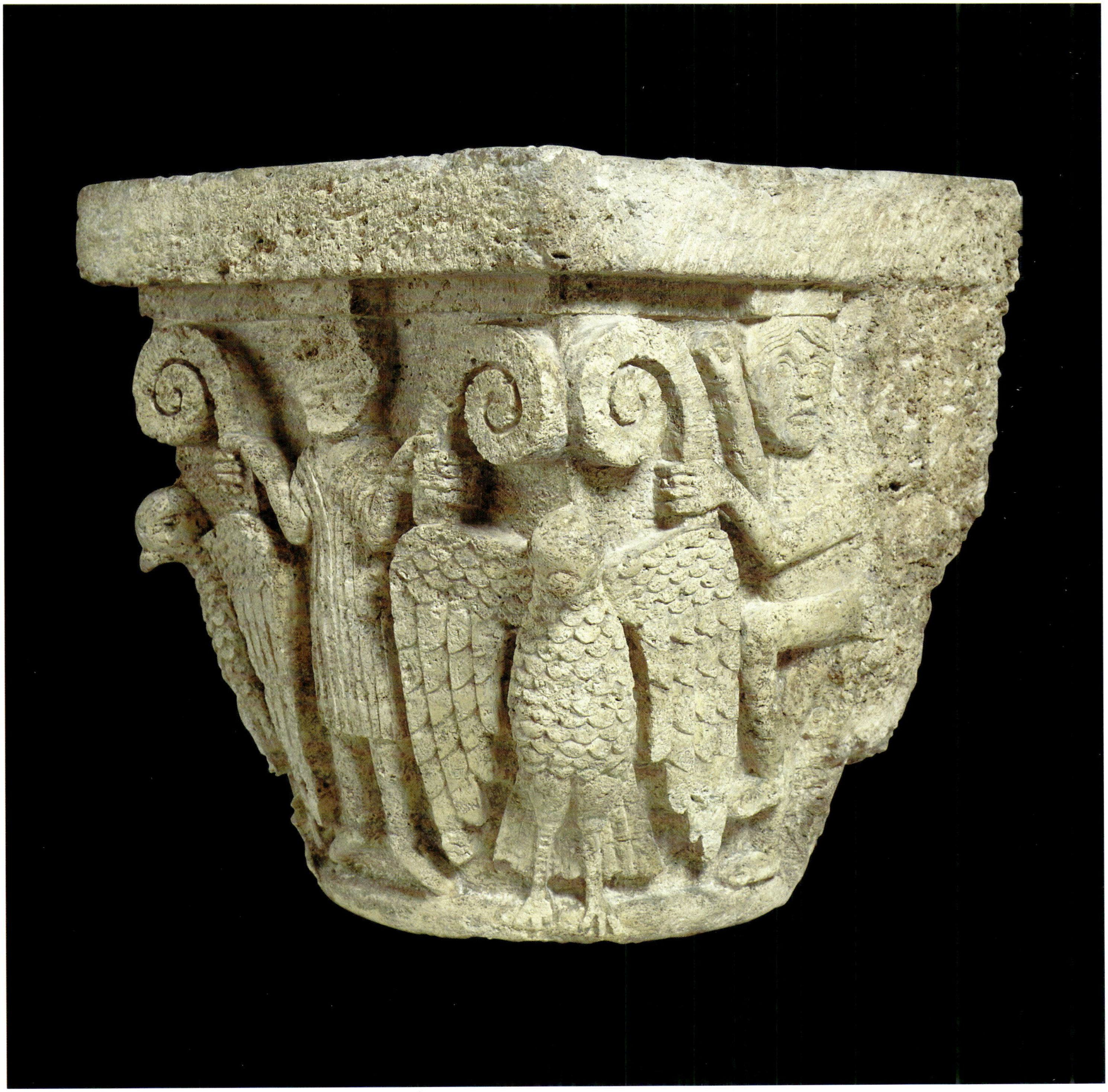

122

124. Voussoir from Ripoll.
Second third of the 12th century
Sandstone. 52.2 × 34.5 × 26 cm
From the monastery of
Santa Maria de Ripoll (Ripollès)
MNAC/MAC 12264

125-126. Details of the pillar from the crossing at Camarasa.
The two historiated capitals are dedicated to the Original Sin,
with Adam and Eve near the Tree of Good and Evil,
and to the Sacrifice of Isaac. First third of the 13th century
Stone. 55 × 50 cm; 55 × 42 cm
From the pillar in the crossing of Sant Miquel de Camarasa Castle (Noguera)
MNAC/MAC 17605/ 17604

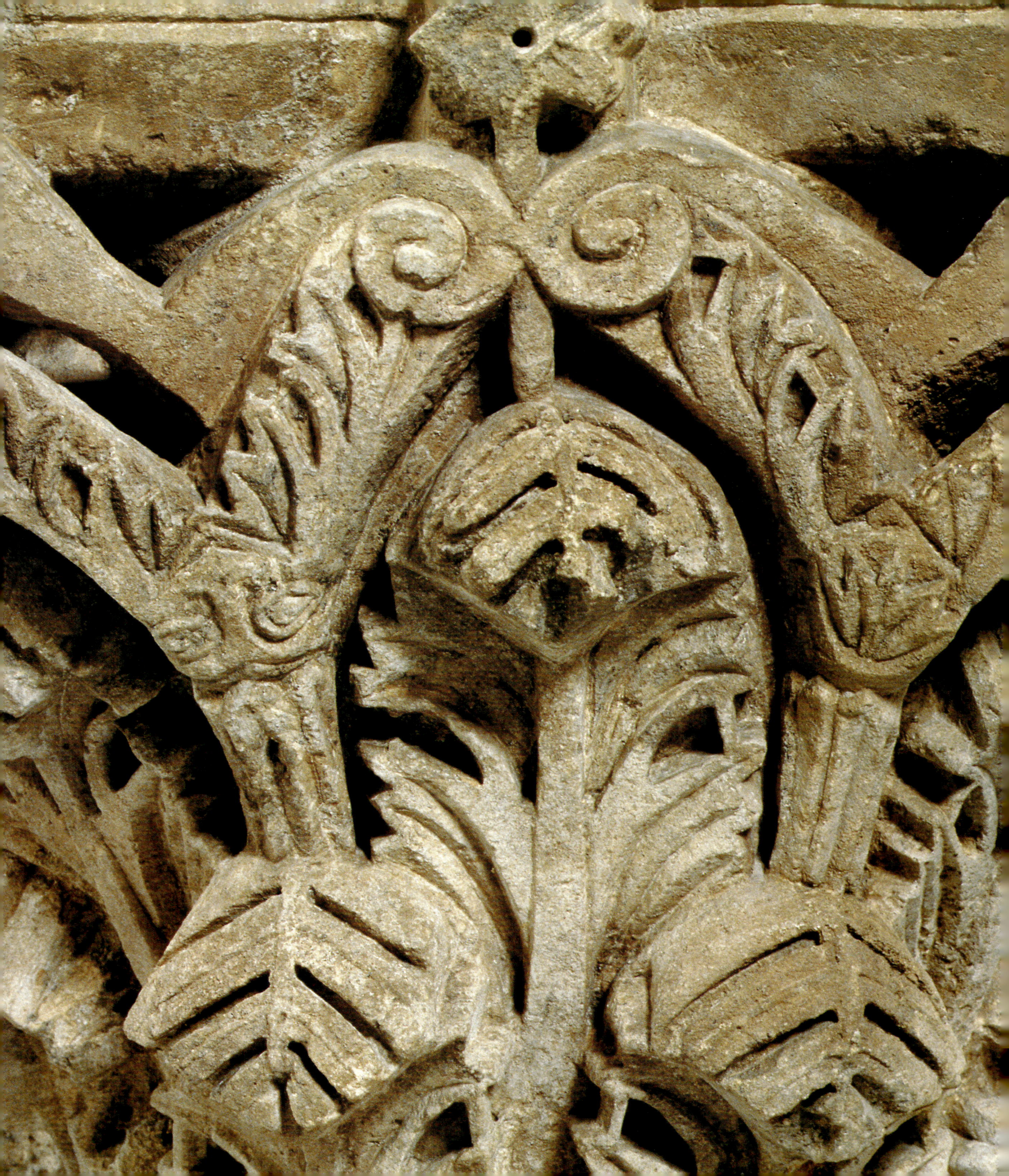

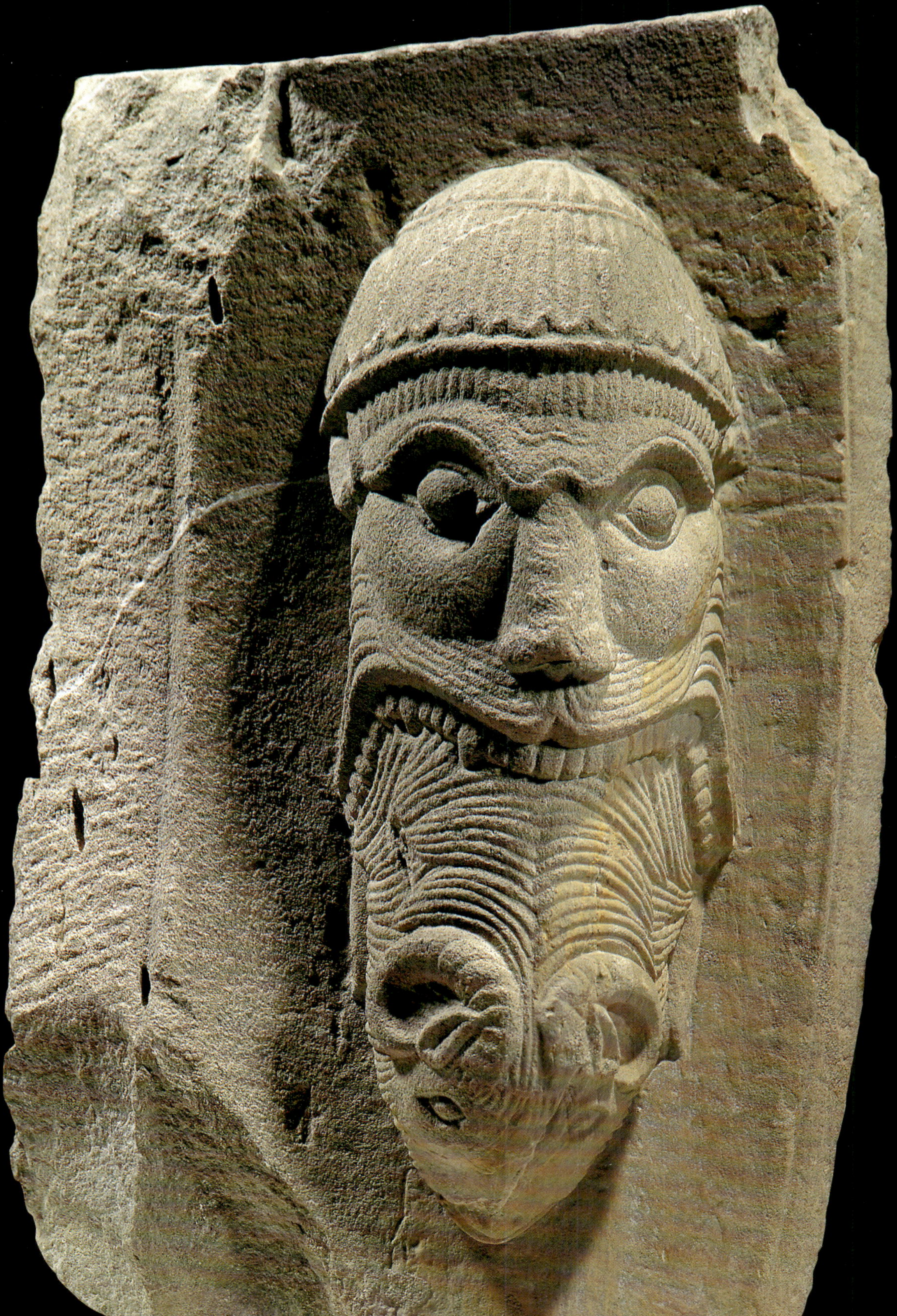

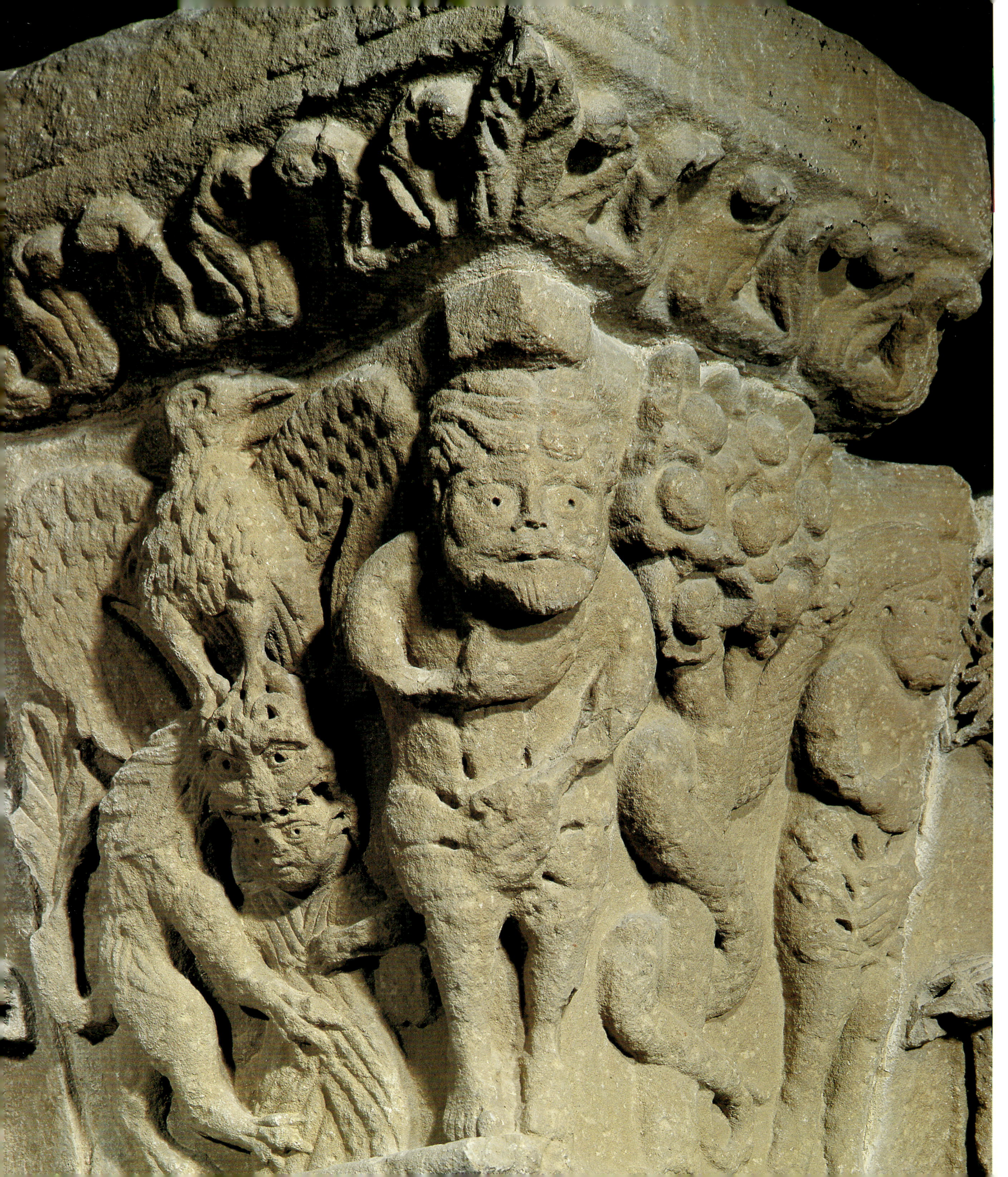

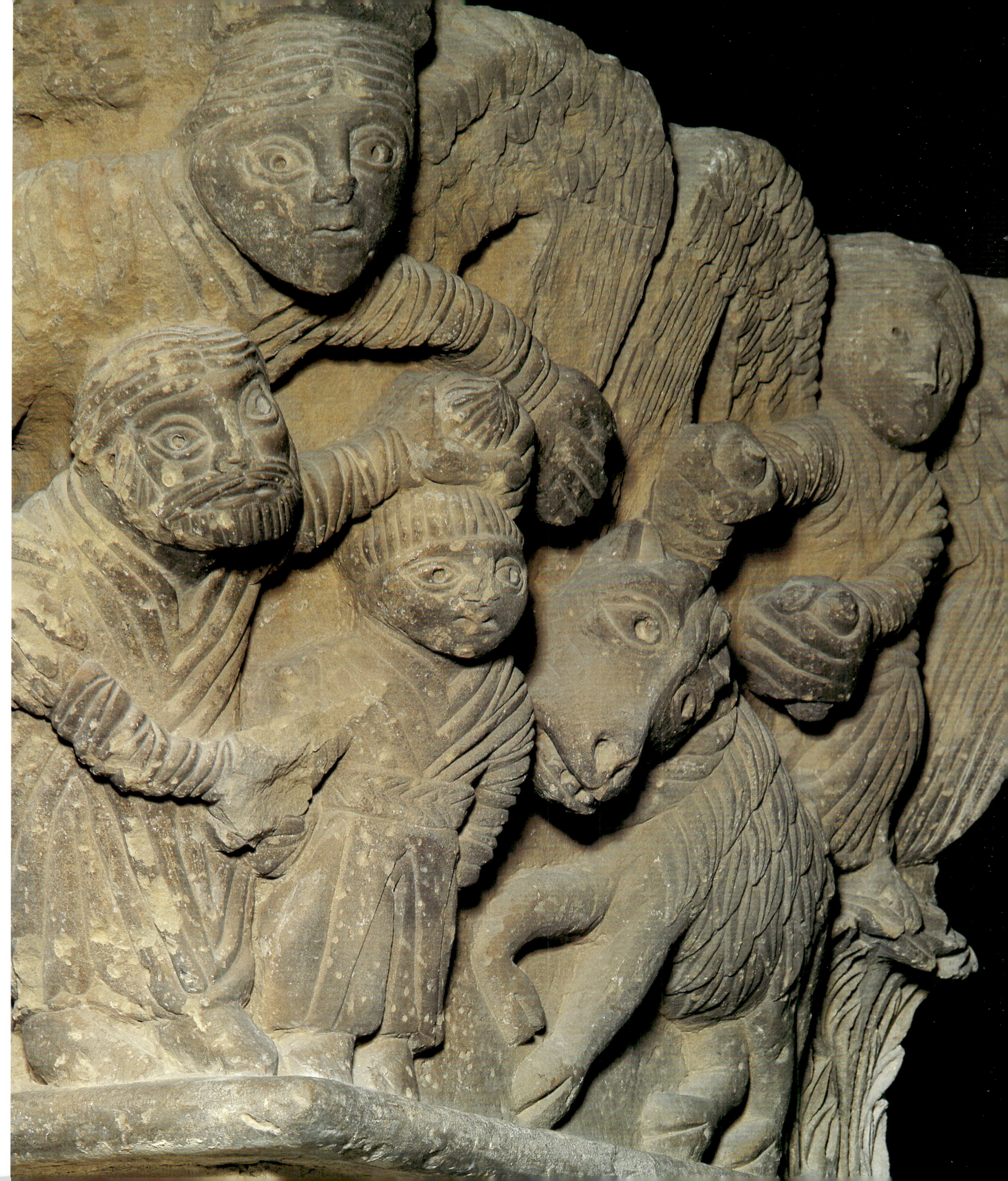

127
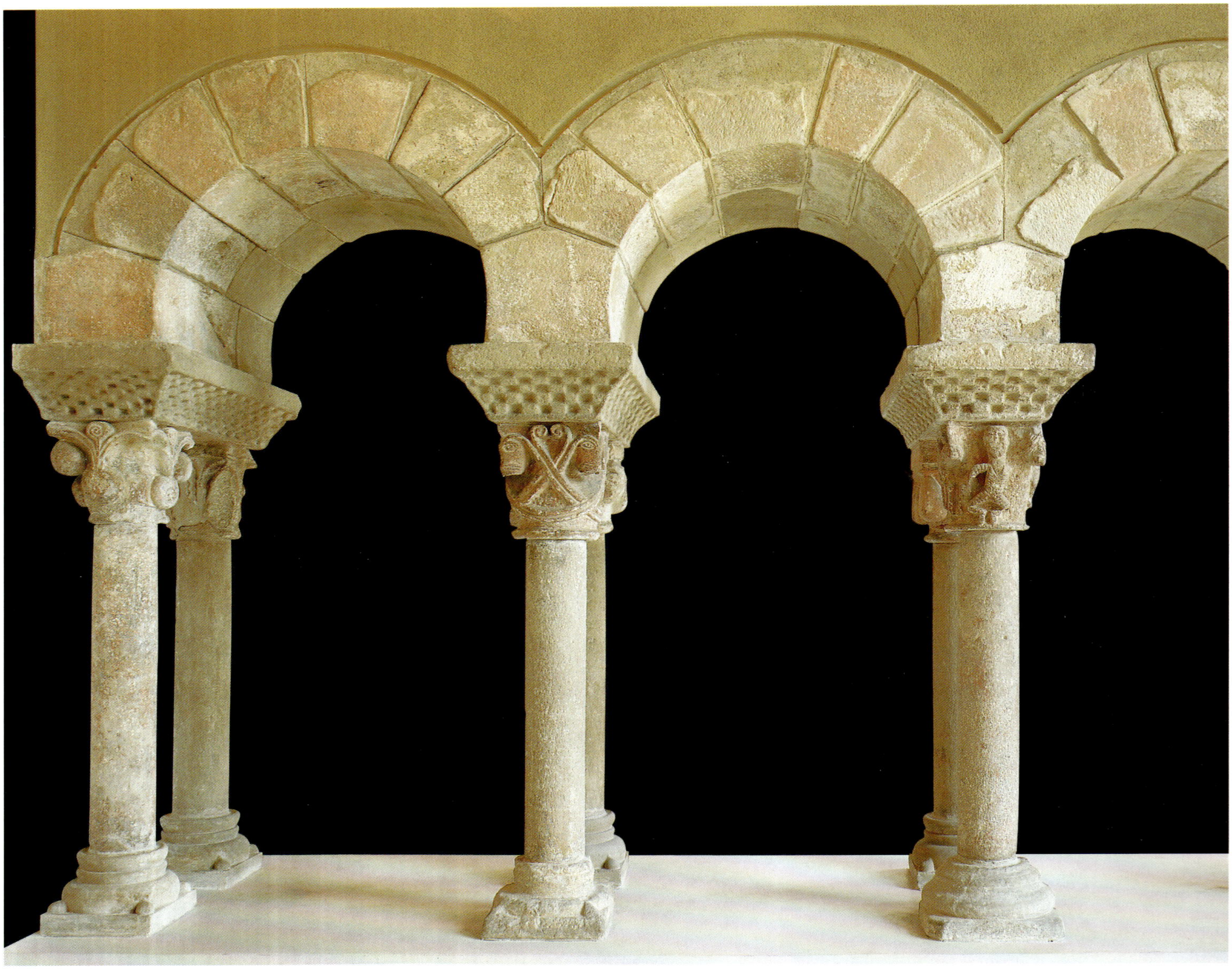

127. Pieces from the cloister of Sant Pere de les Puel·les.
The three arches are an assembly made in the time of Joaquim Folch i Torres from pieces coming from the Barcelona site.
After 1187
Stone, with traces of later polychromy
210 × 347 × 90 cm
From the church of the old monastery of Sant Pere de les Puel·les in Barcelona
MNAC/MAC 113143

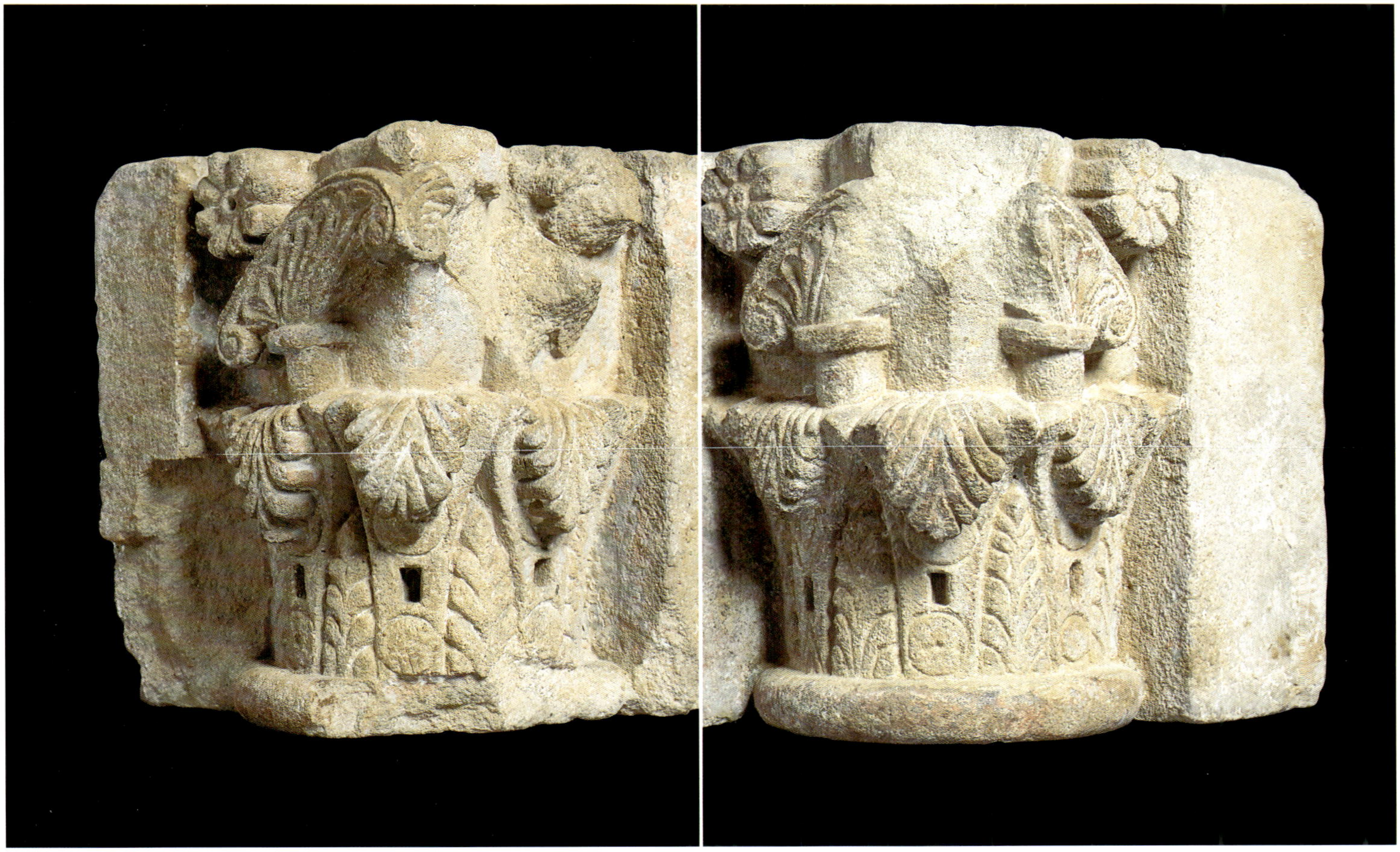

128

128. CAPITALS FROM SANT PERE DE LES PUEL·LES.
Late 12th century
Stone. 32 × 43 × 35.5 cm
32 × 36.5 × 35.5 cm
From a doorway in the old monastery of Sant Pere de les Puel·les in Barcelona
MNAC/MAC 9867/9868

129-130. CAPITALS FROM SANT NICOLAU DE BARCELONA.
Around 1200-1220
Marble. 29 × 23; 29 × 22 cm
From the cloister of the old pilgrims' hospital of Sant Nicolau de Barcelona, later the convent of Sant Francesc
MNAC/MAC 14202/14203

profoundly marked with the imprint of the ancient Roman world, a homogeneity into which Catalonia fits perfectly.

The presence in Besalú, and specifically in Santa Maria, of this sculpture with influences from Late Roman Antiquity contrasts with other options to be seen in other work in the same church (the tympanum of the west portal, for example, kept at the Conventet in Barcelona, next to the monastery of Pedralbes) and in the buildings of Sant Pere and Sant Vicenç, which are far more closely related to the trends deriving from the sculpture of Roussillon and Ripoll, which is very different from those dealt with earlier.

The main centre in the Eastern Pyrenees is undoubtedly the abbey of Santa Maria de Ripoll, where the building from Abbot Oliba's time, which had been consecrated in 1032, underwent extensive work in the second third of the twelfth century. This work culminated in the great portal, a unique work in Europe, the cloister and other buildings and also elements of its liturgical furnishings. The MNAC keeps a voussoir from this important centre, probably once part of a doorway, which is decorated with a head with demonic features apparently devouring a sheep, of which only the front half is visible. This motif can be seen in other parts of the monastery and shows that this repertory, which is common in Romanesque in general, was also known in Ripoll. From the

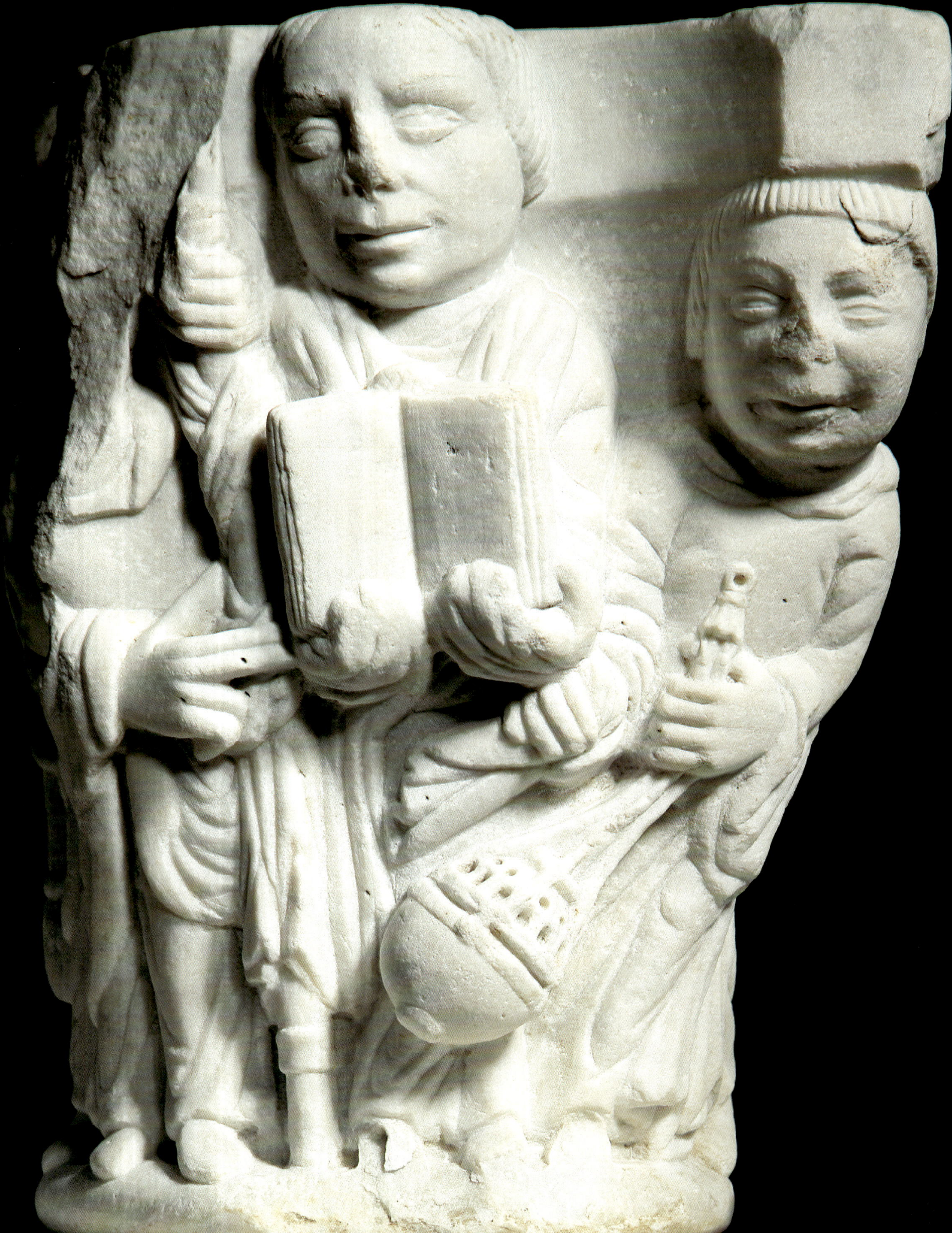

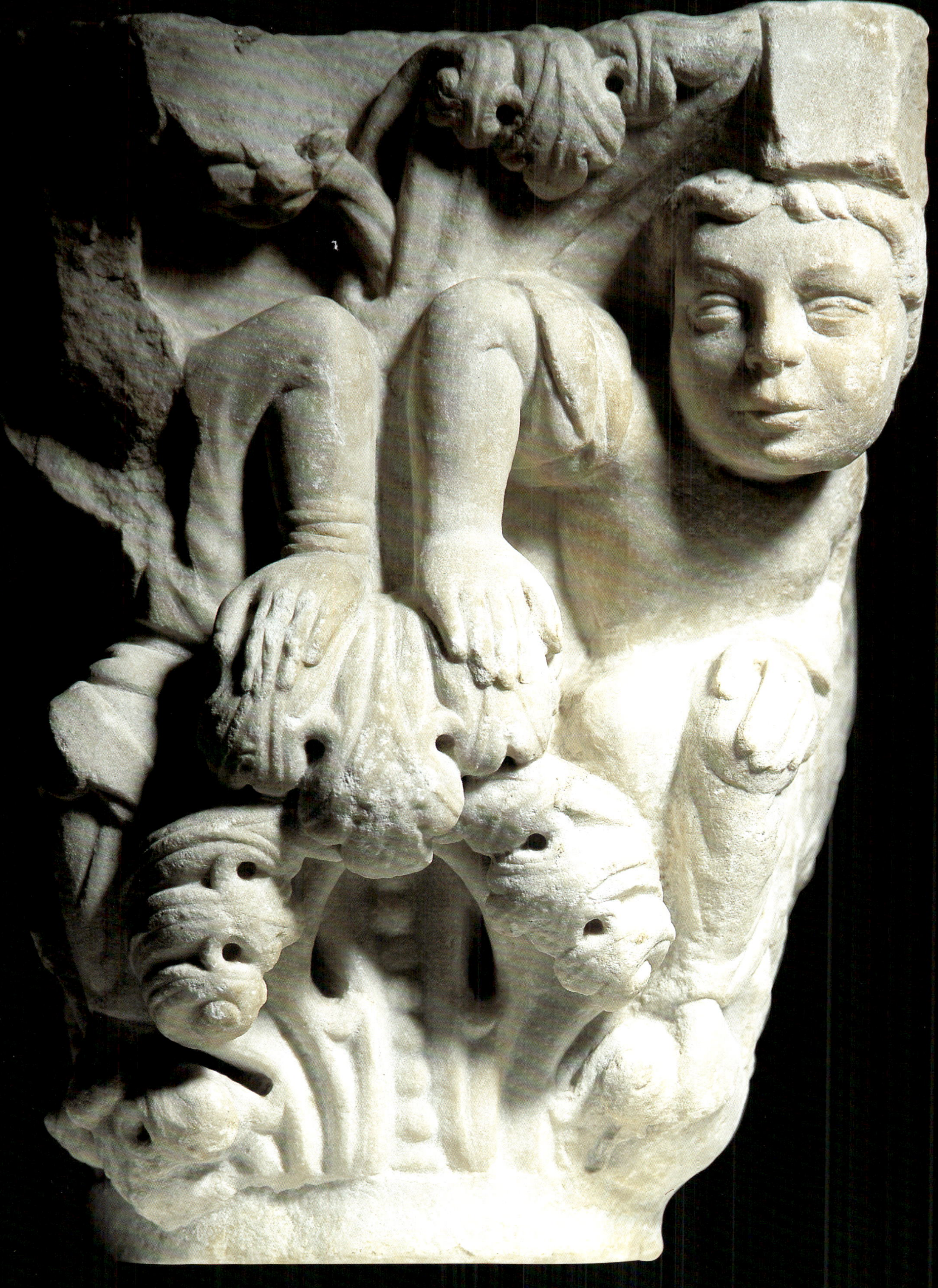

point of view of technique, the work shows a marked sense of detail, built up from very precise and clearly geometrised lines and volumes that convincingly emphasise the ferociousness of the head (pointed ears, large mouth, etc.). Stylistically, it coincides with the general features of the Ripoll doorway, which backs up the belief that this well preserved item is part of the building work done in the second third of the twelfth century. The Museum also keeps another stone carving from Ripoll, a lion's head from one of the bases of the baldachin, also from the same time. The carving from Ripoll, which is substantially based on the abbey's own tradition, reflected for example in the use of storied subject matter based on the eleventh-century bible, also shows points of contact with trends linked to the world of Toulouse and repertories used in the north of Italy. It is continued or reflected in various sites in the surrounding area and in the sculptural decoration of Vic cathedral, which was also renovated in the twelfth century.

Between the end of the twelfth century and the first decades of the thirteenth century a large number of workshops active in Catalonia took part in the renewal that affected Europe from the middle of the twelfth century. On the basis of Byzantine influence, which was renewed under the Komnenos dynasty, and of the presence of a powerful classical component, the figures tend to be more corporeal and the gestures of the characters more realistic. Nevertheless, there is an enormous range of treatments and trends, which responds to a complex network of influences, though it does seem clear that this new taste also has something to do with the growing power of the courtly world, which often appears as the patron of the works.

In Catalonia, these movements coincide with the start of the construction of the Cistercian monasteries, marked by a strong tendency towards austere decoration, but also of the cathedrals of Tarragona and Lleida, as well as other buildings of some size like the churches of Camarasa and Sant Martí Sarroca. These monuments reflect the convergence of workshops and trends that to different degrees and with different stylistic options joined in the 1200 renovation, often stamped with the influence of Roman Antiquity and showing more developed figurative work.

This is the case of the church in the castle of Camarasa (Noguera), which had a broad decorative programme covering the capitals on the interior and exterior of the east end. Of the narrative cycles from the interior of the crossing, the Museum conserves the one from the south-east corner, where the Old Testament subject matter appears on capitals with plant motifs derived once more from ancient Corinthian. Its present installation in the Museum shows the details of the work and demonstrates the idea of monumental architectural sculpture applied to the constituent elements of the Romanesque building. On the left is a representation of the Original Sin, with Adam and Eve on either side of the tree of Paradise and the serpent curled around it symbolising the Devil. This subject matter representing the Fall of Man is complemented with a representation of Isaac's Sacrifice on the same pillar from the crossing. This scene, a common one due to the association between the idea of sacrifice and that of the Eucharist celebrated at the altar, close to the crossing, foreshadows the death of Christ, so that it can also be interpreted as an announcement of the salvation of Mankind. However, the rest of the representations in the crossing, which are preserved *in situ*, with scenes like the Nativity, are needed to give a global explanation to the work. Stylistically, the forms take on a certain sense of relief, though on the basis of simplified volumes and planes, a treatment that in fact derives from the style of the cloister doorway in Tarragona, worked in marble. There are also points in common between the two sites as regards the repertories and the iconography.

Decorative elements from the inside of the large windows of the apse in Camarasa and from the exterior are also preserved. They use a repertory of plants and interlaced elements treated as free and agile forms. Both from this point of view and from that of the items in the interior, the site at Camarasa belongs to a sculptural tendency to be seen in Tarragona and Barcelona from the final decades of the twelfth century and in works in their respective cathedrals. The finest examples of these trends can also be found in Barcelona, in the church of Sant Pau del Camp, and with a more limited technique in the church of the castle of Sant Martí Sarroca.

At some distance and with unequal results, in Sant Pere de les Puel·les, in Barcelona, a similar workshop was also active, of which there are testimonies kept in the MNAC displayed on a structure evoking part of the arch of a cloister. It was built in the days of Joaquim Folch i Torres and consolidated, using the same arrangement, in 1995. The series of arches supported on pairs of columns with carved capitals puts the emphasis on the sculpture's function and brings to mind the exceptional series of Romanesque cloisters preserved in Catalonia. Sant Pere de les Puel·les was once a feminine Benedictine convent in the city. It was abandoned in 1835 and the cloister was demolished in 1879 along with other buildings. Its subject matter is based on plant themes of some simplicity, such as plain leaves crowned by inverted palmettes, interlacing, like that of other sites in Barcelona such as the cloister of Sant Pau del Camp or the remains of two galleries in the Palau Episcopal, amongst others. There are also examples of figurative art, though rather crudely done. To some extent, the connection with these sites in Barcelona agrees with the only information we have about the cloister, from 1187, when Beatriu de Rocafort undertook to have a cloister built opposite the door of the monastery refectory. In fact, the items at the MNAC match the ones to be found scattered around other Catalan museums (Museu de Terrassa, Museu Santacana de Martorell) and in a farmhouse in Sant Antoni de Vilamajor. From the same monastery are two capitals from a portal, decorated with plant themes, with a structure derived from Corinthian, with acanthus leaves.

However, one of the best examples of the standard reached by thirteenth-century sites in Barcelona can be found in the group of three small capitals worked in marble, from the old Hospital de Sant Nicolau. They were discovered as a result of building work in Plaça del Duc de Medinaceli, once the site of the hospital, which in 1232 became the convent of Sant Francesc. In fact, Francis of Assisi stayed at this hospital on his visit to Barcelona in 1214. The first capital, carved on two sides, shows three beardless characters who emerge from a row of very fleshy acanthus leaves. This subject shows a direct relationship between the sculpture on this building and the sculpture derived from the *Pórtico de la Gloria* of Santiago de Compostela cathedral, where it appears on the archivolt of the left portal. Similar representations also appear on buildings in its sphere of influence in Galicia. The second capital shows a scene alluding to a recently identified Saint Nicholas with his entourage, in an iconography also present in other hospitals dedicated to the same saint, such as on the doorway of San Nicolás de Soria (Castile). Amongst the objects present is a sort of pail, which may be an allusion to one of the saint's miracles, that of the resurrection of the three children, a subject that is deployed in the cloister of Tarragona cathedral. The forms show a certain proximity to Gothic formulas, especially as regards the characters' features, for which reason it has been given a later date towards the first decades of the thirteenth century. It's difficult to be certain about the precise function of these items; it has been suggested that they might come from a small cloister there was in Sant Nicolau or from a funerary work. Whatever the case, it's worth noting the small size of the items compared to the ones in the cloisters of the time.

In short, this group of pieces is a clear sign that a workshop in an establishment in Barcelona had links with one of the most important Romanesque sites, the cathedral in Santiago de Compostela, and with one of the works that illustrate the renewal in the arts during the last decades of the twelfth century and the first decades of the thirteenth.

There is another storied capital from this period, of similar size and material to the ones from Sant Nicolau, with which it was associated. Despite the similarities, this item entered the Museum later, to be precise through the purchase of the Plandiura collection, without its origin being specified. It shows a composition presided by two crowned figures on horseback, the one on the left male and the one on the right female. The rest of the figures seem to make up an entourage dominated by expressions of grief and concern. To date the subject matter has not been precisely identified, but what is interesting about the scene is its courtly nature, possibly a reference to a ceremony or episode future research will have to elucidate on. Stylistically, the item fits in with the trends that were current in Catalonia during the first decades of the thirteenth century, in keeping with tendencies that can be seen in the construction of the two new cathedrals. The convincing nature of the gestures and the postures of the characters reach the same standard as other 1200 productions, in the Hispanic sphere as well. As in the case of the items from Sant Nicolau in Barcelona, this capital shows to what extent the treatment of the characters and compositions places some Catalan works on an equal footing with other important Spanish sites in this advanced, or late, stage of Romanesque.

131. CAPITAL.
First quarter of the 13th century
Marble. 28 × 25 × 24.5 cm
Provenance unknown
MNAC/MAC 5290

131

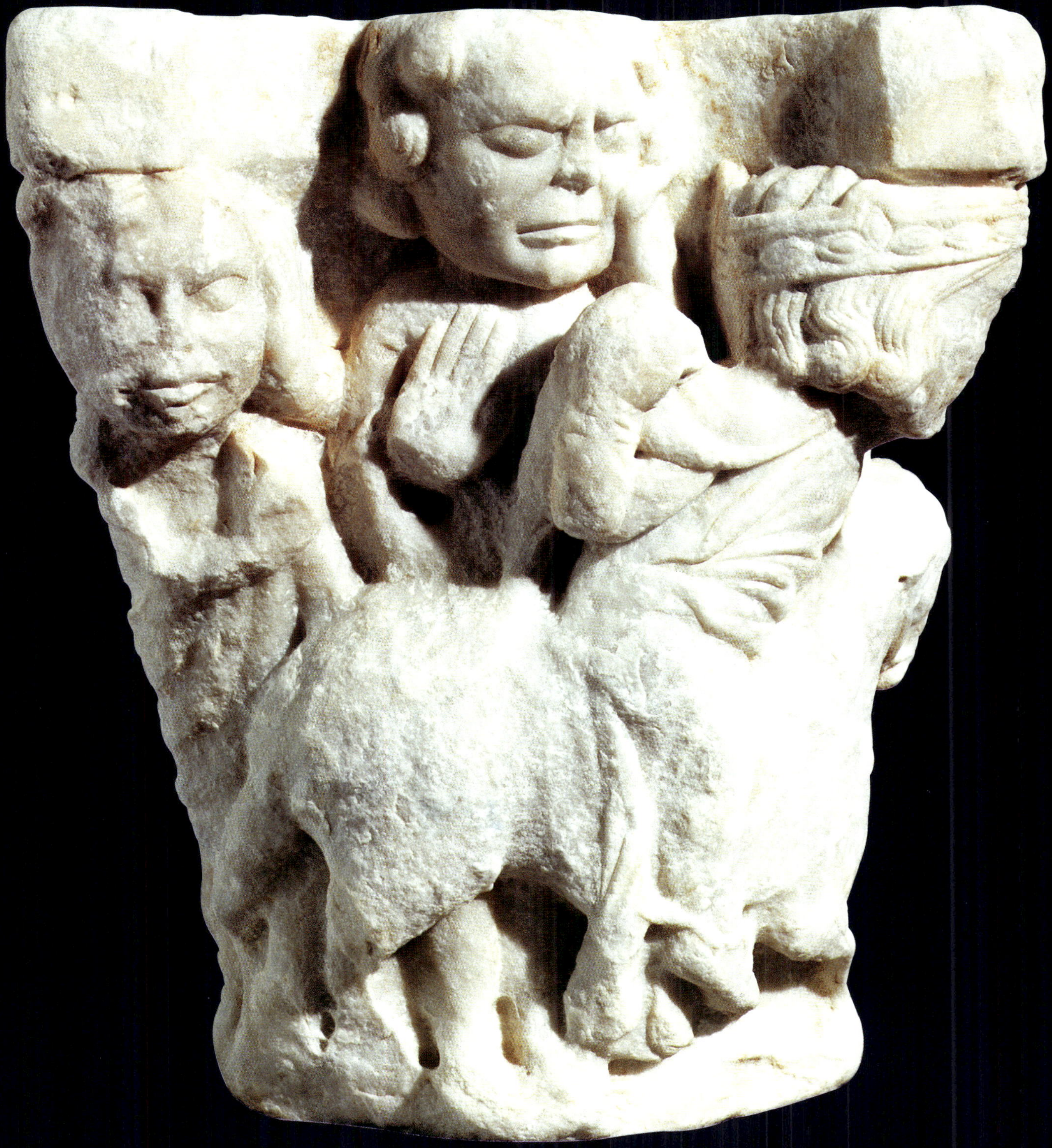

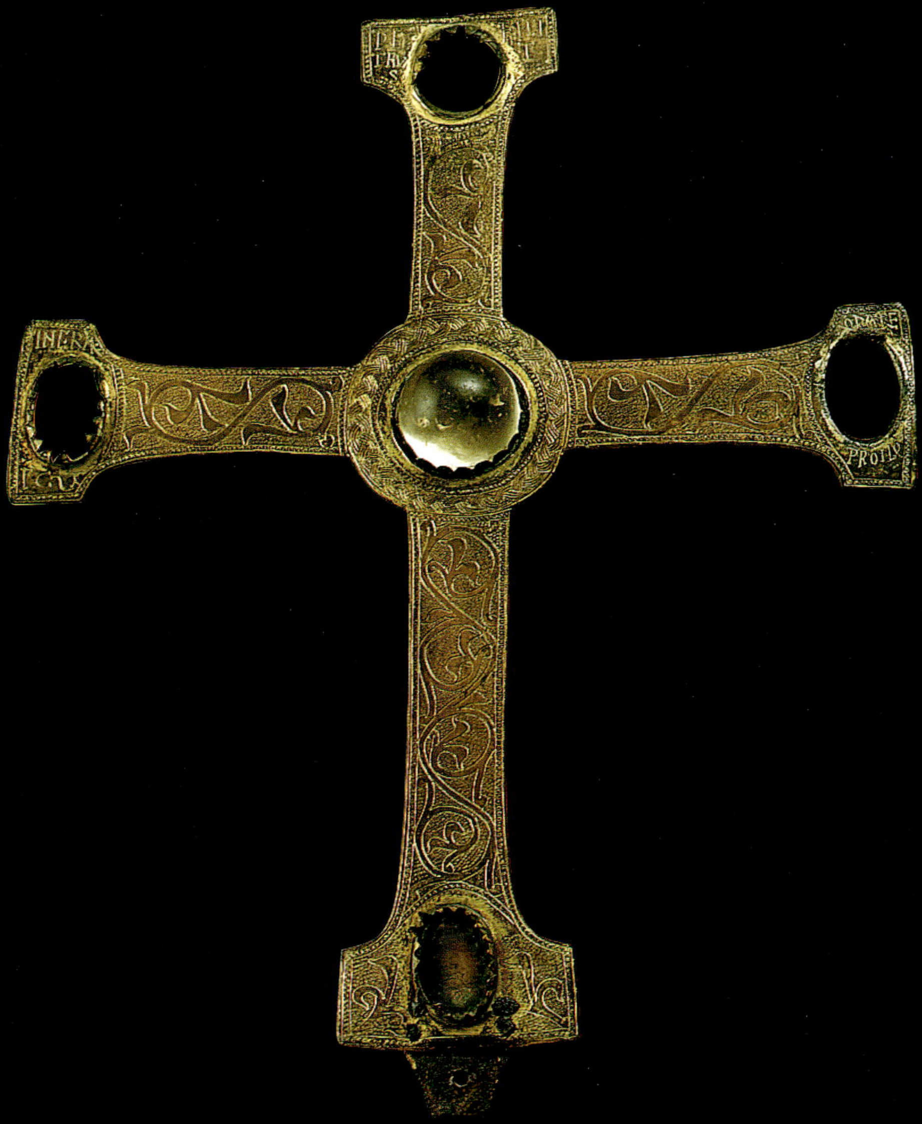

Metalwork: a Romanesque Treasury

Joan Duran-Porta

132. PETRUS CROSS.
Castilian in origin, it is an example of the late continuity, in the Romanesque period, of the tradition of aniconic Hispanic crosses. The five large original rock crystals (four of them are lost) gave it a special richness.
1122 (according to the inscription)
Bronze and rock crystal
47 × 39 × 4 cm
From Castile-León
MNAC/MAC 12180

The MNAC's collection of Romanesque metalwork has not always been given the attention it deserves and has often been overshadowed by the exceptional nature and fame of a large part of the Museum's paintings and carvings. The collection is nevertheless of a high standard that speaks for the diversity and wealth of the objects filling the ancient treasuries of medieval churches, objects that were used in liturgical celebrations but that at the same time made up the churches' material property. In a way, we could even say that they were collected, and exhibited to the faithful, at least on special occasions, in sacristies or in rooms specially reserved for that purpose. The most highly-prized items in these treasuries were the ones made with precious metals, especially gold and silver, which according to the allegorical interpretations typical of medieval thinking were associated with certain Christian virtues or symbols. According to the twelfth-century theologian Honorius of Autun, for example, gold could be thought of as an emblem of the Church's holy martyrs, while silver represented virgins.

In spite of these symbolic values, it goes without saying that in times of financial need spiritual demands took second place and items were melted down so as to reuse the metals for slightly more earthly purposes, especially for minting coin. This already happened, of course, in the medieval period itself, and has later been a constant throughout history. One well-known example in Catalonia is the Romanesque gold frontal in Girona cathedral, which was looted by Napoleon's troops during the Peninsular War at the beginning of the nineteenth century.

The MNAC's collection, like most modern collections of Romanesque metalwork, consists basically of less luxurious items than those of gold and silver which were therefore less greedily looted. This leads us to talk about enamels and their extraordinary importance and widespread presence. Because enamel decoration was enormously successful throughout medieval Europe, especially when it began to be applied to copper objects, which were much more economical than gold or silver ware and which with a coat of gilding on them made the same sumptuous effect. The taste for this kind of material reached Rome, and when the *confessio* (the space beneath the high altar connected with the grave of the Apostle) in Saint Peter's Basilica in the Vatican was renovated at the beginning of the thirteenth century, a large part of the decoration was also done in enamel. The two specialists hired to do the work were from Limoges, the chief production centre of the time.

This Occitanian city's workshops did indeed lead the production of enamels during the Romanesque period and their work was exported and sold all over Europe. Because of all this trade, a truly large number of these items made in Limoges, known during the Middle Ages as 'Oeuvre de Limoges', have come down to us today. As we shall see in a moment, this type of object is by far the most abundant in the Museum's Romanesque treasury.

Interest in medieval metalwork in Catalonia, like the rest of Europe, was aroused during the nineteenth century. The Romantic revaluation of the national past, coinciding with the developing taste for and appreciation of the arts and crafts that mark the scholarly but also practical interests of the men of the *Renaixença*, with the final explosion of *Modernisme*, provided particularly suitable circumstances for the admiration of ancient sumptuous arts. The arousal of interest and public awareness of this type of object (and very especially of the Limoges enamels) was partly a result of big exhibitions of art and antiquities held in Barcelona, as in other European cities, during the second half of the nineteenth century (1867, 1877 and 1888). These exhibitions' catalogues provided information about the exhibits and high-quality illustrations.

Public recognition of Romanesque metalwork meant that its value increased and it immediately drew the attention of the antiques market and leading collectors. A large part of the works still kept in Catalan churches and monasteries were bought then (or plundered) and most of them disappeared without trace, because being small items they were easily transportable and as there was no legislation to protect them there was nothing anyone could do to preserve them *in situ*.

During the years the MNAC was taking shape, in the first decades of the twentieth century, purchases of items of precious metal complemented the more widely known and publicised acquisitions of frontals, mural paintings and wood carvings. These acquisitions were largely a result of expeditions to the Pyrenees by members of the Junta de Museus, who had the opportunity to see some of these items still in place in the churches where they had been kept for centuries. Of course, contact with antiquarians and the art market of the time also played an important role and provided some interesting works. By way of example, an eleventh-century Castilian cross known as the *Petrus Cross* was bought from the Barcelona antiquarian Celestí Dupont in 1906, and another of the Museum's emblematic works, the enigmatic *Ciborium from La Cerdanya*, was purchased in 1918 from the art dealer Amadeu Sales of La Seu d'Urgell.

By 1930 the Romanesque treasury contained about twenty items distributed between two display cases in the museum premises in the Parc de la Ciutadella. Two years later, another forty or so items of Romanesque metalwork entered the Museum with the extensive Plandiura collection, mainly Limoges enamels, most of which apparently came from the Iberian Peninsula. However, we know that Plandiura had bought a lot of these items from a Paris antiquarian in a single lot.

During the years of the Republic, when the decision was taken to move the Museum to Montjuïc, the renovated collection of precious metal was left in an unusual situation. It wasn't included in the new premises inaugurated in 1934 because there were plans to set up a museum devoted exclusively to the sumptuous arts in the chapel of Santa Àgata in Plaça del Rei, which until shortly before had been the home of a state-owned collection of art and archaeology. In 1931 all the works of art as well as the beautiful Gothic chapel itself were transferred to the Junta de Museus, whose intention it was to turn it into 'an equivalent of the Musée de Cluny in Paris', in the

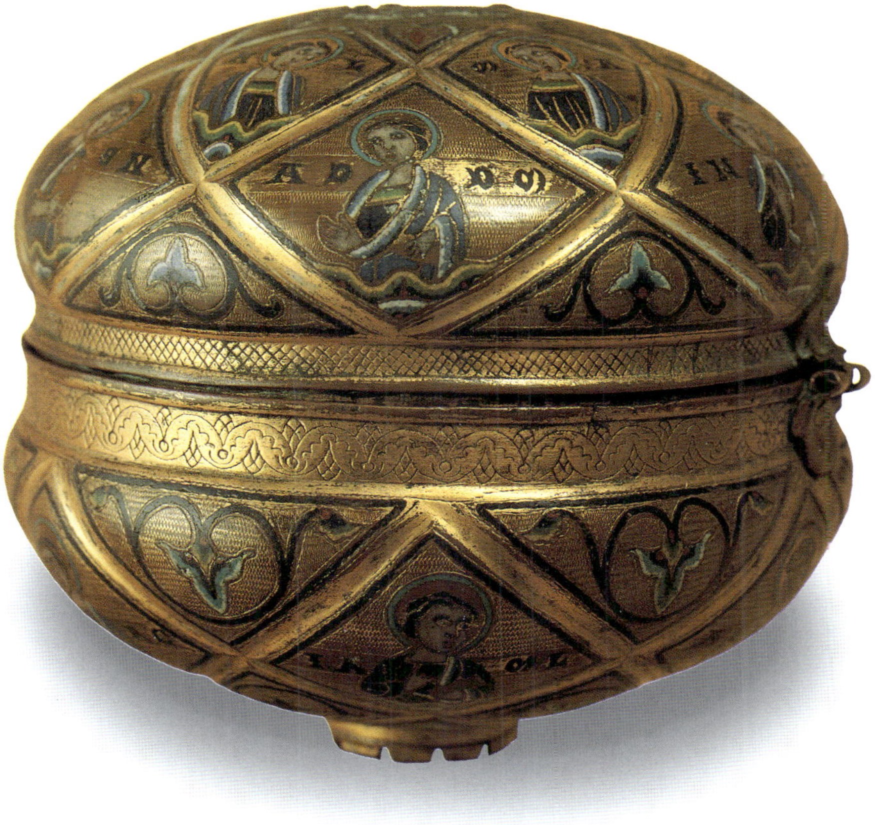

133

133. Ciborium from La Cerdanya. *Although it is conserved in a fragmentary state, it is one of the best pieces of metalwork in the museum. It has been linked to one of the most famous items to come out of the enamellers' workshops of Limoges, the ciborium of Master Alpais. Limoges, between 1195 and 1200. Copper melted, gilded and engraved, with the application of champlevé enamelling. 13.5 × 14 × 14 cm From an unidentified church in La Cerdanya MNAC/MAC 12106*

words of Joaquim Folch i Torres. As we know, the war prevented this project being carried out, as a result of which the Romanesque treasure was stored in boxes for some years, and it wasn't until the spring of 1961 that a large selection of the best items were exhibited in public again.

A long time had also gone by before any further additions were made to the collection in the 1950s. These additions were basically in 1958, with the bequest of the Espona collection, at which time more than sixty items of Romanesque metalwork entered the MNAC. Once again the Limoges enamels predominated, in particular works like the Casket of Saint Stephen and a Bishop's crosier with the scene of Saint Michael and the Dragon. Since then, it has only been possible to make sporadic additions to the collection with new acquisitions, the last one being a seventh-century Visigothic paten which has joined the Museum's small but representative collection of works from the Early Middle Ages but which strictly speaking, of course, isn't part of the Romanesque treasury.

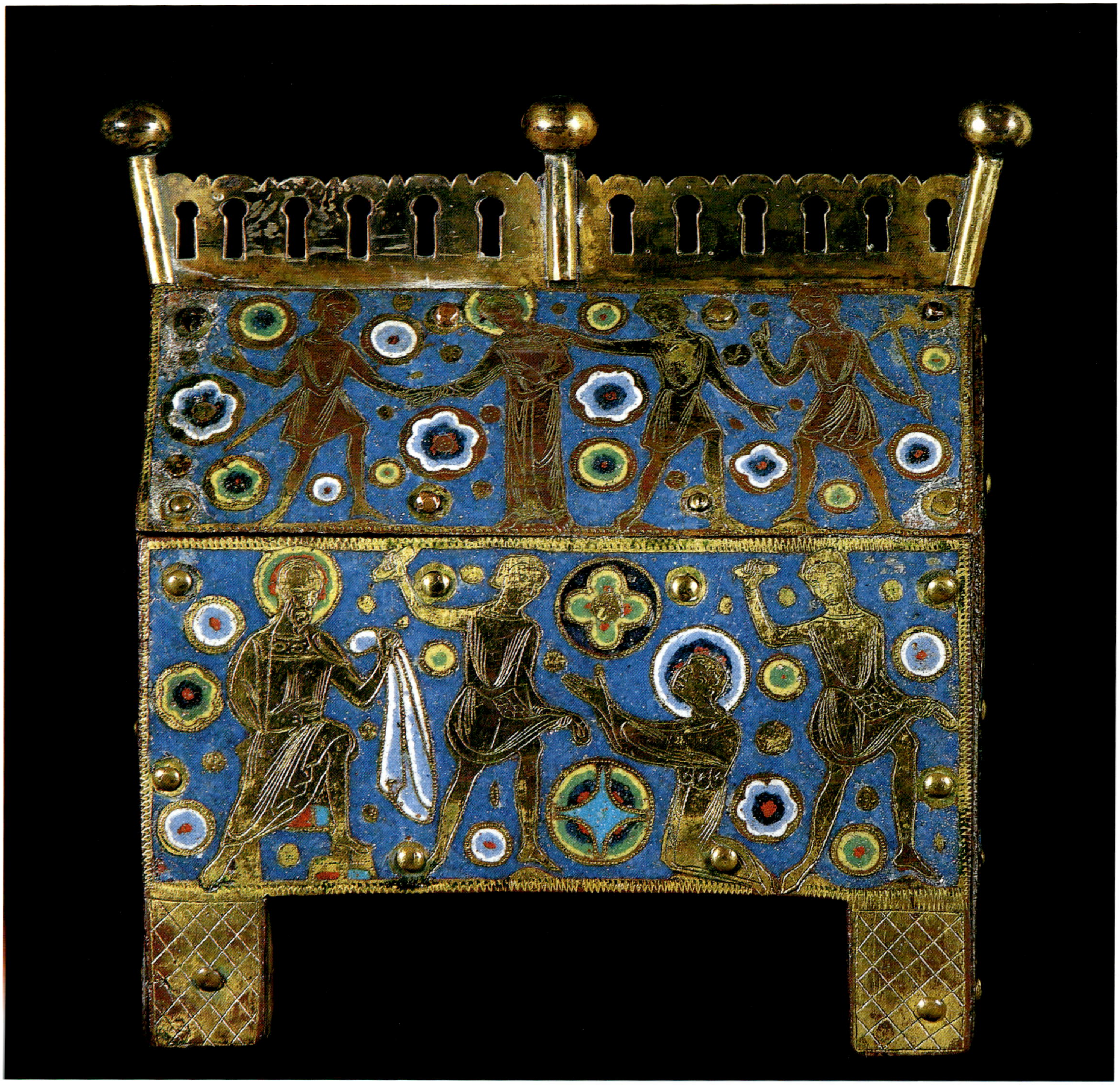

134

135

134. Saint Stephen Casket.
The martyrdom of Saint Stephen is represented quite habitually on caskets from Limoges. Here, the Lapidation on the main body is accompanied, on the lid, by the scene of the saint's arrest.
Limoges, between 1210 and 1220
Copper melted, gilded and engraved on a body of oak wood, with the application of champlevé enamelling
16.5 × 15.5 × 6 cm. MNAC/MAC 65526

135. Bishop's Crosier.
Limoges, between 1230 and 1240
Copper melted, gilded and engraved, with the application of champlevé enamelling, and cast-iron figures in full relief
33 × 7 cm (diameter of the volute) and 3.5 cm (diameter of the knot)
MNAC/MAC 65523

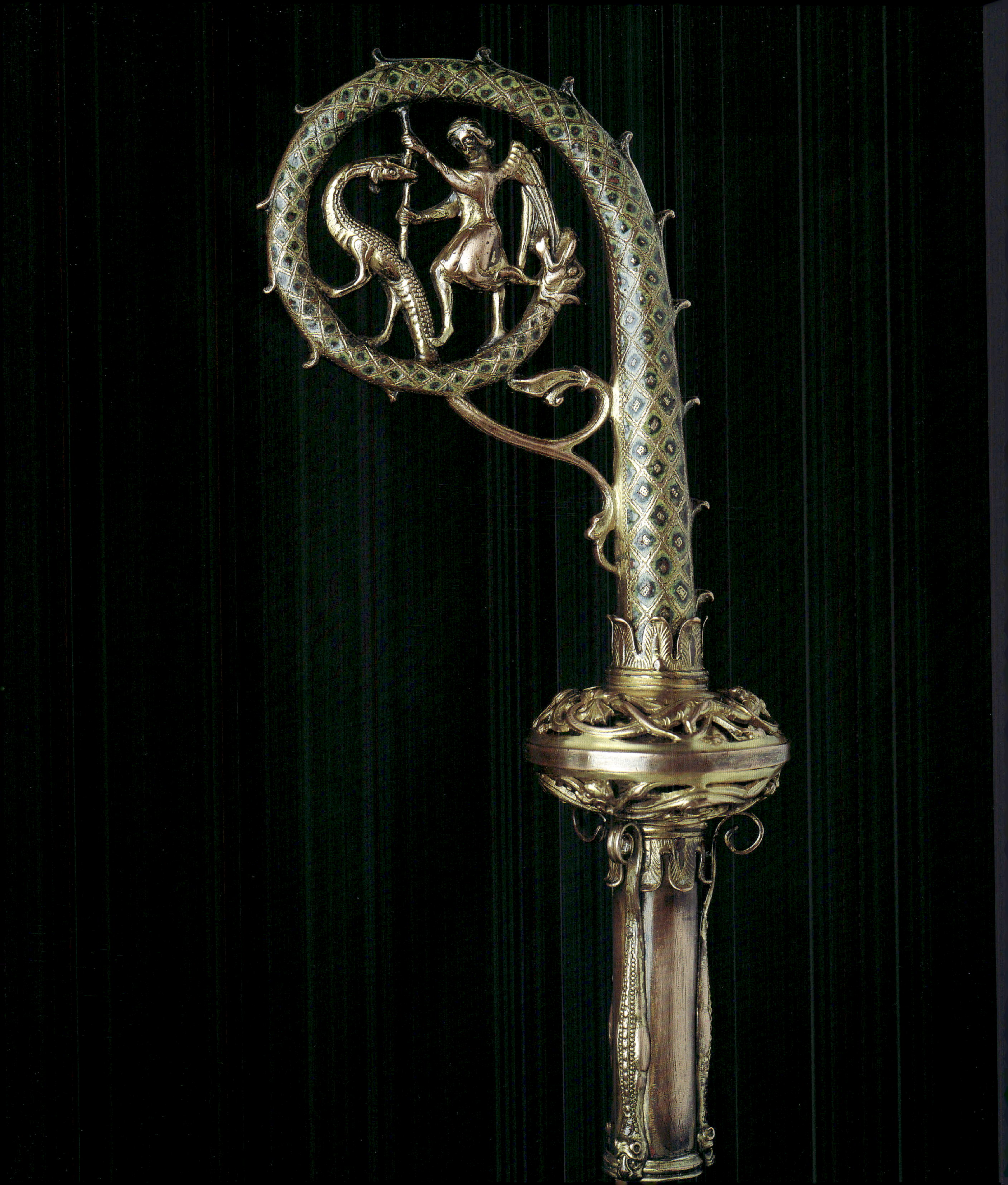

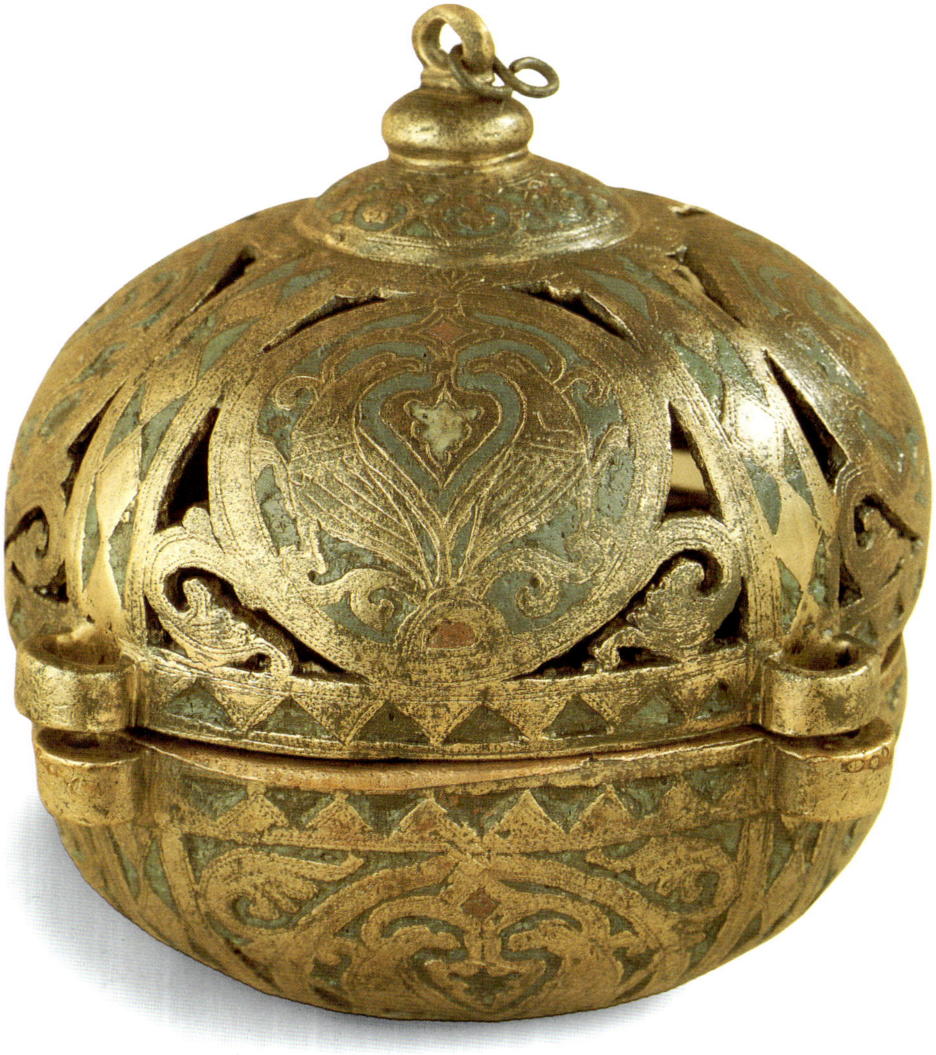

136

136. CENSER.
The possibility of this being one of the few enamelled pieces made in Catalan territory gives this beautiful censer a special significance. The decoration, with pairs of facing birds, follows a scheme with a long history in the East. Catalonia (?), second quarter of the 12th century
Copper melted, gilded and engraved, with the application of champlevé enamelling
13 × 13.5 cm
MNAC/MAC 4581

Romanesque metalworking techniques

The art of metalwork and precious stones was the most highly valued of all the artistic activities of the Middle Ages, as it used the noblest materials. Gold and silver were the most highly prized metals, with which the most luxurious items were made, but we have already seen how common the use of copper was, and the same goes for bronze, tin and other materials that were cheaper and generally easier to work with. Goldsmiths used a wide variety of techniques.

Some elements and small details of carving were done using the casting procedure, heating the metal to its melting-point and then pouring it into previously carved moulds. Usually, however, the metal was worked while cold using the *repoussé* technique, which consists in hammering the thin sheet of metal to give it the desired form.

Next the metal surface had to be treated to give it the right finish, It could be simply burnished (that is, polished), or else gilded with a fine layer of gold, as was done with copper items. It might also be engraved with ornamental or figurative motifs using a range of tools, like the burin (which made small furrows by cutting away the

137. CHRIST FROM MOROR.
An elegant piece with slender features, it shows Christ naked on the cross, with his eyes open and a serene expression. The bronze has kept the original gilt patina, something that reinforces the figure's luxurious and delicate appearance.
Around 1180
Bronze melted, gilded and engraved.
From the church of Sant Miquel de Moror (Pallars Jussà)
19.3 × 19 × 3.5 cm
MNAC/MAC 4581

137

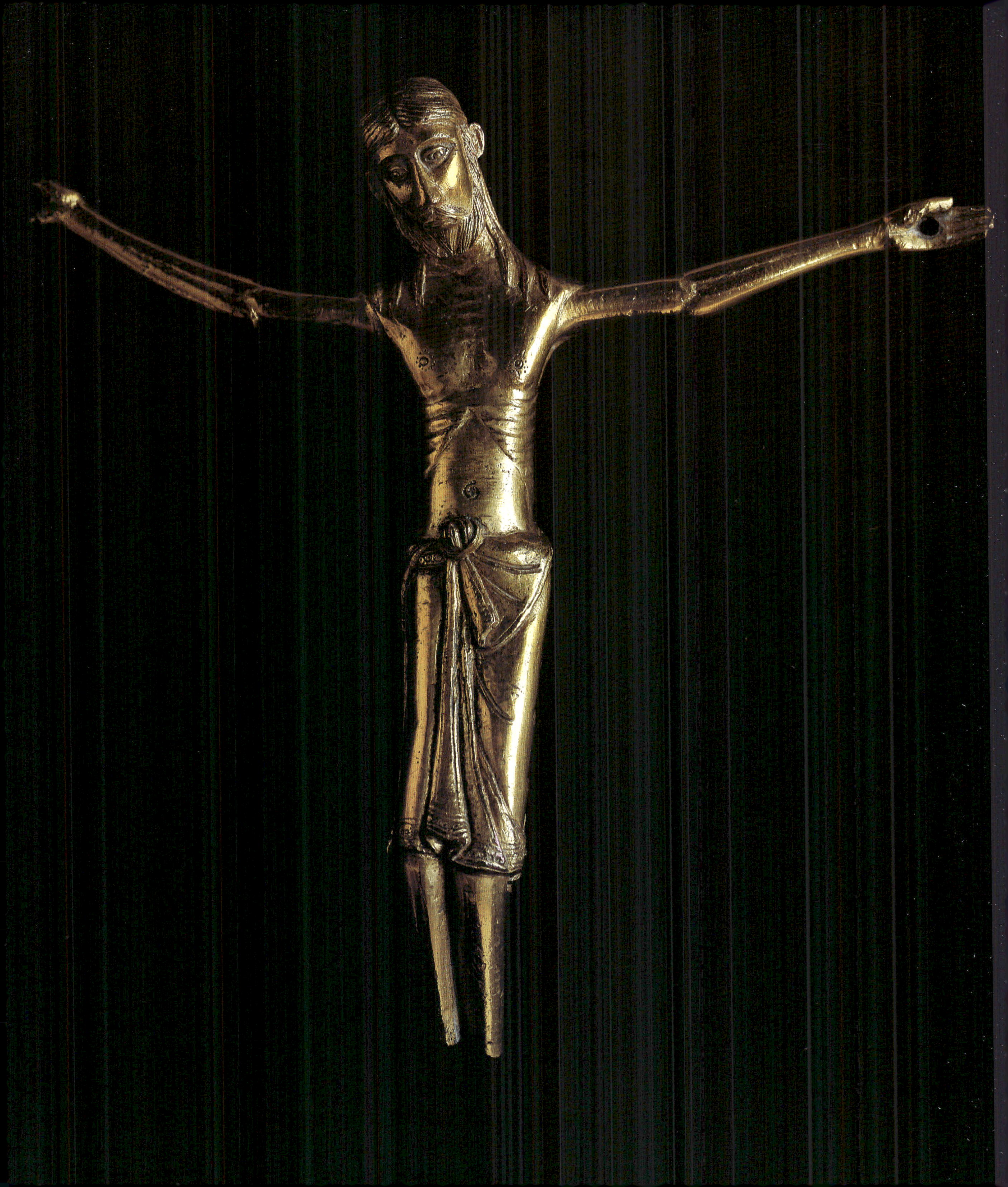

metal) or the chisel (which lowered the surface without removing metal). Though less common, we mustn't forget the filigree technique, which consisted in applying small metal filaments on the surface of the work to create the desired ornamental effects.

Pieces worked in metal might be completed with other materials such as precious or semi-precious stones (rock crystal, balas rubies, pearls) which were attached as decoration. However, as we saw earlier, the commonest and most highly appreciated ornamental technique of the time was enamelling.

Enamel is simply glass paste mixed with something to colour it, which is applied on metal sheets, fundamentally of gold or gold-plated copper. Next it's heated to the paste's melting-point, which is between 700 and 800 degrees Celsius, and on cooling the result is an evenly-coloured surface with a highly characteristic texture and shine. By combining the different colours and the gilded areas that haven't been enamelled (that have been left 'in reserve'), ornamental motifs and storied scenes can be achieved, so that enamels can not only add incomparably rich colours to metalwork but also wide-ranging figurative content.

Two basic techniques were used in the Middle Ages for applying the glass paste to the metal, known by the French names of *cloisonné*, which could be translated as compartmented, and *champlevé*, from the French for 'raised field'.

The earliest technique is *cloisonné* enamel, which consists in soldering small strips of gold onto a gold base to form the outlines of the pattern. The resulting enclosed spaces are filled with the enamel paste with the corresponding colours to make up the desired design. The sheet is then fired and finally the surface is polished. The *cloisonné* technique is very characteristic of Byzantine metalwork and of European metalwork of the Early Middle Ages. The Carolingian enamels, for example, were made using this procedure, which was continued during the Romanesque but which after the middle of the twelfth century was gradually replaced by the *champlevé* technique.

In *champlevé* enamels a different method is used for applying the vitreous material to the metal base. Instead of drawing the design by adding strips of metal, the surface is hollowed out to form small pits. These pits are filled with the enamel paste, after which the procedure is identical to the first: firing of the work followed by polishing.

Although the technique was already known in Antiquity, the real rise of *champlevé* enamel came about during the Romanesque period and after the middle of the twelfth century it became the predominant procedure. The technique is more flexible than *cloisonné* and gives slightly different results. For example, it makes it easier to combine enamelled motifs with large areas left in reserve, or, vice versa, to leave figures and ornaments in reserve and enamel all the background of the scenes.

Another important characteristic of *champlevé* is that instead of applying it to gold sheets it was generally used on copper, a cheaper metal and one that was easier to obtain, but also resistant and suitable for working. Of course, the surface had to be gilded to get the same shiny effect. It was also common to add small carved elements to the composition, either heads of the characters depicted or complete figures. In this way rich and very original combination of pictorial and sculptural ef-

138. CENTRAL PLATE FROM A CROSS.
The oval face and the type of figure of Christ is very characteristic of the enamels from Limoges. Richly attired, it is part of a group of pieces from around 1200 presenting the iconographic type of the 'Majesty'. Limoges, first third of the 13th century. Copper gilded and engraved, figure applied and champlevé *enamelling*
20.8 × 13.5 × 2.6 cm
MNAC/MAC 4556

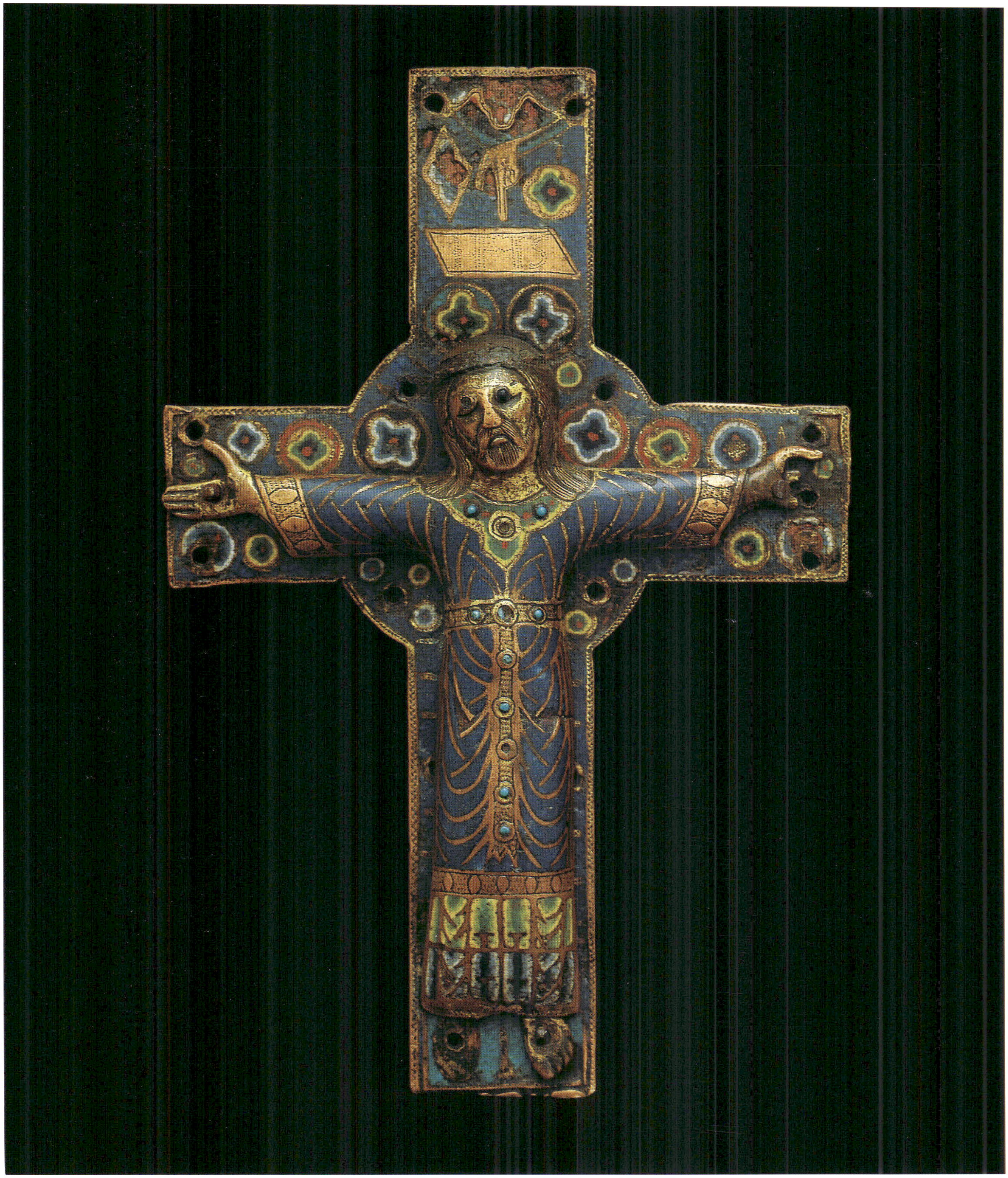

138

fects (thanks to the enamels and the reliefs, respectively) could be obtained on the same item.

The importance of Limoges enamel has already been mentioned above. In fact, almost all the MNAC's enamelled items come from workshops in Limoges or at least connected with the same tradition or the same technical procedures. The commercial success of these workshops, which supplied items of great beauty at moderate prices, meant that by the beginning of the thirteenth century production had already become industrialised and objects were often made in series, with the inevitable loss of quality this always involves.

It's interesting to note that Limoges enamels belong to a style characteristic of the countries of southern Europe and related to other forms of artistic expression in southern Romanesque art. The overriding importance of Roman influence in these regions, and the frequent contact between them, either because of trade or along the pilgrimage routes, gave rise to a Romanesque style with a classical flavour, fond of narratives and with highly characteristic decorative elements. All of this is reflected in the formulas used by enamellers, which have points in common with miniatures and even with the monumental sculpture of the great Occitanian abbeys like Moissac, Souillac and obviously Limoges itself.

The success of Limoges doesn't mean there weren't other regions of Europe with a comparable production in enamels, that flourished especially during the twelfth century. None of them, though, was able in the long run to withstand the competition from Limoges. The main production centres in northern Europe, direct heirs to the rich tradition of Carolingian metalwork, were located in the region of the Middle Rhine, near Cologne, and in the diocese of Liège, on the banks of the Meuse. In the south of the continent, apart from the actual area of Limoges, enamel is known to have been produced in many other parts of Aquitaine, at the abbey of Conques, for example, and also in the north of the Iberian Peninsula, where the presence of one or several workshops in the orbit of the monastery of Silos has long been demonstrated. As far as Catalonia is concerned, there is no definite evidence that enamelled works were also produced here, but there are a series of signs that could suggest this possibility. One is the well documented presence of enamelled work in the eleventh century (like the gold altar frontal in Girona cathedral, mentioned above, which probably had *cloisonné* enamelling), and another is the fact that enamel production in Catalonia during the Gothic period was of the highest quality, something that is difficult to understand without a previously established tradition of some sort.

Romanesque metalwork at the MNAC

Metalwork enjoyed an age of splendour in the Catalan counties during the Romanesque period —that we are sure of—, perhaps more especially during the eleventh century. The willingness on the part of the nobility and the church hierarchies to finance luxury objects can be explained by their great material value but also because of their symbolic value and because of the prestige they brought to their patrons. A

139. Ciborium.
Limoges, between 1220 and 1240
Copper melted, embossed, gilded and engraved, with the application of champlevé enamelling.
31 × 14.5 cm (maximum diameter)
MNAC/MAC 4600

140. Eucharistic dove.
Containers in the shape of a dove to keep consecrated hosts in were a very popular part of the production of Limoges in the 13th century. More than thirty of them have been conserved.
Limoges, first half of the 13th century
Copper melted, gilded and engraved, with the application of champlevé enamelling.
18 × 21 × 7.3 cm (diameter of the bottom disc)
MNAC/MAC 65534

139

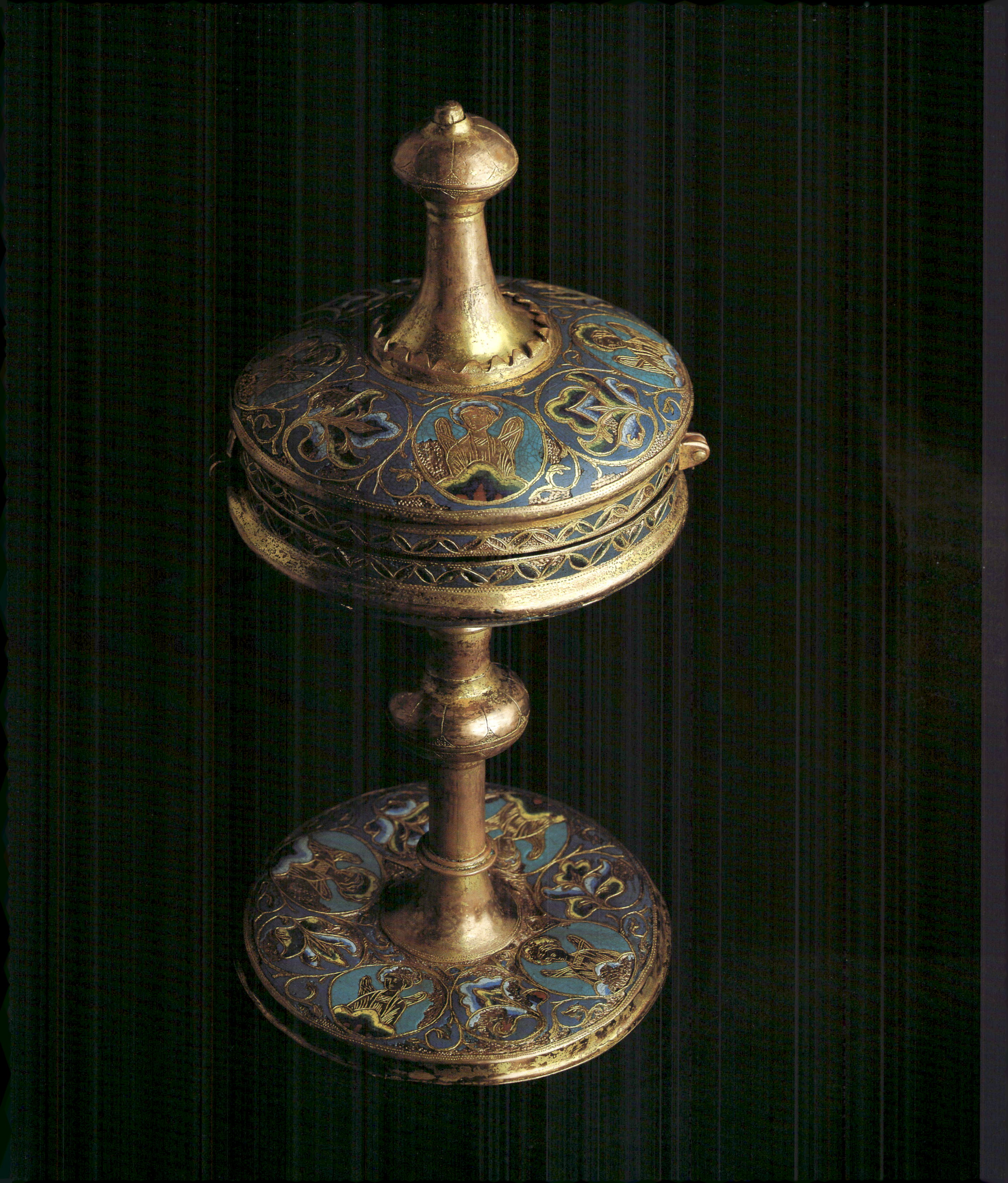

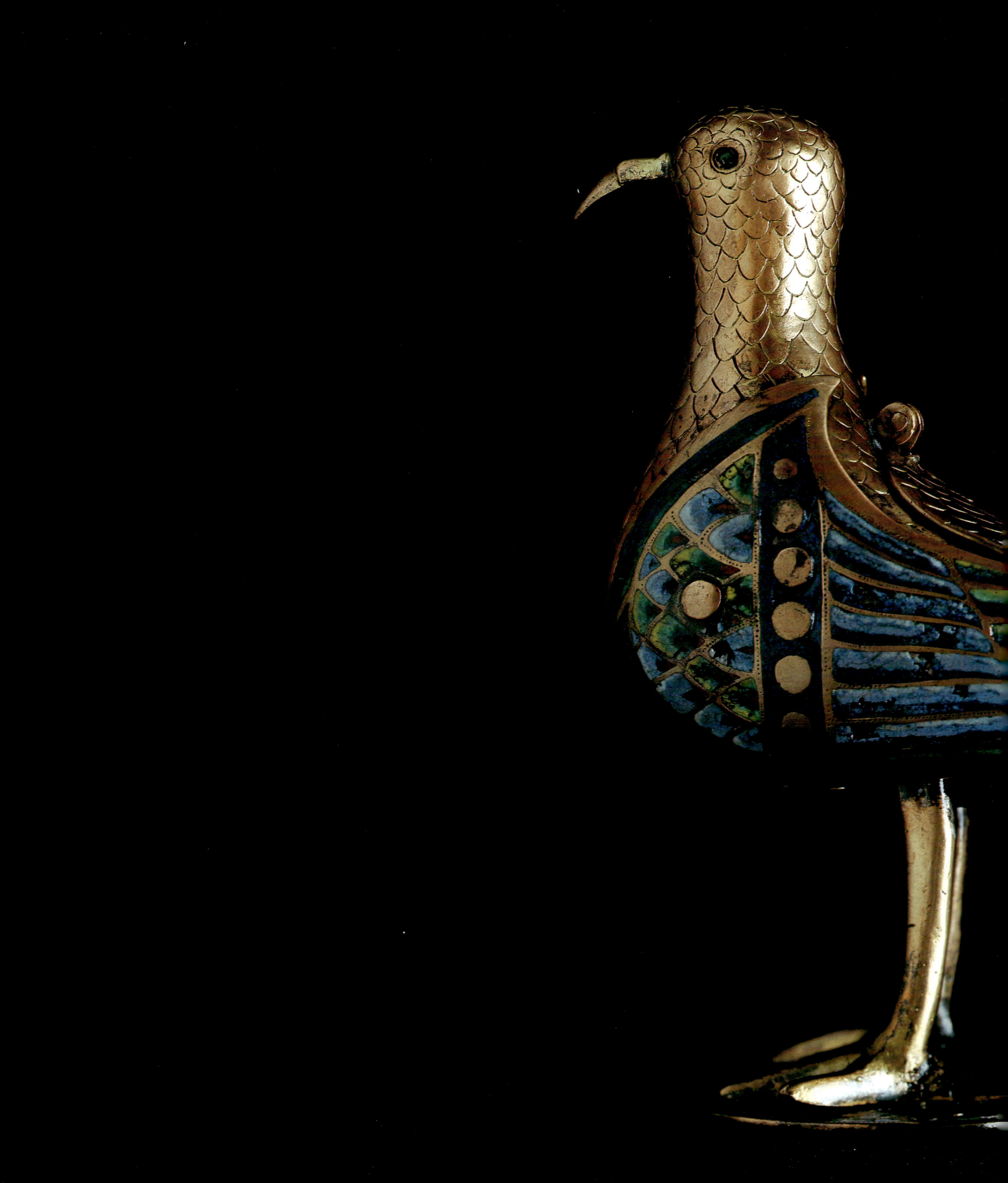

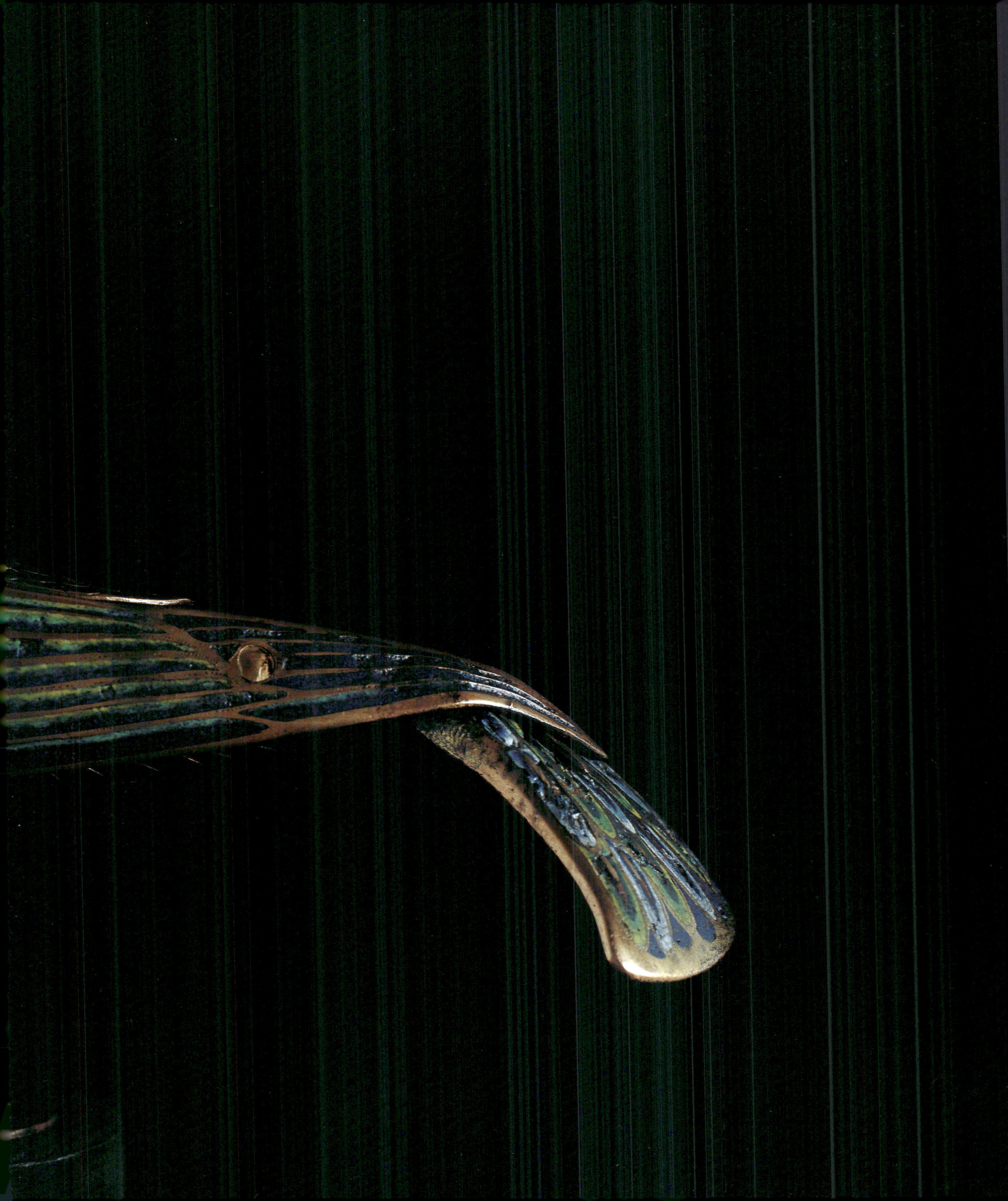

monastery of such importance as Santa Maria de Ripoll, for example, would decorate its high altar with a gold altar frontal covered with precious stones and enamelled sheets, as well as with two silver side panels and a large baldachin of the same material. Even if this type of work in fact had a wooden core and was 'only' coated with metal sheets (which was usual in metalwork in the Middle Ages), the overall impression must have been truly spectacular.

But nothing has survived of either the altar in Ripoll or of other similar works; we only know they existed from written accounts, just as we know of the existence of equally valuable altar crosses, chalices and patens, reliquaries and many types of sumptuous object for use in worship. And we mustn't forget the objects made for secular use: hand-basins, candelabra, items for knights' harnesses, etc.

Although some of the items in the MNAC's collections once formed part of Catalan church property, it's nevertheless very difficult to say if any of them were actually made in Catalonia. Amongst the works with enamel decoration, for example, only an attractive censer decorated with pairs of birds facing each other against a blue background might have originated in the former Catalan counties, amongst other things because it seems to be too early (first half of the twelfth century) to be an export from Limoges. Leaving to one side the thorny question of origins, perhaps the best way to understand the Museum's collection is by analysing the different types of object making it up. But it's important to remember that all these objects weren't purely decorative, as they also played a definite role in the liturgy of the time. We see this in many paintings and miniatures of the same period that illustrate the sacred area of the altar.

A review of the different types of object should perhaps begin with the crosses, the great symbol of the Christian faith, which played an important part in the liturgy. They were placed on the altar presiding the Mass (altar crosses) or headed processions and other acts of worship like baptisms and funerals (processional crosses).

Most of the MNAC's Romanesque crosses are enamelled and came from Limoges, but there are also some that speak of a different tradition, that of the Spanish crosses typical of the Visigothic era which later became symbols of royalty under the Asturian monarchy (ninth century). Despite being Romanesque, the *Petrus Cross* mentioned above is a powerful reminder of this tradition, with its four arms of almost equal length and five encrusted rock crystals, of which only the central one has been preserved. An inscription tells us the date it was consecrated, 1122, and includes the name Petrus, who was either the person who made it or the person who paid for it.

Whereas the oldest crosses hadn't yet included the figure of Christ crucified, during the Romanesque period its presence in the centre gradually came to dominate, sometimes accompanied by other characters or figurative motifs on the arms of the cross. All these figures were carved separately before being literally nailed to the cross; when attached to the structure in this way they are usually called 'applied' figures. Very often these figures have survived separately from the original cross. There are a lot of them in the Museum's collection, of which the most interesting is the splendid *Moror Christ*, a small image of Christ crucified from the church of Sant Miquel de Moror, in Pallars Jussà, purchased in 1920 from the priest of the neighbouring parish of Santa Maria de Mur. The quality of this bronze item from the second half

141. CRUCIFIXION CASKET.
The central image of the Crucifixion, with the Virgin and Saint John flanking Christ on the Cross, and the personification of the Sun and the Moon at the top, is accompanied by two unidentified apostles. On the lid, the Pantocrator sits between two angels. Limoges, between 1210 and 1220
Copper melted, gilded and engraved, with the application of champlevé enamelling and heads in relief
21 × 18 × 8.5 cm
MNAC/MAC 4573

142. CROSIER FROM MONDOÑEDO.
This kind of crosier was part of a bishop's grave goods, to be buried with him. This one must have belonged to the Galician bishop Pelayo de Cebeyra, as in the 18th century it was found beside his tomb, in the sacristy of the church of Santa Maria do Campo, in Ribadeo. Limoges, around 1200
Copper melted, gilded and engraved, with the application of champlevé enamelling, and cast-iron figures in full relief
32 × 15 cm (diameter of the volute) and 8 cm (diameter of the knot)
From the old cathedral of Ribadeo (Galicia)
MNAC/MAC 4544

143. COVER PLATE FROM AN EVANGELIARY (CRUCIFIXION).
Around 1200
Copper gilded and engraved, with the application of champlevé enamelling and figures in relief
25.9 × 13.5 cm
MNAC/MAC 4574

141

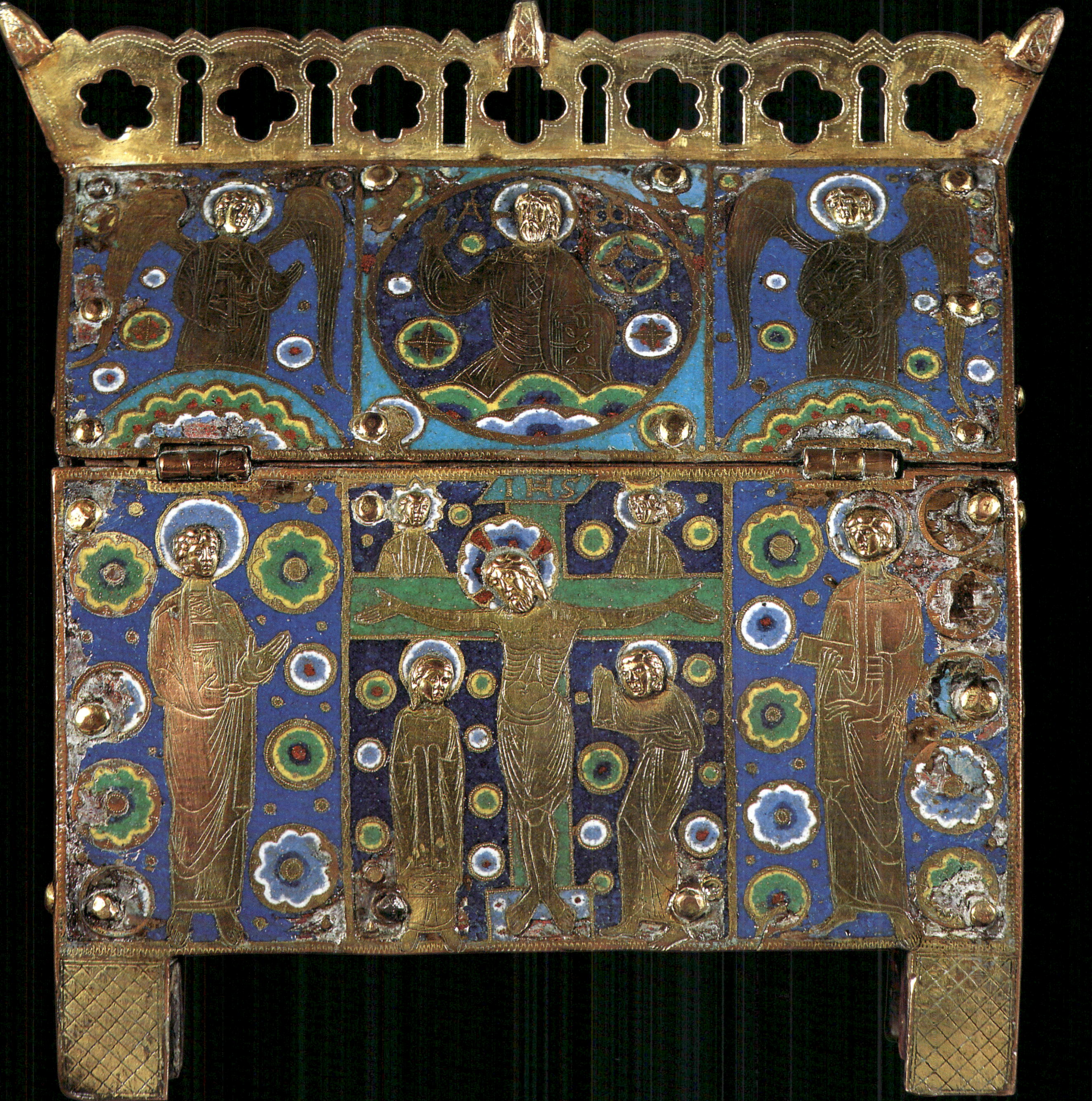
IHS

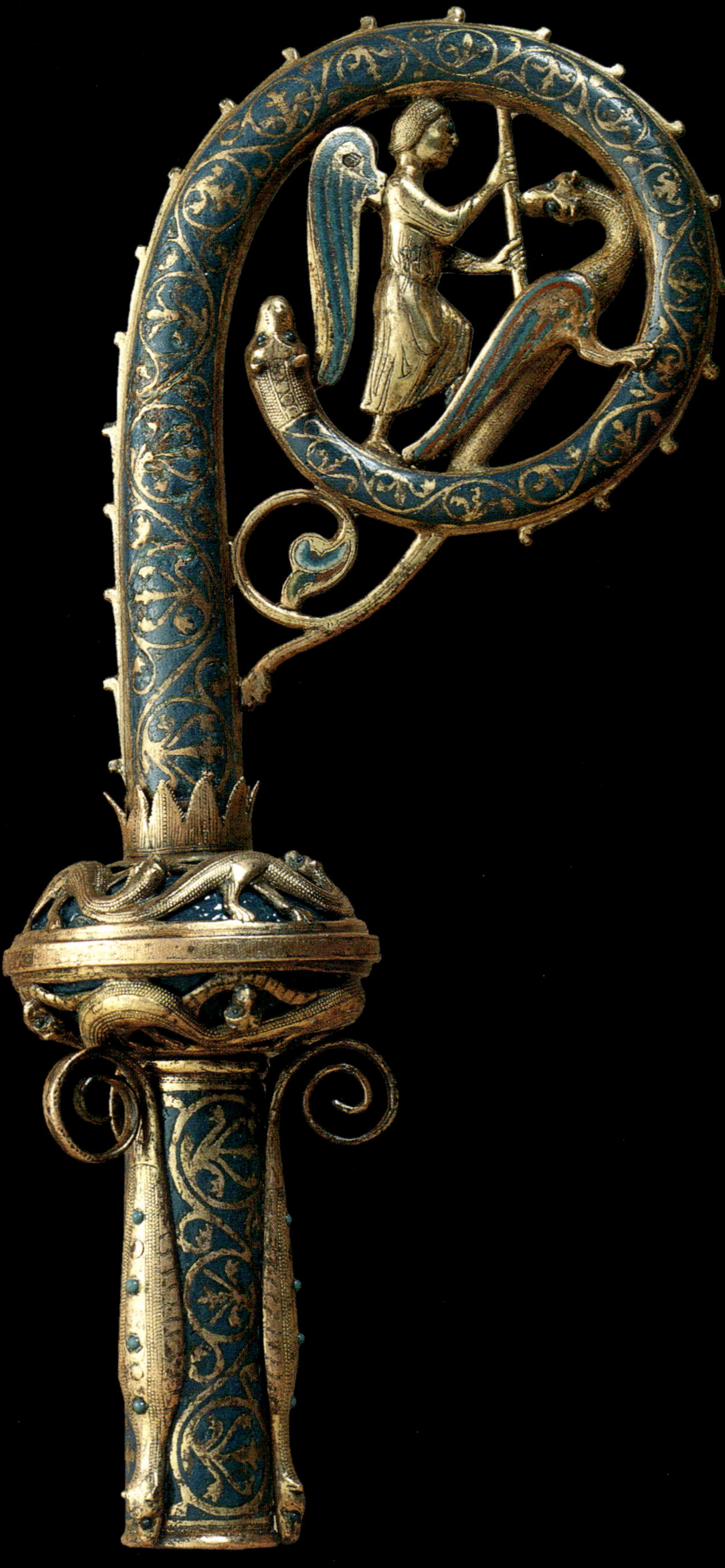

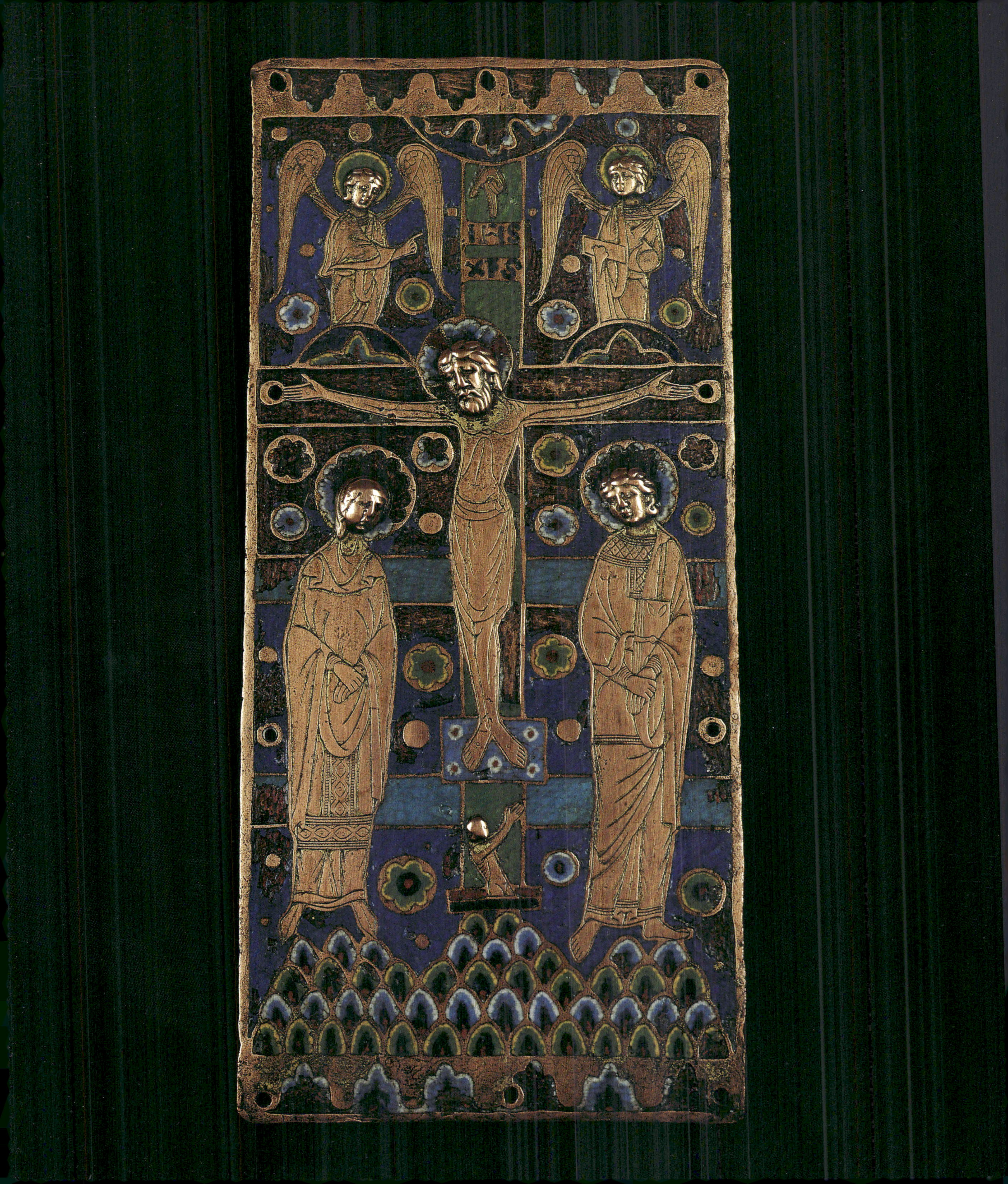

of the twelfth century is perfectly visible in the careful representation of the anatomy and face of Christ, and in the innovative decorative working of the *perizonium*.

In many cases, instead of an applied figure in the centre of the cross, a sheet decorated with enamel and already including a relief figure of the crucified Christ was added. Of this type of item, which was very typical of Limoges work, we have an extremely interesting example in the Museum that came from the former Plandiura collection (fig. p. 193). The figure of Christ is entirely clothed and originally wore a crown (now lost), in keeping with the iconographic type we call *Majestat* in Catalonia. This type was very common in Catalan and Italian wood carving and as we see here also present in metalwork. By studying the relations between the two techniques we might be able to explain the spread of *Majestats* all over southern Europe in the twelfth and thirteenth centuries.

So far we have only spoken of crosses, but the liturgical furnishings of the Romanesque altars included many other types of work. The MNAC's treasury is very complete in this respect, because it contains practically all the objects that were needed for the proper functioning of medieval religious practice: vessels for the Eucharist, candelabra, censers and incense boats, liturgical basins, etc.

Of all these objects, one thing that should perhaps be singled out is the range of forms of the Eucharistic monstrances, the receptacles used to store the consecrated hosts. The commonest, known as pyxes, were small cylindrical vessels with a conical lid. The *ciboria* were larger and more luxurious, in the form of a chalice and always beautifully decorated as we see in the two examples in the Museum's collection. One of them is very well preserved and the other, the mentioned *Ciborium from la Cerdanya*, though badly damaged, is very interesting on account of its rich enamelling and because we know for a fact that it was part of the treasury of a church in this catalan region. Finally, there were also some curious monstrances in the form of a dove, which were hung on chains in front of the altar as an allusion to the presence of the Holy Ghost. Seen in the light of the candles, these doves must have had a striking, almost magical effect.

Candelabra and censers completed the essential ornaments of the Romanesque altar. The candelabra, arranged in pairs above (or beside) the altar, were not only used to light the sacred area but also had a spiritual value, as the light from the candles was considered a symbol of divine light. Censers were small vessels in which incense was burned. They were generally made from bronze or copper and occasionally enamelled (they were also sometimes made from gold or silver). As they were plentiful and cheap, many have survived, most of them spherical and with fretwork decoration (completely perforated on the lid) to release the smoke. Some very particular censers, characteristic of Northern Europe, had an architectural structure instead of the spherical shape to symbolise the image of the Heavenly Jerusalem.

The Romanesque altar wasn't just a place where the Eucharist was celebrated, but also where the sacred relics needed for celebrating the Christian cult were kept. During the early Middle Ages these relics used to be placed in crypts or in small cavities beneath or even inside the altar, but from the eleventh century the spectacular increase in the cult of saints brought these relics out onto the altars, so to speak, where they could be displayed and celebrated during the Mass. In fact, all that remained in sight of the faithful were the reliquaries, objects that had to be especially luxurious, of course, because they contained the precious holy bodies... or at least what was left of them.

The commonest type of Romanesque reliquary took the form of a rectangular casket with a two-sided lid with crestwork on the top. Once again, production of this sort of item was abundant in the workshops of Limoges and the constant repetition of the same compositions and scenes clearly reveals that they were produced in series. Amongst the caskets kept at the MNAC, perhaps the best are the Saint Stephen Casket mentioned above and the Crucifixion Casket, both dating from the beginning of the thirteenth century.

Before ending we have yet to look at one last significant type of Romanesque metalwork, also in a way an object of worship. These are the binding plaques or metal covers that decorated liturgical manuscripts, especially the Gospels that were read during acts of worship. The images most often reproduced in pairs on these front and back plates were of Christ in Majesty and the Crucifixion or Calvary, like the one we see in the Limoges plate reproduced here. As I said earlier, the combination that can be seen of enamelled backgrounds and figures in reserve, to which are added small relief heads, was a very typical procedure in Limoges enamels.

Finally, a review of this sort of the MNAC's collection of precious metals can not overlook another object that used to be very rich and sumptuous: the bishop's crosier. These staffs, a symbol of the bishop's authority, used to end in a spiral or volute inside which a figurative scene could be placed. One magnificent example is the *Mondoñedo Crosier*, discovered in the eighteenth century in the Galician church of Ribadeo and then taken to Mondoñedo cathedral, where it gets its name. The image in the volute, with the Archangel Michael vanquishing the dragon, symbolised the victory of the Church over Evil and is very characteristic of Romanesque crosiers, perhaps because bishops had to fight against the widespread heresies of the twelfth and thirteenth centuries.

Conclusion

Metalwork reflects medieval values better than any other artistic technique: the fondness for noble materials, the aesthetics of light and colours, the importance of detail, the need to dress art in spiritual qualities. Perhaps modern-day interests and tastes, still heirs to the prejudices of the Renaissance, are directed more at painting or sculpture, but in the Middle Ages men delighted in the art of the goldsmith above any other, and the most highly appreciated works were those created with gold, with silver, with enamels and precious stones. This is why, to fully understand the aesthetic principles of the Romanesque, we need to turn to the metalwork and enamel, perhaps even *start* there. And so, rediscover the treasure.

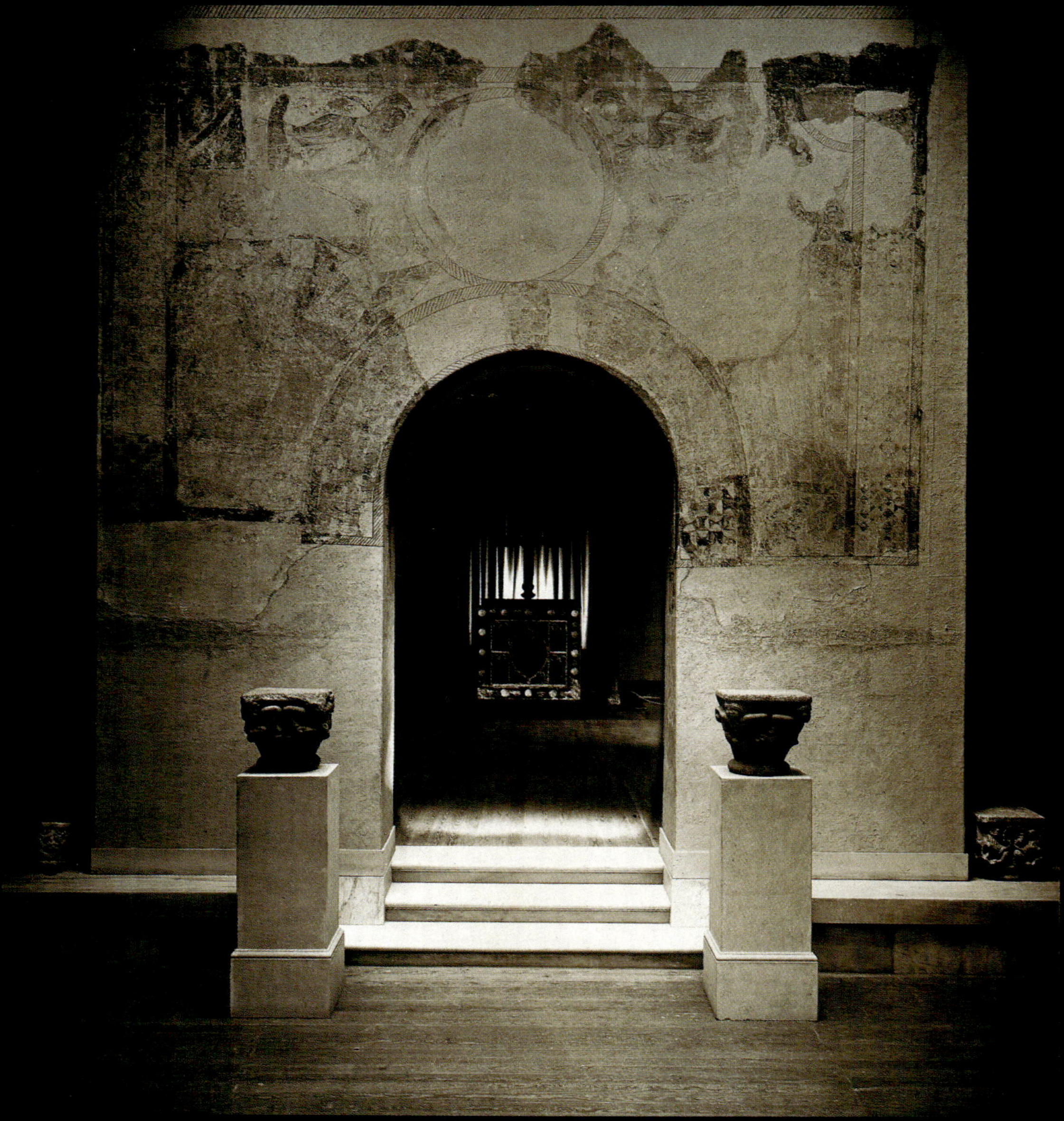

The legacy of Romanesque art: the vision of modernity

Manuel Castiñeiras

'He agreed unhesitatingly that our Romanesque museum would be unique in the world, an essential document for anyone wanting to understand the origins of Western art, an invaluable lesson for the moderns'

C. Capdevila, 'Picasso al Museu', *La Publicitat*, 56, 18.741, 1934

The MNAC's Romanesque collection was recognised as one of Western art's most important legacies in the 1920s. This and its subsequent rise to international status raised its fame beyond its local roots or its diverse artistic quality. Three events seem to have been the catalysts for this process. The first, already described, was the sale of the mural paintings from Santa Maria de Mur and their transfer to the Museum of Fine Arts in Boston between 1919 and 1921. The ensuing reaction by Catalan intellectuals led the Junta de Museus to purchase the Romanesque paintings in the Pyrenees and have them removed and taken to the Museu d'Art i Arqueologia de Barcelona, which was the predecessor to today's Museu Nacional d'Art de Catalunya and was located in the Parc de la Ciutadella. Following this rescue operation, carried out between 1919 and 1923, J. Folch i Torres had the privilege of setting up one of the world's most original museum installations of Romanesque art. With an optimum museographic presentation influenced by Art Deco, many of these works were elevated to the ranks of legend in the debate on Romanesque art. Quite rightly, on the cover of the Museum's first catalogue Folch i Torres unhesitatingly chose the 'Pantocrator' of Sant Climent de Taüll as the new icon *par excellence* of Catalan Romanesque art.

The second event that seems to have been fundamental for the collection's international fame was the interest it drew in the the incipient American art history of the time. A long list of researchers and experts on Spain specialising in the Romanesque, amongst them A. K. Porter, Walter Cook, Walter Kuhn and Chandler Post, wrote a series of articles during the twenties specifically devoted to Spanish medieval art. In them, subjects closely tied to the specific nature of Catalan Romanesque, such as Romanesque painting, panel painting or wood carving (without forgetting stone sculpture), were dealt with exhaustively in all their variety. The fact that they were published in English, in prestigious art history magazines like *The Art Bulletin* or *The Burlington Magazine*, made many of the Museum's Romanesque works (like the *Altar Frontal from La Seu d'Urgell*, the Taüll paintings or the statues of the *Erill la Vall Descent*) into household words in international art historiography. In other words, no discussion of the Romanesque since then is complete unless it mentions these works.

But there was undoubtedly also a third reason for this 'canonisation' of the Romanesque collection of the former Museu d'Art i Arqueologia in the Parc de la Ciutadella, and that was its aesthetic appreciation by the up-and-coming avant-garde painters of the time. These artists saw in Romanesque art the essence of 'the primitive', a category which furthermore was just beginning to be considered a characteristic of Spanish art and, by extension, of the Catalan figurative arts. The first step in the identification of Romanesque art with what was 'savage' or 'primitive' is owed to Fauvism and, more specifically, to the French artist André Derain. In 1906 Derain painted the picture *Dance*, in which the figure of Eve, with legs crossed and arms raised to the left, was inspired by the famous dancing Isaiah in the French church of Souillac (*c.* 1135). The artist was probably familiar with this work through the plaster cast of it kept in the then Musée de Sculpture Comparé in the Trocadero (Paris), now the Musée des Monuments Français. This institution was founded in 1882 by the French architect Eugène Viollet-le-Duc, who was responsible for restoring many Romanesque buildings, and is a leading example of French pride in the country's medieval monuments.

144. Museu d'Art i d'Arqueologia, 1924. Painted portal from Sant Joan de Boí, museographical installation by Joaquim Folch i Torres.

As we shall see, the Romanesque museum in Barcelona, first in La Ciutadella and later on Montjuïc, represents a similar feeling (a mixture of pride and Catalan patriotic feeling) and from the 1920s was to exert a similar fascination for avant-garde artists.

In fact, the interest in the figurative art of the 'Mozarabic' miniature and Peninsular Romanesque art shown early on by Auguste Herbin, Auguste Bataille, Pablo Picasso and Francis Picabia marked a change in the aesthetic appreciation and artistic acknowledgement of these arts. Auguste Herbin (1882) was one of the founders of the 'Abstraction-Création' movement in 1931, along with Theo van Doesburg, Hans Arp and Robert Delaunay. The movement propounded a new artistic alphabet combining pure colours with elemental figures of plane geometry. Years earlier Herbin had been especially fascinated by Cubism, hence his visit in 1913 to the French-Catalan town of Ceret (Vallespir) along with Juan Gris and Pablo Picasso. He returned there in 1918 for a two-year stay, and it was precisely during this time that he formulated his first abstract proposals, heavily influenced by the ornamental repertory of Pyrenean Romanesque art. In particular, one group of paintings in Vallespir from the second quarter of the twelfth century, in the church of Sant Martí de Fonollar (Morellas), very close to the town of Ceret, became the artist's special object of attention. In 1919 he painted a series of watercolours of them that are kept in the Musée d'Art Moderne de Céret. We mustn't forget that in the history of the rediscovery of Catalan Romanesque mural painting the Fonollar cycle, along with that of Pedret, was one of the first to be made public and studied at the end of the nineteenth century. In fact, the French scholar J.-A. Brutails had not only made lengthy commentaries on it in 1895 in a book which in 1901 was translated into Catalan with the title *Notes sobre l'art religiós en el Rosselló*, he had also been particularly fascinated, like Herbin, by its rich repertory of geometrical decorative borders, which he later published in his *Précis d'archéologie du Moyen Age* (Toulouse, Paris, 1908). The Catalan *Modernista* architect Lluís Domènech i Montaner had himself visited the church in 1904 and had painted a series of watercolours of that same group of contorted, angular, outlined figures —the Old Men of the Apocalypse, Saint Joseph, the Magi— and of their varied ornamental repertory.

Nevertheless, the person who marked a turning point for avant-garde appreciation of the Museum's collection of Romanesque art was Francis Picabia (1879-1953). This Cuban-born French artist of Spanish descent, well-known for his involvement in Dada and Surrealism, visited the Museu de Belles Arts in La Ciutadella in 1927 (the Romanesque apses had been installed there in 1924), accompanied by the art dealer Josep Dalmau. This visit led to a series of works in which the impact of the Romanesque mural paintings recently added to the collection and the artist's fascination with them is made abundantly clear. In particular, the themes and motifs of the apses from Santa Maria d'Àneu and Sant Climent de Taüll are superimposed over other compositions like archetypal or dream images. Thus the image of the beautiful six-winged seraph from Àneu is stamped on the characters in the scene of the Original Sin in Picabia's *Adam and Eve* (1927), while in his oil *Barcelona* (1927) a whirlwind of figures inspired in Sant Climent de Taüll (prominent amongst them the *Agnus Dei* and Lazarus's dog) are crowded into a composition whose format brings to mind a bullfight poster. The magnetic force of the *Agnus Dei* of Taüll, accompanied by the four

145. Auguste Herbin,
Sant Martí de Fonollar, 1919.
Watercolour and ink on paper.
Musée d'Art Moderne de Céret,
Céret (France).

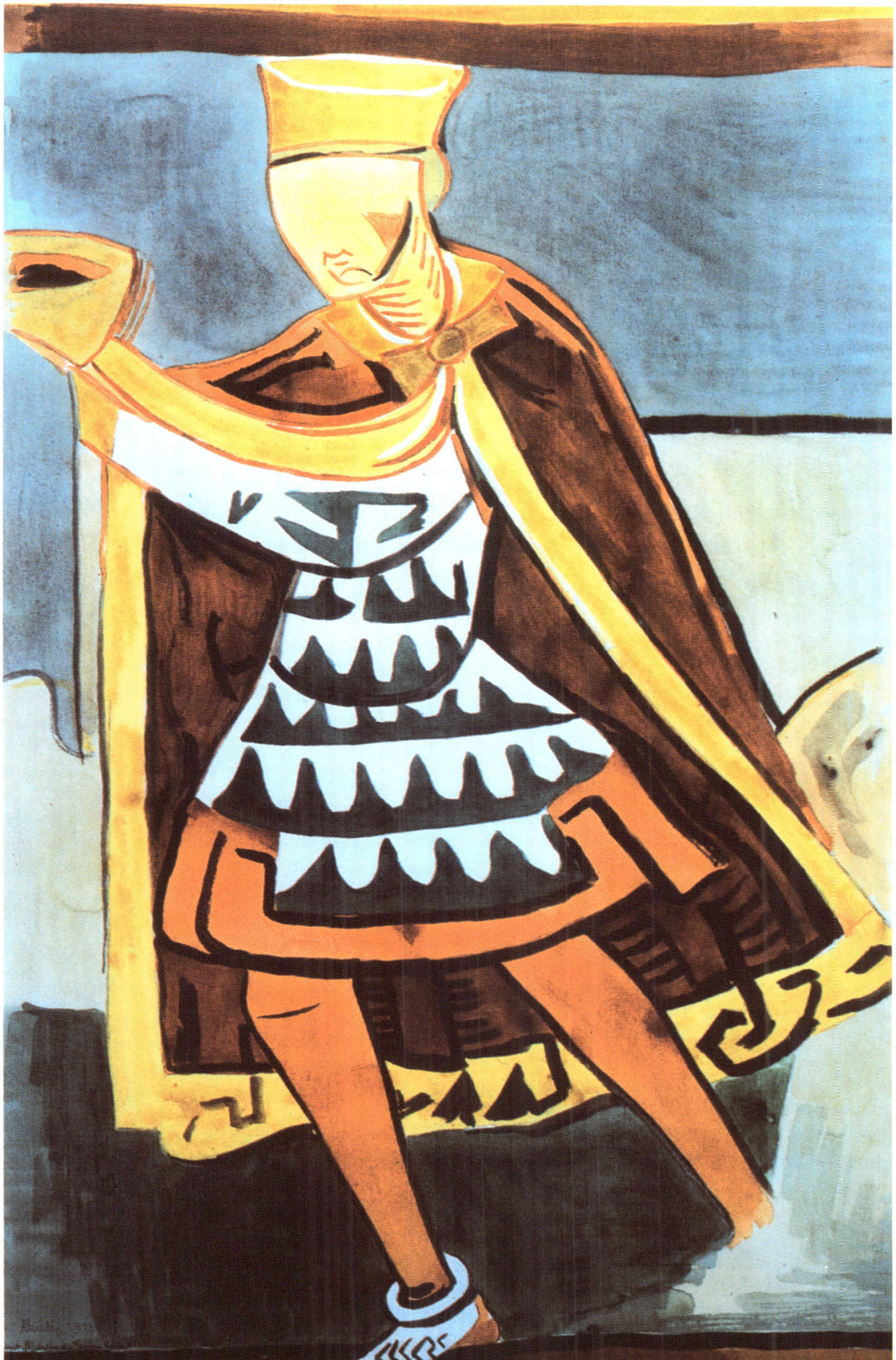

145

wheels from Ezekiel's Vision from Àneu, preside the scene of a kiss in the gouache *Agneau mystique et baiser* (1927), while the outline of the *Madonna of All* is stamped like automatic drawing across the portrait of a beautiful, worldly woman smoking in the gouache *La femme à la cigarrette (Vièrge de Montserrat)* (1928).

Equally fundamental to the incorporation of the dreamlike force of Spanish medieval art imagery into the repertory of the historic avant-gardes was the publication during those same years of an article on the Apocalypse in the manuscript of the Saint-Sever Beatus (Paris, BN, Ms. Lat. 8878). Written by the French philosopher Auguste Bataille (1897-1962) and published in the magazine *Documents*, the author, who in the context of the Surrealist movement was especially interested in the irrational aspects of human nature, discussed, with the help of six illustrations, the expressive power of these eleventh-century miniatures:

> 'C'est l'horreur - c'est-à-dire le sang, la tête coupée, la mort violente et tous les jeux bouleversants des viscères vivants tranchés - qui constitue apparemment l'élément même de ces peintures...' mais 'l'horreur n'entraîne aucune complaisance pathologique'
>
> (*'L'Apocalypse de Saint-Sever'*, Documents, 1, May, 1929, 74-84).

In Bataille's opinion, although this illuminated codex had been made in the South of France, the manuscript followed a Spanish model (known as the *Commentary of the Beatus of Liébana on the Apocalypse*), and he identified the artist, one 'Stephanus Garcia', as a Spaniard. In fact, the taste for brutality, blood and destruction was considered typical of the aesthetics of Spanish art. It should therefore come as no surprise that another Spanish artist, Pablo Picasso (1881-1973), a friend of Bataille and an assiduous reader of the magazine *Documents*, was not only struck by the visual force of this manuscript but even thought to describe the horrors of the Spanish Civil War through similar images. Indeed, a miniature of the Great Flood in the Saint-Sever Beatus (f. 85), more precisely the detail of the drowned bodies floating on the waters, provided him with a source of inspiration for the composition of the bottom part of the famous *Guernica*, the painting he did for the Spanish Republic's pavilion in Paris in 1937, at the height of the Civil War, with the object of denouncing the cruelty and the irrationality of this fratricidal conflict.

Over the years, it became commonplace in foreign publications on Spanish and, by extension, Catalan Romanesque art to comment on its bloodthirsty brutality and, in short, its primitive savagery, In fact, they often analysed especially violent scenes from Catalan Romanesque painting from this peculiar point of view, with the object above all of underlining its true modernity ahead of time. There are examples of this in the fight between David and Goliath in the paintings from Santa Maria de Taüll, in which David clutches Goliath by the hair as he makes a clean cut in his neck that gushes blood, and the martyrdom of Saint Julitta and her son Saint Quiricus on the *Durro Altar Frontal*, in which the mother is cruelly tortured by her executioners, who not only stick nails into her face but also proceed to cut her body in two with a saw.

Not by chance, Picasso, who during his stay in Gósol had already shown clear signs of his interest in Romanesque figurative art, was a friend of Joaquim Folch i Tor-

146. Francis Picabia, Barcelona, 1927. Seattle Art Museum, Eugene Fuller Memorial Collection.

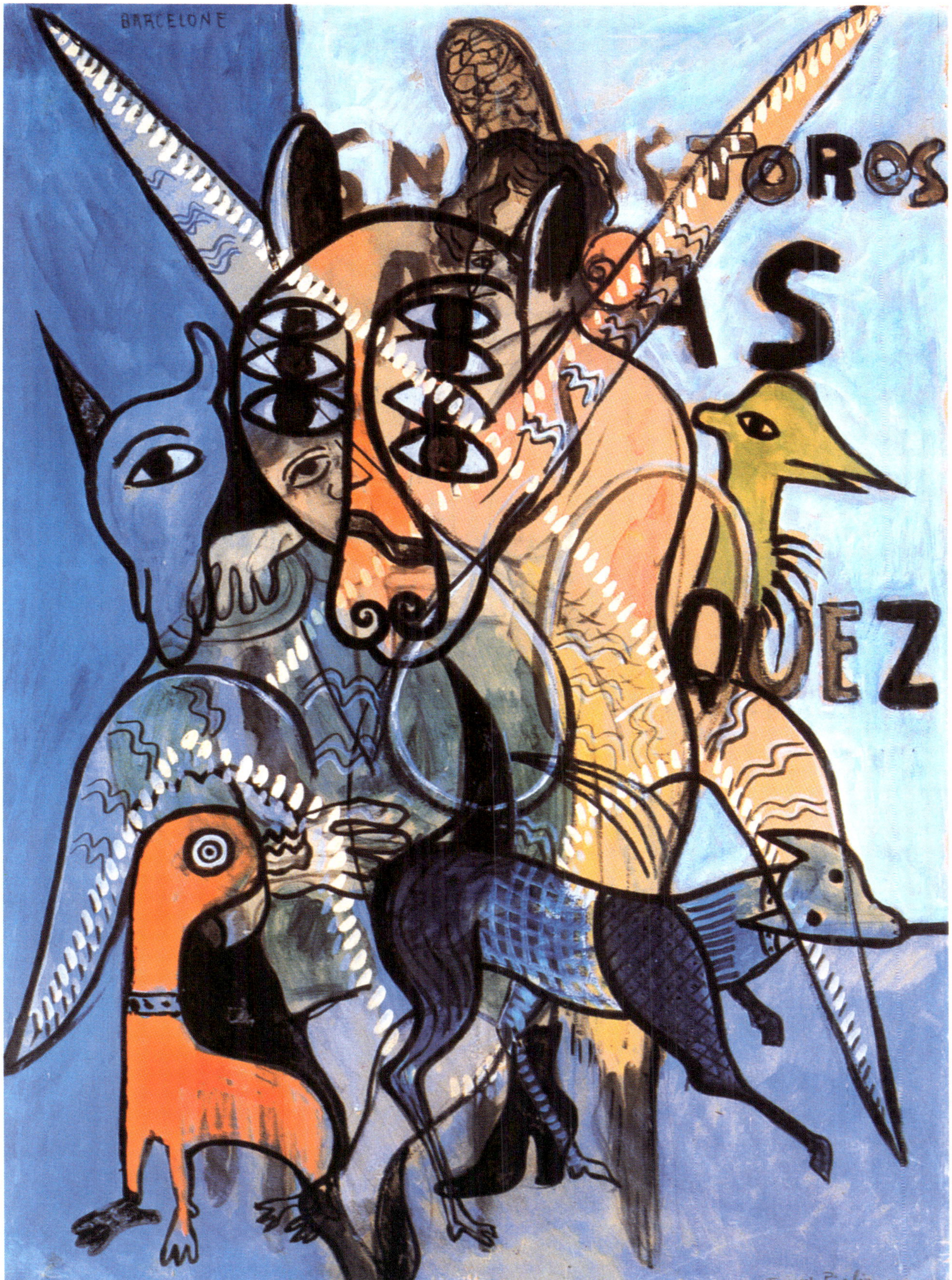

146

res, the first director of the Museum in the Parc de La Ciutadella and, as such, responsible for the first museographic installation of the Romanesque paintings. He too was well aware of the connection between the early medieval universe and contemporary figurative art. In 1931, following Bataille's example, he published an article in *Cahiers d'Art* on the illustration of the 'Mozarabic' Beati of Girona and La Seu d'Urgell, which in his opinion '*révelè nombre de points communs avec l'art contemporain le plus avancé*'. Remember that the French magazine *Cahiers d'Art* had been founded in 1926 by a great student of Picasso, Christian Zervos, who in this way sought to promote avant-garde artists. It's not surprising, then, that when the Romanesque collection was moved to its current home, the Palau Nacional de Montjuïc, inaugurated in 1934, Picasso visited it in the company of Folch i Torres. A delightful press release, signed by C. Capdevila in the Barcelona newspaper *La Publicitat*, comments on their visit to the new Museum on Montjuïc. The great artist acknowledged the undeniable debt that avant-garde art owed to the Romanesque tradition, which was to be seen as a great lesson for contemporary artists:

> 'As he went from one room to another, Picasso, before those incomparable fragments of early Catalan art, admired their power, intensity and skill; the sureness of vision and execution, the aplomb and the conviction with which the hand of the ignorant artist had expressed on those walls the ideas and the feelings that filled his spirit, and he agreed unhesitatingly that our Romanesque Museum would be unique in the world, an essential document for those wanting to understand the origins of Western art, *an invaluable lesson for the moderns.*' (my italics).

Since then the Romanesque collection has become a place of pilgrimage for contemporary artists in search of sources for their work, or rather trying to capture the *genius loci* surrounding its mysterious mural paintings like a talisman. This was the reason behind the visits by Joan Miró in 1955 with Llorens Artigas, in search of inspiration for their gigantic ceramic mural for Place de Fontenoy, home to UNESCO in Paris, or the visit by the writer and film-maker Jean Cocteau. The two visits live on in two eloquent photographs by Francesc Català Roca: a smiling Miró with Artigas under the lively prancing of the minstrels of Sant Joan de Boí and an arrogant pose by Cocteau in the shade of the representation of the boat from the church of Sant Pere de Sorpe. That same year the same photographer took the picture of the Grup Tahull, made up of leading painters of 'matteric informalism', like Antoni Tàpies, Josep Guinovart and Modest Cuixart, who posed for posterity before the southern door of the mural paintings from Santa Maria de Taüll. The Museum's frescoes were to them the symbol of an art rooted in the earth and in historical circumstance but which at the same time was magically universal, as Joan Teixidor pointed out.

Leaving aside the group portrait, for Antoni Tàpies (1923), the contemporary artist who has done most to idealise the Romanesque legacy in his work and writings, the mural painting tradition provided not only the secret to the magic of the symbol but also the access to a 'matteric' density arising from the mixture of powder, pigment and binder. He has referred to these two values since his earliest works. In the 1946

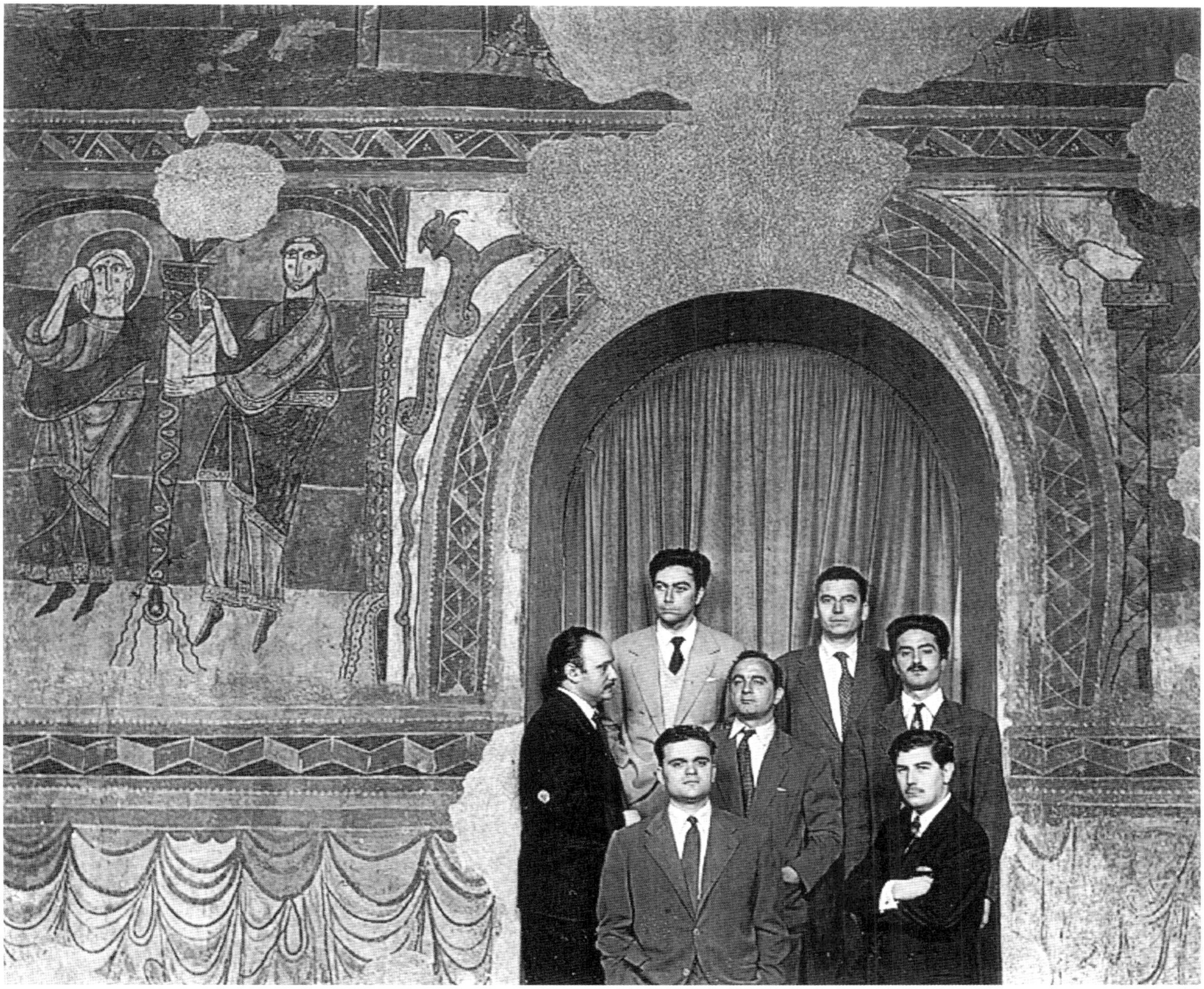

147

147. THE TAHULL GROUP AT THE MUSEU D'ART DE CATALUNYA, 1955 (J. Muxart, A. Tàpies, M. Aleu, J. J. Tartas, J. Mercadé, J. Guinovart, M. Cuixart).

Zoom (Fundació Antoni Tàpies de Barcelona), for example, he has no qualms about showing us his peculiar vision of the world when he plays with the image of a Pantocrator upside down characterised with his own face. Equally striking is his later work, *Pintura romànica i barretina*, done in 1971 and belonging to his private collection. Here he takes the second set of paintings removed from the altar of Santa Maria de Taüll and juxtaposes a *barretina*, the cap that is one of the traditional symbols of Catalan culture, after the fashion of an *objet trouvé*. In fact, in Tàpies's words, the regard for the Romanesque style always involved a return to the purity of the origins:

'It's very likely, then, that this interest in Romanesque art that still shows up in today's tastes can best be explained in the general context of the desire to return to the purity of the "origins" which makes itself felt in so many fields.'

L'arrel romànica, valor de l'art, Barcelona, 1993, p. 159.

And as such it constitutes a lesson from which we can always learn. This is why the artist's private collection includes some extraordinary fragments of Catalan Romanesque mural painting from the church of Santa Maria de Cap d'Aran. Most of this church's apsidal decoration, by the way, is kept at The Cloisters Museum in New York.

However, in the gradual 'canonisation' of the Romanesque collection of the Museo de Arte de Cataluña, as it was called in those days, there was an event of another sort that definitively launched it beyond our borders. In 1961, the isolated Spain of the Franco régime thought up a political and cultural operation directed at obtaining European recognition and consisting in holding a large exhibition to be called *El Arte Románico*. This exhibition would be part of the events organised every year by the Council of Europe on some aspect of European art in a significant location. The last two editions had been held in London (1959), on Romanticism, and in Paris (1960-1961), on the sources of twentieth-century art, so obviously an event devoted to the Romanesque in Spain had to have two prestigious venues, the Museo de Arte de Cataluña of the time, which housed the world's most magnificent series of apses with original removed mural painting, and Santiago de Compostela cathedral, as it was the most thoroughly studied and the most international of Spain's Romanesque monuments. The general curator of the exhibition would be none other than Joan Ainaud Lasarte (1919-1995), director of the MAC, with an assistant curator in Compostela, Manuel Chamoso Lamas (1909-1985), curator of the Servicio de Defensa del Patrimonio Nacional.

As the general object of these exhibitions was to demonstrate Europe's cultural 148
unity, the Dictatorship took advantage of the occasion to run a press campaign intending to put a more open and pro-European face on the régime. A remarkable number of works were exhibited, both in Santiago and in Barcelona, something unequalled before then and difficult to match in a contemporary event. Whereas in Santiago the connecting thread was the art of the *Camino de Santiago* (Saint James's Way), from Compostela to Toulouse, in the Palau Nacional in Barcelona, in the midst of the ancient Romanesque collection of painted apses and altar frontals, a splendid group of masterpieces was set up, amongst which the most outstanding were a monumental Irish cross, the relief of the Last Supper from the Musée Archéologique de Dijon, a metope from Ferrarra cathedral, two capitals from Autun attributed to Gislebertus, two capitals from Vézelay and various bits of sculpture from Cluny. I ought to emphasise that most of the foreign loans went to the Barcelona venue, where the exhibition discourse was richer and more articulate. By way of example, it included a reunited *Erill la Vall Descent from the Cross* (a group of wood carvings split between the Museu Episcopal de Vic and the Museu d'Art de Catalunya) and a room devoted to the so-called 'Cabestany Master'.

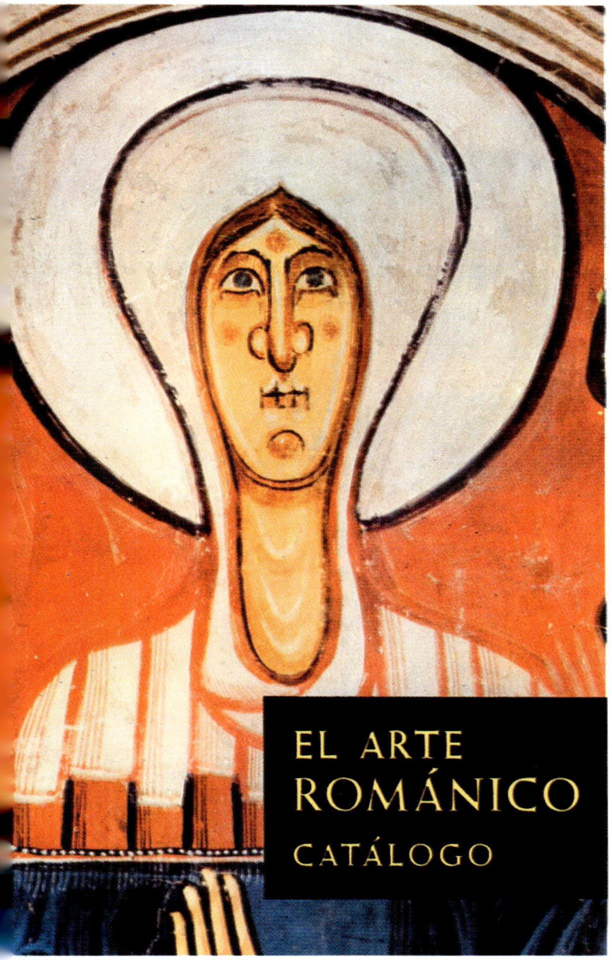

148. COVER OF THE CATALOGUE FOR THE 1961 *exhibition held in Barcelona and Santiago de Compostela: El Arte románico, Barcelona, 1962.*

In short, all of this not only succeeded in bringing the Romanesque to the attention of the general public (attendance figures reached 150,000), it also led to important publicity and research for a heritage that for decades had been hoarded in Barcelona. A stamp was issued with the famous Pantocrator from Sant Climent de Taüll and a voluminous catalogue was published, most of it consisting of the collections of the museums in Santiago and Barcelona, with 700 pages and 1,914 entries and an international scientific committee of advisers. As Josep Bracons has pointed out, for Catalonia this event was above all a boost to the fame of Catalan Romanesque painting, which in the space of a few years was the object of several monographs published in various languages and signed by J. Ainaud (1962, 1963, 1965), F. Hermann (1962), J. Gudiol (1965) and M. Bucci (1966).

All this growing enthusiasm over the reception of the collection of Romanesque art during the course of the twentieth century must not, however, obscure the misgivings and polemic aroused in Barcelona by the arrival of the recently removed paintings from the Pyrenees between 1919 and 1923 and their subsequent installation in La Ciutadella in 1924. Who better than Josep Pla to remind us of certain reactions against the rusticity of Romanesque painting on the part of Barcelona society, which in the twenties had a tendency to frippery and frivolity. Indeed, his words are unequivocal as he describes the adverse effects produced in some people on seeing the Pantocrator from Sant Climent de Taüll, the indisputable symbol of the collection:

> 'That Pantocrator! Before his figure, people were first left stunned and breathless, then their faces contorted, and finally they reacted irately against it... That rigid scarecrow air it has, the stiff, grave severity, eventually stirred people's indignation and anger.'

Nevertheless, those 'rigid, monstrous, deformed' figures, which according to Pla seemed to live outside time, eventually convinced all and sundry of their incomparable genius. Their images, which have reached the status of icons in our mass culture, have not only become an inevitable reference in Catalan and European Romanesque art, they have also brought such fame to their original churches that UNESCO in 2000 was led to declare them World Heritage Sites. A long, epic, fruitful path with no turning back.

BIBLIOGRAPHY

Compiled by Laia Pérez

Publications by the Museum and about the collections

AINAUD, J., *Art Romànic. Guia*, Barcelona, 1973 [guide to the Museu Nacional d'Art de Catalunya].

AINAUD, J., *Museo de Arte de Cataluña. Arte Románico*, Madrid, 1980 (Grandes Pinacotecas. Museos de España, 2).

L'Art Catalan du xe au xve siècle, Paris, 1937 [catalogue for the exhibition held at the Museé National du Jeu de Paume, Paris, March-April 1937].

L'Art Catalan à Paris, Paris, 1937 [double catalogue for the exhibitions held at the Musée National du Jeu de Paume and at the Musée National de Maisons-Laffite].

El Arte Románico. Exposición organizada por el Gobierno Español bajo los auspicios del Consejo de Europa. Catálogo. Barcelona y Santiago de Compostela 1961, Barcelona, 1962.

BARRAL, X. (coor.), *Prefiguració del Museu Nacional d'Art de Catalunya*, Barcelona, 1992.

BARRAL, X. (coor.), *Un any d'adquisicions, donacions i recuperacions*, Barcelona, 1993 [catalogue for the exhibition held at the Museu Nacional d'Art de Catalunya].

BARRAL, X., *El Museu Nacional d'Art de Catalunya i l'art romànic català. Història d'una gran col·lecció*, Barcelona 1994, pp. 195-234 (Catalunya Romànica, I)

BORONAT I TRILL, M. J., *La política d'adquisicions de la Junta de Museus, 1890-1923,* Barcelona, 1999.

CAMPS, J. *et al.*, *Guia Visual. Art romànic*, Barcelona, 2002 [guide to the Museu Nacional d'Art de Catalunya].

CARBONELL, E., *et al.*, *Guia. Art Romànic*, Barcelona, 1997 [guide to the Museu Nacional d'Art de Catalunya].

FOLCH I TORRES, J., *Museo de la Ciudadela. Catálogo de la sección de arte románico*, Barcelona, 1926.

GUDIOL I CUNILL, J., 'La col·lecció Plandiura', in *Gaseta de les Arts*, Barcelona, 1928, 2nd period, year 1, 2, pp. 2-14.

JUNTA DE MUSEUS, *Legado Espona. Catalogo-guía*, Barcelona, 1958.

JUNTA DE MUSEUS, *Catàleg del Museu d'Art de Catalunya. Primera part. Art Romànic - Art Gòtic - Art del Renaixement - Art Barroc*, Barcelona, 1936.

JUNTA DE MUSEUS, 'L'Adquisició de la col·lecció Plandiura', in *Butlletí dels Museus d'Art de Barcelona*, Barcelona, 1932, 19, II, pp. 353-395.

MANOTE, R. (ed.), *Bagliori del Medioevo. Arte romanica e gotica dal Museu Nacional d'Art de Catalunya*, Rome, 1999.

Romanesque art. General and Catalonia

AINAUD, J., *Catalogne romane*, Sainte-Marie de la Pierre-qui-vire (Yonne), 1994 (3rd edition revised).

AVRIL, F. *et al.*, *Le monde roman. 1060-1220. Le Temps des Croisades,* Paris, 1982.

AVRIL, F. *et al.*, *Le monde roman. 1060-1220. Les Royaumes d'Occident*, Paris, 1983.

BRUTAILS, J. A., *L'art religiós en el Rosselló*, Barcelona, 1901 (1895).

CARBONELL, E., *L'art romànic a Catalunya. Segle XII*, 2 vols., Barcelona, 1974-1975.

CASTIÑEIRAS, M.; CAMPS, J. (coor.), *El romànic i la Mediterrània. Catalunya, Toulouse i Pisa. 1120-1180*, Barcelona, 2008 [catalogue for the exhibition held at the MNAC].

Catalunya Romànica, 27 vols., Barcelona, 1984-1998.

DURLIAT, M., *L'art roman*, Paris, 1982 [Spanish edition: *El Arte románico*, 1992].

DALMASES, N. DE; JOSÉ PITARCH, A., *L'època del Císter. Segle XIII*, Barcelona, 1986, (Història de l'art català, II).

DALMASES, N. DE; JOSÉ PITARCH, A., *Els inicis i l'art romànic. Segles IX-XII*, Barcelona, 1986 (Història de l'art català, I).

ERLANDE-BRANDENBURG, A., *L'art roman. Un défi européen*, Paris, 2005.

ESPAÑOL, F.; YARZA, J., *El romànic català*, Manresa, 2007.

GUDIOL I CUNILL, J., *Nocions d'arqueologia sagrada catalana*, Vic, 1902 (2nd ed., 1931-1932).

GUDIOL RICART, J.; GAYA NUÑO, J.-A., *Arquitectura y escultura románicas*, Madrid, 1948 (Ars Hispaniae, V).

JUNYENT, E., *Catalogne romane*, 2 vols., Sainte-Marie-de-la-Pierre-qui-vire (Yonne), 1960-1961.

Milone, A.; Polo D'Ambrosio, L., *Medioevo. 1000-1400: l'arte europea dal Romanico al Gotico*, Milan, 2006.
Petzold, A., *Romanesque Art*, London, 1995.
Puig i Cadafalch, J. *et al.*, *L'arquitectura romànica a Catalunya*, 3 vols., Barcelona, 1909-1918, [facsimile editions, 1983 and 2001].

1. Mural Painting

Ainaud, J., *La pintura catalana. La fascinació del romànic,* Geneva-Barcelona, 1989.
Ainaud, J., 'Les col·leccions de pintura romànica del Museu Nacional d'Art de Catalunya', in *Butlletí del MNAC*, Barcelona, 1993, I, 1, pp. 57-69.
Alcoy, R., 'Les pintures bizantinizants de Sant Esteve d'Andorra la Vella en el món europeu del 1200', in *Lambard*, Barcelona, 1989-1991, V, pp. 23-47.
Alcoy, R., 'El taller de Lluçà i el seu cercle', in *De l'inici a l'italianisme*, Barcelona, 2005, pp. 38-43 (L'art gòtic a Catalunya. Pintura 1).
Alcoy, R., 'Ferrer Bassa y el Salterio Anglo-Catalán', in *Salterio Anglo-Catalán*, Barcelona, 2006, pp. 59-120.
Alfani, E., 'Relations iconographiques entre Catalogne et Orient: mobilité des modèles', in *Les Cahiers de Saint-Michel de Cuxa*, Prades-Codalet, 2007, XXXVIII, pp. 57-70.
Barral, X., 'Histoire et chronologie de la peinture murale romane du Musée Nacional d'Art de Catalogne', in *Académie des Inscriptions & Belles-Lettres. Comptes rendus des séanles de l'annéé 1994,* Paris, 1994, pp. 821-848.
Bousquet, J., 'Le thème des "archanges à l'étendard" de la Catalogne à l'Italie et à Byzance', in *Les Cahiers de Saint-Michel de Cuxa*, Prades-Codalet, 1974, V, pp. 7-27.
Borrás, G. M.; García, M., *La pintura románica en Aragón*, Zaragoza, 1978.
Camps, J. *et al.*, *Puig i Cadafach i la col·lecció d'art romànic del MNAC,* Barcelona, 2001 [catalogue for the exhibition held at the MNAC].
Carbonell, E., *L'ornamentació en la pintura romànica catalana,* Barcelona, 1981.
Castiñeiras, M.; Ylla-Català, G., 'Lluís Domènech i Montaner i la descoberta del Romànic', Graner, E.; Ramon, T. (coor.), in *Lluís Domènech i Montaner, Arquitectura romànica a Catalunya*, Barcelona, 2006, pp. 287-306.
Cennino Cennini, *Il libro dell'arte,* Vicenza, 2003.
Cook, W. W. S.; Gudiol Ricart, J., *Pintura e imaginería románicas,* Madrid, 1950 (Ars Hispaniae, VI) [2nd edition revised, Madrid, 1980].
Dodwell, C. R., *Artes pictóricas en Occidente, 800-1200,* Madrid, 1995.
Durliat, M., 'L'iconographie d'abside en Catalogne', in *Les Cahiers de Saint-Michel de Cuxa*, Prades-Codalet, 1974, V, pp. 99-116.
Folch i Torres, J., *Museo de la Ciudadela. Catálogo de la Sección de Arte Románico*, Barcelona, 1926.
Giannini, C., *L'attimo fulgente. Storie di collezionisti e mercanti,* Bérgamo, 2002.
Giannini, c., *Giovanni Secco Suardo alle origini del restauro moderno*, Florencia, 2006.
Goering, J., *The Virgin and the Grail. Origins of a Legend*, New Haven-London, 2005.
Guardia, M. *et al.*, *La descoberta de la pintura mural romànica catalana. La col·lecció de reproduccions del MNAC,* Barcelona, 1993.
Guardia, M., '*Ioculatores et saltator*. Las pinturas con escenas de juglaría de Sant Joan de Boí', in *Locus Amoenus*, Bellaterra, 2000-2001, pp. 11-32.
Guardia, M., 'Enluminure et peinture murale du nord au sud des Pyrénées: la syntaxe ornamentale et ses thèmes', in *Les Cahiers de Saint-Michel de Cuxa*, Prades-Codalet, 2007, XXXVIII, pp. 175-196.
Guardia, M., 'Una regió meridional de la pintura romànica', in *El romànic i la Mediterrània. Catalunya, Toulouse i Pisa. 1120-1180*, Barcelona, 2008, pp. 149-157 [catalogue for the exhibition held at the MNAC]
Gudiol i Cunill, J., *La pintura mig-eval catalana. Els Primitius*, 2 vols., Barcelona, 1927.

KUHN, C., *Romanesque Mural Painting of Catalonia,* Cambridge, 1930.

MANCHO, C., 'Les peintures de Sant Pere de Sorpe: prémices d'un ensemble presque ignoré', in *Revue de Comminges et des Pyrénées Centrales*, Saint-Gaudens, 2000, CXVI, pp. 545-572.

MANCHO, C., 'Els grans conjunts de pintura mural del segle XII', in *El romànic i la Mediterrània. Catalunya, Toulouse i Pisa. 1120-1180*, Barcelona, 2008, pp. 159-167 [catalogue for the exhibition held at the MNAC].

MAZZINI, F., 'Per la storia del restauro bergamasco: gli Steffanoni', in *Bergamo e il Novecento: istituzioni, protagonisti, luoghi*, Bérgamo, 2001, pp. 65-77.

MORER, A.; FONT-ALTABA, M., 'Materials pictòrics medievals. Investigació de les pintures murals romàniques a Catalunya', in *Butlletí del MNAC*, Barcelona, 1993, I, 1, pp. 71-105.

OAKESHOTT, W. F., *Sigena: Romanesque paintings in Spain & the Winchester bible artists*, London, 1972.

OCÓN, D., 'Une salle capitulaire pour une reine: les peintures du Chapitre de Sigena', in *Les Cahiers de Saint-Michel de Cuxa*, Prades-Codalet, 2007, XXXVIII, pp. 81-94.

ORRIOLS, A., 'Temes i intencions en la pintura mural de temps romànics', in *Magister Sancta Columba. La pintura mural romànica del Mestre de Santa Coloma i la seva època*, Barcelona, 2003, pp. 39-70.

PAGÈS, M., *Sobre pintura romànica catalana,* Barcelona, 2005.

PAGÈS, M., *La pintura mural romànica de les Valls d'Àneu,* Barcelona, 2008.

PIJOAN, J., *Pintures murals catalanes*, 4 inst., Barcelona, 1907-1921.

PIJOAN, J.; GUDIOL RICART, J., *Les pintures murals romàniques de Catalunya,* Barcelona, 1948 (Monumenta Cataloniae, VI).

PIVA, G. (ed), *L'arte del restauro. Il restauro dei dipinti nel sistema antico e moderno secondo le opere di Secco-Suardo e del Prof. R. Mancia*, Milan, 1984.

PIVA, P. (ed.), *Pittura murale del Medievo Lombardo (Ricerche iconografiche: l'alta Lombardia, secoli XI-XIII)*, Milan, 2006.

POST, CH. R., *A History of Spanish Painting*, 14 vols., Cambridge, 1930-1966.

SUREDA, J., *La pintura romànica a Catalunya,* Barcelona, 1981.

SUREDA, J., *La pintura románica en España (Aragón, Navarra, Castilla-León y Galicia),* Madrid, 1985.

WUNDERWALD, A.; BERENGUER, M., 'Les circustàncies sobre la venda de les pintures murals de Santa Maria de Mur', in *Butlletí del MNAC*, Barcelona, 2001, 5, pp. 121-129.

YARZA, J., 'San Quirze de Pedret, pintura', in *El Berguedà*, Barcelona, 1985, pp. 218-234 (Catalunya Romànica, XII).

YARZA, J., 'Un cycle de fresques romanes dans la paroisse de Santa Maria de Taüll', in *Les Cahiers de Saint-Michel de Cuxa*, Barcelona, 1999, pp. 121-140.

THEOPHILUS, *On divers arts,* J. G. HAWTHORNE, C. STANLEY SMITH (ed.), New York, 1979.

2. PAINTING ON WOOD

AINAUD, J., *La pintura catalana. La fascinació del romànic,* Geneva-Barcelona, 1989.

Álbum de detalles artísticos y plástico-decorativos de la Edad Media (Sociedad Artístico-Arqueológica Barcelonesa), Barcelona, 1882.

ALCOY, R., 'Mestre dels Arcàngels o primer Mestre de Sant Pau de Casserres', in *Prefiguració del Museu Nacional d'Art de Catalunya*, Barcelona, 1992, pp. 171-174, cat. no 26 [catalogue for the exhibition held at the MNAC].

ALCOY, R., 'Les taules pintades a Catalunya i els corrents anglesos a la fi del romànic', in *Lambard*, Barcelona, 1993-1994, VII, pp. 139-156.

BARRAL, X., 'La pintura sobre taula', in *Pintura antiga i medieval*, Barcelona, 1998, pp. 126-135 (Art de Catalunya. Ars Cataloniae, 8).

BLASCO, A. M., *La pintura romànica sobre fusta*, Barcelona, 1984.

CARBONELL-LAMOTHE, Y., 'Les devants d'autel peints de Catalogne: bilan et problèmes', in *Les Cahiers de Saint-Michel de Cuxa*, Prades-Codalet, 1974, 51, pp. 71-86.

CASELLAS, R., *Catálogo descriptivo parcial de las secciones de pintura románica y gótica del Museo de Arte y Arqueología de Barcelona,* Barcelona, no date [unpublished].

CASTIÑEIRAS, M., 'The Catalan Romanesque Painting Revisited (with Technical Report by A. Morer and J. Badia)', in *Spanish medieval Art, Recent Studies*, Tempe (Arizona), 2007, pp. 119-153.

CASTIÑEIRAS, M. (coor.), *El cel pintat. El Baldaquí de Tost*, Vic, 2008 [catalogue for the exhibition held at the Museu Episcopal de Vic].

CASTIÑEIRAS, M., 'Entorn als orígens de la pintura romànica sobre taula a Catalunya: els frontals d'Urgell, Ix, Esquius i Planès', in *Butlletí del MNAC, 9*, Barcelona [forthcoming].

COOK, W. W. S., 'The Earliest Painted Panels of Catalonia (I)', in *The Art Bulletin*, New York, 1923, V, 4, pp. 85-101.

COOK, W. W. S., 'The Earliest Painted Panels of Catalonia (II)', in *The Art Bulletin*, New York, 1923, VI, 2, pp. 31-60.

COOK, W. W. S., 'The Earliest Painted Panels of Catalonia (III)', in *The Art Bulletin*, New York, 1925-1926, VIII, 2, pp. 57-104.

COOK, W. W. S., 'The Earliest Painted Panels of Catalonia (IV)', in *The Art Bulletin*, New York, 1926, X, 4, pp. 228-234.

COOK, W. W. S., 'The Earliest Painted Panels of Catalonia (V)', in *The Art Bulletin*, New York, 1928, X, 4, pp. 153-204.

COOK, W. W. S., 'A Catalan Altar Frontal in the Worcester Museum', in *Archaeologica Orientalia in Memoriam Ernst Herzfeld*, New York, 1952, pp. 5-65.

COOK, W. W. S., *La pintura románica sobre tabla en Cataluña*, Madrid, 1960.

COOK, W. W. S.; GUDIOL RICART, J., *Pintura e imaginería románicas,* Madrid, 1950 (Ars Hispaniae, VI) [2nd edition revised, Madrid, 1980].

FOLCH I TORRES, J., 'La tècnica del pastillatge en els frontals romànics catalans', in *Gaseta de les Arts*, Barcelona, 1924, I, 10, pp. 1-12.

FOLCH I TORRES, J., 'Peinture et orfèvrerie: les origines de la peinture sur panneaux', in *La Catalogne à l'époque romane. Conférences en Sorbonne*, Paris, 1932, pp. 143-155.

FOLCH I TORRES, J., 'La Peinture sur panneaux', in *La Catalogne à l'époque romane. Conférences en Sorbonne*, Paris, 1932, pp. 129-142.

FOLCH I TORRES, J., *La pintura romànica catalana sobre fusta*, Barcelona, 1956 (Monumenta Cataloniae, IX).

GUDIOL I CUNILL, J., *Els Primitius. Segona part. La pintura sobre fusta*, Barcelona, 1929.

JUNTA DE MUSEUS, *Frontales románicos catalanes del Museu d'Art de Catalunya*, Barcelona, 1934 [2nd edition enlarged, 1944].

MONTEIRA, I., 'Los musulmanes como verdugos de los personajes sagrados en la iconografía románica. Una interpretación actualizada de las escrituras para combatir en Islam en la Edad Media', in *Codex Aquilarensis,* 23, 2007, pp. 67-87.

MORER, A., FONT-ALTABA, M., 'Resultats analítics dels materials i de la tècnica pictòrica del frontal d'Urgell', in *Butlletí del MNAC*, Barcelona, 1994, 2, pp. 118-124.

MORER, A. *et al.*, 'Noves aportacions a l'estudi de les tècniques pictòriques: la Majestat Batlló, la Majestat d'Organyà i el Frontal de Planès', in *El romànic i la Mediterrània. Catalunya, Toulouse i Pisa. 1120-1180*, Barcelona, 2008, pp. 221-229 [catalogue for the exhibition held in the MNAC].

MUÑOZ, A., 'Pittura romanica catalana: I paliotti dipinti dei Musei de Vich e di Barcellona', in *Anuari de l'Institut d'Estudis Catalans*, Barcelona, 1907, I, pp. 89-118.

ORRIOLS, A., 'Hagiographie et art roman en Catalogne', in *Les Cahiers de Saint-Michel de Cuxa*, Prades-Codalet, 1998, XXIX, pp. 121-142.

PAGÈS, M., 'La pintura romànica de les esglésies de Cerdanya', in *Sobre pintura romànica catalana,* Abadia de Montserrat, 2005, pp. 47-66.

PATTON, P. A., 'An Islamic Envelope-Flap Binding in the Cloister of Tudela: another "Muslim Connection" for Iberian Jews?', in *Spanish Medieval Art, Recent Studies*, Tempe (Arizona), 2007, pp. 65-88.

PUIGGARÍ, J., 'Catálogo Razonado de las Láminas de este Álbum', in *Álbum de la Sección Arqueológica de la Exposición Universal de Barcelona*, Barcelona, 1988, pp. 107-109.

SANPERE, S., *La pintura mig-eval catalana. L'Art Barbre*, Barcelona, 1908.

SUREDA, J., *La pintura romànica a Catalunya*, Barcelona, 1981.

THOMPSON, D. V. JR., *The Practice of Tempera Painting. Materials and Methods*, New York, 1962 (1936).

3. WOOD CARVING

BASTARDES, R., *Les talles romàniques del Sant Crist a Catalunya*, Barcelona, 1978.

BASTARDES, R., *Els davallaments romànics a Catalunya*, Barcelona, 1980.

BARRACHINA, J., 'La talla [Obra romànica dispersa en col·leccions no tractada fins ara. El col·leccionisme a Catalunya]', in *Tortosa i les Terres de l'Ebre, la llitera i el Baix Cinca. Obra no arquitectònica. Dispersa i restaurada*, Barcelona, 1997, p. 351-352.

BARRACHINA, J., 'Introducció [Obra romànica dispersa en col·leccions no tractada fins ara. El col·leccionisme a Catalunya]', in *Tortosa i les Terres de l'Ebre, la llitera i el Baix Cinca. Obra no arquitectònica. Dispersa i restaurada*, Barcelona, 1997, p. 335-385.

BRACONS, J., 'Els davallaments romànics a Catalunya i l'heretgia albigesa. Propostes d'interpretació i aproximació a la seva datació', in *Miscel·lània en homenatge a Joan Ainaud de Lasarte*, Barcelona, 1998, I, pp. 197-205.

CAMPS, J., *Diàleg d'obres disperses. Davallament d'Erill la Vall. Publicació editada amb motiu de l'exposició del conjunt complet del Davallament d'Erill la Vall*, Vic, 2002.

CAMPS, J., 'Le mobilier d'autel en Catalogne à l'époque romane: devants d'autel et structures de retables sculptés', *in Autour de l'autel roman catalan*, Paris, 2008, pp. 125-148.

CAMPS, J.; DECTOT, X. (coor.), *Obres mestres del romànic. Escultures de la vall de Boí*, Barcelona, 2004 [catalogue for the exhibition held at the MNAC and the Musée national du Moyen Âge-Musée de Cluny].

COOK, W. W. S.; GUDIOL RICART, J., *Pintura e imaginería románicas*, Madrid, 1950 (Ars Hispaniae, VI) [2nd edition revised, 1980].

DELCOR, M., *Les Vierges romanes de Cerdagne et de Conflent dans l'Histoire et dans l'Art*, Barcelona, 1970.

DURLIAT, M., *Christs romans. Roussillon. Cerdagne*, Perpignan, 1956.

DURLIAT, M., 'La signification des Majestés catalanes', in *Cahiers Archéologiques*, Paris, 1989, 37, pp. 69-95.

FERRARI, M. C.; MEYER, A. (ed.), *Il Volto Santo in Europa. Culto e immagini del Crocifisso nel Medioevo. Atti del Convegno internazionale di Engelberg (13-16 settembre 2000)*, Luca, 2005.

FORSYTH, I. H., *The Throne of Wisdom. Wood sculptures of the Madonna in Romanesque France*, Princeton, 1972

JUNYENT, E., 'La imatgeria', in *L'Art Català*, Barcelona, 1957, I, pp. 191-204.

MAINAR, J., *El moble català*, Barcelona, 1976.

NOGUERA, A., *Les marededéus romàniques de les terres gironines*, Barcelona, 1977.

SCHÄLICKE, B., *Die Ikonographie der monumentalen Kreuzabnahmegruppen des Mittelalters in Spanien*, Berlin, 1975.

TRENS, M., *Les majestats catalanes*, Barcelona, 1966 (Monumenta Cataloniae, XIII).

YARZA, J., 'L'escultura romànica', in *Art Català. Estat de la Qüestió, Vè Congrés del CEHA*, Barcelona, 1984, pp 102-122.

4. STONE SCULPTURE

BARRAL, X., 'Preromànic i romànic', in *Escultura antiga i medieval*, Barcelona, 1997, pp. 94-206 (Art de Catalunya. Ars Cataloniae, 6).

CAMPS, J., 'Els precedents immediats de l'escultura gòtica', in *Escultura I. La configuració de l'estil*, Barcelona, 2007, pp. 34-42 (L'art gòtic a Catalunya).

CAMPS, J., 'L'escultura dels claustres. Del segle XI al segle XIII', in *Visió de síntesi, restauracions i noves troballes, bibliografia, índexs generals*, Barcelona, 1998, pp. 103-115 (Catalunya Romànica, XXVII).
CASTIÑEIRAS, M., 'Un passaggio al passato: il portale di Ripoll', in *Medioevo: il tempo degli antichi, VI Convegno Internazionale di Studi di Parma, 24-28 settembre 2003*, Milan, 2006, pp. 365-381.
DURLIAT, M., *La sculpture romane en Roussillon*, 5 vols., Perpignan, 1948-1957.
DURLIAT, M., 'La Méditerranée et l'art roman', in *Les Cahiers de Saint-Michel de Cuxa*, Prades-Codalet, 1975, 6, pp. 116.
LORÉS, I., 'Transmission de modèles toulousains dans la sculpture monumentale en Catalogne dans la première moitié du XIIe siècle: anciens et nouvelles problématiques', in *Les Cahiers de Saint-Michel de Cuxa*, Prades-Codalet, 2006, XXXVII pp. 91-102.
LORÉS, I. *El monestir de Sant Pere de Rodes*, Bellaterra/Barcelona/Girona/Lleida, 2002.
PORTER, A. K., *La escultura románica en España*, Barcelona, 1928.
PUIG I CADAFALCH, J., *L'escultura romànica a Catalunya*, 3 vol., Barcelona, 1949-1954 (Monumenta Cataloniae, V, VI, VII).
YARZA, J., 'L'escultura romànica', in *Art Català. Estat de la Qüestió, Vè Congrés del CEHA*, Barcelona, 1984, pp. 102-122.

5. METALWORK: THE ROMANESQUE TREASURY

ALCOLEA, S., *Los esmaltes en la orfebrería catalana*, Barcelona, 1962.
BARRACHINA, J., 'Romànic. Arts sumptuàries', in *Art Català. Estat de la qüestió, Ve Congrés del CEHA*, Barcelona 1994, pp. 149-167.
BARRACHINA, J., 'Cruz de altar, siglo XI. Museu Nacional d'art de Catalunya', in *Butlletí del MNAC*, Barcelona, 2000, 4, pp. 95-104.
BIRON, I., 'Les apports du laboratoire à la connaisance de l'émail limousin', in *L'Oeuvre de Limoges. Art et Histoire au temps des Plantagenêts, Actes du Colloque*, Paris, 1998, pp. 83-106.
CABESTANY, J.-F., 'Les arts sumptuàries i artesanals', in *Introducció a l'estudi de l'art romànic català. Fons d'art romànic català del Museu Nacional d'Art de Catalunya*, Barcelona, 1994, pp. 119-132 (Catalunya Romànica, I).
ESPAÑOL, F., 'Los esmaltes de Limoges en España', in *De Limoges a Silos*, Madrid, 2001, pp. 87-111.
FOLCH I TORRES, J., 'Copó esmaltat del Rin (segle XIII)', in *Anuari de l'Institut d'Estudis Catalans*, Barcelona, 1920, VI, pp. 774-780.
FOLCH I TORRES, J., 'Imitation de l'orfèvrerie dans les devants d'autel et les retables catalans de l'époque romane', in *Gazette des Beaux-Arts*, Paris, 1930, 30 [offprint].
FOLCH I TORRES, J., 'El què era i el què serà el museu de Santa Àgata', in *Butlletí dels Museus d'Art de Barcelona*, Barcelona, 1932, II, pp. 173-176.
FOLCH I TORRES, J., 'Los esmaltes de Limoges en la colección Plandiura', in *La Vanguardia*, 4/6/1936.
FRANCO, Á., 'El tesoro románico', in *Boletín del Museo Arqueológico Nacional*, Madrid, 1999, XVII, 1-2, pp. 201-225.
GAUTHIER, M.-M., 'La clôture émaillée de la confession de Saint Pierre au Vatican, lors du Concile de Latran, IV, 1215', in *Syntrhonon, Art et Archéologie de la fin de l'Antiquité et du Moyen Âge*, Paris, 1968, pp. 237-246.
GAUTHIER, M.-M., *Émaux du moyen âge occidental*, Fribourg, 1972.
GAUTHIER, M.-M., *Émaux meridionaus. Catalogue international de l'Oeuvre de Limoges. 1. L'époque romane*, Paris, 1987.
GAUTHIER, M.-M., 'L'Espagne, reconquêtes et pèlerinages de l'Oeuvre de Limoges', in *L'Oeuvre de Limoges. Art et Histoire au temps des Plantagenêts. Actes du Colloque*, Paris, 1998, pp. 297-432.
GOUSSET, M.-T., 'Un aspect du symbolisme des encensoirs romans: la Jérusalem Céleste', in *Cahiers Archéologiques*, Paris, 1982, 30, pp. 81-106.
GUARDIA, M., 'Vas litúrgic', in *Un any d'adquisicions, donacions i recuperacions*, Barcelona, 1992, pp. 34-38.
GUDIOL I CUNILL, J., 'L'orfebreria en l'exposició hispano-francesa de Saragoça', in *Anuari de l'Institut d'Estudis Catalans*, Barcelona, 1908, pp. 103-149.

GUDIOL I CUNILL, J., *El mobiliari litúrgich. Resum arqueològic*, Vic, 1920.
HILDBURGH, W. L., 'Concerning a questionable identification of medieval Catalan champlevé enamels', in *The Art Bulletin*, New York, 1945, 27, 4, pp. 247-259.
LASKO, P., *Ars sacra 800-1200*, New Haven, 1994 (2nd ed.)
MARQUÉS, J., 'El frontal de oro de la seo de Gerona', in *Annals de l'Institut d'Estudis Gironins*, Girona, 1959, 13, pp. 213-231.
MATAS, T., *Els esmalts romànics a Catalunya. 1. Arquetes*, Barcelona, 1982.
SITGES, X., *L'Argenteria i l'orfebreria al Bages: Segles* X-XVIII, Manresa, 2001.
SUBÍAS GALTER, J., 'Els Pal·lis: or i argent a l'orfebreria romànica catalana', in *Miscel·lània Puig i Cadafalch*, Barcelona, 1947-1951, 1, pp. 373-382.

6. THE LEGACY OF ROMANESQUE ART: THE VISION OF MODERNITY

Agnus Dei. L'art romànic i els artistes del segle XX, Barcelona, 1995 [catalogue for the exhibition held at the MNAC].
BARRAL, X., 'Joan Miró i l'art romànic català', in *Revista de Catalunya*, Barcelona, 1994, 87, pp. 90-103.
BARRAL, X, 'Historiografia i bibliografia del romànic català', *Introducció a l'estudi de l'art romànic català. Fons d'art romànic català del Museu Nacional d'Art de Catalunya*, Barcelona, 1999, pp. 169-188 (Catalunya Romànica, I).
BATAILLE, G., 'L'Apocalypse de Saint-Sever', in *Documents*, Paris, 1929, 1, pp. 74-84.
BLUNT, A., *Picasso's "Guernica"*, New York, 1969.
BORRÀS, M. L., 'Picabia al Museu de Belles Arts', in *Agnus Dei. L'art romànic i els artistes del segle* XX, Barcelona, 1995, pp. 62-67 [catalogue for the exhibition held at the MNAC].
BRACONS, J., *L'exposició internacional d'art romànic de 1961*, Barcelona, 2005 [2005-2006 inaugural lecture, Amics de l'Art Romànic].
BURGARD, T. A., 'Picasso's Night Fishing at Antibes. Autobiography, Apocalypse, and the Spanish Civil War', in *The Art Bulletin*, New York, 1986, 68, 4, pp. 657-672.
CAPDEVILA, C., 'Picasso, al Museu', in *La Publicitat*, Barcelona, 6/11/1934.
CASTIÑEIRAS, M., 'Tre miti storiografici sul romanico ispanico: Catalogna, il Cammino di Santiago e il fascino dell'Islam', in *Medioevo: Arte e Storia, I Convegni di Parma, 10, Parma, 18-22 settembre 2007*, Milan, 2008, p.86-107.
CASTIÑEIRAS, M.; YLLA-CATALÀ, G., 'Lluís Domènech i Montaner i la descoberta del Romànic', in E. GRANELL, T. RAMON (ed.), *Lluís Domènech i Montaner, Arquitectura romànica a Catalunya*, Barcelona, 2006, pp. 287-306.
CAVINESS, M. H., 'The Politics of Taste. An Historiography of "Romanesque" Art in the Twentieth Century', C. HOURIHANE, *Romanesque. Art and Thought in the Twelfth Century*, The Index of Christian Art, Occasional Papers, X, Princeton University, 2008, p. 57-81.
FOLCH I TORRES, J., 'Les miniatures des commentaires aux Apocalypses de Gerona et de Seu d'Urgell', in *Cahiers d'Art*, Paris, 1931, VI, pp. 331-334.
GARCÍA DE CARPI, L., 'Imágenes milenaristas en el arte de vanguardia', in *Anales de Historia del Arte*, Madrid, 2003, 13, pp. 257-285.
GUARDIA, M. *et al.*, *La descoberta de la pintura romànica catalana. La col·lecció de reproduccions del MNAC*, Barcelona, 1993 (Los dossieres del Museu Nacional d'Art de Catalunya, 1).
LARREA, J., *Guernica: Picasso*, New York, 1947.
PARCERISAS, P., 'L'avantguarda i el romànic al segle XX', in *Agnus Dei. L'art romànic i els artistes del segle* XX, Barcelona, 1995, pp. 8-37 [catalogue for the exhibition held at the MNAC].
PLA, J., 'El Museu', in *Obra completa. Primera volada. Tres ciutats*, Barcelona, 1966, III, pp. 405-408.
TÀPIES, A., 'L'Arrel Romànica', in *Valor de l'art*, Barcelona, 1993, pp. 157-159.

Photographs

MNAC- Museu Nacional d'Art de Catalunya, Barcelona, 2008
(Calveras/Mérida/Sagristà):
12, 13, 15, 20, 23, 25, 27, 30, 31, 33, 40, 41, 44-45, 46, 47, 48, 51, 57, 60, 61, 62, 63, 64-65, 67, 69, 71, 77, 82, 83, 84, 85, 86, 87 bottom left, 87 top right, 87 top left, 96, 97, 98-99, 105, 109, 110, 111, 114-115, 118-119, 121, 122, 123, 124, 125, 127, 129, 133, 134, 135, 148, 159, 163, 169, 170, 171, 172, 176, 177, 183, 184, 187, 190 193, 200, 204, 213

Matías Briansó:
19, 26, 28, 29, 34-35, 36, 37, 38, 39, 42-43, 52, 53, 54, 55, 58, 59, 73, 74, 75, 78-79, 81, 87 top left, 88, 89, 90, 92-93, 94, 95, 100, 101, 102, 103, 106, 107, 112-113, 117, 130, 131, 149, 151, 164, 166, 167, 189, 191,195, 196-197, 201

Domi Mora:
49, 136, 139, 141, 143, 146, 147, 152, 154, 155, 157, 160, 161, 173, 174, 175, 178, 179, 183, 188, 199

Institut Amatller d'Art Hispànic – Arxiu Mas:
8, 22

Musée d'Art Moderne de Cëret, Ceret (Photo: Gibernau):
207

Arxiu Català Roca:
211

Seattle Art Museum, Eugene Fuller Memorial Collection (Photo: Susan Dirk):
209

ECSA (Photo: F. Bedmar):
11